"This book is a definitive overview of the important research on aging. It provides an up-to-date review of the latest research on aging, a demographic reality that should be on everyone's radar and one of the largest challenges of our time."

David Aaker, *Professor Emeritus, Haas School of Business,*
University of California, Berkeley, USA

"A remarkable synthesis of the latest thinking, theories, and findings about our maturing population, and its ramifications for both business and society. The book is remarkable both for its breadth of perspective—psychological, sociological, neuroscientific, economic, political—and detailed discussions of how the graying demographic will impact our collective future."

Itamar Simonson, *Sebastian S. Kresge Professor,*
Stanford Graduate School of Business, Stanford University, USA

THE AGING CONSUMER

The Aging Consumer: Perspectives from Psychology and Marketing, 2nd edition takes stock of what is known around age and consumer behavior, identifies gaps and open questions within the research, and outlines an agenda for future research.

There has been little systematic research done with respect to the most basic questions related to age and consumer behavior, such as whether older adults versus young and middle-age adults respond to marketing activities including pricing, promotions, product design, and distribution. Written by experts, *The Aging Consumer* compiles research on a broad range of topics on consumer marketing, from an individual to a societal level of analysis. This second edition provides new versions of chapters contained in the 2010 volume that have been updated to reflect the latest psychological and marketing research and thinking. Included also are ten new chapters which cover exciting new ground, such as changes in metacognition in older adults, motivated cognition of the aging consumer, and a global perspective on aging and the economy across cultures.

This updated volume is beneficial for researchers and practitioners in marketing, consumer behavior, and advertising. Additionally, *The Aging Consumer, 2nd edition* will appeal to professionals in other fields such as psychology, decision sciences, gerontology, and gerontological social work, and those who are concerned with normal human aging and its implications for the everyday behavior of older individuals. It will also be of interest to those in fields concerned with the societal implications of an aging population, such as economics, policy, and law.

Aimee Drolet, MA, AM, and Ph.D. is the Marion Anderson Chair of Management, The Anderson School at the University of California, Los Angeles, USA (UCLA). She specializes in consumer decision-making. Her research looks at the mental processes underlying consumers' choices, specifically focusing on decision-making among older consumers. Her latest research focuses on the development of habits and on the preference for moderation.

Carolyn Yoon, MBA, Ph.D., is Professor of Marketing at the Stephen M. Ross School of Business, University of Michigan, USA. Her research investigates psychological and neural mechanisms underlying decision processes across the lifespan, with a focus on generating insights that facilitate improvements in life satisfaction and well-being among older consumers.

MARKETING AND CONSUMER PSYCHOLOGY SERIES

Curtis P. Haugtvedt, Ohio State University
Series Editor

Titles in the Series:

For a complete list of all books in this series, please visit the series page at: https://www.routledge.com/Marketing-and-Consumer-Psychology-Series/book-series/LEAMCPS

THE AGING CONSUMER

Perspectives from Psychology and Marketing

2nd edition

Edited by Aimee Drolet and Carolyn Yoon

Routledge
Taylor & Francis Group

NEW YORK AND LONDON

Second edition published 2021
by Routledge
52 Vanderbilt Avenue, New York, NY 10017

and by Routledge
2 Park Square, Milton Park, Abingdon, Oxon, OX14 4RN

Routledge is an imprint of the Taylor & Francis Group, an informa business

© 2021 Taylor & Francis

First edition published 2010 by Routledge

Library of Congress Cataloging-in-Publication Data
Names: Drolet, Aimee Leigh, editor. | Yoon, Carolyn, 1960- editor.
Title: The aging consumer: perspectives from psychology and marketing /
edited by Aimee Drolet and Carolyn Yoon.
Description: 2nd edition. | New York: Routledge, 2020. | Revised edition
of The aging consumer, c2010. | Includes bibliographical references
and index. |
Identifiers: LCCN 2020020060 (print) | LCCN 2020020061 (ebook) |
ISBN 9780367360948 (hardback) | ISBN 9780367360931 (paperback) |
ISBN 9780429343780 (ebook)
Subjects: LCSH: Older consumers. | Consumer behavior. | Consumption
(Economics) | Marketing–Psychological aspects.
Classification: LCC HF5415.332.O43 A455 2020 (print) | LCC
HF5415.332.O43 (ebook) | DDC 658.8/3420846–dc23
LC record available at https://lccn.loc.gov/2020020060
LC ebook record available at https://lccn.loc.gov/2020020061

ISBN: 978-0-367-36094-8 (hbk)
ISBN: 978-0-367-36093-1 (pbk)
ISBN: 978-0-429-34378-0 (ebk)

Typeset in Bembo
by Deanta Global Publishing Services, Chennai, India

CONTENTS

CONTRIBUTORS

Nishaat Mukadam currently works as the lab manager at Boston University's Aphasia Research Laboratory, where she studies bilingualism and cognitive reserve in post-stroke aphasia, and runs a weekly aphasia resource group. She has a master's degree in Clinical Psychology from Mumbai University (India), and four years of clinical and research experience working on the diagnosis, rehabilitation, and management of Parkinson's disease and other neurodegenerative conditions. Prior to joining the Aphasia Laboratory, she completed her second master's degree in Experimental Psychology from Brandeis University, where she worked on research related to self-reference memory and aging.

Krystal Leger is currently a Psychology Ph.D. student at Brandeis University. She earned her BS in Psychology at the University of Massachusetts Amherst, where she completed an honors thesis investigating the neural underpinnings of object perception and memory. She also worked as a summer research fellow in a robotics lab at the University of Vermont Complex Systems Center. Her current research uses behavioral and neuroimaging techniques to study mechanisms underlying cross-cultural differences in cognition.

Angela Gutchess is currently an associate professor of Psychology at Brandeis University, with appointments in Neuroscience and the Volen Center for Complex Systems. She attended Boston University for her BA/BS degrees and the University of Michigan for her Ph.D. Her research investigates the influence of age and culture on memory and social cognition using behavioral, neuroimaging (Functional magnetic resonance imaging—fMRI, Event Related Potentials—ERP), and patient (amnestic mild cognitive impairment) methods. Dr. Gutchess was elected to the Governing Board of the Psychonomic Society and the Memory

Disorders Research Society and currently serves as Associate Editor at *Cognition* and the *Journal of Gerontology: Psychological Sciences*. She recently published *The Cognitive and Social Neuroscience of Aging* and is co-editing *The Cambridge Handbook of Cognitive Aging: A Life Course Perspective*, both published through the Cambridge University Press.

Alexander Siegel, MA, is a Ph.D. candidate in the Department of Psychology at the University of California, Los Angeles. He received his undergraduate degree at Tufts University and will be a postdoctoral research fellow at the University of Southern California School of Gerontology in 2020. His research interests focus on memory, attention, emotion, metacognition, and aging.

Mary Whatley, MA, is a Ph.D. student in the Department of Psychology at the University of California, Los Angeles. She received her undergraduate degree at the University of North Carolina at Chapel Hill in 2016 and worked as a research assistant for Teledyne Scientific Company and 3C Institute for Social Development before joining the Ph.D. program at UCLA. Her research interests focus on memory, attention, education, decision-making, metacognition, and aging.

Mary B. Hargis is an assistant professor of Cognitive Psychology at Texas Christian University. She received her Ph.D. at the University of California, Los Angeles in 2019. Her research focuses on how younger and older adults learn, with applications in clinical, educational, and marketing domains.

Alan D. Castel is a professor of Cognitive Psychology at the University of California, Los Angeles. His research focuses on how younger and older adults selectively attend to important information, and how memory changes with age, with applications in clinical, legal, educational, and marketing domains. He received his Ph.D. from the University of Toronto in 2004 and completed a postdoctoral fellowship at Washington University in St. Louis. His research has been supported by the National Institute on Aging. He received the Springer Early Career Achievement Award in Research on Adult Development and Aging from the American Psychological Association (Division 20). His book *Better with Age: The Psychology of Successful Aging* was recognized as one of the "Best Books on Aging Well" by *The Wall Street Journal*.

Mary B. Hargis is an assistant professor of Cognitive Psychology at Texas Christian University. She received her Ph.D. at the University of California, Los Angeles in 2019. Her research focuses on how younger and older adults learn, with applications in clinical, educational, and marketing domains.

Mary Whatley, MA, is a Ph.D. student in the Department of Psychology at the University of California, Los Angeles. She received her undergraduate degree at the University of North Carolina at Chapel Hill in 2016 and worked as a research assistant for Teledyne Scientific Company and 3C Institute for Social Development before joining the Ph.D. program at UCLA. Her research interests focus on memory, attention, education, decision-making, metacognition, and aging.

Alexander Siegel, MA, is a Ph.D. candidate in the Department of Psychology at the University of California, Los Angeles. He received his undergraduate degree at Tufts University and will be a postdoctoral research fellow at the University of Southern California School of Gerontology in 2020. His research interests focus on memory, attention, emotion, metacognition, and aging.

Alan D. Castel is a professor of Cognitive Psychology at the University of California, Los Angeles. His research focuses on how younger and older adults selectively attend to important information, and how memory changes with age, with applications in clinical, legal, educational, and marketing domains. He received his Ph.D. from the University of Toronto in 2004 and completed a post-doctoral fellowship at Washington University in St. Louis. His research has been supported by the National Institute on Aging. He received the Springer Early Career Achievement Award in Research on Adult Development and Aging from the American Psychological Association (Division 20). His book *Better with Age: The Psychology of Successful Aging* was recognized as one of the "Best Books on Aging Well" by *The Wall Street Journal*.

Pär Bjälkebring is a researcher in the Department of Psychology at the University of Gothenburg as well as the Cognitive and Affective Influences in Decision Making (CAIDe) lab at the University of Oregon. He is also a member of the Center for Aging and Health (AgeCap) in Sweden. His research focuses on the interplay of affect and deliberation (for example, numeracy) in judgments and decision-making. He is particularly interested in understanding changes in decision-making that occur as people age and how decision-making skill can shape a person's life trajectory of happiness and satisfaction. He has published in outlets such as the *Journal of Personality and Social Psychology*, *Emotion*, and *Aging and Mental Health*. He has been awarded the Carin Mannheimer Award for Emerging Scholars. Finally, he has received several grants and stipends including a three-year international postdoctoral grant from the Swedish Research Council.

Ellen Peters is the Philip H. Knight Chair and Director of the Center for Science Communication Research in the School of Journalism and Communication at the University of Oregon. She studies the basic building blocks of human judgment and decision-making and their links with effective communication techniques. She is particularly interested in how affective, intuitive, and deliberative processes help people perceive risks and make decisions. She has published more than 150 peer-reviewed papers in outlets such as *Psychological Science*, PNAS, *JAMA*, *Annual Review of Public Health*, and *Nature Climate Change*. She is former President of the Society for Judgment and Decision Making and a fellow of the American Association for the Advancement of Science, Association for Psychological Science, the American Psychological Association, and the Society for Experimental Social Psychology. She has worked extensively with federal agencies to advance decision and communication sciences in health and health policy, including being Chair of FDA's Risk Communication Advisory Committee and member of the NAS's Science of Science Communication committee. She has been awarded the Jane Beattie Scientific Recognition Award and an NIH Group Merit Award. Finally, she has received extensive funding from the National Science Foundation and National Institutes of Health.

William Hampton is co-director of TechX Lab and International Postdoctoral Fellow of the Institute of Marketing at the University of St. Gallen. He first joined in the research community at Dartmouth College where he worked in the neurology department studying neurodegenerative diseases using rodent models. He then earned a bachelor's *cum laude* from the University of Pennsylvania where he studied Psychology and Neuroscience. After postbaccalaureate neuroeconomics research, he completed an interdisciplinary Ph.D. in Decision Neuroscience from Temple University, focusing on intertemporal choice, aging, and modeling neural white matter connectivity. He was then an affiliated research scholar at the Center for Decision Sciences at Columbia Business School before joining St. Gallen as a postdoctoral fellow. His research leverages a diverse toolset ranging from behavioral and self-report measures to neuroimaging to study real-world decision-making behaviors, particularly those relating to reward in the context of aging, technology, and consumer behavior.

Vinod Venkatraman is currently an associate professor in Marketing and Director of the Center for Applied Research in Decision Making at the Fox School of Business, Temple University. Dr. Venkatraman joined Temple in July 2011 after completing his Ph.D. in Psychology and Neuroscience at Duke University. His research involves the use of behavioral, eye tracking, neurophysiological, and neuroimaging methodologies to study the effects of context, state, and individual traits on decision preferences. A core emphasis of his research is in the application of findings from the laboratory to real-world decisions in the areas of consumer financial decision-making, public policy, and marketing communications. Dr. Venkatraman received the Early Career Award from the Society of Neuroeconomics in 2016 for his contributions to the area of decision neuroscience. His research has been published in leading scientific journals including *Journal of Marketing Research*, *Journal of Neuroscience*, *Neuron*, and *Journal of Consumer Psychology*, and featured in popular media outlets including BBC, Forbes, NPR, *LA Times*, and *Newsweek*. Several of his recent research projects have been funded through grants and collaborations with the industry. He has also been an academic advisor and Fellow at IPSOS, a leading market research company.

Professor Anand V. Bodapati's research is at the intersection of consumer psychology, decision-making, statistics, marketing, and computer science. His interests lie in the development of statistical models, methodologies, and decision support systems to address marketing problems in value creation, value communication, customer acquisition, customer development, customer retention, and the assessment of customer response to marketing. He has worked on customer acquisition targeting, product optimization, consumer preference assessment, conjoint analysis, segmentation, advertising response, direct marketing, customer relationship management, Bayesian statistics, and experimental design. Professor Bodapati's domain-specific interests are in advertising, retailing, direct marketing, digital marketing, and social marketing for health and public policy.

Aimee Drolet is the Marion Anderson Chair of Management. She specializes in consumer decision-making. Her research looks at the mental processes underlying consumers' choices, specifically focusing on decision-making among older consumers (age 50 or older), consumer habits, and meta-preferences. Her latest research focuses on the development of habits and on moderation—that is, avoiding excess in consumption.

Jill Steinberg is an Emeritus Professor of Psychology at San Jose State University, licensed clinical psychologist, Salzburg Fellow, author, and founder of MyRetirementWorks.com. Her research and publications focus on "achieving success," e.g., *Climbing the Ladder of Success in High Heels: Backgrounds of Professional Women* (UMI Press), and the "imposter phenomenon." Since retiring, Dr. Steinberg has been teaching classes and presenting her research on successful retirement to universities, Google, and other professional organizations, and enjoying ocean kayaking with her retirement dog Herbie.

Raphaëlle Lambert-Pandraud is Professor of Marketing at the Paris campus of Ecole Supérieure de Commerce de Paris (ESCP) Business School, the oldest business school in the world, est. 1819. After graduating from ESCP, she worked as a senior product manager at L'Oréal in the UK, where she test marketed and launched the French anti-aging skincare range Plénitude.

She then earned a Ph.D. in Consumer Behavior at HEC, Paris, and a Habilitation à Diriger des Recherches (HDR) at Paris-Dauphine University. Professor Lambert-Pandraud's current research is focused on the influence of age on consumers' brand memory, consideration, and choice. She has published her research in international journals, such as the *Journal of Marketing, Marketing Letters, RAM Recherches et Applications en Marketing*, and *International Journal of Market Research*. She has presented papers in international conferences such asSociety of Consumer Psychology (SCP), European Marketing Academy (EMAC), Association for Consumer Research (ACR), and Marketing Science. She also participated to the 6th and 7th Invitational Choice Symposiums. The workshop participants co-authored joint papers on cognition and decision-making in older consumers in *Marketing Letters* (2005; 2008).

Gilles Laurent is Research Fellow at ESSEC Business School, Cergy-Pontoise, France. Over the years, he has done research on consumer involvement profiles, brand awareness, sales promotion, older consumers, price from the consumer's point of view, luxury, and a variety of other topics. His research has been published in *Management Science, Journal of Marketing Research, Journal of Marketing, International Journal of Research in Marketing, Marketing Science, Journal of Consumer Research, Marketing Letters, Journal of the Academy of Marketing Science,* and other journals. He was editor-in-chief of *International Journal of Research in Marketing* in a previous millennium. He organized the Marketing Science Conference (1987) and the Invitational Choice Symposium (1998), in both cases for the first time outside North America. In 2012, he received the EMAC Distinguished Marketing Scholar Award from the European Marketing Academy. In 2020, he was awarded the title of Distinguished Emeritus Professor by HEC Paris.

Carolyn M. Bonifield is an associate professor of Marketing at the University of Vermont Grossman School of Business. She holds degrees from the University of Iowa (Ph.D.), Michigan State University (MBA), and Ohio University (BA). Dr. Bonifield teaches courses in Marketing Communications, Consumer Behavior, and Marketing Management. Her research interests include consumer decision-making, services marketing, consumer responses to mobile technology, and consumer engagement with social media. She has published articles in a number of top business journals including the *Journal of the Academy of Marketing Science, Journal of Business Research,* and *Marketing Letters,* among others. She serves on the Editorial Board of The Service Industries Journal. Prior to pursuing her Ph.D., she was a product manager for Unilever, and launched a small business, which she later sold.

Catherine Cole graduated with a Ph.D. in Marketing from the University of Wisconsin at Madison. Currently she is a professor of Marketing at the University of Iowa and a Henry B. Tippie Research Fellow. She has broad research interests in consumer behavior including elderly adults' use of consumer information; advertising effects on consumer affect, cognition, and behavioral intent; and public policy and consumer decision-making. She has published in the *Journal of Marketing, Journal of Marketing Research, Journal of Consumer Research, Journal of Consumer Psychology,* and *Management Science.*

Sanjay Sood is a professor of Marketing and the Chairman of the UCLA Anderson School. Sanjay Sood holds an MBA from Kellogg and a Ph.D. from

Stanford. Sood's academic research focuses on two areas, brand management and behavioral decision-making. Sood helped develop what is now UCLA Anderson's Center for Management of Enterprise in Media, Entertainment & Sports. Using psychological principles in his research, Sood examines how firms can best build, manage, and leverage strong brand names. This includes investigating what brand names mean to consumers, how to manage brand portfolios, how to use brand naming strategies to launch new products and how to protect brand names from becoming diluted over time and across geographical boundaries. In his latest work on decision-making, he studies the differences between how people make decisions about products versus how they make decisions about experiences—like buying a DVD versus going to see the movie in a cinema.

Harry R. Moody is a graduate of Yale University and received his Ph.D. in Philosophy from Columbia University. He has taught philosophy at Columbia University, Hunter College, New York University, and the University of California at Santa Cruz. He recently retired as Vice President and Director of Academic Affairs for AARP in Washington, DC. He is currently Visiting Professor at Tohoku University in Japan and Distinguished Visiting Professor at Fielding Graduate University. Dr. Moody previously served as Executive Director of the Brookdale Center on Aging at Hunter College and Chairman of the Board of Elderhostel (now Road Scholar). Moody is the author of over 100 scholarly articles, as well as a number of books including *Abundance of Life: Human Development Policies for an Aging Society* (Columbia University Press, 1988) and *Ethics in an Aging Society* (Johns Hopkins University Press, 1992). His most recent book, *The Five Stages of the Soul*, was published by Doubleday Anchor Books and has been translated into seven languages worldwide. He is the editor of a newsletter, "Human Values in Aging," reaching 10,000 subscribers each month. In 2011, he received the Lifetime Achievement Award from the American Society on Aging and in 2008 he was named by *Utne Reader Magazine* as one of "50 Visionaries Who Are Changing Your World."

Neil Charness is William G. Chase Professor of Psychology and Director of the Institute for Successful Longevity at Florida State University. He received his BA from McGill University (1969) and MS and Ph.D. from Carnegie Mellon University (1971, 1974) in Psychology. Neil's research focuses on human factors approaches to age and technology use. He has held grants from the Natural Science and Engineering Council of Canada, the Social Sciences and Humanities Research Council of Canada, the Retirement Research Foundation, the National Science Foundation, and the National Institute on Aging. He has published over 200 journal articles, book chapters, proceedings papers, and technical reports, and also co-authored books *Designing Telehealth for an Aging Population: A Human Factors Perspective* and *Designing for older adults: Principles and creative human factors approaches (3rd Edition)*. He is a Fellow of the American Psychological Association, the Association for Psychological Science, and the Gerontological Society of America. He received the Jack A. Kraft Innovator award, the Franklin V. Taylor Award, the M. Powell Lawton award, the APA Prize for Interdisciplinary Team Research, Grandmaster of the International Society for Gerontechnology, and APA's Committee on Aging award for the Advancement of Psychology and Aging.

Jong-Sung Yoon is an assistant professor of Psychology and Cognitive Neuroscience at the University of South Dakota. He received his BA and MA from Yonsei University (in South Korea) and Ph.D. from Florida State University in Cognitive Psychology. Prior to joining the faculty at the University of South Dakota, he was a postdoctoral fellow in the Institute of Successful Longevity at Florida State University, working as a member of the multi-disciplinary Center for Research and Education on Aging and Technology Enhancement (CREATE). His research is grounded in the study of expert performance and cognitive aging. His research interests include the development of training activities and technology-based interventions that can help older adults remain independent; older adults' attitude toward and adoption of new technology; and how to apply the expert-performance approach to the study of medical education and neural evidence of deliberate practice.

Hellen Pham is a master's candidate in Cognitive Psychology at Florida State University with an interest in human factors and human-computer interaction. She is currently working on a project investigating the impact of negative media coverage regarding advanced driver assistance systems (ADAS) and autonomous vehicle (AV) system failures on aging drivers' current attitudes and willingness to use ADAS and AV technology.

Alessandro M. Peluso is an associate professor of Business Management at the Department of Management and Economics of the University of Salento, Lecce (Italy), where he has been teaching Business Management, Marketing, Marketing Research, Tourist Destination Marketing, and Place Marketing. He has been Adjunct Professor of Advertising, Marketing, and Marketing Strategies at the LUISS University, Rome (Italy), and has taught Marketing Research, Customer Analytics, and Big Data for Marketing at the LUISS Business School. His research activity focuses on older consumers' behavior, sustainable consumption, and social communication. He has published three books, more than 50 scientific articles in peer-reviewed journals, such as the *European Journal of Marketing*, *International Journal of Advertising*, *International Journal of Research in Marketing*, *Journal of Business Ethics*, *Journal of Business Research,* Journal of Consumer Research, *Journal of Marketing Research*, *Research Policy*, and many others, in addition to several contributions in edited books and conference proceedings. He is a member of the Association for Consumer Research, the Academy of Marketing Science, and the European Marketing Academy.

Cesare Amatulli is an associate professor of Business Management at the University of Bari, Italy, where he has been teaching Marketing, Tourism Marketing, and Luxury Marketing. He has been Adjunct Professor of Distribution and Sales, Trade and Retail Marketing, Social Advertising, Branding, and Advanced Marketing Management at the LUISS University, Rome (Italy). He has been Adjunct Professor of Sustainable Luxury Development at the EMC Business School, Paris (France), and Adjunct Professor of Luxury Product Development & Management and Retail Marketing and Operations at the International University of Monaco (Principality of Monaco). He has been Visiting Researcher at the Ross School of Business (USA) and at the University of Hertfordshire (UK). Most of his ongoing research focuses on cognitive age and older consumers, sustainable consumption, luxury consumption, luxury tourism, the role of emotions, and WOM. He has published three books and more than 50 scientific articles in major academic journals such as the *Journal of Consumer Research*, *International Journal of Research in Marketing*, *Journal of Business Ethics*, *European Journal of Marketing*, *Journal of Business Research*, and *Psychology & Marketing*. He has presented several papers at international conferences.

Carolyn Yoon is a professor of Marketing at the Stephen M. Ross School of Business, University of Michigan. She is also a faculty associate at the Institute for Social Research. Her research focuses on understanding psychological and neural mechanisms underlying judgment and decision processes across the lifespan in consumer domains and socio-cultural contexts. Her research has been published in journals such as the *Journal of Marketing Research*, *Journal of Consumer Research*, *Journal of Consumer Psychology*, *Journal of Personality and Social Psychology*, *Psychological Science*, *Psychology and Aging,* and *Journal of Neuroscience*. She is an associate editor at the *Journal of Marketing Research* and serves on the editorial review boards of a number of journals. She also serves on the Policy Board of the *Journal of Consumer Research* and the Board of the Society for Neuroeconomics. She is a recipient of the *Journal of Consumer Research* Best Paper Award and a Fellow of the Association for Psychological Science.

Gianluigi Guido (Ph.D., University of Cambridge, UK) is a professor of Marketing at the University of Salento, Italy. He has been a professor at the University of Padua, Sapienza and LUISS University of Rome, Italy, and a visiting researcher at the University of Florida at Gainesville, and Stanford University, USA. He has published 20 books and more than 250 articles in major scholarly journals in the field of marketing and consumer behavior.

Abby Yip holds a BA in Psychology with a minor in Music Performance from Mills College and a Ph.D. in Developmental Psychology from Cornell University. From 2014 to 2019, she was a member of Dr. Corinna Löckenhoff's Healthy Aging Laboratory, where she studied individual differences in affective experiences and their associations with decision-making and health outcomes across age groups and different cultures. She has also worked at the Life-Span Development Laboratory at Stanford University and the Motivation and Emotion Laboratory at the Chinese University of Hong Kong. Abby is currently an associate in Mercer's Workforce Strategy and Analytics practice, where she uses data to generate evidence-based solutions to help clients better manage their human capital.

Julia Nolte received a BS in Psychology in 2014 from Heidelberg University, Germany, followed by an MS in Psychology in 2017. Since then, Julia Nolte has been a Ph.D. student at Cornell University's Department of Human Development, where she is a member of Dr. Corinna Löckenhoff's Healthy Aging Laboratory. Julia first joined the Human Development Department as Cornell's 2015–2016 Heidelberg Exchange Fellow and a Fulbright grantee. Before returning to Cornell, Julia worked with the Funke Lab for Problem-Solving at Heidelberg University (2013–2017) and Valerie F. Reyna's Rational Decision Making Lab at Cornell University (2015–2016). In addition, she completed research visits with the Nock Lab at Harvard University (2016), the Cognition and Health Research Group at Oxford University (2016), and Cambridge University's Winton Center for Risk and Evidence Communication (2017). Julia's research interests span risk perception, decision-making, lifespan development, and health. Specifically, Julia's research explores age differences in the acquisition, construal, and use of decision-relevant information.

Corinna E. Loeckenhoff is a professor in the Department of Human Development at Cornell University and in Gerontology in Medicine at Weill Cornell Medical. Her research focuses on age differences in time horizons, personality, and emotional experiences and their influence on health-related decisions and outcomes across the life span. She received her undergraduate degree from the University of Marburg, Germany and her Ph.D. from Stanford University. She completed a postdoctoral fellowship in the intramural research program of the National Institute on Aging before joining Cornell University in 2009. Dr. Loeckenhoff is a Fellow of the Gerontological Society of America. She was recognized as a Rising Star by the Association for Psychological Science in 2011 and received the Margret M. and Paul B. Baltes Foundation Award in Behavioral and Social Gerontology from the Gerontological Society of America in 2014. Her efforts in teaching gerontology were honored by a SUNY Chancellors Award for Teaching Excellence in 2013 and a KON Award for Excellence in Advising in 2018.

Stephanie M. Carpenter is the Associate Director of the Data Science for Dynamic Decision-Making (d3) Lab and a Fellow in the Quantitative Methodology Program at the University of Michigan Institute for Social Research. She received a joint Ph.D. in Social Psychology and Business Administration from the University of Michigan and was previously a NIMH postdoctoral trainee at the University of

Wisconsin-Madison Department of Psychology. Her research examines the role of emotion and cognition in decision-making, with special interests in the psychology of aging and health behavior change.

Rebecca Chae is a Ph.D. candidate in Marketing at the Stephen M. Ross School of Business, University of Michigan. Her substantive research interests are in judgment and decision-making, and culture with a focus on consumer behavior that can contribute to individual and societal well-being. She is a recipient of the Association of Consumer Research/Sheth Foundation Dissertation Award. Prior to joining the Ph.D. program at Ross, she earned her MS in Marketing from Columbia University and her BS in Economics from University of Pennsylvania.

Yeonjin Sung is a Ph.D. candidate in Marketing at the Stephen M. Ross School of Business, University of Michigan. Her research interests are time perception, digital consumption, and branding. She received a BA in Economics and Psychology and an MS from Seoul National University.

Carolyn Yoon is a professor of Marketing at the Stephen M. Ross School of Business, University of Michigan. She is also a faculty associate at the Institute for Social Research. Her research focuses on understanding psychological and neural mechanisms underlying judgment and decision processes across the lifespan in consumer domains and socio-cultural contexts. Her research has been published in journals such as the *Journal of Marketing Research, Journal of Consumer Research, Journal of Consumer Psychology, Journal of Personality and Social Psychology, Psychological Science, Psychology and Aging*, and *Journal of Neuroscience*. She is an associate editor at the *Journal of Marketing Research* and serves on the editorial review boards of a number of journals. She also serves on the Policy Board of the *Journal of Consumer Research* and the Board of the Society for Neuroeconomics. She is a recipient of the *Journal of Consumer Research* Best Paper Award, and a Fellow of the Association for Psychological Science

Cassandra Denise Davis is an assistant professor of Marketing at Wayne State University. Her research broadly encompasses the domain of consumer well-being, with research spanning topics such as nutrition, aging, and tobacco. Dr. Davis also has a particular interest in stigmatized and stereotyped identities, particularly when these identities negatively affect consumer health and safety. She has published in journals such as the *Journal of Business Ethics, Journal of Advertising, Journal of Public Policy and Marketing*, and the *Journal of Business Research*. She has also received grants from organizations such as the American Marketing Association and the Morrison Family Center for Marketing and Data Analytics. Dr. Davis is a member of the Ph.D. Project, an organization that seeks to increase workplace diversity by increasing the diversity of business school faculty and has recently co-edited a special issue on diversity and marketing education in the *Journal of Marketing Education*.

Alexandra Polyakova is an assistant professor in Marketing at the Department of Strategy and Marketing at the University of Sussex. She received her Ph.D. from Bocconi University. She has been a Visiting Scholar at Erasmus University Rotterdam and the University of California Los Angeles. She worked in marketing departments in diverse institutions (including non-profit associations. Her research interests include consumer entitlement, consumer emotions, services marketing, and unethical behavior.

Professor Anand V. Bodapati's research is at the intersection of consumer psychology, decision-making, statistics, marketing, and computer science. His interests lie in the development of statistical models, methodologies, and decision support systems to address marketing problems in value creation, value communication, customer acquisition, customer development, customer retention, and the assessment of customer response to marketing. He has worked on customer acquisition targeting, product optimization, consumer preference assessment, conjoint analysis, segmentation, advertising response, direct marketing, customer relationship management, Bayesian statistics, and experimental design. Professor Bodapati's domain-specific interests are in advertising, retailing, direct marketing, digital marketing, and social marketing for health and public policy.

Aimee Drolet is the Marion Anderson Chair of Management. She specializes in consumer decision-making. Her research looks at the mental processes underlying consumers' choices, specifically focusing on decision-making among older consumers (age 50 or older), consumer habits, and meta-preferences. Her latest research focuses on the development of habits and on moderation—that is, avoiding excess in consumption.

Noah J. Webster is an assistant research scientist in the Life Course Development Program at the University of Michigan's Institute for Social Research. Dr. Webster's research focuses on examining the role of the lived environment (e.g., community, built, natural) in shaping social relations and their impact on multiple health outcomes. This includes recent work to develop social network-based interventions for specific environmental contexts (e.g., senior housing communities). Dr. Webster also served as Assistant Director for Society 2030, a platform for establishing new, innovative combinations of science, technology, and engineering to meet the needs of Society in 2030. The Society 2030 Consortium is a model for the rational organization of resources of modern interdisciplinary science and technology to meet the needs of individuals and families by harnessing and/or developing resources from multiple sources to efficiently meet current and evolving needs—much as outlined in the concept of smart living.

Jess Francis is a gerontechnologist and postdoctoral research fellow in the Life Couse Development Program at the University of Michigan's Institute for Social

Research. Her research focuses on how technology use impacts the well-being of older adults. Specifically, Dr. Francis explores how emerging technology use can promote both connection and independence in order to foster healthy aging. She is particularly passionate about conducting research related to individuals from a variety of backgrounds and life experiences in order to highlight the diversity of needs among some of the various sub-populations of older adults in the United States. In addition to her research, Dr. Francis has also served as an industry consultant with OhmniLabs, a technology company out of the Bay Area as well as OscarSenior a technology company located in the Czech Republicboth of which develop technology specifically for the older adult population.

Toni C. Antonucci is the Elizabeth M. Douvan Collegiate Professor of Psychology, Program Director and Research Professor in the Life Course Development Program at the Institute for Social Research, all at the University of Michigan, USA. Her research focuses on social relations and health (physical/psychological/cognitive functioning) across the life span. Professor Antonucci studies all types of social relations including close social relations, peer and family relations, caregiving, and social media. She is interested in family multigenerational relations, and child and adult development. In 2011, while she was Senior Associate Vice President for Research and with Dr. Noah Webster as Assistant Director, Dr. Antonucci launched Society 2030, a platform for establishing new, innovative combinations of science, technology, and engineering to meet the needs of society in 2030. The Society 2030 Consortium is a model for the rational organization of resources of modern interdisciplinary science and technology to meet the needs of individuals and families by harnessing and/or developing resources from multiple sources to efficiently meet current and evolving needs—much as outlined in the concept of smart living.

PREFACE

Population aging is a worldwide phenomenon. At present, nearly 55 million Americans—one out of six—are over the age of 65.[1] Over the next several decades, the proportion of adults aged 65 and older will continue to increase in all major industrial countries as the share of the total adult population declines. The economic ramifications of an aging population are serious and potentially enormous. As the median age of the world continues to rise and is expected to reach 42 by 2050,[2] the labor force will shrink, leaving fewer younger workers to sustain growth and trying the strength of economies all over the world, in both developing and developed countries. In brief, the economic woes of population aging will be far greater than anything experienced at present or in the past. Yet, many social science researchers appear unaware of the phenomenon of population aging and the gravity of its societal consequences.

Population aging originates from two sources. First, for the past two hundred years, people everywhere have been living longer, healthier lives. At present, a typical person in the developed world is expected to live to 79, and an average person from a developing country is expected to live to 71.[3] Second, in addition to a longer lifespan, people are having fewer children. Fertility rates are in dramatic decline worldwide as the cost of raising children has increased along with access to contraception. According to some forecasts, the world population will peak at nine billion and then decline. In summary, as more people reach retirement age, there will be fewer younger workers left to replace them in the workforce.

Declining fertility rates at a time when a large portion of the population is nearing retirement age is a trend that is being experienced in most developed countries. Many developed countries, especially in Europe,[4] are already on an inescapable path to population aging, having faced low fertility rates for decades. For some countries, mostly in the developing world, a younger population may stave off population aging in the meantime. However, increasing longevity and decreasing birth rates are universal trends, and these countries will face the same set of problems eventually.

Indeed, some countries, notably Japan, are experiencing "super-aging."[5] Since the end of World War II, the median age of Japan has doubled from the low 20s to the high 40s. In the last forty years, the number of Japanese adults aged 65 or older has nearly quadrupled. Once hailed for its innovation and industry, the age cohort that has brought the country enormous growth until the 1980s is retiring and expiring. The country's current population of 126 million people is projected to drop to 97 million by 2050. Like women in other developed countries, Japanese women are increasingly postponing marriage and childbirth in favor of longer working hours.[6] The Japanese government has been actively pursuing numerous initiatives to avert the graying of the country,[7,8] including a state-sponsored dating service.[9] However, these government efforts to encourage higher birth rates have met with little success and, as of yet, there are no signs of a reversal of fewer children and more elderly people. A key reason for failure is increased fatigue among women. Indeed, Japanese women say they do not have enough energy to go on a date, let alone stay awake during it.[10]

One way countries can forestall the problems of population aging is immigration. For example, until recently, an intersection of welcoming labor markets and flexible immigration policies enabled the United States to maintain a younger workforce and have a fertility rate close to an equilibrium point between the birth rate and death rate. However, over the last three years, the Trump administration's antagonistic immigration policies have reduced immigration by more than 11 percent.

In addition to its overall effect on the economy, population aging may alter the consumer market in several ways. According to the life-cycle theory of savings, people will vary their consumption habits depending on their age, marital status, and economic resources. People will try to save more during their middle years and spend more in their old age. However, current research has painted a more nuanced portrait of the life-cycle theory of savings, whereby consumption varies depending on the types of goods. For some goods like transportation services, vacations, and food, people tend to decrease their spending as they age. For other goods like health care, donations, and gifts, people tend to increase their spending as they reach old age.[11] As population aging takes hold in countries everywhere, some goods more than others may be positioned to benefit from the different consumption habits of older adults.

In summary, population aging presents a problem never before seen. Despite the significant demographic shift, consumer researchers have paid relatively little attention to older consumers. This is surprising since the increasing population of older consumers corresponds to the wealthiest segment of the population. Although there is much debate over the impact of and solutions to population aging, what we do know is that fertility rates are getting lower, people are living longer, and the world population is getting older.

Overview

The Aging Consumer: Perspectives from Psychology and Marketing (2020) is both an update and extension of research reported in *The Aging Consumer: Perspectives from Psychology and Economics* (2010; Eds. Drolet, Scwarz, and Yoon). The present edition contains a total of 16 chapters, six of which are updated versions of chapters that appeared in the previous edition (Chapters 1, 4, 8, 9, 10, and 11). These chapters have been updated to reflect the latest psychological and marketing research and thinking with respect to their specific topics. The present edition also contains ten new chapters which cover exciting new ground (Chapters 2–3; 12–16) or older ground in deep new detail (Chapters 5–7).

This book is divided into four parts (I–IV). Part I considers the neurological and cognitive changes as people age. In particular, in Chapter 1 ("Cognitive Neuroscience of Aging"), Mukadam, Leger, and Gutchess review several age-related changes that reflect typical developmental processes, many of which emerge gradually after young adulthood and continue throughout later life. Chapter 1 focuses first on changes that occur to the structure and function of the brain, considering widespread systems. It focuses next on domain-specific changes, highlighting changes to in sensory and memory abilities. Last, Mukadam et al. discuss the possibility of preserved social and emotional abilities, relating these to changes reviewed in other cognitive abilities.

In Chapter 2 ("Changes in Memory and Metacognition in Older Adulthood"), Siegel, Whatley, Hargis, and Castel discuss the broad changes in memory that occur across the lifespan. In general, older (vs. young) adults have a smaller memory capacity, decreased episodic and source memory, and rely more on gist-memory and feelings of familiarity. However, alongside these impairments, the authors discuss memory abilities that are preserved with age and that help older adults offset these declines. For example, in some circumstances, older adults can minimize age-related deficits by relying on schematic knowledge of what "should have" occurred. Siegel et al. review a growing body of work that shows how the ability to effectively prioritize information in memory may also help older adults remember high-value or critical information just as accurately as young adults. In addition, Siegel et al. consider the effect of aging on use of metacognitive processes that allow individuals to assess memory quality and adjust their behavior to regulate memories. These processes become more important with increasing age due to an increase in the frequency of memory errors. Chapter 2 details how and why metacognition changes in older adulthood may contribute to older adults' memory abilities and behaviors.

In Chapter 3 ("Motivated Cognition and Curiosity in the Aging Consumer"), Hargis, Whatley, Siegel, and Castel consider what motivates younger and older people to learn new information and skills through the lens of multiple theories of cognitive aging. After discussing knowledge, emotion, and control as motivating factors, they examine the roles of curiosity and interest in motivated cognition, suggesting that curiosity may not always benefit older consumers. Chapter 3 also examines older adults' perceptions of risk, gains, and losses, and how those perceptions may affect consumer behavior. Last, Hargis et al. discuss applications of their research. Specifically, they discuss (1) older adults' perceptions about and use of so-called "brain training" techniques; (2) how age-related changes may affect novelty-seeking; and (3) how situations that induce stereotype threat and anxiety may also motivate older adults' cognition differently from that of younger adults.

Part II consists of three chapters that each examine how age influences the decision-making process of older (vs. young) adults. In particular, in Chapter 4 ("Aging-related Changes in Decision-Making), Bjälkebring and Peters discuss the age-related differences in cognition, affect, and goals that interact to influence the decision-making of older adults. In general, older adults process information differently compared to young adults. Although declines in deliberative processes imply that older (vs. young) adults make worse decisions, the implications may be oversimplified because older adults appear to use their deliberative capacity selectivity. Furthermore, because accumulated experience can partly compensate for age-related declines and the ability to manage emotions increases with age, older adults may be better decision makers than younger adults in some situations.

In Chapter 5 ("Effects of Age on Risky and Intertemporal Choices: Decision Strategies and Real-World Implications"), Hampton and Venkatraman focus on two types of decisions that are particularly critical for older adults. The first is risky choice and the second type is intertemporal choice. Whereas some research shows that risk seeking and delay discounting tend to decline with age, there are exceptions to this trend. Chapter 5 reviews both changes in decision-making strategies with age, as well as the role that emotion may play in governing these age-related changes in risky choice and intertemporal choice. Hampton and Venkatraman then discuss the everyday implications of older adults' risky choices and discounting, as well as some possible routes for interventions to improve decision-making across the lifespan. Last, they address the corpus of cognitive neuroscience research in the last two decades that has begun to reveal the neural correlates and mechanisms underlying an array of decisions.

In Chapter 6 ("Effects of Age on Spending Behavior for Consumer Packaged Goods"), Bodapati and Drolet report the results of an analysis of age effects on consumer buying behaviors across a total of 29 different consumer package good categories, several of which one would expect to change with age (e.g., categories related to workforce participation). Specifically, in terms of spending behaviors, they looked at buying volume, brand loyalty, unit size, mean volume per shopping occasion, size loyalty, shopping trip frequency, inter-trip gap stability, time of day, day of week, store loyalty, and preferred store size. Their analysis reveals large differences across categories in terms of whether age had a significant increasing, decreasing, or no effect. In addition, Bodapati and Drolet investigate the effect of age on consumer responsiveness to marketers' promotional activities, including feature advertising, in-store displays, and price promotions, which is a novel aspect of their investigation. Taken together, the results reveal few age differences in consumer response to key promotional activities.

Chapter 7 ("Successful Retirement: From Retiring to Rewiring) centers on the notion of "successful retirement." Having sufficient financial resources, a sense of control, being goal-directed, planning for retirement, implementing some projects before retiring, having concrete strategies to deal with goals and losses, and having supportive social and tech connections are all factors associated with having a more purposeful and successful retirement, including better health and being better prepared for dealing with changes in their finances, time, health, and relationships. Steinberg reviews these factors and also addresses often-overlooked quality of life factors that are important for a successful retirement, such as how older adults spend their time and money, find purpose, and maintain friendships and social connections.

Part III consists of four chapters that are focused on the implications of psychological and marketing research for communicating effectively with older versus younger consumers. In Chapter 8 ("Impact of Age on Brand Choice"), Lambert-Pandraud and Laurent review research on age-related differences among consumers in brand loyalty. Specifically, they discuss several underlying psychological processes that lead older consumers to choose from smaller consideration sets, spend less time searching for product information, repeat their choices more often, and prefer older brands. Their review suggests that brand choice among older adults is influenced by a variety of mechanisms, including cognitive decline, biological aging, aversion to change, innovativeness, socioemotional selectivity, attachment, expertise, habits, nostalgia, and cohort effects.

In Chapter 9 ("Comprehension of and Vulnerability to Persuasive Marketing Communications among Older Consumers"), Bonifield and Cole identify the individual, task, and contextual characteristics that influence older consumers' comprehension of marketing communications. They then present a set of research propositions based on this review. Whereas Bonifield and Cole draw primarily on applications for marketing communications, they also discuss applications for product warnings. Chapter 9 concludes with a review of how and when these characteristics interact to increase older adults' vulnerability to persuasive communications. Based on this review, Bonifield and Cole outline a set of hypotheses related to age differences in susceptibility to persuasive appeals.

Chapter 10 ("Age Branding") by Sood and Moody focuses on age branding, which refers to the primary brand message underlying products targeted at older consumers (e.g., hearing aids). Using numerous case studies (e.g., Thrive by Kaiser Permanente and Chico's), Sood and Moody outline four categories of age brands: age-denial, age-adaptive, age-irrelevant, and age-affirmative. They then discuss how this typology offers useful insights and helpful advice for marketers and public policy makers.

In Chapter 11 ("Designing Products for Older Consumers: A Human Factors Perspective"), Charness, Yoon, and Pham discuss typical human factors approaches to design and introduce the Center for Research and Education on Aging and Technology Enhancement (CREATE) framework for understanding person-system fit. They then review normative changes with age in perceptual, cognitive, and psychomotor abilities that have implications for product design. Charness et al. provide conceptual heuristics for understanding age-related changes in performance and describe design issues for a variety of products. Last, they discuss how usability testing and modeling can help in design decisions.

Part IV's five chapters discuss new directions in aging research. Chapter 12 ("Subjective Age and Older Consumers") focuses on the construct of "subjective age," which refers to how old an individual perceives oneself to be, versus chronological age, which refers to how old an individual actually is. At older ages, people's perception of their own age tends to be lower than their chronological age. Peluso, Amatulli, Yoon, and Guido focus on the discrepancy between subjective age and chronological age. They reveal that this discrepancy is malleable, varying in magnitude across cultural contexts, age groups, individuals, and situations. Finally, Peluso et al. consider the main consequences of this discrepancy for marketers who seek to target older consumers.

Chapter 13 ("Aging Across the World: The Interplay of Demographic, Economic, Historical, and Cultural Factors") begins with a broad overview of the potential mechanisms underlying cross-national differences in aging experiences and outcomes. Yip, Nolte, and Löckenhoff illustrate the interplay among such factors with respect to three key types of outcomes: (1) perceptions and attitudes toward aging and older adults; (2) age-related shifts in socioemotional functioning; and (3) patterns of cognitive aging. Yip, Nolte, and Löckenhoff consider the implications of their insights for consumers. They conclude with a discussion of the limitations of existing research and potential directions for future research.

In Chapter 14 ("The Influence of Creativity on Objective and Subjective Well-being in Older Adulthood"), Carpenter, Chae, Sung, and Yoon examine involvement in creative processes as a promising way to increase older adults' well-being, even among those who suffer from severe physical and cognitive declines or mental illness. Carpenter et al. propose a framework for understanding how both objective well-being (mental health, physical health, cognitive outcomes) and subjective well-being (psychosocial, emotional, life satisfaction) is influenced by involvement in a number of creative processes. Furthermore, they review ways in which older adults can benefit from the positive effects of involvement in creative activities with respect to their everyday consumption experiences. They also discuss some caveats to the benefits of creativity on older adults' well-being, including possible drawbacks. Chapter 14 concludes with a discussion of future directions for research on creativity and well-being in older adulthood.

Chapter 15 ("Are Young Adults More Narcissistic Than Older Adults?") addresses the question of whether young adults are generally more narcissistic than older adults. Older generations often characterize younger generations as relatively egoistic versus altruistic. For example, the Depression-era generation labeled its Baby Boomer offspring the "Me Generation" which is essentially the same label that the Baby Boomer generation now uses to characterize its own Millennial offspring ("Generation Me"). Davis, Polyakova, Bodapati, and Drolet review various past research findings on the nature of the relationship between age and (sub-clinical) narcissism. Although these findings are mixed, studies suggest that *both* older adults and young adults view young adults as more narcissistic compared to older adults. Understanding differences due to age in narcissistic tendencies is important from a marketing perspective. For example, by targeting consumers' egoistic (vs. altruistic) values, advertisers can increase felt involvement with a product and in turn the effectiveness of their persuasive appeals.

Finally, in Chapter 16 ("Smart Living for Older People and the Aging Consumer"), Webster, Francis, and Antonucci discuss changes in population demographics not only due to age but also race and ethnicity. They also discuss changes in the individual life span and in family structure. Together, these changes result in older adults having very different experiences, needs, and preferences. Webster et al. propose "smart living" as a new approach to adapting to these changes. They describe several examples from a variety of smart living settings, including the home, workplace, and public domain. They then discuss how these developments can promote healthy aging, improve the functioning of the workforce, and facilitate transportation. Smart living provides a new perspective on design and consumption that addresses the needs of an aging society across multiple domains including prevention, intervention, adaptation, and rehabilitation.

Notes

1 "Fact Sheet: Aging in the United States," *Population Reference Bureau* (www.prb.org), 7/15/19.
2 "Projected Median Age of the U.S. Population, through 2060," *Atlas* (www.theatlas .com).
3 "Life Expectancy in Developed and Developing Countries," *Statista* (www.statista .com).
4 "Population Structure and Ageing–Statistics Explained," (http://ec.europa.edu/eur ostat/statistics-explained/index.php/Population_structure_and_ageing). *Ec.europa.edu.* 12/28/17.
5 Muramatsu, Naoko (8/1/11), "Japan: Super-Ageing Society Preparing for the Future," *The Gerontologist*, 51(4): 425–432.
6 "Marriage Process and Fertility of Japanese Married Couples," *National Institute of Population and Social Security Research (IPSS)* (2011). (http://www.ipss.go.jp/site-ad/ index_english/nfs14/Nfs14_Couples_Eng.pdf), 9–14.
7 "Japan Baby Boom: City's policies turn around population decline," (https://www.yo utube.com/watch?v=MMA3eDNS0jw). *TRT World*, 9/14/19.
8 "Urgent Policies to Realize a Society in Which All Citizens are Dynamically Engaged," (http://www.kantei.go.jp/jp/topics/2015/ichiokusoukatsuyaku/kinkyujisshitaisaku_ en.pdf). 11/26/15.

9 "Young Japanese 'decline to fall in love'" (https://www.bbc.co.uk/news/world-1 6500768). *BBC News*, 1/11/12.

10 Ishimura, Sawako, "60% of tired women do not want to love!? Cause of fatigue" second place work content, first place?)" *Cocoloni Inc.*, 10/24/17.

11 Hurd, M.D., and Rohwedder, S. (2010). Spending patterns in the older population. *The aging consumer: Perspectives from psychology and economics*, 25–50.

PART I

Cognitive Changes with Age

1

COGNITIVE NEUROSCIENCE OF AGING

Nishaat Mukadam, Krystal Leger, and Angela Gutchess

Cognitive Neuroscience of Aging

Many people think about the cognitive and neural changes that occur with age as being due to neurodegenerative diseases such as dementia. However, healthy aging is also associated with widespread changes to the brain and many cognitive abilities. In this chapter, we will review some of the age-related changes that reflect typical developmental processes, many of which emerge gradually after young adulthood and continue throughout later life. The chapter focuses first on changes that occur to the structure and function of the brain, considering widespread systems. Next, the chapter focuses on domain-specific changes, considering changes to abilities such as sensation and memory. Finally, we discuss the possibility of preserved social and emotional abilities, relating these to changes reviewed in other cognitive abilities.

Neural Changes with Age

Changes to the brain with age are widespread, impacting the structure of both gray and white matter in the brain (Driscoll et al., 2009; Resnick, Pham, Kraut, Zonderman, and Davatzikos, 2003) as well as the function of the brain. All of these changes have implications for cognitive and other abilities. This section focuses on these structural and functional changes that are seen in healthy aging and how these changes influence older adults' cognitive abilities, including implications for their behavior as consumers.

Structural Changes

Gray Matter

Just as other organs undergo age-related decline, so too does the brain. Structural changes in gray matter that occur with age involve a reduction in the volume of gray matter and thinning of the cortex (C. D. Good et al., 2001; Salat et al., 2004). As seen in Figure 1.1, these changes result in atrophy, or shrinkage of the overall brain size (Driscoll et al., 2009) and enlargement of the ventricles, the spaces through which cerebrospinal fluid flows (Kwon, Jang, and Yeo, 2014; Resnick et al., 2003). Gray matter volume and cortical thickness may predict cognitive performance on some tasks. Not only is the amount of gray matter considered, but also the rate of change from one time point to another. Some studies have found that healthy individuals undergo significant amounts of brain shrinkage even in a short period of time (Raz, Ghisletta, Rodrigue, Kennedy, and Lindenberger, 2010). Thus, it may be the case that the rate of change over only a few years could

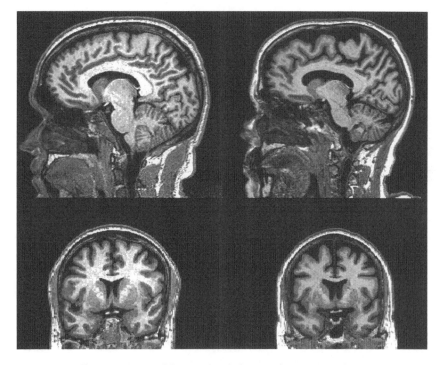

FIGURE 1.1   Illustrates some of the structural changes that occur with age. Compared to the younger adult brain (left), the older adult brain (right) shows loss of tissue volume. This atrophy can be seen in the enlargement of spaces around the cortex, including the ventricles (dark space in the center of each image).

serve as an important predictor of who is at risk for accelerated cognitive decline with age or perhaps already exhibiting signs of disorder.

Gray matter loss typically occurs in a progressive and slow manner with age and is not uniform across different regions of the brain (Raz et al., 2005b; Resnick et al., 2003). Patterns of loss tend to be linear, at a consistent rate over time, in some regions and non-linear (e.g., the rate potentially accelerating at a faster rate in later years) in other regions (Raz et al., 2005a). Through the use of magnetic resonance imaging (MRI), both cross-sectional (studying different groups of individuals at different ages) and longitudinal (studying the same individuals over time as they age) studies have consistently found that the most prominent loss occurs in regions of the prefrontal cortex, particularly the inferior and orbitofrontal regions (Driscoll et al., 2009; Farokhian, Yang, Beheshti, Matsuda, and Wu, 2017; C. Good et al., 2001; Raz et al., 2010; Raz et al., 1997; Resnick et al., 2003). Other gray matter changes also include loss in the insular, cingulate, superior parietal cortices (Driscoll et al., 2009; Farokhian et al., 2017; Resnick et al., 2003), pre and post central gyri (C. Good et al., 2001), the caudate, the cerebellum, and the hippocampus (Raz et al., 2010; Raz et al., 2005b). In contrast, there tends to be more preservation in the occipito-parietal, subcortical (Farokhian et al., 2017; C. Good et al., 2001), entorhinal (Raz et al., 2005b), and the mesial temporal (Resnick et al., 2003) regions.

These age-related declines in gray matter were initially attributed to neuronal death, though more recent work suggests that the number of neurons may be relatively consistent with age. Instead, losses of volume may actually reflect reductions in neuron size, the number of synapses, or synaptic spikes (Esiri, 2007; Freeman et al., 2008). Age-related gray matter changes are also responsible for many of the types of changes with age in cognitive functioning that are reviewed in a later section of this chapter.

White Matter

The white matter in the brain plays a role in connecting regions, allowing for the transmission of information across the brain. Figure 1.2 depicts some white matter tracts. White matter consists of myelinated and unmyelinated axons of neurons and myelin-producing glial cells. Myelin is the fatty substance wrapped around the axon of some neurons which helps to speed transmission of neural signals down the axon; myelinated axons form the majority of white matter. White matter, like gray matter, also undergoes global volume loss with age (Resnick et al., 2003). Despite the amount of attention paid to gray matter, imaging studies have shown that white matter change is actually *more* pronounced in normal aging than gray matter changes (Liu et al., 2017). Age-related white matter changes involve the loss of myelin, known as demyelination. This loss is most significant in the anterior thalamic radiations (Farokhian et al., 2017; C. Good et al., 2001) the optic radiations, frontal regions (C. Good et al., 2001), and the prefrontal cortex

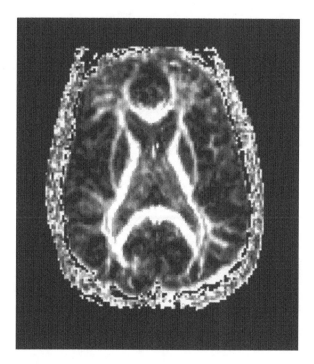

FIGURE 1.2   Depicts white matter tracts in the brain. These can serve as short- or long-range connections between regions of cortex. With aging, the integrity of these tracts can be reduced, which can impact the communication between regions. Reprinted from Madden et al. 2004, Diffusion tensor imaging of adult age differences in cerebral white matter: Relation to response time. *NeuroImage*, Vol 21, p. 1174–1181, Copyright 2004, with permission from Elsevier.

(Raz et al., 2005b; Salat et al., 2004). Although there is significant white matter loss seen in aging, there is also some white matter preservation in the posterior frontal lobes, cerebellum, and right temporal lobes (C. Good et al., 2001) and even an increase in the white matter volume in the pericentral and occipital areas (Farokhian et al., 2017). Changes in white matter with age also involve the development of white matter hyperintensities (Habes et al., 2016) which are lesions in the brain that show up as bright spots on T2 weighted MRI scans and seem to be linked to reduced cerebrovascular health.

Structural changes in white matter seen in normal aging play an important role in the age-related cognitive decline observed in the older adult population (Valdes Hernandez Mdel et al., 2013). Because of the role that myelin plays in the speed of signal transmission, demyelination and white matter hyperintensities seen with age lead to a decline in the speed at which neuronal signals are transmitted, and is manifested cognitively as slower speed of processing. This further influences other cognitive processes as well. For example, a greater number of white matter hyperintensities seem to be linked to impairments in cognitive performance (Gunning-Dixon, Brickman, Cheng, and Alexopoulos, 2009).

Although both gray and white matter show notable and more or less uniform changes in the aging population, there is some degree of individual variability seen in the rate and magnitude of progression of gray and white matter (Raz et al., 2005b; Resnick et al., 2003). This variability can be attributed to early life experiences and opportunities which we will discuss in a later section.

Functional Changes

Neural Activation

In addition to the effects of age on the brain's physical tissue, neural activity also changes with age. This includes changes in the onset, intensity, location, and extent of activation, all of which have implications for cognitive processing and behavior.

There are a couple of notable patterns of activation change with age. One observed difference between younger and older adults is in the bilaterality of neural activations (Cabeza et al., 1997; Grady et al., 1995; Reuter-Lorenz et al., 2000). This refers to the activation of regions in both hemispheres rather than only in one hemisphere. Younger adults generally activate left *or* right prefrontal cortex during tasks such as working memory, due to the largely lateralized activity for verbal tasks (left prefrontal cortex) or visuospatial tasks (right prefrontal cortex). In contrast, older adults are more likely to activate the same region in *both* hemispheres. Regions tend to be recruited in both hemispheres that are homologous to one another—i.e., the same region in each hemisphere. This framework of age-related neural change is known as the hemispheric asymmetry reduction in older adults—or HAROLD—model. Another characterization of age-related changes is the posterior-anterior shift in aging, or PASA. This model posits a relationship between increases in frontal lobe activity and decreases in occipital lobe activation (S. W. Davis, Dennis, Daselaar, Fleck, and Cabeza, 2008).

A prevailing explanation for these changes is that the increases in activation in certain areas are compensatory. This explains the HAROLD pattern such that older adults are recruiting resources in both hemispheres in order to achieve performance comparable to what young adults achieve with unilateral activation. For the PASA pattern, increased activation in the frontal lobes in response to decreased occipital lobe activity with age also aligns with the compensatory explanation. As visual processing becomes more difficult and less precise with age, higher-order frontal lobe processes (such as attention, or regions reflecting increased cognitive effort) need to be called upon to compensate for the impoverished sensory information. Indeed, these explanations are supported by data comparing different performance levels (e.g., Cabeza, Anderson, Locantore, and McIntosh, 2002; Gutchess et al., 2005) and reaction times (e.g., Madden et al., 1997).

However, it should be noted that increased activation as a compensatory response is not a completely straightforward process, especially when considering aging disorders (e.g., Alzheimer's disease) and the typical approach of comparing between groups. Thus, researchers have specified criteria for differentiating successful compensation from *attempts* at compensation. Though the relationship between increased neural activity and brain atrophy reflects compensation as a response to cognitive decline, this mechanism cannot be sustained as the brain continues to deteriorate with age or as tasks become too demanding. Additionally, in order to be considered a successful attempt at compensation, the activity must be related to task performance and occur in a brain region known to be relevant for that particular task.

Other frameworks have emerged to explain how aging affects demands on cognitive resources. According to the compensation-related utilization of neural circuits hypothesis (CRUNCH), increased neural activity in response to task demands should occur at lower levels of task difficulty for older adults than for younger adults (Reuter-Lorenz and Cappell, 2008). A similar model known as the scaffolding theory of aging and cognition (STAC) also purports that the cognitive and neural challenges that accompany aging require additional resources and further explains that individual factors such as fitness and social and intellectual engagement over the lifespan can affect the availability and utilization of these neural resources (D. C. Park and Reuter-Lorenz, 2009; Reuter-Lorenz and Park, 2014).

Reduced Specificity of Neural Responses

In addition to quantifying activation, changes in neural response with age can also be examined in terms of the clarity of information processing, that is, the extent to which neural representations are specific and devoid of noise. One challenge with age to having clear and distinct neural responses that map on to specific representations is dedifferentiation, referring to a reduction in the specificity of response in neural regions. Dedifferentiated patterns of activity have primarily been observed in sensory regions. Areas of cortex that are narrowly tuned in younger adults to respond to certain classes of visual stimuli (e.g., faces, places, objects) do not exhibit that same specificity in older adults but respond more generally across categories (D. C. Park et al., 2004). Motor cortices are also affected by aging, as lateralization (i.e., left motor cortex responding to movement in the right side of the body and vice versa) is reduced (Carp, Park, Hebrank, Park, and Polk, 2011).

Other processes beyond sensory systems experience age-related loss of specificity. A possible culprit for this is older adults' reduced ability to suppress the default network, so named because the neural regions in this network tend to be more engaged at rest as opposed to when performing tasks. During tasks that demand external attention, older adults do not suppress this network as much as younger adults (Grady et al., 2010; Persson, Lustig, Nelson, and Reuter-Lorenz, 2007). This inability to suppress this network, alongside a general reduction in the ability to distinguish neural signal from noise (Backman, Nyberg, Lindenberger, Li, and Farde, 2006; S. C. Li, Lindenberger, and Sikstrom, 2001), could contribute to older adults' poorer quality of information processing. The default network will be discussed further in the section below as a specific system impacted by aging.

Connectivity

As we discuss activation of different areas of the brain, it is important to keep in mind that these regions do not operate in isolation. The connectivity between the regions and the ability to operate as a network are also affected with age. Researchers distinguish between two different types of connectivity. Structural connectivity refers to the white matter pathways that connect regions of gray matter, essentially the physical wiring of the brain. Functional connectivity is when regions activate in tandem (e.g., when you make a decision to reach for something, both prefrontal and motor cortices activate). Both structural and functional connectivity are affected by aging, and changes that occur in one domain of connectivity can affect the other.

As discussed earlier in this chapter, older adults demonstrate increased bilateral activation of the prefrontal cortex. This change in functional connectivity has been found to be related to the integrity in the corpus callosum, which is a thick bundle of white matter connecting the left and right hemispheres of the brain and moreover, connecting homologous regions in each hemisphere to each other (Davis et al., 2012). This pattern of connectivity makes sense in the context of recruiting homologous regions in both hemispheres as a compensatory response. That is, when older adults experience difficulty with a task, the intact white matter tracts can support functioning via the connectivity between hemispheres.

Though there are findings for stronger connectivity within anterior regions with age, this is not the case for all brain regions. Long-range connections tend to be more affected by aging, and this includes fronto-temporal and temporal-parietal regions involved in memory (L. Wang, Li, Metzak, He, and Woodward, 2010). Additionally, connectivity efficiency in older adults is also affected by increases in the length of the shortest path and changes in the centrality of regions in a network (L. Wang et al., 2010).

Researchers that look more broadly at network organization and coordination have found that although younger adults tend to have highly organized and distinct modules for different brain systems, this tight modularity breaks down with age (Chan, Park, Savalia, Petersen, and Wig, 2014). Older adults have weaker connections within system and stronger connections between systems, giving rise to reduced distinction between modules. This relates to ideas presented earlier about reduced capacity for distinguishing neural signal from noise, and indeed, this is seen in memory performance such that better segregation of association systems relates to better performance (Chan et al., 2014).

Neurotransmitters

In addition to the structural and activation changes, the brain also undergoes chemical changes with age. Neurotransmitter levels can be affected in a number of ways, including changes in receptor binding or overproduction or under-production of a particular chemical. The systems mediating dopamine, serotonin, and acetylcholine have been shown to decline with age, affecting learning, motivation, mood, and motor functioning (see review by S. C. Li et al., 2013).

Of these neurotransmitters, dopamine is the most studied with age, and as it is implicated in a number of processes—most notably motor abilities and reward response. Positron emission tomography (PET) scanning has revealed a reduced number of D_2 receptors in the striatum with age, and this receptor availability is related to performance on neuropsychological tests of motor and cognitive functions (Volkow et al., 1998). Another study showed age-related reductions in D_1 receptor binding potential in the regions such as caudate nucleus and dorsolateral prefrontal cortex affect working memory capacity (Backman et al., 2011).

The role of dopamine in the reward response system has been demonstrated in studies on delay discounting (see Chapter 5 by Hampton and Venkartraman, 2020). This phenomenon refers to the tendency to discount rewards that will be received at a later time rather than immediately (e.g., receiving $2 in a month versus receiving $1 tomorrow). Though no age differences were found behaviorally, younger adults' mesolimbic dopamine activity was heightened in response to a sooner reward while the manipulation had less of an effect on older adults (Samanez-Larkin et al., 2011). This result has been interpreted as a reflection of older adults' substantial experience with receiving delayed rewards over a lifetime, although it could also reflect changes in the dopamine system with age.

Specific Systems Affected by Aging

In this section, we move from discussing the ways in which overall brain systems are impacted by aging to consider more specific cognitive abilities and the corresponding brain regions. Although we review a number of abilities that change with age that may account for many challenges in information processing that occur with age, this review is by no means exhaustive in reviewing the types of changes that occur with age.

Sensory Systems

Age-related deficits occur across sensory domains, including audition, vision, gustation, olfaction, and balance. Declines in auditory sensitivity, temporal processing, and spatial localization are among the problems that occur in the auditory system. In visual perception, age-related declines occur in a number of abilities beyond simply visual acuity, including contrast sensitivity, which is the difference between black and white that is needed to perceive an item, or scotopic vision, which is the ability to see under low lighting conditions. Deficits in taste and smell have been linked to atrophic changes in the olfactory bulb, while balance problems are believed to be due to changes in the vestibular system. Each of these sensory issues—individually and when they occur together—can dramatically impact an older adult's quality of life, cognitive ability, and task performance. Beyond the limitations these deficits place on sensorimotor and perceptual abilities, they also place a burden on cognitive resources as older adults are likely to recruit higher-order prefrontal regions in order to compensate for reduced sensory abilities.

In addition to the changes in the sensory systems themselves, the cortical regions associated with sensory perception and processing become less specialized with age. That is, neural responses to particular stimuli become less distinct from one another. This phenomenon observed across a number of brain modalities and in the domain of visual perception, has been demonstrated in the fusiform face area. What this means is that in older adults, this region responds less selectively to individual face identities compared to distortions based on morphing the individual face identities with others (Goh, Suzuki, and Park, 2010). Similarly, para-hippocampal gyrus does not respond as selectively to places as it does in younger adults, but instead, the region responds more generally to places and other categories of visual stimuli, such as faces (Park et al., 2004).

With these age-related changes in mind, it is important to consider the effect on older adults' cognitive abilities and their engagement in complex environments in everyday life. What might at first appear to be a deficit in a higher-order process (such as attention or comprehension) may, in fact, be simply an issue of sensory processing. For example, if an older adult is having trouble understanding the plot of a movie, it may be that they are having difficulty distinguishing between characters' faces or distinguishing speech from background noise in order to understand what the characters are saying. In expending neural resources to compensate, they are sacrificing attention to other information.

Speed of Processing

Speed of processing, or the speed at which cognitive and motor tasks are performed, declines with age (Damoiseaux et al., 2008; Eckert, Keren, Roberts, Calhoun, and Harris, 2010; Verhaeghen, Kliegl, and Mayr, 1997). This slowing may reflect changes in the frontal and cerebellar networks (Eckert et al., 2010) seen in aging. The extensive gray and white matter loss that occurs in frontal and prefrontal regions and the development of white matter hyperintensities in the frontal lobes and corpus callosum with age (Papp et al., 2014) help to explain the slower processing speed among older adults. Additionally, given the role of myelin in speeding up the transmission of signals between neurons, demyelination of axons in the brain with age also contributes to the slower processing speeds seen in older adults.

Speed of processing influences the performance of other cognitive and motor abilities including decision-making. Older adults are able to make better decisions compared to younger adults for decisions that rely on their experience and existing knowledge (Fein, McGillivray, and Finn, 2007). However, when it comes to making decisions about newer or more complex issues, older adults tend to take longer and have more difficulty, possibly because it takes them longer to review individual pieces of information and searching for new information is more cognitively taxing for them (Fein et al., 2007). Furthermore, slower processing speed makes the information subject to distortion or loss as signals are transmitted across neural networks, so older adults might be making even rather simple perceptual judgments based on degraded information. These declines in the ability and speed of making decisions influence the behavior of older adults as consumers. Older adults tend to make more inconsistent decisions and more comprehension errors with increased task complexity (Finucane, Mertz, Slovic, and Schmidt, 2005). Additionally, when under time pressure, older adults tend to have even more difficulty with decision-making (Earles, Kersten, Berlin Mas, and Miccio, 2004). Due to the potential for degraded information, speed of processing changes with age can have profound effects on other cognitive abilities, included perception and memory.

Executive Functioning

Executive functioning has been described as a set of mental processes that are important for the control and management of simple cognitive functions and for goal-oriented behaviors. These functions can be mapped to the functioning of prefrontal cortex in the brain (Diamond, 2013 Three primary mental processes comprise executive functioning: inhibition, working memory, and mental flexibility (Miyake, Friedman, Emerson, Witzki, and Howerter, 2000). These core processes form the basic building blocks for higher-order cognitive processes such as reasoning, problem solving, organizing, decision-making, judgment, and planning. Several studies show the connection between aging and decline in these abilities (Carey et al., 2008; Damoiseaux et al., 2008) with specific impact on decision-making (Carpenter and Yoon, 2011), judgment and reasoning (Denburg et al., 2007; Fein et al., 2007), inhibition (Hasher, Stoltzfus, Zacks, and Rypma, 1991), and cognitive flexibility (Kray and Lindenberger, 2000). Age-related gray and white matter changes in the frontal lobes and corpus callosum (Papp et al., 2014), in particular, can to a large extent, explain this decline in functioning.

The decline in executive functioning in older adults influences their behaviors as consumers. As discussed earlier, the decision-making abilities of older adults suffer due to the decrease in processing speed seen with aging. In addition to the influence of speed, the declines in executive functioning can lead to impaired judgment and reasoning abilities, which in turn influence decision-making abilities. The reduced ability to inhibit irrelevant information and environmental stimuli also influences older adults' abilities to make decisions as consumers, especially when presented with a large number of choice options or variables to consider in order to make a decision.

Memory

Memory decline is perhaps the most often discussed hallmark of aging. However, "memory" is a vast domain, encompassing many different subtypes and relying upon a number of different brain regions. Not all aspects of memory are affected equally by aging; even within memory types, there are still caveats and variability to consider.

Age-related changes in working memory, the type of memory used for keeping information in mind and active for a short period of time, are an example of this. The ability to manipulate information in working memory (e.g., performing a computation in one's head) is more impacted by age than simple rehearsal (e.g., repeating back a phone number) (Craik and Jennings, 1992; Craik and Rabinowitz, 1984). Long-term explicit memory is also affected by aging in a number of ways. Researchers in this area delineate between recollection (vividly remembering the details of an experience, allowing one to relive the experience) and familiarity (the vague feeling of having encountered a stimulus before). Although initial studies suggested that only recollection is impaired with aging (e.g., Hay and Jacoby, 1999), later studies measuring electrophysiological response in the brain revealed that both can be impacted by age (Angel et al., 2013; Duarte et al., 2010).

Furthermore, older adults are more prone to false memories, remembering events that did not occur or remembering those events with substantial alterations. This effect is observed most strongly in tasks where new items are related to previously studied items (e.g., falsely remembering seeing the word "cow" on a word list comprised of other farm animals) (Koustaal and Schacter, 1997; Tun et al., 1998). Interestingly, these false memories invoke the same neural regions relied upon by accurate memories: visual regions responsible for feature perception, frontal and temporal regions associated with semantic knowledge, and the hippocampus, which is involved in a variety of memory processes, including binding the various types of information together into a memory (Gutchess and Schacter, 2012; Schacter and Slotnick, 2004). The neural correlate of these false memories is believed to be age-related increases in the engagement of the superior temporal gyrus (Dennis et al., 2007). This activity reflects the "gist," or theme, component of memory that could explain behavior such as falsely recalling "cow" as being among a list of other related farm animals.

Autobiographical memory, the personal memories from one's past, also declines with age, becoming less detailed. This is particularly true for episodic details (e.g., the rich details of events), while semantic details (e.g., facts such as names of friends, names of places where one has lived) tend to remain intact with age. Neuroimaging results have attributed this loss of episodic detail to reduced activity in medial-temporal regions (St. Jacques et al., 2012). Also, in line with concepts discussed previously in this chapter regarding dedifferentiation of brain regions with age, networks for autobiographical and episodic memory were found to be more differentiated and distinct in younger adults than older adults (St-Laurent et al., 2011).

Prefrontal regions and their associated control processes also play a role in memory, and age impacts these mechanisms as well. Corroborating the previously discussed theories of compensatory "top-down" recruitment, findings demonstrate that older adults are more likely to engage prefrontal regions during retrieval than younger adults (Velanova et al., 2007). Moreover, older adults experience a deficit in inhibition—that is, they have difficulty "filtering out" irrelevant information. However, poorer inhibition may paradoxically increase memory. In experimental tasks in which older adults are supposed to ignore some aspects of the information (e.g., ignoring a picture presented behind a word, when the word should be the target of attention), older adults sometimes perform better than younger adults on memory tests of stimuli designated to be ignored (e.g., the pictures) (Campbell et al., 2012).

Resting State

Resting state, the brain activity observed during periods when an individual is not specifically engaged in a particular external task, has been a growing area of interest in recent years. The regions that are consistently activated during rest but not activated while performing other tasks include a network of systems from the motor cortex, the visual cortex, and the dorsal and ventral attention systems. These sub-networks that activate during periods of non-engagement have come to be known as the default mode network (Beckmann, DeLuca, Devlin, and Smith, 2005; Damoiseaux et al., 2006; Fox, Corbetta, Snyder, Vincent, and Raichle, 2006; Raichle et al., 2001). This network has been associated with spontaneous self-thought (Raichle et al., 2001) and mind-wandering (Mason et al., 2007).

Imaging studies examining the activation and function of the default mode network in older versus younger adults have found differences between these two groups. Compared to younger adults, older adults have decreased activity, efficiency, and connectivity in this network during non-task performance (Damoiseaux et al., 2008; Geerligs, Renken, Saliasi, Maurits, and Lorist, 2015). Furthermore, they exhibit more difficulty suppressing this network (Grady et al., 2010; Persson, Lustig, Nelson, and Reuter-Lorenz, 2007).

A number of studies have found a link between age-related decreases in the default mode network connectivity and decreased cognitive abilities like memory, executive functioning, and processing speed (Andrews-Hanna et al., 2007;

Geerligs et al., 2015; Geerligs, Saliasi, Maurits, and Lorist, 2012). Along these lines, taking into account the importance of executive functioning in self-thought, Damoiseaux et al. (2008) have proposed a connection between decreased spontaneous self-thought and decreased executive functioning in the older adult population.

Modifiers of Aging

Thus far, we have reviewed some of the types of general and specific changes that occur to different systems and processes with age. Although these changes generally characterize the majority of people as they age, there is substantial variability in the rates of change. A large body of research has identified which factors help people to achieve better outcomes with aging, whether they are relatively fixed biological factors (e.g., genes) or experiences that can be adopted at any time point during one's life. We will review some of the major factors that have been demonstrated to impact cognitive aging across individuals in different ways.

Early Life Experiences

Individual differences in age-related cognitive changes have been linked to early life experiences and opportunities. There has been some work showing the associations between cognitive preservation and engagement in (1) *intellectually stimulating activities* such as reading, group discussions, puzzles, learning to play a musical instrument (Crowe, Andel, Pedersen, Johansson, and Gatz, 2003; Verghese et al., 2003), more years of formal education (Stern, 2012; Wilson et al., 2009), and challenging occupations (Stern, 2012); (2) *physical activities* such as sports, exercise, and dance; and (3) *social activities* such as traveling, exposure to different cultures, and socializing with friends (Scarmeas, Levy, Tang, Manly, and Stern, 2001; Stern, 2012). Socioeconomic status, typically defined based on income and mother's level of education, is another factor that has been found to be related to individual differences in cognitive abilities (Fotenos, Mintun, Snyder, Morris, and Buckner, 2008).

It has been theorized that these early life opportunities contribute toward a cognitive reserve that protects against brain degeneration (Stern, 2002, 2012). Stern (2002) considers two ways in which reserve can be defined: an *active process* through which the brain actively tries to compensate for degeneration, or a *passive process* in which reserve is the amount of damage that can be sustained before the individual presents clinical symptoms (e.g., such as memory decline from Alzheimer's disease). The passive explanation holds that the more connections that are formed between neurons through stimulating activities or advantageous early life experiences, the more connections that need to be lost before the damage can result in the presentation of symptoms. According to the active explanation, the brain uses pre-existing resources and knowledge to cope with lost connections.

That means that even though there may be loss of some neuronal function in people with higher intelligence and higher educational qualifications, the damage for them takes longer to present itself clinically.

There has been extensive work on the role that cognitive reserve plays in preventing degeneration. However, there is still debate about whether it truly does prevent degeneration and if it does, how it can be defined independently from the effects on behavior and cognition, and whether it is an active or passive process or a combination of both active and passive processes.

Individual Differences

A number of individual traits—both physical and psychological—can influence the effects of aging. Many genes affect neurotransmitter levels, most notably dopamine and serotonin which are implicated in emotional, cognitive, and learning processes (S.C. Li et al., 2013 for review; Waring, Addis, and Kensinger, 2013). Sex differences have also been observed in brain aging. Some data indicate that men are more likely to lose volume in parietal regions, implicated in language and integration of sensory information, whereas women are more likely to exhibit degradation in temporal regions, implicated in memory function (Carne et al., 2006).

Beyond these innate physical factors that can affect the brain, personality traits can also moderate the neurological changes brought about by age. Personality research has focused on the Big Five traits (extraversion, neuroticism, agreeableness, conscientiousness, and openness) (Costa and McCrae, 1987). High levels of neuroticism have been associated with lower levels of white and gray matter volume and thinner cortex in superior and inferior frontal cortex (Jackson et al., 2011; Wright, Feczko, Dickerson, and Williams, 2007). Extraversion and conscientiousness have been associated with greater cortical thickness.

External life factors also impact aging, stress being one of the most relevant and often researched factors. Stress has been linked to atrophy in the hippocampus, which possibly contributes to memory impairment (see review by McEwen, 2006). Stress has also been shown to have an impact on decision-making; in an experimental task, older adults were more impaired by the stress condition than younger adults (Mather, Gorlick, and Lighthall, 2009). One stressor that is important to consider in the aging population is loneliness. Associated with a number of psychological and physical conditions (see reviews by Cacioppo, Hawkley, and Thisted, 2010; Wilson and Bennett, 2017), perceived loneliness plagues many older adults as individuals in their close social circles pass away or they become more isolated by physical, sensory, or cognitive impairments.

It is important to note that much of this research on individual differences is in its initial stages. However, these preliminary findings still offer important insights on factors, both in and out of an individual's control, that influence how aging affects the brain and cognition. As these topics are further researched, ways in which unhealthy aging can be slowed or prevented may be gleaned.

Cognitive Training and Physical Activity

With an increasingly aging population, solutions to combat some of the afore-mentioned cognitive declines with age have become both popular and market-able. However, it is important to be informed about the validity and possible pitfalls of such "cognitive training" regimens. Most notably, there is little evidence of transferability—doing a lot of crossword puzzles may make one better at cross-word puzzles but is unlikely to improve memory. The most successful of these types of training are those which target cognitive domains most broadly, and research is still needed to determine long-term effects.

Beyond cognitive puzzles, exercise and meditation are among the most stud-ied interventions and have yielded some promising results. One study demon-strated that older adults with higher levels of physical activity showed higher levels of variability in brain engagement (a marker of healthy brain functioning) (Burzynska et al., 2015). Practicing meditation has been linked to slowed pro-gression of brain degeneration and improved resting state connectivity and con-nection among regions (Luder and Cherbin, 2016; Prakash, De Leon, Patterson, Schirda, and Janssen, 2014). However, in considering this body of research, we should keep in mind that these sorts of studies often include small samples and/or self-selected individuals who have chosen to adopt the activity or lifestyle. Thus, it may be the case that those who choose to exercise or meditate regularly also possess other traits that support healthy cognitive aging.

Emotion and Social Processes

Although we have focused on the numerous types of changes that occur across domains with age, there may be some exceptions to the general pattern of age-related loss. Some evidence indicates that social and emotional processes may be more preserved with age, or at least undergo different trajectories of change with age. In this section, we will discuss some of these findings.

Connection Between Socioemotional and Cognitive Abilities

Information that is emotionally or socially meaningful often receives prioritized processing. For example, emotional information can capture attention and evoke additional cognitive processing and relating information to oneself enhances its memorability (Gutchess and Kensinger, 2018). Due to the potential for socioemo-tional processes to enhance cognition, the potential preservation of these mecha-nisms with age has been of considerable interest. The evidence indicates that these socioemotional abilities continue to operate in older adults much like younger adults. For example, information that is emotionally arousing or personally mean-ingful is remembered better in both younger and older adults. Interestingly, when performing socioemotional tasks, the engagement of neural resources also appears to be similar in younger and older adults. Regions such as medial prefrontal cortex are activated more when making judgments about the self compared to making judgments about other people, and the region also contributes to memory formation for self-referential information (Kelley et al., 2002; Macrae et al., 2004). Older adults continue to engage this region similarly to younger adults (Gutchess et al., 2007, 2015), a pattern that contrasts the increases and reductions in neural activity with age that occur for many cognitive processes.

Despite the potential for preserved socioemotional processing with age, social and emotional processes may intersect with cognitive abilities such that benefits for these types of information likely draw on the same mechanisms as other cognitive information (Kensinger and Gutchess, 2017). For example, forming detailed, accurate memories of personally meaningful social events likely draws on many of the same functions mediated by the hippocampus as memories that do not have socioemotional relevance. Thus, cognitive changes with age will also affect some aspects of socioemotional processing. For example, some work has suggested that theory of mind, the ability to put oneself in another's shoes or consider information from their perspective, may rely on cognitive abilities to some extent (Moran, 2013; Phillips, MacLean, and Allen, 2002).

One important difference between cognitive and socioemotional domains is that cognitive tasks typically vary in the amount of demand placed on cognitive resources. For example, as a person is asked to hold more items in working memory, the load will start to approach the person's capacity; older adults may approach that limit faster than younger adults. Many socioemotional tasks studied thus far do have clear variation in the amount of demand placed on processing resources. This feature may account for the relative similarity in neural engagement for younger and older adults on socioemotional tasks.

When age differences *do* emerge on these tasks, it may reflect the divergent ways in which younger and older adults approach the task. For example, older adults may prioritize the processing of positive over negative information (Cassidy et al., 2013; LeClerc and Kensinger, 2008) or think about the self in a more relative manner (considering the self in comparison to others) (Gutchess et al., 2015) than younger adults. These strategy differences evoke different patterns of neural engagement that do not so much reflect differences in ability with age, but differences in approach to the task. See Gutchess (2019) and Gutchess and Samanez-Larkin (2019) for further discussion of these ideas. In future work, it will be important to constrain or explicitly assess strategies, alongside variability in the amount of demand, in order to fully understand the effects of aging on socioemotional abilities.

Summary

In this chapter, we reviewed some of the changes that occur with age. In addition to widespread changes to the structure and functional engagement of the brain, there are many specific abilities that change, including memory, speed of processing, and executive functioning. Recent research illuminates that socioemotional abilities may be more preserved with age, but before embracing this idea, it is necessary to further understand the interplay of socioemotional and cognitive domains as well as further probe the ways in which strategy differences and task demands intersect in socioemotional tasks. We provide a neuroscientific perspective on age-related changes in processing that may be helpful for promoting better insights, advancing theory, and generating practical insights about consumer behavior and decision-making across the lifespan.

References

Andrews-Hanna, J. R., Snyder, A. Z., Vincent, J. L., Lustig, C., Head, D., Raichle, M. E., & Buckner, R. L. (2007). Disruption of large-scale brain systems in advanced aging. *Neuron, 56*(5), 924–935.

Angel, L., Bastin, C., Genon, S., Balteau, E., Phillips, C., Luxen, A., Maquet, P., Salmon, E., & Collette, F. (2013). Differential effects of aging on the neural correlates of recollection and familiarity. *Cortex, 49*(6), 1585–1597.

Backman, L., Karlsson, S., Fischer, H., Karlsson, P., Brehmer, Y., Rieckmann, A., MacDonald, S. W., Farde, L., & Nyberg, L. (2011). Dopamine D(1) receptors and age differences in brain activation during working memory. *Neurobiol Aging, 32*(10), 1849–1856. doi:10.1016/j.neurobiolaging.2009.10.018.

Backman, L., Nyberg, L., Lindenberger, U., Li, S. C., & Farde, L. (2006). The correlative triad among aging, dopamine, and cognition: Current status and future prospects. *Neurosci Biobehav Rev, 30*(6), 791–807. doi:10.1016/j.neubiorev.2006.06.005.

Beckmann, C. F., DeLuca, M., Devlin, J. T., & Smith, S. M. (2005). Investigations into resting-state connectivity using independent component analysis. *Philos Trans R Soc Lond B Biol Sci, 360*(1457), 1001–1013. doi:10.1098/rstb.2005.1634.

Burzynska, A. Z., Wong, C. N., Voss, M. W., Cooke, G. E., Gothe, N. P., Fanning, J., McAuley, E., & Kramer, A. F. (2015). Physical activity is linked to greater Moment-to-Moment variability in spontaneous brain activity in older adults. *PLoS One, 10*(8), e0134819.

Cabeza, R., Anderson, N. D., Locantore, J. K., & McIntosh, A. R. (2002). Aging gracefully: Compensatory brain activity in high-performing older adults. *Neuroimage, 17*(3), 1394–1402. doi:10.1006/nimg.2002.1280.

Cabeza, R., Grady, C. L., Nyberg, L., McIntosh, A. R., Tulving, E., Kapur, S., Jennings, J. M., Houle, S., & Craik, F. I. M. (1997). Age-related differences in neural activity during memory encoding and retrieval: A positron emission tomography study. *J Neurosci, 17*(1), 391.

Cacioppo, J. T., Hawkley, L. C., & Thisted, R. A. (2010). Perceived social isolation makes me sad: 5-year cross-lagged analyses of loneliness and depressive symptomatology in the Chicago Health, Aging, and Social Relations Study. *Psychol Aging, 25*(2), 453.

Campbell, K. L., Grady, C. L., Ng, C., & Hasher, L. (2012). Age differences in the frontoparietal cognitive control network: Implications for distractibility. *Neuropsychologia, 50*(9), 2212–2223.

Carey, C. L., Kramer, J. H., Josephson, S. A., Mungas, D., Reed, B. R., Schuff, N., Weiner, M. W., & Chui, H. C. (2008). Subcortical lacunes are associated with executive dysfunction in cognitively normal elderly. *Stroke, 39*(2), 397–402. doi:10.1161/STROKEAHA.107.491795.

Carne, R. P.,Vogrin, S., Litewka, L., & Cook, M. J. (2006). Cerebral cortex:An MRI-based study of volume and variance with age and sex. *J Clin Neurosci, 13*(1), 60–72.

Carp, J., Park, J., Hebrank, A., Park, D. C., & Polk, T. A. (2011). Age-related neural dedifferentiation in the motor system. *PLoS One, 6*(12), e29411. doi:10.1371/journal. pone.0029411.

Carpenter, S. M., & Yoon, C. (2011). Aging and consumer decision making. *Ann NY Acad Sci, 1235*, E1–E12. doi:10.1111/j.1749-6632.2011.06390.x.

Cassidy, B. S., Leshikar, E. D., Shih, J.Y., Aizenman, A., & Gutchess, A. H. (2013).Valence-based age differences in medial prefrontal activity during impression formation. *Soc Neurosci, 8*(5), 462–473. doi:10.1080/17470919.2013.832373.

Chan, M. Y., Park, D. C., Savalia, N. K., Petersen, S. E., & Wig, G. S. (2014). Decreased segregation of brain systems across the healthy adult lifespan. *Proc Natl Acad Sci U S A, 111*(46), E4997–E5006.

Costa, P. T., & McCrae, R. R. (1987). Neuroticism, somatic complaints, and disease: Is the bark worse than the bite? *J Pers, 55*(2), 299–316.

Craik, F. I. M., & Jennings, J. M. (1992). Human memory. In: F. I. M. Craik & T. A. Salthouse (Eds.), *The Handbook of Aging and Cognition* (pp. 51–110). Hillsdale, NJ England: Lawrence Erlbaum Associates, Inc.

Craik, F. I. M., & Rabinowitz, J. C. (1984). Age differences in the acquisition and use of verbal information:A tutorial review. *Atten Perform X, 10*, 471–499.

Crowe, M.,Andel, R., Pedersen, N. L., Johansson, B., & Gatz, M. (2003). Does participation in leisure activities lead to reduced risk of Alzheimer's disease? A prospective study of Swedish twins. *J Gerontol B Psychol Sci Soc Sci, 58*(5), 249–255. doi:10.1093/ geronb/58.5.p249.

Damoiseaux, J. S., Beckmann, C. F., Arigita, E. J., Barkhof, F., Scheltens, P., Stam, C. J., Smith, S. M., & Rombouts, S. A. (2008). Reduced resting-state brain activity in the "default network" in normal aging. *Cereb Cortex, 18*(8), 1856–1864. doi:10.1093/ cercor/bhm207.

Damoiseaux, J. S., Rombouts, S. A., Barkhof, F., Scheltens, P., Stam, C. J., Smith, S. M., & Beckmann, C. F. (2006). Consistent resting-state networks across healthy subjects. *Proc Natl Acad Sci U S A, 103*(37), 13848–13853. doi:10.1073/pnas.0601417103.

Davis, S.W., Dennis, N. A., Daselaar, S. M., Fleck, M. S., & Cabeza, R. (2008). Que PASA? The posterior-anterior shift in aging. *Cereb Cortex, 18*(5), 1201–1209.

Davis, S. W., Kragel, J. E., Madden, D. J., & Cabeza, R. (2012). The architecture of cross-hemispheric communication in the aging brain: Linking behavior to functional and structural connectivity. *Cereb Cortex, 22*(1), 232–242.

Denburg, N. L., Cole, C. A., Hernandez, M., Yamada, T. H., Tranel, D., Bechara, A., & Wallace, R. B. (2007).The orbitofrontal cortex, real-world decision making, and normal aging. *Ann NY Acad Sci, 1121*, 480–498. doi:10.1196/annals.1401.031.

Dennis, N. A., Kim, H., & Cabeza, R. (2007). Effects of aging on true and false memory formation:An fMRI study. *Neuropsychologia, 45*(14), 3157–3166.

Diamond, A. (2013). Executive functions. *Annual Review of Psychology, 64*, 135–168. doi: 10.1146/annurev-psych-113011-143750

Driscoll, I., Davatzikos, C., An,Y., Wu, X., Shen, D., Kraut, M., & Resnick, S. M. (2009). Longitudinal pattern of regional brain volume change differentiates normal aging from MCI. *Neurology, 72*(22), 1906–1913. doi:10.1212/WNL.0b013e3181a82634.

Duarte,A., Graham, K. S., & Henson, R. N. (2010). Age-related changes in neural activity associated with familiarity, recollection and false recognition. *Neurobiol Aging, 31*(10), 1814–1830.

Earles, J. L., Kersten, A. W., Berlin Mas, B., & Miccio, D. M. (2004). Aging and memory for self-performed tasks: Effects of task difficulty and time pressure. *J Gerontol B Psychol Sci Soc Sci, 59*(6), 285–293.

Eckert, M. A., Keren, N. I., Roberts, D. R., Calhoun, V. D., & Harris, K. C. (2010). Age-related changes in processing speed: Unique contributions of cerebellar and prefrontal cortex. *Front Hum Neurosci, 4*, 10. doi:10.3389/neuro.09.010.2010.

Esiri, M. M. (2007). Ageing and the brain. *J Pathol, 211*(2), 181–187. doi:10.1002/path.2089.

Farokhian, F., Yang, C., Beheshti, I., Matsuda, H., & Wu, S. (2017). Age-related gray and white matter changes in normal adult brains. *Aging Dis, 8*(6), 899–909. doi:10.14336/AD.2017.0502.

Fein, G., McGillivray, S., & Finn, P. (2007). Older adults make less advantageous decisions than younger adults: Cognitive and psychological correlates. *J Int Neuropsychol Soc, 13*(3), 480–489. doi:10.1017/S135561770707052X.

Finucane, M. L., Mertz, C. K., Slovic, P., & Schmidt, E. S. (2005). Task complexity and older adults' decision-making competence. *Psychol Aging, 20*(1), 71–84. doi:10.1037/0882-7974.20.1.71.

Fotenos, A. F., Mintun, M. A., Snyder, A. Z., Morris, J. C., & Buckner, R. L. (2008). Brain volume decline in aging: Evidence for a relation between socioeconomic status, preclinical Alzheimer disease, and reserve. *Arch Neurol, 65*(1), 113–120. doi:10.1001/archneurol.2007.27.

Fox, M. D., Corbetta, M., Snyder, A. Z., Vincent, J. L., & Raichle, M. E. (2006). Spontaneous neuronal activity distinguishes human dorsal and ventral attention systems. *Proc Natl Acad Sci U S A, 103*(26), 10046–10051. doi:10.1073/pnas.0604187103.

Freeman, S. H., Kandel, R., Cruz, L., Rozkalne, A., Newell, K., Frosch, M. P., Hedley-Whyte, E. T., Locascio, J. J., Lipsitz, L. A., & Hyman, B. T. (2008). Preservation of neuronal number despite age-related cortical brain atrophy in elderly subjects without Alzheimer disease. *J Neuropathol Exp Neurol, 67*(12), 1205–1212. doi:10.1097/NEN.0b013e31818fc72f.

Geerligs, L., Renken, R. J., Saliasi, E., Maurits, N. M., & Lorist, M. M. (2015). A brain-wide study of age-related changes in functional connectivity. *Cereb Cortex, 25*(7), 1987–1999. doi:10.1093/cercor/bhu012.

Geerligs, L., Saliasi, E., Maurits, N. M., & Lorist, M. M. (2012). Compensation through increased functional connectivity: Neural correlates of inhibition in old and young. *J Cogn Neurosci, 24*(10), 2057–2069. doi:10.1162/jocn_a_00270.

Goh, J. O., Suzuki, A., & Park, D. C. (2010). Reduced neural selectivity increases fMRI adaptation with age during face discrimination. *Neuroimage, 51*(1), 336–344.

Good, C. D., Johnsrude, I. S., Ashburner, J., Henson, R. N., Friston, K. J., & Frackowiak, R. S. (2001). A voxel-based morphometric study of ageing in 465 normal adult human brains. *Neuroimage, 14*(1 Pt 1), 21–36. doi:10.1006/nimg.2001.0786.

Grady, C. L., McIntosh, A. R., Horwitz, B., Maisog, J. M., Ungerleider, L. G., Mentis, M. J., Pietrini, P., Schapiro, M. B., & Haxby, J. V. (1995). Age-related reductions in human recognition memory due to impaired encoding. *Science, 269*(5221), 218.

Grady, C. L., Protzner, A. B., Kovacevic, N., Strother, S. C., Afshin-Pour, B., Wojtowicz, M., Anderson, J. A., Churchill, N., & McIntosh, A. R. (2010). A multivariate analysis of age-related differences in default mode and task-positive networks across multiple cognitive domains. *Cereb Cortex, 20*(6), 1432–1447. doi:10.1093/cercor/bhp207.

Gunning-Dixon, F. M., Brickman, A. M., Cheng, J. C., & Alexopoulos, G. S. (2009). Aging of cerebral white matter: A review of MRI findings. *Int J Geriatr Psychiatry, 24*(2), 109–117. doi:10.1002/gps.2087.

Gutchess, A., & Kensinger, E. A. (2018). Shared mechanisms may support mnemonic benefits from self-referencing and emotion. *Trends Cogn Sci, 22*(8), 712–724.

Gutchess, A., & Samanez-Larkin, G. R. (2019). Social function and motivation in the aging brain. In: G. Samanez-Larkin (Ed.), *The Aging Brain: Functional Adaptation Across Adulthood* (pp. 165–184). Washington, DC: APA.

Gutchess, A. H. (2019). *Cognitive and Social Neuroscience of Aging*. New York, NY: Cambridge University Press.

Gutchess, A. H., Kensinger, E. A., & Schacter, D. L. (2007). Aging, self-referencing, and medial prefrontal cortex. *Soc Neurosci, 2*(2), 117–133. doi:10.1080/17470910701399029.

Gutchess, A. H., & Schacter, D. L. (2012). The neural correlates of gist-based true and false recognition. *Neuroimage, 59*(4), 3418–3426.

Gutchess, A. H., Sokal, R., Coleman, J. A., Gotthilf, G., Grewal, L., & Rosa, N. (2015). Age differences in self-referencing: Evidence for common and distinct encoding strategies. *Brain Res, 1612*, 118–127. doi:10.1016/j.brainres.2014.08.033

Gutchess, A. H., Welsh, R. C., Hedden, T., Bangert, A., Minear, M., Liu, L. L., & Park, D. C. (2005). Aging and the neural correlates of successful picture encoding: frontal activations compensate for decreased medial-temporal activity. *Journal of Cognitive Neuroscience, 17*(1), 84–96. doi: 10.1162/0898929052880048

Habes, M., Erus, G., Toledo, J. B., Zhang, T., Bryan, N., Launer, L. J., Rosseel, Y., Janowitz, D., Doshi, J., Van der Auwera, S., von Sarnowski, B., Hegenscheid, K., Hosten, N., Homuth, G., Völzke, H., Schminke, U., Hoffmann, W., Grabe, H. J., & Davatzikos, C. (2016). White matter hyperintensities and imaging patterns of brain ageing in the general population. *Brain, 139*(Pt 4), 1164–1179. doi:10.1093/brain/aww008.

Hasher, L., Stoltzfus, E. R., Zacks, R. T., & Rypma, B. (1991). Age and inhibition. *J Exp Psychol Learn Mem Cogn, 17*(1), 163.

Hay, J. F., & Jacoby, L. L. (1999). Separating habit and recollection in young and older adults: Effects of elaborative processing and distinctiveness. *Psychol Aging, 14*(1), 122.

Jackson, J., Balota, D. A., & Head, D. (2011). Exploring the relationship between personality and regional brain volume in healthy aging. *Neurobiol Aging, 32*(12), 2162–2171. doi:10.1016/j.neurobiolaging.2009.12.009.

Kelley, W. M., Macrae, C. N., Wyland, C. L., Caglar, S., Inati, S., & Heatherton, T. F. (2002). Finding the self? An event-related fMRI study. *J Cogn Neurosci, 14*(5), 785–794.

Kensinger, E. A., & Gutchess, A. H. (2017). Cognitive aging in a social and affective context: Advances over the past 50 years. *J Gerontol B Psychol Sci Soc Sci, 72*(1), 61–70. doi:10.1093/geronb/gbw056.

Koutstaal, W., & Schacter, D. L. (1997). Gist-based false recognition of pictures in older and younger adults. *J Mem Lang, 37*(4), 555–583.

Kray, J., & Lindenberger, U. (2000). Adult age differences in task switching. *Psychol Aging, 15*(1), 126–147.

Kwon, Y. H., Jang, S. H., & Yeo, S. S. (2014). Age-related changes of lateral ventricular width and periventricular white matter in the human brain: A diffusion tensor imaging study. *Neural Regen Res, 9*(9), 986–989. doi:10.4103/1673-5374.133152.

Leclerc, C. M., & Kensinger, E. A. (2008). Age-related differences in medial prefrontal activation in response to emotional images. *Cogn Affect Behav Neurosci, 8*(2), 153–164. doi:10.3758/CABN.8.2.153.

Li, S. C., Lindenberger, U., & Sikstrom, S. (2001). Aging cognition: from neuromodulation to representation. *Trends Cogn Sci, 5*(11), 479–486.

Li, S. C., Papenberg, G., Nagel, I. E., Preuschhof, C., Schroder, J., Nietfeld, W., Bertram, L., Heekeren, H. R., Lindenberger, U., & Backman, L. (2013). Aging magnifies the effects of dopamine transporter and D2 receptor genes on backward serial memory. *Neurobiol Aging*, *34*(1), 358.e351–358.e310. doi:10.1016/j.neurobiolaging.2012.08.001.

Liu, H., Yang, Y., Xia, Y., Zhu, W., Leak, R. K., Wei, Z., Wang, J., & Hu, X. (2017). Aging of cerebral white matter. *Ageing Res Rev*, *34*, 64–76. doi:10.1016/j.arr.2016.11.006.

Luders, E., & Cherbuin, N. (2016). Searching for the philosopher's stone: Promising links between meditation and brain preservation. *Ann N Y Acad Sci*, *1373*(1), 38–44. doi:10.1111/nyas.13082.

Macrae, C. N., Moran, J. M., Heatherton, T. F., Banfield, J. F., & Kelley, W. M. (2004). Medial prefrontal activity predicts memory for self. *Cereb Cortex*, *14*(6), 647–654. doi:10.1093/cercor/bhh025.

Madden, D. J., Turkington, T. G., Provenzale, J. M., Hawk, T. C., Hoffman, J. M., & Coleman, R. E. (1997). Selective and divided visual attention: Age-related changes in regional cerebral blood flow measured by H2(15)O PET. *Hum Brain Mapp*, *5*(6), 389–409. doi:10.1002/(SICI)1097-0193(1997)5:6<389::AID-HBM1>3.0.CO;2-#.

Madden, D. J., Whiting, W. L., Huettel, S. A., White, L. E., MacFall, J. R., & Provenzale, J. M. (2004). Diffusion tensor imaging of adult age differences in cerebral white matter: Relation to response time. *Neuroimage*, *21*(3), 1174–1181. doi:10.1016/j.neuroimage.2003.11.004.

Mason, M. F., Norton, M. I., Van Horn, J. D., Wegner, D. M., Grafton, S. T., & Macrae, C. N. (2007). Wandering minds: The default network and stimulus-independent thought. *Science*, *315*(5810), 393–395.

Mather, M., Gorlick, M. A., & Lighthall, N. R. (2009). To brake or accelerate when the light turns yellow? Stress reduces older adults' risk taking in a driving game. *Psychol Sci*, *20*(2), 174–176.

McEwen, B. S. (2006). Protective and damaging effects of stress mediators: Central role of the brain. *Dial Clin Neurosci*, *8*(4), 367.

Miyake, A., Friedman, N., Emerson, M., Witzki, A., Howerter, A., & Wager, T. D. (2000). The unity and diversity of executive functions and their contributions to complex "frontal lobe" tasks: A latent variable analysis. *Cogn Psychol*, *41*(1), 49–100.

Moran, J. M. (2013). Lifespan development: The effects of typical aging on theory of mind. *Behav Brain Res*, *237*, 32–40. doi:10.1016/j.bbr.2012.09.020.

Papp, K. V., Kaplan, R. F., Springate, B., Moscufo, N., Wakefield, D. B., Guttmann, C. R., & Wolfson, L. (2014). Processing speed in normal aging: Effects of white matter hyperintensities and hippocampal volume loss. *Neuropsychol Dev Cogn B*, *21*(2), 197–213. doi:10.1080/13825585.2013.795513.

Park, D. C., Polk, T. A., Park, R., Minear, M., Savage, A., & Smith, M. R. (2004). Aging reduces neural specialization in ventral visual cortex. *Proc Natl Acad Sci U S A*, *101*(35), 13091–13095.

Park, D. C., & Reuter-Lorenz, P. A. (2009). The adaptive brain: Aging and neurocognitive scaffolding. *Annu Rev Psychol*, *60*, 173–196.

Persson, J., Lustig, C., Nelson, J. K., & Reuter-Lorenz, P. A. (2007). Age differences in deactivation: A link to cognitive control? *J Cogn Neurosci*, *19*(6), 1021–1032.

Phillips, L. H., MacLean, R. D., & Allen, R. (2002). Age and the understanding of emotions: Neuropsychological and sociocognitive perspectives. *J Gerontol B Psychol Sci Soc Sci*, *57*(6), 526–530. doi:10.1093/geronb/57.6.P526.

Prakash, R. S., De Leon, A. A., Patterson, B., Schirda, B. L., & Janssen, A. L. (2014). Mindfulness and the aging brain: A proposed paradigm shift. *Front Aging Neurosci, 6, 120.*

Raichle, M. E., MacLeod, A. M., Snyder, A. Z., Powers, W. J., Gusnard, D. A., & Shulman, G. L. (2001). A default mode of brain function. *Proc Natl Acad Sci U S A, 98*(2), 676–682.

Raz, N., Ghisletta, P., Rodrigue, K. M., Kennedy, K. M., & Lindenberger, U. (2010). Trajectories of brain aging in middle-aged and older adults: Regional and individual differences. *Neuroimage, 51*(2), 501–511. doi:10.1016/j.neuroimage.2010.03.020.

Raz, N., Gunning, F. M., Head, D., Dupuis, J. H., McQuain, J., Briggs, S. D., Loken, W. J., Thornton, A. E., & Acker, J. D. (1997). Selective aging of the human cerebral cortex observed in vivo: Differential vulnerability of the prefrontal gray matter. *Cereb Cortex, 7*(3), 268–282. doi:10.1093/cercor/7.3.268.

Raz, N., Lindenberger, U., Rodrigue, K. M., Kennedy, K. M., Head, D., Williamson, A., Dahle, C., Gerstorf, D., & Acker, J. D. (2005). Regional brain changes in aging healthy adults: General trends, individual differences and modifiers. *Cereb Cortex, 15*(11), 1676–1689. doi:10.1093/cercor/bhi044.

Resnick, S. M., Pham, D. L., Kraut, M. A., Zonderman, A. B., & Davatzikos, C. (2003). Longitudinal magnetic resonance imaging studies of older adults: A shrinking brain. *J Neurosci, 23*(8), 3295–3301.

Reuter-Lorenz, P. A., & Cappell, K. A. (2008). Neurocognitive aging and the compensation hypothesis. *Curr Dir Psychol Sci, 17*(3), 177–182. doi:10.1111/j.1467-8721.2008.00570.x.

Reuter-Lorenz, P. A., Jonides, J., Smith, E. E., Hartley, A., Miller, A., Marshuetz, C., & Koeppe, R. A. (2000). Age differences in the frontal lateralization of verbal and spatial working memory revealed by PET. *J Cogn Neurosci, 12*(1), 174–187.

Reuter-Lorenz, P. A., & Park, D. C. (2014). How does it STAC up? Revisiting the scaffolding theory of aging and cognition. *Neuropsychol Rev, 24*(3), 355–370. doi:10.1007/s11065-014-9270-9.

Salat, D. H., Buckner, R. L., Snyder, A. Z., Greve, D. N., Desikan, R. S. R., Busa, E., Morris, J. C., Dale, A. M., & Fischl, B. (2004). Thinning of the cerebral cortex in aging. *Cereb Cortex, 14*(7), 721–730.

Samanez-Larkin, G. R., Mata, R., Radu, P. T., Ballard, I. C., Carstensen, L. L., & McClure, S. M. (2011). Age differences in striatal delay sensitivity during intertemporal choice in healthy adults. *Front Neurosci, 5*, 126. doi:10.3389/fnins.2011.00126.

Scarmeas, N., Levy, G., Tang, M. X., Manly, J., & Stern, Y. (2001). Influence of leisure activity on the incidence of Alzheimer's disease. *Neurology, 57*(12), 2236–2242. doi:10.1212/wnl.57.12.2236.

Schacter, D. L., & Slotnick, S. D. (2004). The cognitive neuroscience of memory distortion. *Neuron, 44*(1), 149–160.

St Jacques, P. L., Rubin, D. C., & Cabeza, R. (2012). Age-related effects on the neural correlates of autobiographical memory retrieval. *Neurobiol Aging, 33*(7), 1298–1310.

St-Laurent, M., Abdi, H., Burianová, H., & Grady, C. L. (2011). Influence of aging on the neural correlates of autobiographical, episodic, and semantic memory retrieval. *J Cogn Neurosci, 23*(12), 4150–4163.

Stern, Y. (2002). What is cognitive reserve? Theory and research application of the reserve concept. *J Int Neuropsychol Soc, 8*(3), 448–460.

Stern, Y. (2012). Cognitive reserve in ageing and Alzheimer's disease. *Lancet Neurol, 11*(11), 1006–1012. doi:10.1016/S1474-4422(12)70191-6.

Tun, P. A., Wingfield, A., Rosen, M. J., & Blanchard, L. (1998). Response latencies for false memories: Gist-based processes in normal aging. *Psychol Aging, 13*(2), 230–241.

Valdes Hernandez Mdel, C., Booth, T., Murray, C., Gow, A. J., Penke, L., Morris, Z., Maniega, S. M., Royle, N. A., Aribisala, B. S., Bastin, M. E., Starr, J. M., Deary, I. J., & Wardlaw, J. M. (2013). Brain white matter damage in aging and cognitive ability in youth and older age. *Neurobiol Aging, 34*(12), 2740–2747. doi:10.1016/j.neurobiolaging.2013.05.032.

Velanova, K., Lustig, C., Jacoby, L. L., & Buckner, R. L. (2007). Evidence for frontally mediated controlled processing differences in older adults. *Cereb Cortex, 17*(5), 1033–1046. doi:10.1093/cercor/bhl013.

Verghese, J., Lipton, R. B., Katz, M. J., Hall, C. B., Derby, C. A., Kuslansky, G., Ambrose, A. F., Sliwinski, M., & Buschke, H. (2003). Leisure activities and the risk of dementia in the elderly. *N Engl J Med, 348*(25), 2508–2516. doi:10.1056/NEJMoa022252.

Verhaeghen, P., Kliegl, R., & Mayr, U. (1997). Sequential and coordinative complexity in time-accuracy functions for mental arithmetic. *Psychol Aging, 12*(4), 555–564.

Volkow, N. D., Gur, R. C., Wang, G.-J., Fowler, J. S., Moberg, P. J., Ding, Y.-S., Hitzemann, R., Smith, G., & Logan, J. (1998). Association between decline in brain dopamine activity with age and cognitive and motor impairment in healthy individuals. *Am J Psychiatry, 155*(3), 344–349.

Wang, L., Li, Y., Metzak, P., He, Y., & Woodward, T. S. (2010). Age-related changes in topological patterns of large-scale brain functional networks during memory encoding and recognition. *Neuroimage, 50*(3), 862–872.

Waring, J. D., Addis, D. R., & Kensinger, E. A. (2013). Effects of aging on neural connectivity underlying selective memory for emotional scenes. *Neurobiol Aging, 34*(2), 451–467. doi:10.1016/j.neurobiolaging.2012.03.011.

Wilson, R. S., & Bennett, D. A. (2017). How does psychosocial behavior contribute to cognitive health in old age? *Brain Sci, 7*(6). doi:10.3390/brainsci7060056.

Wilson, R. S., Hebert, L. E., Scherr, P. A., Barnes, L. L., Mendes de Leon, C. F., & Evans, D. A. (2009). Educational attainment and cognitive decline in old age. *Neurology, 72*(5), 460–465. doi:10.1212/01.wnl.0000341782.71418.6c.

Wright, C. I., Feczko, E., Dickerson, B. C., & Williams, D. (2007). Neuroanatomical correlates of personality in the elderly. *Neuroimage, 35*(1), 263–272.

2

CHANGES IN MEMORY AND METACOGNITION IN OLDER ADULTHOOD[1]

Alexander L. M. Siegel, Mary C. Whatley,
Mary B. Hargis, and Alan D. Castel

Changes in Memory and Metacognition in Older Adulthood

We use our memory in a variety of settings. As people age, older adults often have difficulty remembering and retrieving names, and rely on habits, prior knowledge, strategies, and emotional processes, and these age-related changes can influence individual behavior. While there are some aspects of memory that may decline with age, older adults can utilize contextual factors (Hess, 2005) and goals-based strategies to selectively remember important information (Castel et al., 2012). In this chapter, we review how different forms of memory are influenced by the aging process, and how one's perspective and awareness of memory abilities (metamemory) can play a role in how older adults remember information.

It is well established that our ability to perform various cognitive processes may decline with advancing age (for review see Craik and Salthouse, 2008). Empirical research has shown a steady decline in working memory capacity, executive functioning, processing speed, and explicit memory ability across the adult lifespan (McCabe, Roediger, McDaniel, Balota, and Hambrick, 2010). However, some processes (such as vocabulary knowledge) appear to be impervious to, or even improve with, the aging process. Many theories have been suggested in order to explain why these selective cognitive deficits occur including a general decline in processing speed (general slowing theory), a reduction in the amount of cognitive resources available (reduced resources theory), the inability to inhibit irrelevant information (inhibition deficit theory), and the accelerated deterioration of pre-frontal brain regions (prefrontal theory). In all likelihood, the confluence of these different factors contributes to age-related decline in cognitive ability.

In general, aging is accompanied by marked declines in episodic memory (Hultsch, Hertzog, Small, McDonald-Miszczak, and Dixon, 1992; Zacks, Hasher, and Li, 2000). One of the major complaints of older adults as they age is that they notice an increase in their forgetting of information and that their memory is declining (Schweich et al., 1992; Weaver Cargin, Collie, Masters, and Maruff, 2008). Indeed, our explicit memory capacity and rate of cognitive processing declines over time—from one's early 20s on, steep declines in working, short-term, and long-term memory ability are observed (Park et al., 2002). Simply put, older adults have poorer memory capacity, quality, and accuracy as compared to younger adults (Koriat and Goldsmith, 1996). However, as extensive research has shown, not all types of memory are equally impaired and older adults often use strategies to compensate for age-related memory deficits.

In this chapter, we will discuss how our memory ability changes as we age, including deficits in recollecting specific details and the source of information. We'll also review the way in which various memory abilities are preserved in old age, with older adults' reliance on schematic support and preserved ability to prioritize important information. Finally, older adults' metacognitive and in particular, metamemory, abilities will be reviewed. Importantly, the work discussed in this chapter will focus on cognitively healthy older adults who are experiencing nonpathological aging, in contrast to those with mild cognitive impairment (MCI), Alzheimer's disease, Parkinson's disease, or other neurocognitive disorders that affect cognition in older age (for reviews on various neurocognitive disorders in aging, see Caballol, Martí, and Tolosa, 2007; Carlesimo and Oscar-Berman, 1992; Petersen et al., 2001).

Memory Impairments in Healthy Aging

Recollection and Familiarity

One of the memorial consequences of growing older is a reduction in the amount and strength of recollective details (Koen and Yonelinas, 2014), as our memories may move away from the verbatim and toward more gist-based representations. Consider the following example: Imagine that you are walking down the main thoroughfare in your hometown. As you cross the street, you look up and make eye contact with someone crossing from the other side. As you walk toward him, you are overtaken by a feeling of familiarity that you have seen this man before, but are unable to remember his name or any other details about him. Still, this lingering feeling of "I've seen this man before" remains. As you pass by him, you flash a polite smile and carry on with your day. Later on, it suddenly dawns upon you: John was the coach of your son's baseball team a few years ago. You can now remember various details that you previously learned about John (e.g., his wife, Lisa, is a member of the parent-teacher association, his son was #7 on the team, etc.).

This example (similar to the classic "butcher-on-the-bus" example put forth by Mandler, 1980) demonstrates the concept of recognition memory, a type of declarative memory. In contrast to recall memory in which information is retrieved without any external stimulus cue, recognition memory involves matching an encountered stimulus or event to related information in long-term memory. Recognition memory can be further subdivided into two categories: familiarity and recollection. Events depicted in the above example provide an illustration of how this distinction might manifest in daily life. Familiarity is associated with a vague "feeling of knowing" that one has encountered a stimulus before, but with the absence of any related details. When you encounter the man crossing the street, your initial reaction (i.e., the feeling of "I've seen this man before") represents familiarity-based recognition. Recollection, however, is associated with retrieval of specific details associated with a previously learned fact or experienced event. Your ability to retrieve specific details about the man (i.e., his name, profession, where you first met him, etc.) represents a conscious, recollective experience.

While situations like the one detailed in the introduction provide an intuitive way for us to understand the distinction between familiarity and recollection, they do not lend themselves very well to scientific inquiry. After Mandler (1980) formally described the familiarity-recollection distinction, Canadian psychologist Endel Tulving was the first to establish a procedure that could operationalize this distinction in an experimental setting. The "remember-know" paradigm (herein referred to as R/K paradigm; Tulving, 1985) was designed to allow for researchers to probe recognition memory in a controlled, methodical manner. In a typical R/K paradigm, participants are asked to study a list of sequentially presented stimuli (usually semantically unrelated words). Then, after a certain delay, participants' memory for that information is tested. Importantly, unlike a free-recall test in which participants are just asked to recall as many words as possible from the previous list, the R/K paradigm tests for recognition memory by sequentially presenting participants with previously viewed stimuli (targets) and new, not previously viewed stimuli (non-targets or lures).

Participants' memory for each stimulus is evaluated using a two-step process during testing. First, participants are required to make an objective old/new judgment about the stimulus, with "old" indicating that the stimulus was previously presented during the study period and "new" indicating that the stimulus was not previously presented. Then, if participants indicate that a stimulus was old, they are to make a subjective remember/know judgment about the quality of their memory for that stimulus. "Remember" indicates that there is a conscious, recollective experience associated with that stimulus, whereas "know" indicates that the participants have a sense of familiarity for the stimulus, but the absence of any explicit detail associated with its presentation. For example, during study, participants may have been presented with a list of words containing the following string: CRATE-DECOY-FRONT. When tested, if prompted with "DECOY," participants should provide an old response, then determine whether they consciously remember seeing the word (and thus provide a "remember" response) or if they simply know the word was presented due to a feeling of familiarity, but in the absence of any explicit memory of its presentation (and thus provide a "know" response). In some paradigms, participants are given a third option "guess" to indicate that their old response was the result of a random guess, which has been shown to increase participants' ability to correctly discriminate between old and new information (Eldridge, Sarfatti, and Knowlton, 2002). Further, if prompted with the word "SPEAR" during the test, participants should provide a new response to indicate that the word was not presented during the study period.

Much research has examined how recollection and familiarity change across the adult life span. In a large meta-analysis, Koen and Yonelinas (2014) investigated 25 empirical studies that sought to clarify the role of recollective and familiarity-based memory in cognitively healthy aging. Across all of the examined studies, moderate to large deficits in the ability to recollect information were observed. The effects of aging on familiarity-based memory was more mixed: Some studies found no impairment in familiarity (e.g., Cohn, Emrich, and Moscovitch, 2008; Parkin and Walter, 1992; Yonelinas, 2002), while others observed declines in the accuracy of familiarity-based episodic memory (Friedman, de Chastelaine, Nessler, and Malcolm, 2010; Prull, Dawes, Martin, Rosenberg, and Light, 2006; Wang, de Chastelaine, Minton, and Rugg, 2012). This apparent discrepancy in findings was attributed to the type of paradigm utilized, with deficits observed in those using the previously described R/K paradigm, but not those using other methods (Koen and Yonelinas, 2014). Regardless, these results suggest that aging is associated with a large decline in the amount of recollective details remembered, with smaller (or perhaps no) deficits in familiarity-based memory.

From a neurocognitive perspective, this dissociation between declines in recollection and familiarity can be partly explained by differences in the structural and functional deterioration of various brain regions. It is well established that within the medial temporal lobe (MTL), the hippocampus is integral in recollection, while surrounding areas like the perirhinal cortex are responsible for familiarity (Diana, Yonelinas, and Ranganath, 2007; Eichenbaum, Yonelinas, and Ranganath, 2007; Yonelinas, Aly, Wang, and Koen, 2010). While aging is associated with widespread and complex changes in neural functioning, there is generally a decrease in hippocampal volume (Driscoll et al., 2003; Raz et al., 2005) accompanied by hippocampally-dependent memory processes, like recollection (Westerberg et al., 2013; Wolk, Dunfee, Dickerson, Aizenstein, and DeKosky, 2011). However, other MTL areas like the perirhinal cortex exhibit relatively less volumetric decline (Raz, Rodrigue, Head, Kennedy, and Acker, 2004; Yonelinas et al., 2007) and may correlate with relatively intact familiarity (Wolk et al., 2011; Yonelinas et al., 2007). As such, these differences in recollection and familiarity appear to map onto structural changes in relevant brain areas that occur with age. This impaired ability to recollect specific details associated with an event can have a pervasive impact on older adults' daily lives. For example, as will be discussed in the following section, older adults may experience source memory deficits in which they are unable to correctly remember the context in which information was learned.

Source Memory

Consider the previously-mentioned example of John, the baseball coach. The inability to place the familiar face with its source is an example of a deficit in source memory. When recalling information, it is often important to remember the source of that information, as this can provide clues about credibility and help us decide how to act on that information. While item memory refers to memory for content (e.g., a word, image, or fact), source memory is memory for the context (e.g., who, what, where) in which an item was encountered (see Johnson, Hashtroudi, and Lindsay, 1993 for a review). Contextual information can be perceptual in nature, such as an item's visual location, or more conceptually tied to the item, like the truth of a statement. We encounter source information in many everyday situations. For example, when running into someone you've met before, you might want to not only remember that you've seen that person, but also who introduced you, where you met, or other contextual information so you know how to interact.

In studies of source memory, participants are typically presented with an item, such as a word, image, or phrase, that is paired with a source (e.g., a word spoken by a specific voice, an image that appears in a certain location on a computer screen). When their memory is tested, participants must not only recall seeing the item before, but also the source it was paired with. This task is more difficult than remembering the item alone, but is particularly difficult for older adults, who show specific impairments in source memory (Burke and Light, 1981; Park and Puglisi, 1985; Rabinowitz, 1989). In one study of source memory, older and younger adults studied a list of fictional, non-famous names, like "Sebastion Weisdorf." A week later, participants were tested on the names they had studied (as well as new names) and asked to identify the source of the names. Both younger and older adults made source mistakes, such that they attributed names they had seen in the experiment to those of actual famous people, but older adults were significantly more likely than younger adults to make this mistake. Older adults seemed to recognize the non-famous names as familiar, but they couldn't correctly recall the source of these names, which led to falsely believing the names were famous (Dywan and Jacoby, 1990). In another study, McIntyre and Craik (1987) showed that older adults were more likely than younger adults to falsely attribute the source of trivia questions they had learned in an experiment to a source outside the experiment (e.g., TV, book, magazine, friend, etc.). These findings not only highlight the difficulty of remembering source information for older adults, but also demonstrate how familiarity can sometimes negatively impact the ability to accurately remember source information.

One proposed hypothesis for source memory deficits in older age is that source memory largely depends on previously discussed recollection processes (Yonelinas, 1999; cf. Addante, Ranganath, and Yonelinas, 2012; Mollison and Curran, 2012). When recalling seeing a word on a computer screen, for example, recollection would involve distinctly remembering what the word looked like (e.g., font, color, size), what you were feeling and doing at the time, and maybe even what was presented beforehand or afterward. In other words, recollection often involves context-rich memories. Familiarity, on the other hand, usually includes a vague "feeling of knowing" but without knowledge of the contextual details or a very strong memory of the event itself. While remembering sources and contextual details tends to rely more heavily on recollection processes, older adults typically experience familiarity more often when remembering (see Koen and Yonelinas, 2014 for a meta-analysis), which may partially explain age differences in source memory.

Some evidence suggests that declines in executive functioning and associative memory may also contribute to source memory deficits (Shing et al., 2013). Executive functioning largely relies on an area of the brain called the prefrontal cortex (PFC) and includes tasks like focusing attention when distractors are present, holding information in memory to manipulate or use later, and adapting cognitive processes to different situations or perspectives (see Diamond, 2013 for a review). The ability to successfully integrate information with one or more sources for successful source retrieval is thought to depend on executive functioning abilities and the PFC (Mitchell and Johnson, 2009). With increasing age, the volume of and connectivity in the PFC tends to decrease, and older adults show less activity in this area compared to younger adults during source memory tasks (Dennis et al., 2008; Dulas and Duarte, 2011).

In addition, successful source memory depends on the ability to bind two or more pieces of information together in memory (i.e., an item and its contextual details), known as associative binding or associative memory. Associative memory also declines in older age (Chalfonte and Johnson, 1996; Naveh-Benjamin, 2000; Siegel and Castel, 2018) and is reliant on many brain areas but especially the hippocampus. Older adults show reduced hippocampal activity in source memory tasks compared to younger adults (Dennis et al., 2008), which may also account for some of the difficulty in performing these tasks. While both associative binding and executive functioning are important for successful memory performance in general, they seem to be required to a greater degree in the successful integration of items with their sources.

Although there is ample evidence supporting a source memory deficit in older adults, there seem to be some instances in which age differences in source memory are reduced. In one study, for example, older and younger adults studied statements that were read by either a male or female voice. One of the voices (e.g., the female voice) always indicated that the statement was true, whereas the other voice always indicated that the statement was false. When tested after a delay on which voice was paired with each statement, older adults were less accurate than younger adults, which was in line with prior work showing age-related deficits in source memory. However, when tested on the truth of the statements, there were no age differences in performance, indicating that older adults were able to remember more conceptual or meaningful contextual information (Rahhal, May, and Hasher, 2002). Another study extended these findings by examining memory for source information about various food items. As expected, older adults were worse at remembering the perceptual details of the foods than younger adults. Interestingly, older adults also showed lower performance than younger adults in remembering a conceptual detail that was neutral in nature (serving temperature), but were just as good as younger adults at remembering an emotional conceptual detail (whether the food would make people sick or not; May, Rahhal, Berry, and Leighton, 2005). These findings suggest that memory for conceptual, meaningful context, particularly information that is emotional or socially important in nature, is more likely to be preserved in older age.

In these cases, remembering the truth of statements or safety of food items may have also been more in line with older adults' goals than remembering the perceptual details. Other work has supported the role of goals or motivation in improving age-related deficits in source memory. For example, age differences are reduced or even eliminated when participants relate the items to themselves (Hamami, Serbun, and Gutchess, 2011; Leshikar and Duarte, 2012) or when source information is central to task goals and affects gains or losses (Bell, Giang, Mund, and Buchner, 2013). These findings are in line with theories of aging that suggest motivational shifts occur in older age (e.g., Carstensen, 2006), and older adults may become more selective with their limited resources and focus on meaningful or valuable information to optimize outcomes (e.g., Hess, 2014). As will be discussed below, these ideas have been further supported by work showing that older adults are able to selectively allocate their attention and cognitive resources to information that is important, valuable, or meaningful, both subjectively and objectively, and are able to successfully remember this information (e.g., Castel, 2008; Castel, McGillivray, and Friedman, 2012; Siegel and Castel, 2018). Overall, it seems that while older adults may experience deficits in memory for source information, they retain the ability to focus on contextual details that are in line with emotional or meaningful goals.

Preserved Memory Abilities in Old Age

Value-Directed Remembering

Often the information that we are attempting to remember varies in importance. For example, it is usually more important to remember your doctor's office phone number as compared to your neighbor's, or the location of your wallet as compared to your pen. The value or importance of this information, then, can influence what we pay attention to and remember. In particular, as we age, we tend to become more selective in the information that we attempt to (and later do) remember. This can be viewed as an adaptive strategy in order to offset an age-related impairment in memory capacity—that is, older adults may think to themselves: "Well, I cannot remember all of the information present, so I may as well remember what is most important." Younger adults, on the other hand, may not routinely utilize such selective strategies and attempt to remember as much information as possible.

As previously discussed, older adults often experience marked declines in various types of memory. However, in some cases, older adults are able to use strategies to compensate for age-related memory deficits. The selection, optimization, and compensation model (SOC; Baltes and Baltes, 1990) posits that older adults, aware of their overall memory deficits, are able to selectively focus on specific information in an effort to alleviate those memory deficits. The model predicts that older adults *select* important information to which they can focus cognitive resources toward in order to *optimize* potential gains and *compensate* for potential losses. The SOC model predicts that older adults may be able to selectively focus on and later remember information that they deem important. Given clear memory deficits, this strategy represents an efficient use of cognitive resources by older adults.

Empirical research in the domain of memory selectivity has shown that older adults are in fact able to focus on high-value information at the expense of competing low-value information, a process termed value-directed remembering (VDR; Castel, Benjamin, Craik, and Watkins, 2002; Castel, 2008). In this experimental paradigm, older and younger adults were shown a list of 12 unrelated words, each paired with a point value 1–12. Participants were told that they would receive the point value associated with a word if they correctly remembered it and that their goal was to maximize their score (the summation of all the points associated with correctly remembered words). The results showed that although older adults remembered a lower proportion of the lower value words (values 1–9), they remembered the same proportion of high-value words (values 10–12) as the younger adults. The author suggests that the older adults, aware of their limited memory capacity, were able to selectively focus on the high-value words in order to maximize their score. So, while older adults remembered a lower proportion of words overall, they were able to compensate for age-related memory deficits by focusing on the important information to boost their point scores.

While the VDR paradigm defines value using a point-based system, what makes information valuable in the real world can vary from the likelihood of using that information in the future (e.g., your new doctor's phone number) to the consequences of not remembering that information (e.g., severe symptoms resulting from a failure to take your medication). Other research has also shown that older adults can employ VDR strategies in more applied contexts. Hargis and Castel (2017) presented younger and older participants with photos of people that they met at a fictional party and were designated as less important (i.e., they would not be seen or interacted with again), broadly important (i.e., they would be seen, but not interacted with, again), or personally important (i.e., they would be seen and interacted with again). In addition, each person was paired with a name and occupation. While younger adults recalled more relevant information for less important people, there was no difference in memory between younger and older adults for broadly and personally important people, extending previous VDR findings to an applied social context. Further research has demonstrated older adults' memory selectivity for important medication side effects (Friedman, McGillivray, Murayama, and Castel, 2015; Hargis and Castel, 2018), memory for people who owe them money (Castel, Friedman, et al., 2016), and memory for important items in varying spatial locations (Siegel and Castel, 2018). Thus, when presented with more information than they can remember, older adults may focus on the most important information in a variety of different contexts to offset their limited memory capacity.

While both younger and older adults can selectively prioritize information in memory, the mechanism underlying this selectivity may be different, as evidenced by neuroscientific studies. Advancing age is linked to a decline in dopaminergic modulation (Bäckman, Nyberg, Lindenberger, Li, and Farde, 2006; Kaasinen et al., 2000) and many of the cognitive impairments associated with age have been associated with a degradation of dopaminergic systems (Volkow et al., 1998). Importantly, the activation of dopaminergic reward systems has been proposed as a possible explanation for VDR effects, at least in younger adults. Cohen, Rissman, Suthana, Castel, and Knowlton (2014) examined the neural correlates of VDR, using pairs of words and point values that were tested via free recall. Younger adults were given a standard VDR paradigm while undergoing fMRI which revealed greater activation in dopaminergic reward regions (i.e., the ventral tegmental area and nucleus accumbens) on high-value relative to low-value trials. These results indicate that, for younger adults, episodic memory benefited from reward anticipation. In addition, there was greater activation in the left ventrolateral prefrontal cortex (left VLPFC; an area associated with deep semantic processing) when encoding high-value words and a significant correlation of activity in this area with a measure of memory selectivity, suggesting that explicit usage of deep semantic processing strategies may also contribute to the selective encoding of high-value information in the context of this task.

When examining older adults, it was found that similar semantic processing regions were associated with memory selectivity, but that the pattern of activation in such areas differed from younger adults (Cohen, Rissman, Suthana, Castel, and Knowlton, 2016). Specifically, older adults were *less* likely to engage areas associated with semantic processing (e.g., the left VLPFC) during the presentation of low-value information, whereas younger adults were *more* likely to engage these areas during the presentation of high-value information. Interestingly, activation in dopaminergic reward regions was not modulated by the value of information in older adults. These findings highlight the importance of semantic processing areas but call into question the role of dopaminergic reward systems, at least for older adults, in VDR tasks. Given that older adults often show equivalent (or in some cases, enhanced) selectivity on VDR tasks (Castel, 2008; Castel et al., 2002), future research should investigate the extent to which activation in dopaminergic reward systems and engagement of fronto-temporal regions during explicit strategy use contribute to older adults' selectivity on these reward-based tasks.

Reliance on Schematic Knowledge

The usage of schemas, cognitive heuristics based on prior experience that dictate what information is likely to be part of a given event, aids in the encoding and retrieval of memories. Take, for example, ordering a meal at a restaurant. Based on your prior experiences, you probably have some generalized knowledge about the typical sequence of events: You take a seat at the table, review the menu, place your order with the waiter, and then receive your meal. If you are unable to retrieve the exact details of a particular restaurant experience, then, you can rely on this "ordering at a restaurant" schema to infer what events most likely occurred. In this sense, schemas are particularly useful, allowing us to encode and retrieve memories of typical events with relative ease. However, much like other cognitive heuristics, the usage of schemas can lead to errors, especially for atypical events (events that are inconsistent with a schema), causing us to remember an event how it "should have" occurred rather than the actual details of an experienced event. In any case, the role of schematic knowledge in memory has been extensively researched in the aging population, suggesting that, with fewer remembered episodic details, older adults may be more reliant on schemas to aid memory (Castel, 2005; Craik and Bosman, 1992; Hess and Slaughter, 1990), even in cases of pathological aging like Alzheimer's disease (Rusted, Gaskell, Watts, and Sheppard, 2000; Zacks, Speer, Vettel, and Jacoby, 2006). This can be beneficial when newly learned information is consistent with schematic knowledge helping to reduce memory deficits, but particularly detrimental when information is inconsistent with older adults' prior knowledge and experience.

An early seminal study examined the role of schematic knowledge in remembering places in younger adults (Brewer and Treyens, 1980). In this study, participants were asked to wait in what they were told was a graduate student's office prior to their participation in an experiment. The waiting room was carefully constructed to include objects that were schema-consistent (e.g., a desk, typewriter, and coffee pot) and schema-inconsistent (e.g., a skull and toy top). Crucially, there were also schema-consistent items that were intentionally omitted from the room—that is, there were no books in the offices when most graduate student offices would certainly contain books of some variety. When later asked to recall the contents of the room, while most people correctly remembered schema-consistent information that was present like the typewriter and coffee pot, many participants falsely recalled the presence of books. Participants were also less likely to remember the presence of schema-inconsistent information within the room like the skull or toy top. These findings suggest that participants were relying on a schema to remember what objects were present within the office and that participants' expectations of what is typically present in academic offices altered their recall of the scene, leading to errors in memory in this circumstance.

Older adults' reliance on schematic knowledge has since been demonstrated in a variety of different contexts. Hess and Slaughter (1990) also explored how memory for visual scenes would be influenced by schemas in younger and older adults. In this task, younger and older adults were presented with drawings of objects varying in typicality depending on the context. Spatial configurations were also varied, such that in an organized condition, participants were shown a kitchen scene containing objects in typical locations (e.g., the refrigerator next to the stove, the window above the stove, etc.), while in an unorganized condition, objects were randomly presented within the array. The results indicated older adults' attentional allocation processes (examined via fixation duration) and subsequent memory (tested via object recognition tests) for the information within the scene were disrupted to a greater extent by a lack of organization relative to younger adults. Further, the likelihood of an object being present within the scene had a greater effect on object recognition performance for older adults, with more accurate memory for more likely objects. Other related work suggests that when older adults are able to use schema-based spatial information, age-related memory deficits may be reduced or eliminated (Dai, Thomas, and Taylor, 2018; Waddell & Rogoff, 1981) and that older adults recruit similar brain regions to younger adults (e.g., the ventromedial prefrontal cortex; vmPFC) when retrieving schema-specific visual information (Webb and Dennis, 2019). Taken together, these findings demonstrate that the use of schemas in visual scene recognition persists in old age and suggest that the removal of schema-based spatial information is particularly detrimental for older adults, highlighting their reliance on schematic knowledge in these tasks.

Outside of the visual memory literature, other work exploring the role of schematic knowledge in price evaluations has found that older adults' memory may benefit when the prices of various items are consistent with previously formed schemas about the value of those items (Castel, 2005). Younger and older adults were presented with grocery items and associated prices that were either underpriced (e.g., $0.39 for a jar of pickles), overpriced ($17.89 for a jug of milk), or market value ($1.89 for a head of broccoli). On a cued recall test for the prices, younger adults outperformed older adults on underpriced and overpriced items. However, there were no differences in memory performance when examining market value items. This finding suggests that, for market price items, older adults were able to rely on their schematic knowledge of what items "should" be worth in order to aid their memory performance, while they were not able to do so for items that were underpriced or overpriced. In fact, in this task involving naturalistic materials, older adults' reliance on schematic knowledge eliminated age-related memory deficits for price information. This memorial benefit of schematic support for older adults has been demonstrated in a variety of other contexts including higher memory performance for statements made by a doctor (relative to a bank teller) after a medical schema was activated during encoding (Besken and Gülgöz, 2009), for faces that were presented with congruent ages (relative to incongruent ages; McGillivray and Castel, 2010), when statements were consistent with previously held stereotypes (Mather, Johnson, and De Leonardis, 1999), and for typical actions read in prose passages (Hess and Pullen, 1996). In each of these tasks, older adults' memory performance is significantly negatively impacted when schematic support is removed or otherwise made unavailable, suggesting that older adults may rely on schemas to remember information in a variety of contexts.

It is important to note, however, that there is also work suggesting that older adults' usage of schematic knowledge may not reduce observed memory deficits (Arbuckle, Cooney, Milne, and Melchior, 1994; Morrow, Menard, Stine-Morrow, Teller, and Bryant, 2001) and may even hinder it in some instances by increasing errors (Balota et al., 1999; Mather et al., 1999; Norman and Schacter, 1997; Tun, Wingfield, Rosen, and Blanchard, 1998). For example, a sample of airline pilots, ranging in age from 20 to 75 years old, were asked to listen to simulated air traffic control messages describing a route (e.g., "Climb and maintain 7000 feet," "Increase speed to 220 knots") while referring to a visual chart of the airspace (Morrow et al., 2001). Later, they were asked to recall the specific routes described by the messages by reciting the messages and drawing the routes on a map. Younger pilots recalled flight-related information more accurately than the older pilots, indicating that age-related memory deficits were not reduced for pilots, even though they could rely on their schematic knowledge. This was the case even though the older pilots had more experience than their younger pilot counterparts. Another study found that although older adults were more negatively affected by the violation of a typical house layout schema, age-related memory deficits were still present when tested on their memory for typical house layouts (Arbuckle et al., 1994).

This over-reliance on schemas has also been shown to produce more memory errors in older adults. Take, for example, the Deese-Roediger-McDermott (DRM; Deese, 1959; Roediger and McDermott, 1995) task, in which participants study semantically associated words (e.g., *sill, curtain, view, pane, glass*). In this task, participants are likely to recall a semantically associated, but non-presented target word (e.g., *window*). Prior work has shown that older adults are more likely to remember this non-presented target word, as well as other non-presented, but semantically related words (Balota, et al., 1999; Norman and Schacter, 1997; Tun et al., 1998). These results suggest that the activation of a particular schema (in this case, information related to the word "window") caused older adults to falsely remember information that was unpresented at a higher rate than younger adults. Further, in investigating memory for stereotypical information (a form of a social-based schema), older adults were more likely than younger adults to falsely attribute an unpresented statement (e.g., "The federal government must do more to protect our environment") to a stereotype-consistent individual (e.g., a Democrat) as compared to a stereotype-inconsistent individual (e.g., a Republican; Mather et al., 1999).

In sum, older adults' ability to apply schematic knowledge and rely on schematic support remains intact across the lifespan and this reliance can aid memory in certain circumstances like remembering market price grocery items or typical spatial layouts. However, in atypical or unusual cases, this dependence on schemas can lead to memory errors for older adults who may experience fewer episodic details and rely more on schematic support as they age.

Metacognitive Changes in Older Adulthood

Metacognition, the ability to monitor and control our cognitive processes, is a crucial aspect of daily functioning. Metamemory, the metacognitive processes associated with memory, allows us to assess memory quality or strength and adjust our behavior to regulate our memories. For example, when learning information for an upcoming exam, it is imperative for a successful student to accurately evaluate their knowledge of the material (e.g., "How well do I know this piece of information?") and adjust their behavior to account for this evaluation (e.g., "I do not know it that well, so I need to study this information in more depth"). Metacognitive functioning is also critical in old age when memory errors may be more frequent. For example, older adults must remember which medications they have taken in a given day and must be able to adjust their behavior in order to account for this assessment (e.g., "I forgot to take my blood pressure medication earlier, so I must do so now"). As such, it is important for younger and older adults to accurately monitor their memory performance and subsequently control their behaviors to maximize this performance.

Metamemory is generally subdivided into two separate, but closely related processes: monitoring and control (Nelson, 1996). Monitoring involves checking in on or assessing the strength or accuracy of one's own knowledge and is measured by feelings of knowing (FOK), judgments of learning (JOL), and confidence judgments (for a review of these different measures, see Schwartz, 1994). Accurate monitoring is particularly crucial as it informs us of what we know and how well we know it and allows us to adjust future behaviors to improve memory performance. Control, on the other hand, involves the manipulation and regulation of memory processes including changes in study decisions. It is evident that these two processes are intrinsically linked with monitoring affecting the subsequent control of memory. Much like memory itself, metamemory is also prone to errors—for example, when learning a new acquaintance's phone number, we may *think* we know the information well and adjust our behavior to account for this knowledge (no longer trying to memorize the digits), but ultimately misremember the number representing both memory (i.e., misrecalling the number) and metamemory (i.e., inaccurately assessing your knowledge) errors.

Importantly, while aging is accompanied by declines in memory performance, this does not necessarily definitively imply metamemory deficits. That is, despite committing more memory errors, one could be equally as accurate in assessing their knowledge. Effective metacognitive functioning may become more important as we age due to an increase in the frequency of episodic memory errors (Hertzog and Dixon, 1994). Thus, the ability to monitor when information will be later remembered or forgotten may be a particularly important skill for older adults. In contrast to well-documented episodic memory deficits that occur with advancing age (for a review, see Hess, 2005; Zacks and Hasher, 2006), metacognitive processes associated with memory may experience little to no age-related decline in some circumstances (Castel, Middlebrooks, and McGillivray, 2016; Hertzog and Dunlosky, 2011; Siegel and Castel, 2019). Various metamemory studies utilizing judgments of learning to examine how well participants can assess whether information will be later recalled have found negligible differences in JOL accuracy between younger and older adults (Hertzog, Sinclair, and Dunlosky, 2010; Hines, Touron, and Hertzog, 2009). Additional work has shown that older adults are equally as accurate as younger adults in determining when and how much information they may have forgotten between initial encoding and retrieval (Halamish, McGillivray, and Castel, 2011).

Importantly, this lack of age-related differences in JOL accuracy may only be the case when judgments are made on a local, item-by-item basis. Other work has demonstrated that, when asked to make global predictions about recall performance on an entire set of to-be-remembered materials, age-related differences are observed, as older adults may be overconfident in their memory performance (Bruce, Coyne, and Botwinick, 1982; Connor, Dunlosky, and Hertzog, 1997; Hertzog, Saylor, Fleece, and Dixon, 1994; cf. Kavé and Halamish, 2015). In one study examining predictions of performance on a VDR task, older adults were overconfident in the number of words they would remember on an upcoming list, displaying inferior metacognitive accuracy relative to younger adults (Siegel and Castel, 2019). However, when predicting how many points they would earn in a separate experiment, older adults were equally as accurate suggesting that the type of information being monitored may affect metacognitive accuracy. Older adults may also be overconfident in predicting how much information will be accompanied by recollective experience (as compared to feelings of familiarity or knowing), suggesting that there are also age-related declines in the monitoring of recollection (Soderstrom, McCabe, and Rhodes, 2012). Thus, while older adults' item-by-item metacognitive processing may be relatively unimpaired, the application of the information gained from this monitoring to make a global assessment may be difficult for older adults.

Conclusion

In general, our ability to remember information as we age tends to decline. Older adults notice an increase in forgetting and often complain that their memory is declining (Schweich et al., 1992; Weaver, Cargin, Collie, Masters, and Maruff, 2008). In particular, aging is accompanied by deficits in remembering details associated with particular events and a shift to more gist-based representations, as demonstrated by studies comparing recollection and familiarity-based memory (Koen and Yonelinas, 2014). Older adults also have difficulties in binding the source of information, like the context in which it was experienced (Johnson, Hashtroudi, and Lindsay, 1993). Despite these overall declines, in some circumstances older adults can engage in strategies to mitigate these effects by relying on schematic knowledge or knowing what "should have" occurred during a particular event (Hess and Slaughter, 1990). Thus, these age-related declines can also be conceptualized in terms of age-related changes, and some of these changes can be predictable and based on interference or use of prior knowledge. Further, the ability to prioritize information in memory appears to remain relatively constant or even improve with age, allowing older adults to selectively remember important information (Castel, 2008; Castel et al., 2012). This maintained prioritization reflects older adults' effective metacognitive monitoring and control which, in some cases, is comparable to younger adults' (Hertzog and Dunlosky, 2011). As such, while there are certainly declines in memory ability in aging, these declines may be partially offset by changes in strategy use and metacognitive awareness of one's capabilities as we age.

Note

1 Author Note: This work was supported in part by the National Institutes of Health (National Institute on Aging), Award Number R01AG044335.

References

Addante, R. J., Ranganath, C., & Yonelinas, A. P. (2012). Examining ERP correlates of recognition memory: Evidence of accurate source recognition without recollection. *Neuroimage, 62*(1), 439–450.

Arbuckle, T.Y., Cooney, R., Milne, J., & Melchior, A. (1994). Memory for spatial layouts in relation to age and schema typicality. *Psychology and Aging, 9*(3), 467–480.

Bäckman, L., Nyberg, L., Lindenberger, U., Li, S. C., & Farde, L. (2006). The correlative triad among aging, dopamine, and cognition: Current status and future prospects. *Neuroscience and Biobehavioral Reviews, 30*(6), 791–807.

Balota, D. A., Cortese, M. J., Duchek, J. M., Adams, D., Roediger, H. L., III, McDermott, K. B., & Yerys, B. E. (1999). Veridical and false memories in healthy older adults and in dementia of the Alzheimer's type. *Cognitive Neuropsychology, 16*(3–5), 361–384.

Baltes, P. B., & Baltes, M. M. (1990). Psychological perspectives on successful aging: The model of selective optimization with compensation. *Successful Aging: Perspectives from the Behavioral Sciences, 1*, 1–34.

Bell, R., Giang, T., Mund, I., & Buchner, A. (2013). Memory for reputational trait information: Is social-emotional information processing less flexible in old age? *Psychology and Aging, 28*(4), 984–995.

Besken, M., & Gülgöz, S. (2009). Reliance on schemas in source memory: Age differences and similarity of schemas. *Aging, Neuropsychology, and Cognition, 16*(1), 1–21.

Brewer, W. F., & Treyens, J. C. (1980). Role of schemata in remembering places. *Cognitive Psychology*, *13*, 207–230.

Bruce, P. R., Coyne, A. C., & Botwinick, J. (1982). Adult age differences in metamemory. *Journal of Gerontology*, *37*(3), 354–357.

Burke, D. M., & Light, L. L. (1981). Memory and aging: The role of retrieval processes. *Psychological Bulletin*, *90*(3), 513–546.

Caballol, N., Martí, M. J., & Tolosa, E. (2007). Cognitive dysfunction and dementia in Parkinson disease. *Movement Disorders: Official Journal of the Movement Disorder Society*, *22*(S17), S358–S366.

Carlesimo, G. A., & Oscar-Berman, M. (1992). Memory deficits in Alzheimer's patients: A comprehensive review. *Neuropsychology Review*, *3*(2), 119–169.

Carstensen, L. L. (2006). The influence of a sense of time on human development. *Science*, *312*(5782), 1913–1915.

Castel, A. D. (2005). Memory for grocery prices in younger and older adults: The role of schematic support. *Psychology and Aging*, *20*(4), 718–721.

Castel, A. D. (2008). The adaptive and strategic use of memory by older adults: Evaluative processing and value-directed remembering. In: A. S. Benjamin & B. H. Ross (Eds.), *The Psychology of Learning and Motivation* (Vol. *48*, pp. 225–270). London: Academic Press.

Castel, A. D., Benjamin, A. S., Craik, F. I., & Watkins, M. J. (2002). The effects of aging on selectivity and control in short-term recall. *Memory and Cognition*, *30*(7), 1078–1085.

Castel, A. D., Friedman, M. C., McGillivray, S., Flores, C. C., Murayama, K., Kerr, T., & Drolet, A. (2016). I owe you: Age-related similarities and differences in associative memory for gains and losses. *Aging, Neuropsychology, and Cognition*, *23*(5), 549–565.

Castel, A. D., McGillivray, S., & Friedman, M. C. (2012). Metamemory and memory efficiency in older adults: Learning about the benefits of priority processing and value-directed remembering. In: M. Naveh-Benjamin & N. Ohta (Eds.), *Memory and Aging: Current Issues and Future Directions* (pp. 245–270). New York, NY: Psychology Press.

Castel, A. D., Middlebrooks, C. D., & McGillivray, S. (2016). Monitoring memory in old age: Impaired, spared, and aware. In: J. Dunlosky & S. Tauber (Eds.), *The Oxford Handbook of Metamemory*. Oxford, UK: Oxford University Press.

Chalfonte, B. L., & Johnson, M. K. (1996). Feature memory and binding in young and older adults. *Memory and Cognition*, *24*(4), 403–416.

Cohen, M. S., Rissman, J., Suthana, N. A., Castel, A. D., & Knowlton, B. J. (2014). Value-based modulation of memory encoding involves strategic engagement of fronto-temporal semantic processing regions. *Cognitive, Affective, and Behavioral Neuroscience*, *14*(2), 578–592.

Cohen, M. S., Rissman, J., Suthana, N. A., Castel, A. D., & Knowlton, B. J. (2016). Effects of aging on value-directed modulation of semantic network activity during verbal learning. *NeuroImage*, *125*, 1046–1062.

Cohn, M., Emrich, S. M., & Moscovitch, M. (2008). Age-related deficits in associative memory: The influence of impaired strategic retrieval. *Psychology and Aging*, *23*(1), 93–103.

Connor, L. T., Dunlosky, J., & Hertzog, C. (1997). Age-related differences in absolute but not relative metamemory accuracy. *Psychology and Aging*, *12*(1), 50–71.

Craik, F. I. M., & Bosman, B. A. (1992). Age-related changes in memory and learning. In: H. Bouma & J. A. M. Graafmans (Eds.), *Gerontechnology* (pp. 79–92). Amsterdam, The Netherlands: IOS Press.

Craik, F. I. M., & Salthouse, T. A. (Eds.) (2008). *The Handbook of Aging and Cognition* (3rd ed.). New York, NY: Psychology Press.

Dai, R., Thomas, A. K., & Taylor, H. A. (2018). Age-related differences in the use of spatial and categorical relationships in a visuo-spatial working memory task. *Memory and Cognition, 46,* 809–825.

Deese, J. (1959). On the prediction of occurrence of particular verbal intrusions in immediate recall. *Journal of Experimental Psychology, 58*(1), 17–22.

Dennis, N. A., Hayes, S. M., Prince, S. E., Madden, D. J., Fleck, M. S., & Cabeza, R. (2008). Effects of aging on the neural correlates of successful item and source memory encoding. *Journal of Experimental Psychology: Learning, Memory, and Cognition, 34*(4), 791–808.

Diamond, A. (2013). Executive functions. *Annual Review of Psychology, 64,* 135–168.

Diana, R. A., Yonelinas, A. P., & Ranganath, C. (2007). Imaging recollection and familiarity in the medial temporal lobe: A three-component model. *Trends in Cognitive Sciences, 11*(9), 379–386.

Driscoll, I., Hamilton, D. A., Petropolous, H., Yeo, R. A., Brooks, W. M., Baumgartner, R. N., & Sutherland, R. J. (2003). The aging hippocampus: Cognitive, biochemical, and structural findings. *Cerebral Cortex, 13*(12), 1344–1351.

Dulas, M. R., & Duarte, A. (2011). The effects of aging on material-independent and material-dependent neural correlates of contextual binding. *Neuroimage, 57*(3), 1192–1204.

Dywan, J., & Jacoby, L. (1990). Effects of aging on source monitoring: Differences in susceptibility to false fame. *Psychology and Aging, 5*(3), 379–387.

Eichenbaum, H., Yonelinas, A. P., & Ranganath, C. (2007). The medial temporal lobe and recognition memory. *Annual Review of Neuroscience, 30,* 123–152.

Eldridge, L. L., Sarfatti, S., & Knowlton, B. J. (2002). The effect of testing procedure on remember-know judgments. *Psychonomic Bulletin and Review, 9*(1), 139–145.

Friedman, D., de Chastelaine, M., Nessler, D., & Malcolm, B. (2010). Changes in familiarity and recollection across the lifespan: An ERP perspective. *Brain Research, 1310,* 124–141.

Friedman, M. C., McGillivray, S., Murayama, K., & Castel, A. D. (2015). Memory for medication side effects in younger and older adults: The role of subjective and objective importance. *Memory and Cognition, 43*(2), 206–215.

Halamish, V., McGillivray, S., & Castel, A. D. (2011). Monitoring one's own forgetting in younger and older adults. *Psychology and Aging, 26*(3), 631–635.

Hamami, A., Serbun, S. J., & Gutchess, A. H. (2011). Self-referencing enhances memory specificity with age. *Psychology and Aging, 26*(3), 636–646.

Hargis, M. B., & Castel, A. D. (2017). Younger and older adults' associative memory for social information: The role of information importance. *Psychology and Aging, 32*(4), 325–330.

Hargis, M. B., & Castel, A. D. (2018). Younger and older adults' associative memory for medication interactions of varying severity. *Memory, 26*(8), 1151–1158.

Hertzog, C., & Dixon, R. A. (1994). Metacognitive development in adulthood and old age. In: J. Metcalfe & A. Shimamura (Eds.), *Metacognition: Knowing about Knowing* (pp. 227–251). Cambridge, MA: Bradford.

Hertzog, C., & Dunlosky, J. (2011). Metacognition in later adulthood: Spared monitoring can benefit older adults' self-regulation. *Current Directions in Psychological Science, 20*(3), 167–173.

Hertzog, C., Saylor, L. L., Fleece, A. M., & Dixon, R. A. (1994). Metamemory and aging: Relations between predicted, actual and perceived memory task performance. *Aging, Neuropsychology, and Cognition, 1*(3), 203–237.

Hertzog, C., Sinclair, S. M., & Dunlosky, J. (2010). Age differences in the monitoring of learning: Cross-sectional evidence of spared resolution across the adult life span. *Developmental Psychology, 46*(4), 939–948.

Hess, T. M. (2005). Memory and aging in context. *Psychological Bulletin, 131*(3), 383–406.

Hess, T. M. (2014). Selective engagement of cognitive resources: Motivational influences on older adults' cognitive functioning. *Perspectives on Psychological Science: A Journal of the Association for Psychological Science, 9*(4), 388–407.

Hess, T. M., & Pullen, S. M. (1996). Memory in context. In: F. Blanchard-Fields & T. M. Hess (Eds.), *Perspectives on Cognitive Change in Adulthood and Aging* (pp. 387–427). New York, NY: McGraw-Hill.

Hess, T. M., & Slaughter, S. J. (1990). Schematic knowledge influences on memory for scene information in young and older adults. *Developmental Psychology, 26*(5), 855–865.

Hines, J. C., Touron, D. R., & Hertzog, C. (2009). Metacognitive influences on study time allocation in an associative recognition task: An analysis of adult age differences. *Psychology and Aging, 24*(2), 462–475.

Hultsch, D. F., Hertzog, C., Small, B. J., McDonald-Miszczak, L., & Dixon, R. A. (1992). Short-term longitudinal change in cognitive performance in later life. *Psychology and Aging, 7*(4), 571–584.

Johnson, M. K., Hashtroudi, S., & Lindsay, D. S. (1993). Source monitoring. *Psychological Bulletin, 114*(1), 3–28.

Kaasinen, V., Vilkman, H., Hietala, J., Någren, K., Helenius, H., Olsson, H., Farde, L., & Rinne, J. O. (2000). Age-related dopamine D2/D3 receptor loss in extrastriatal regions of the human brain. *Neurobiology of Aging, 21*(5), 683–688.

Kavé, G., & Halamish, V. (2015). Doubly blessed: Older adults know more vocabulary and know better what they know. *Psychology and Aging, 30*(1), 68–73.

Koen, J. D., & Yonelinas, A. P. (2014). The effects of healthy aging, amnestic mild cognitive impairment, and Alzheimer's disease on recollection and familiarity: A meta-analytic review. *Neuropsychology Review, 24*(3), 332–354.

Koriat, A., & Goldsmith, M. (1996). Monitoring and control processes in the strategic regulation of memory accuracy. *Psychological Review, 103*(3), 490–517.

Leshikar, E. D., & Duarte, A. (2012). Medial prefrontal cortex supports source memory accuracy for self-referenced items. *Social Neuroscience, 7*(2), 126–145.

Mandler, G. (1980). Recognizing: The judgment of previous occurrence. *Psychological Review, 87*(3), 252–271.

Mather, M., Johnson, M. K., & De Leonardis, D. M. (1999). Stereotype reliance in source monitoring: Age differences and neuropsychological test correlates. *Cognitive Neuropsychology, 16*(3–5), 437–458.

May, C. P., Rahhal, T., Berry, E. M., & Leighton, E. A. (2005). Aging, source memory, and emotion. *Psychology and Aging, 20*(4), 571–578.

McCabe, D. P., Roediger III, H. L., McDaniel, M. A., Balota, D. A., & Hambrick, D. Z. (2010). The relationship between working memory capacity and executive functioning: Evidence for a common executive attention construct. *Neuropsychology, 24*(2), 222–243.

McGillivray, S., & Castel, A. D. (2010). Memory for age-face associations in younger and older adults: The role of generation and schematic support. *Psychology and Aging, 25*(4), 822–832.

McIntyre, J. S., & Craik, F. I. M. (1987). Age differences in memory for item and source information. *Canadian Journal of Psychology/Revue Canadienne De Psychologie, 41*(2), 175–192.

Mitchell, K. J., & Johnson, M. K. (2009). Source monitoring 15 years later: What have we learned from fMRI about the neural mechanisms of source memory? *Psychological Bulletin, 135*(4), 638–677.

Mollison, M. V., & Curran, T. (2012). Familiarity in source memory. *Neuropsychologia, 50*(11), 2546–2565.

Morrow, D. G., Menard, W. E., Stine-Morrow, E. A. L., Teller, T., & Bryant, D. (2001). The influence of expertise and task factors on age differences in pilot communication. *Psychology and Aging, 16*(1), 31–46.

Naveh-Benjamin, M. (2000). Adult age differences in memory performance: Tests of an associative deficit hypothesis. *Journal of Experimental Psychology: Learning, Memory, and Cognition, 26*(5), 1170–1187.

Nelson, T. O. (1996). Consciousness and metacognition. *American Psychologist, 51*(2), 102–116.

Norman, K. A., & Schacter, D. L. (1997). False recognition in younger and older adults: Exploring the characteristics of illusory memories. *Memory and Cognition, 25*(6), 838–848.

Park, D. C., Lautenschlager, G., Hedden, T., Davidson, N. S., Smith, A. D., & Smith, P. K. (2002). Models of visuospatial and verbal memory across the adult life span. *Psychology and Aging, 17*(2), 299–320.

Park, D. C., & Puglisi, J. T. (1985). Older adults' memory for the color of pictures and words. *Journal of Gerontology, 40*(2), 198–204.

Parkin, A. J., & Walter, B. M. (1992). Recollective experience, normal aging, and frontal dysfunction. *Psychology and Aging, 7*(2), 290–298.

Petersen, R. C., Doody, R., Kurz, A., Mohs, R. C., Morris, J. C., Rabins, P. V., Ritchie, K., Rossor, M., Thal, L., & Winblad, B. (2001). Current concepts in mild cognitive impairment. *Archives of Neurology, 58*(12), 1985–1992.

Prull, M. W., Dawes, L. L. C., Martin, A. M., Rosenberg, H. F., & Light, L. L. (2006). Recollection and familiarity in recognition memory: Adult age differences and neuropsychological test correlates. *Psychology and Aging, 21*(1), 107–118.

Rabinowitz, J. C. (1989). Judgments of origin and generation effects: Comparisons between young and elderly adults. *Psychology and Aging, 4*(3), 259–268.

Rahhal, T. A., May, C. P., & Hasher, L. (2002). Truth and character: Sources that older adults can remember. *Psychological Science, 13*(2), 101–105.

Raz, N., Lindenberger, U., Rodrigue, K. M., Kennedy, K. M., Head, D., Williamson, A., Dahle, C., Gerstorf, D., & Acker, J. D. (2005). Regional brain changes in aging healthy adults: General trends, individual differences and modifiers. *Cerebral Cortex, 15*(11), 1676–1689.

Raz, N., Rodrigue, K. M., Head, D., Kennedy, K. M., & Acker, J. D. (2004). Differential aging of the medial temporal lobe: A study of a five-year change. *Neurology, 62*(3), 433–438.

Roediger, H. L., III, & McDermott, K. B. (1995). Creating false memories: Remembering words not presented in lists. *Journal of Experimental Psychology: Learning, Memory, and Cognition, 21*(4), 803–814.

Rusted, J., Gaskell, M., Watts, S., & Sheppard, L. (2000). People with dementia use schemata to support episodic memory. *Dementia and Geriatric Cognitive Disorders, 11*(6), 350–356.

Schwartz, B. L. (1994). Sources of information in metamemory: Judgments of learning and feelings of knowing. *Psychonomic Bulletin and Review, 1*(3), 357–375.

Schweich, M., Van der Linden, M., Brédart, S., Bruyer, R., Nelles, B., & Schils, J. P. (1992). Daily-life difficulties in person recognition reported by young and elderly subjects. *Applied Cognitive Psychology, 6*(2), 161–172.

Shing, Y. L., Werkle-Bergner, M., Brehmer, Y., Muller, V., Li, S.-C., & Lindenberger, U. (2013). Episodic memory across the lifespan: The contributions of associative and strategic components. *Neuroscience and Biobehavioral Reviews, 34*(7), 1080–1091.

Siegel, A. L. M., & Castel, A. D. (2018). Memory for important item-location associations in younger and older adults. *Psychology and Aging, 33*(1), 30–45.

Siegel, A. L. M., & Castel, A. D. (2019). Age-related differences in metacognition for memory capacity and selectivity. *Memory, 27*(9), 1236–1249.

Soderstrom, N. C., McCabe, D. P., & Rhodes, M. G. (2012). Older adults predict more recollective experiences than younger adults. *Psychology and Aging, 27*(4), 1082–1088.

Tulving, E. (1985). Memory and consciousness. *Canadian Psychology/Psychologie Canadienne, 26*(1), 1–12.

Tun, P. A., Wingfield, A., Rosen, M. J., & Blanchard, L. (1998). Response latencies for false memories: Gist-based processes in normal aging. *Psychology and Aging, 13*(2), 230–241.

Volkow, N. D., Gur, R. C., Wang, G. J., Fowler, J. S., Moberg, P. J., Ding, Y. S., Hitzemann, R., Smith, G., & Logan, J. (1998). Association between decline in brain dopamine activity with age and cognitive and motor impairment in healthy individuals. *The American Journal of Psychiatry, 155*(3), 344–349.

Waddell, K. J., & Rogoff, B. (1981). Effect of contextual organization on spatial memory of middle-aged and older women. *Developmental Psychology, 17*(6), 878–885.

Wang, T. H., de Chastelaine, M., Minton, B., & Rugg, M. D. (2012). Effects of age on the neural correlates of familiarity as indexed by ERPs. *Journal of Cognitive Neuroscience, 24*(5), 1055–1068.

Weaver Cargin, J., Collie, A., Masters, C., & Maruff, P. (2008). The nature of cognitive complaints in healthy older adults with and without objective memory decline. *Journal of Clinical and Experimental Neuropsychology, 30*(2), 245–257.

Webb, C. E., & Dennis, N. A. (2019). Differentiating true and false schematic memories in older adults. *Journal of Gerontology: Psychological Sciences, 74*, 1111–1120.

Westerberg, C. E., Mayes, A. R., Florczak, S. M., Chen, Y., Creery, J., Parrish, T., Weintraub, S., Mesulam, M. M., Reber, P. J., & Paller, K. A. (2013). Distinct medial temporal contributions to different forms of recognition in amnestic mild cognitive impairment and Alzheimer's disease. *Neuropsychologia, 51*(12), 2450–2461.

Wolk, D. A., Dunfee, K. L., Dickerson, B. C., Aizenstein, H. J., & DeKosky, S. T. (2011). A medial temporal lobe division of labor: Insights from memory in aging and early Alzheimer disease. *Hippocampus, 21*(5), 461–466.

Yonelinas, A. P. (1999). The contribution of recollection and familiarity to recognition and source-memory judgments: A formal dual-process model and an analysis of receiver operating characteristics. *Journal of Experimental Psychology: Learning, Memory, and Cognition, 25*(6), 1415–1434.

Yonelinas, A. P. (2002). The nature of recollection and familiarity: A review of 30 years of research. *Journal of Memory and Language, 46*(3), 441–517.

Yonelinas, A. P., Aly, M., Wang, W. C., & Koen, J. D. (2010). Recollection and familiarity: Examining controversial assumptions and new directions. *Hippocampus, 20*(11), 1178–1194.

Yonelinas, A. P., Widaman, K., Mungas, D., Reed, B., Weiner, M. W., & Chui, H. C. (2007). Memory in the aging brain: Doubly dissociating the contribution of the hippocampus and entorhinal cortex. *Hippocampus, 17*(11), 1134–1140.

Zacks, J. M., Speer, N. K., Vettel, J. M., & Jacoby, L. L. (2006). Event understanding and memory in healthy aging and dementia of the Alzheimer type. *Psychology and Aging, 21*(3), 466–482.

Zacks, R. T., & Hasher, L. (2006). Aging and long-term memory: Deficits are not inevitable. In: E. Bialystok & F. I. M. Craik (Eds.), *Lifespan Cognition: Mechanisms of Change* (pp. 162–177). Oxford: Oxford University Press.

Zacks, R. T., Hasher, L., & Li, K. Z. H. (2000). Human memory. In: F. I. M. Craik & T. A. Salthouse (Eds.), *The Handbook of Aging and Cognition* (pp. 293–357). Mahwah, NJ: Lawrence Erlbaum Associates.

3

MOTIVATED COGNITION AND CURIOSITY IN THE AGING CONSUMER[1]

Mary B. Hargis, Mary C. Whatley,
Alexander L. M. Siegel, and Alan D. Castel

Across the lifespan, our goals often include learning new things, building relationships with loved ones, and being healthy and active. Older age is often associated with changes in what motivates us, but younger and older adults often have many goals in common. People of all ages set goals, and assessing what factors influence goal pursuit (as well as how those factors may change with age) can lead to interesting insights about how individuals across the lifespan interact with products, learn new things, and make important decisions.

Some theories of motivation in older age focus largely on the shift from knowledge acquisition goals in younger adulthood to emotion regulation goals in older adulthood. While the empirical evidence to support this shift is strong, it is also worth examining the situations in which older adults do continue to seek knowledge. Many older consumers are retired but being in this phase of life does not necessarily mean that they stop pursuing goals that promote the acquisition of new information in their daily lives. For example, many older people have hobbies such as birdwatching, in which an expert may acquire knowledge about migration patterns, habitats, and food sources. Many are curious about how memory changes with age, and how they can do their best to stay cognitively healthy. In this chapter, we will discuss what motivates younger and older people to learn new skills and new information through the lens of several theories of cognitive aging. After discussing knowledge, emotion, and control as motivating factors, we will examine the roles of curiosity and interest in motivated cognition—including a suggestion that curiosity may not always benefit older consumers. We will then turn to older adults' perceptions of risk, gains, and losses, and how those perceptions may affect consumer behavior. Throughout this chapter, we will also consider older adults' use of and perceptions about so-called "brain training" techniques, examine how age-related changes may affect variety-seeking, and discuss how situations that induce stereotype threat and anxiety may also motivate the cognition of older adults differently from younger adults.

Knowledge, Emotion, and Control as Motivating Factors

Several theories of healthy cognitive aging focus on changes in people's goals. These theories propose differences in the way older adults attend to, remember, and make decisions about the world around them.

Socioemotional Selectivity Theory

Socioemotional selectivity theory holds that aging is associated with a positivity effect in memory, such that older adults remember positive over negative information, and also that there is a general shift in goal pursuit across the adult lifespan. Younger adults focus on acquiring knowledge, often to succeed in school and at work, while older adulthood is associated with a lower priority assigned to pursuing knowledge-based goals and a higher priority assigned to pursuing goals that regulate emotions and build social relationships (Carstensen, Isaacowitz, and Charles, 1999; Carstensen, Fung, and Charles, 2003).

Motivation is intricately tied to memory, especially in aging; if more of older adults' goals are related to emotion, their memory for emotional items may be preserved, in contrast to other declines in memory. Prior work suggests that older adults remember products' slogans more accurately if those slogans had an emotional component (Fung and Carstensen, 2003). For example, "Capture those special moments," as compared to "Capture the unexplored world," was more preferred and better remembered by older adults when used in an advertisement for a camera. However, when older participants were asked to imagine that a medication existed that would extend their life by 20 years, their preferences and memory were more similar to that of younger adults' (Fung and Carstensen, 2003; cf. Uttl and Graf, 2006).

Lifespan Theory of Control

The lifespan theory of control holds that humans have a basic desire to control their environment, and because losing this control causes discomfort in the individual, loss of control is avoided if at all possible (Heckhausen and Schulz, 1995). Primary control is the attempt to change the external world so that it fits with the individual's goals, while secondary control is the attempt to modify internal processes so that one can mesh with the environment, and is identified as being a largely internal cognitive process, as opposed to the external primary control. According to Heckhausen and Schulz (1995), primary control has greater adaptive value than secondary control, and the latter mostly exists to support the former. Which type of control is utilized more strongly is dependent upon both biological and societal factors, as biological changes and shifts in normative social constraints across the lifespan promote the use of secondary control over primary control.

Older adults do, however, report decreased ability to exert primary control over their environment (Heckhausen and Schulz, 1995). When older adults face events in their lives in which they have very limited opportunities to exert primary control—for example, when facing serious health problems—coping strategies are "likely to be focused on regulating emotion" rather than pursuing goals in the external environment (Heckhausen and Schulz, 1995; p. 296). Preserved emotion regulation is a key component of socioemotional selectivity theory, as discussed above.

Curiosity and Interest as Motivating Factors

Consumers across the lifespan are more likely to pursue information in which they are interested, and this tendency can have implications for which products they seek to learn more about and, perhaps, purchase. Curiosity, or the seeking out of some new information, has been studied extensively in young children (Engel, 2011; Smock and Holt, 1962), but it remains a motivating factor into older adulthood. In fact, Sakaki, Yagi, and Murayama (2018) argue that curiosity in older age supports physical, mental, and cognitive health. However, some measurements of curiosity and related factors (e.g., openness to experience; Kashdan et al., 2004, 2009) do show a general decline with age (Kashdan et al., 2004, 2009).

Socioemotional selectivity theory, as discussed above, suggests that our goals change as we age from primarily knowledge-based pursuits in younger adulthood to primarily socioemotional relationship building in older adulthood. This general pattern can help explain why curiosity may decline with age (Sakaki et al., 2018): While learning new things and encountering novel environments is a common goal among younger adults, it becomes less important as we age, when we prefer to spend time with those we already know well.

While some measures of curiosity may decline across the lifespan (see Robinson et al., 2017), maintaining curiosity is associated with positive outcomes in memory and well-being (Sakaki et al., 2018). Successful aging, Sakaki and colleagues (2018) argue, can benefit from a person's interest in learning new information. Further evidence supports this notion of curiosity as a protective factor: In a large-scale study of older adults, those who were more curious were more likely to survive over a five-year period than those who were not (Swan and Carmelli, 1996). It is interesting to consider the benefits of curiosity from a consumer psychology perspective: If older consumers are less curious than their younger counterparts in some domains but not in others, perhaps further examination of domains of preserved curiosity can uncover novel and innovative ways to market products. For example, work examining purchasing decisions suggests that aging is negatively related to gathering information about alternatives and positively related to brand loyalty (e.g., when purchasing a car, Evanschitzky and Woisetschläger, 2008), and lack of social influence from others may contribute to this conservative behavior (East, Uncles, and Lomax, 2014). The growing body of literature suggests that incorporating older adults' curiosity as a relevant factor in models of preferences with aging may help explain brand loyalty.

Age-related memory differences can be overcome—or at least reduced—when older adult participants are interested in the information (see Zacks and Hasher, 2006), possibly related to the reduced load on attentional resources that is needed to study interesting material (McDaniel, Waddill, Finstad, and Bourg, 1990). Additionally, when specific information is of interest to the participant, their memory performance is not just enhanced for that information; information presented in the same context also gets remembered with higher accuracy (for example, Gruber et al., 2014). In the context of marketing, future research may investigate whether curiosity or interest drives younger and older adults' memory for information peripheral to the product being advertised. For example, if marketing a new medication that is meant to provide some interesting and novel therapeutic benefit (e.g., scoring well on exams might be of interest to undergraduate students, and extending the lifespan might be interesting to older adults), a memory test for the product's name and purpose can be accompanied by items assessing peripheral information such as dosage instructions, side effects, and even the name of the hypothetical prescribing physician. Memory accuracy and preference judgments can be compared between products that younger and older individuals find interesting and those that they do not.

McGillivray and colleagues (2015) investigated the role of interest in memory for trivia questions, e.g., "What was the first country to allow women the right to vote?" (Answer: New Zealand.) Participants rated how interesting they found the answer once it was presented, as well as how likely they felt it would be for them to remember the information at a later time. Interestingly, older adults' recall accuracy after a one-week delay was strongly predicted by the ratings they gave after learning the answers to the trivia questions, while younger adults' recall was less strongly predicted by this factor. These findings may be driven by attention, as attention is shifted away from uninteresting items and toward more interesting items (Castel, 2008), which has notable implications for learning in other domains (e.g., see Hargis, Siegel, & Castel, 2019). Many older adults seek out activities in which they will learn new information: For example, many older adults who attend formal lifelong learning classes (Kim and Merriam, 2004) and those who participate in massive open online learning courses ("MOOCs"; Xiong and Zuo, 2019) report that they engage in such programs to learn new things.

Variety-Seeking

Curiosity and interest could also be related to how much people choose to try different options or stick to the usual choice. When making decisions about which car to purchase or which dessert to order at a restaurant, we are often faced with various options. Will we order our favorite dish again or choose something that will be different from our usual choice, but might be less satisfying? Variety-seeking refers to the tendency to vary choices such as where to eat, what to buy, or what to do with spare time, even if it means choosing the less enjoyable option (Ratner, Kahn, and Kahneman, 1999). While there are individual differences in variety-seeking behavior, people generally prefer to vary their choices. This is perhaps due, at least in part, to memory: People tend to remember an experience overall more favorably if it includes variety than if it does not (Ratner, Kahn, and Kahneman, 1999).

Early investigation into how variety-seeking behaviors change in older age suggested that certain forms of variety-seeking may decrease with age. For example, a desire to travel and seek new experiences tends to decline with age, but there are no age differences in preferences for variety in everyday activities, and older and younger adults both report a tendency to become bored when things are unchanging (Zuckerman and Neeb, 1980). This suggests that there is a shift in the amount of variety people prefer as they get older, but older adults do not necessarily stop engaging in varied behaviors. There is also evidence that even though variety-seeking behavior declines with age, this decrease is not reflective of an overall decline in engagement, especially in activities that are meaningful or social in nature. For example, older adults spend more time volunteering than younger or middle-aged adults, despite being involved in fewer volunteer organizations and activities than either age group (Hendricks and Cutler, 2004).

Particularly relevant to consumer psychology, some research has examined variety-seeking behaviors in relation to how people make decisions about what product to purchase, what music to listen to, or what food to consume. Research on how these decisions change with age suggests that there are no age differences in how many options people choose for immediate consumption, but older adults choose fewer options for future consumption than younger adults do (Novak and Mather, 2007). These age-related differences are not due to memory declines or age differences in preference for the options themselves. Novak and Mather (2007) suggest that older adults may be willing to try more options while their mood is positive. However, they only selected their favorite options for future consumption to avoid choices that might lead to negative or uncertain future experiences. Other work further supports the role of emotion regulation in variety-seeking behaviors in older adults. For example, when given the opportunity to experience events in any order, older adults are more likely than younger adults to save the best (i.e., rated most positive) for last and to separate the negative and positive events with a neutral event to create a more positive experience overall (Drolet, Lau-Gesk, and Scott, 2011). These findings are in line with predictions from socioemotional selectivity theory (discussed previously in this chapter), which suggests a greater focus on emotion regulation in older age.

Other motivational factors can also influence the extent to which older adults choose to use their limited cognitive resources, and this can influence variety-seeking behavior. For example, older adults prefer to have fewer available options when making decisions (Reed, Mikels, and Lockenhoff, 2013) and place lower value on having ample choice options than young adults (Mikels, Reed, and Simon, 2009). Further, when given many options from which to choose, older adults engage in less information search than younger adults do (Mata and Nunes, 2010). These findings may reflect a preference for reducing the need to engage cognitive resources, as effortful cognitive processing is required for weighing the relative pros and cons of every option (see Shah and Oppenheimer, 2008). This explanation is in line with some theories of cognitive aging that suggest that older adults, aware of their limited resources, choose to selectively allocate attention and cognitive resources accordingly to optimize outcomes (Baltes and Baltes, 1990; Hess, 2014) and avoid losses (Heckhausen and Schulz, 1995). Despite a decline in information search and preference for fewer options, older adults tend to make fairly high-quality decisions (Mata and Nunes, 2010), indicating that older adults are able to use their limited resources to successfully achieve their goals.

This reduction in information search and preference for fewer options may also manifest in brand loyalty behaviors. While older adults tend to show greater brand loyalty for some types of purchases more than others (i.e., greater loyalty for cars than toiletries; Schewe, 1984; Lambert-Pandraud and Laurent, 2010), research has shown that older adults consider fewer brands than younger adults (Lambert-Pandraud, Laurent, and Lapersonne, 2005). Brand loyalty may be related to memory for truth and meaningfulness in older age. For example, Rahhal, May, and Hasher (2002) found that while older adults struggled compared to younger adults to remember perceptual source information, they did remember whether a person was truthful (see also Cassidy, Hedden, Yoon, and Gutchess, 2014; Mitchell and Hill, 2019), suggesting that meaning can be extracted without memory for specific details. Others have established that the meaningfulness of a message can particularly affect older adults' memory performance (Skinner and Price, 2019). Perhaps older adults' preserved ability to remember character-related information is linked with their brand loyalty, such that remembering that a brand has treated them fairly in the past (i.e., that it is trustworthy) leads to increased likelihood to continue purchasing products produced by that brand (see Yoon et al., 2005; Yoon, Cole, and Lee, 2009).

Brain-Training Games

The power of curiosity (and, perhaps, motivational changes in variety-seeking) could help explain the increasing popularity of so-called "brain-training games." Brain-training is predicted to be a six billion dollar industry in 2020 (SharpBrains, 2015). Older adults may be particularly interested in ways to keep their minds "healthy," and brain-training games are compellingly advertised as a solution, or at least a supplement, for cognitive health. Types of "brain games" subject to previous empirical investigation include *NeuroRacer*, a 3-D video game that measures perceptual discrimination ability in a visuomotor tracking task (Anguera et al., 2013); a mix of cognitive tasks including reasoning and speed of processing (Ball et al., 2002); fluid intelligence (Baltes, Sowarka, and Kliegl, 1989); and programs such as *Cogmed*, which adaptively trains working memory (Brehmer, Westerberg, and Backman, 2012). A recent meta-analysis (Melby-Lervag and Hulme, 2013) on games such as those mentioned above suggests that the evidence is mixed at best for the effectiveness of these programs; there is little to no long-term retention of gains or transfer of them into related domains. It is important to note, however, that these games are not at all likely to be harmful to the player (unless they take time away from another thing the person could be doing to stay in good cognitive shape, such as taking a walk with a friend). In fact, many people enjoy the feeling of solving complex problems on a computer or tablet, which should be encouraged for many who would not otherwise be using their skills in this way.

Though the scientific evidence for the effectiveness of brain-training programs on broader cognitive functioning is certainly not settled (see Simons et al., 2016 for a discussion), many consumers seem to trust the notion that brain training actually works. In fact, Rabipour and colleagues (2015, 2018) have found that people generally believe brain-training programs to be effective, which Rabipour, Andringa, Boot, and Davidson (2018) suggest may be related to extensive advertising campaigns meant to illustrate the potential of brain training to maintain or enhance positive functioning (Farah, 2015). Older adults in particular seem to be optimistic about brain training (Rabipour and Davidson, 2015), and it may be that curiosity is part of what drives this interest in and optimism about brain training. Perhaps some older adults are more susceptible to the messaging in these advertisements in the real world due to their interest in cognitive health (though reminding older people of their declining abilities could induce stereotype threat, as discussed below). A younger person's curiosity might not be especially piqued when an advertisement asserts that a given product can help users remember where they put their glasses, but older adults may find this interesting, may direct more attentional resources toward that information, and may therefore be more optimistic about and perhaps more likely to remember that information. Future research can examine whether curiosity about how the brain works is piqued in such advertisements as those touting the "science of neuroplasticity," and whether curiosity (about how memory works, for example) is a driving factor in purchasing a subscription.

While evidence supporting far transfer and long-term benefits from brain training is not very convincing, there is some evidence to suggest that engaging in the learning of challenging skills might be an effective way to stay sharp in older age. For example, Park and colleagues (2014) designed an intervention to improve cognitive functioning in older adults in which participants either received intensive training in a new domain (photography, quilting, or both) or were in a control group where activities included things like watching documentaries, playing word games, and participating in social activities. Learning a new skill (e.g., photography) was considered cognitively demanding, because it required learning not only new physical and motor skills like operating a camera or working a sewing machine, but also learning the software required for photo editing or understanding how to weave together complex patterns for quilt making.

Park and colleagues found that those in the training conditions showed greater improvement on cognitive assessments compared to controls, particularly in speed of processing and episodic memory. Other work has found similar improvements in older adults who learn a new language (Schroeder and Marian, 2012) or learn to use new technology, such as an Apple iPad (Chan, Haber, Drew, and Park, 2016), suggesting that engaging in mentally challenging activities in older age may be an effective way to improve memory. Like brain training, the extent of the effects from this type of skill learning is still unknown, such as how long the benefits last or whether improvements apply to everyday situations like remembering where one left their keys. In addition, engaging in these activities did not produce widespread improvements in all cognitive abilities, and complex skill learning may not in itself be more effective than computerized brain-training games. However, pursuing new hobbies such as photography and quilting might be more likely to be continued long-term and on a regular basis if participants are actually interested in them, thus potentially fostering greater long-term benefits. Participating in hobbies and other skill learning could also encourage older adults to engage in other behaviors that are known to improve memory and cognitive functioning, such as exercising or social activities. For example, an interest in photography might encourage more nature walks to take pictures or one might want to find others who are also interested in photography. In this way, more realistic behavior-based methods to improve cognitive functioning might be a more viable way to stay sharp than brain-training games that encourage people to spend more time on their computers or phones.

A Potential Pitfall of Curiosity and Interest

While curiosity may be a protective factor in cognitive aging (Sakaki et al., 2018), it could also shed light on a common problem among older adults. With aging comes an increased risk of financial exploitation (James, Boyle, and Bennett, 2014): Previous work has found that of older adults surveyed, 4.5 percent reported being defrauded in the past five years (Lichtenberg, Stickney, and Paulson, 2013). Those who are psychologically vulnerable—for example, those with diagnoses of depression or mild cognitive impairment—may be at even higher risk of financial victimization (Han, Boyle, James, Yu, and Bennett, 2015; Lichtenberg et al., 2013). Established frameworks include older adults' cognitive functioning as an important facet of susceptibility to exploitation (e.g., Pinsker, McFarland, and Pachana, 2010; see Shao, Zhang, Ren, Li, and Lin, 2019, for a review), such that difficulties in cognitive functioning are associated with greater likelihood of victimization (James et al., 2014). While greater curiosity is certainly not considered a negative aspect of aging, perhaps for an older adult who is a target in a scam, being curious or interested in learning more about the "opportunity" could actually lead to adverse effects (see also Yoon et al., 2009). For example, bogus claims about anti-aging supplements that purportedly prevent or cure various ills may pique the interest of older adults who are concerned about the negative aspects of aging (perhaps particularly if they subscribe to some negative stereotypes regarding aging discussed below).

Scams in the medical domain may be particularly harmful to older adults' physical and financial health. Many older adults take more than five medications or supplements regularly (Qato et al., 2008). Common supplements such as ginseng or Gingko bilboa, which may be considered beneficial for those who are getting older, could lead to adverse reactions when taken with other medications (Marinac, Buchinger, Godfrey, Wooten, Sun, and Willsie, 2007). As many older adults who consume such supplements reported interest in the "general health purposes" of the supplements (Marinac et al., 2007; p. 18), there are perhaps pitfalls to interest in taking steps to "ward off" specific illnesses or the aging process more generally. While the overall direction of curiosity research in cognitive aging seems to suggest that it is a beneficial and protective factor, it is also important to assess whether those who are more interested in anti-aging medicine may be more susceptible to products marketed as anti-aging but that do not actually help, and could in fact be harmful to patients, such as the victims of a fake Botox scam who lost millions of dollars (*Arizona Daily Sun*, 2005).

Risk, Gains, and Losses as Motivating Factors

When we select and pursue goals, we must make a series of decisions, some of which carry more risk than others (e.g., "should I take notes on the information my physician is giving me, or should I simply expect that I will remember the information that is important?"). The underlying processes of decision-making, particularly in light of risk, may change across the lifespan. Risk can be a powerful motivating factor: For example, the risk of losing resources, the risk of forgetting important information, and the risk of offending a social partner can all influence behavior. Some research suggests that certain types of decisions are made fairly similarly by younger and older adults (e.g., those that involve strategic thinking to understand how others make decisions; Kovalchik, Camerer, Grether, Plott, and Allman, 2005), but the introduction of risk can cause younger and older adults to behave differently.

Selective Optimization with Compensation Model

As we age, evidence suggests that we shift away from accumulating resources, and toward conserving resources and avoiding losses (Fruend, 2008). That is, instead of pursuing goals that would allow one to gain resources, older adults pursue goals that would allow them to avoid losing resources. At its core, the selective optimization with compensation (SOC) model involves the prioritization of goals by their relevance (selection) in order to increase gains (optimization) and avoid losses (compensation; Baltes and Baltes, 1990; Freund, 2008).

Baltes' (1997) example of an individual engaging in SOC-based strategies is outlined as follows: A famous pianist, in response to a question about how he managed to maintain a high level of performance in his craft, suggested that he played fewer pieces (selection), practiced those few pieces more often (optimization), and managed the music such that the sections that needed to be played quickly seemed quicker than he was able to produce them (compensation).

To expand, selection—the first component of the theory—is based on the fact that when faced with a large number of potential actions and a limited capacity for engaging in them, individuals across the lifespan engage in a selective amount. This can be shaped by culture, such as infants who are born with the ability to recognize different sounds produced by all languages, but are shaped by exposure to focus on a certain subset necessary for communicating in whatever language(s) they learn.

Optimization, or the shift toward doing things more effectively, is also thought to be relevant across the lifespan; for example, practicing to learn a particular set of items, and engaging effortfully in learning or acquiring skills. When we choose to optimize is based largely on our goals, as we use our limited resources to pursue them. Compensation occurs when the individual is unable to pursue a given set of avenues, but uses other strategies to maintain success in a given domain (e.g., using external aids such as lists to remember activities that need to be done). This compensation can be engaged in response to a lack of available resources, a change in context, or a readjustment of one's goals. The process of selecting, optimizing, and compensating is thought to lead to the maximization of gains and the minimization of losses (gains and losses are dependent upon the developmental and environmental state of the individual), the attainment of goals, and/or the maintenance of functioning of the organism (Baltes, Staundinger, and Lindenberger, 1999).

Much of the empirical support for SOC comes from self-report studies (Freund, 2008). A set of behaviors identified as "SOC strategies" tend to decline in frequency of use across the lifespan, but using these strategies into old age is related to positive outcomes (Freund, 2008). SOC-related behaviors have been found to correlate with a number of indicators of successful aging, including satisfaction with age, lack of agitation, absence of loneliness, and positive emotions (Freund and Baltes, 1998). Perhaps the adaptive shifts that occur with age are at least partly a result of an increasing awareness of and ability to effectively deal with physical and cognitive decline associated with normal (non-pathological) aging.

The SOC model has been used to explain findings from memory studies, in which older adults show lower performance overall but relatively accurate memory for information that is important, valuable, or meaningful. For example, when asked to remember words paired with varying point values, older adults remember fewer words than younger adults, but often remember the highest value words in order to optimize their score (Castel, 2008; Castel, McGillivray, and Friedman, 2012). This reflects an SOC-based strategy in which to compensate for declines in capacity, older adults select the most important or valuable information to remember in order to optimize the outcome (i.e., point score).

Risk-Aversion in Older Adulthood?

Laboratory-based tasks that measure participants' decision-making and willingness to risk money suggest that, as we age, we act in ways that reduce risk (Deakin, Aitken, Robbins, and Sahakian, 2004; cf. Dror, Katona, and Mungur, 1998; but see Kovalchik, Camerer, Grether, Plott, and Allman, 2005; MacPherson, Phillips, and Della Sala, 2002). As discussed in this chapter, there is also a common stereotype that older adults are cautious (Okun, 1976). However, the evidence supporting the notion that older adults are risk-avoidant is mixed (see Mather, 2006). Real-world financial decisions often have potential for gains and losses, such as deciding whether to pursue an investment strategy that is risky versus one that is more conservative. Some studies indicate that risk-seeking behavior with one's own investments increases into older age but starts to decrease after approximately 65 years of age (Knoll, 2010; Schooley and Worden, 1999), while in another study, the older employees of financial organizations made riskier decisions than the younger employees (Brouthers, Brouthers, and Werner, 2000).

Castel and colleagues (2016) examined how important financial information— in this case, being owed or owing others varying amounts of money—may affect learning. They found that the more money an individual owed the participant, the more likely that both younger and older participants would remember how much that individual owed. The risk of losing resources that would be associated with forgetting who owes one a fairly large sum of money can be a strong motivating factor for younger and older people, and cognitive resources seem to be allocated accordingly to avoid this risk. Older adults seem to be especially focused on remembering who owes them money (gains), but less likely to remember people to whom they owe money (losses), suggesting a difference in approach to remembering gains and losses relative to younger adults (see also Freund, 2008). These age-related differences can have implications regarding how older adults remember information related to financial decisions and investments (Benartzi and Castel, 2016).

In addition, the risk of forgetting (in some sense, *losing*) important information may lead us to depend on external sources (such as a calendar, a to-do list, or smartphone application) to do the remembering for us. What we offload onto such external sources is influenced by our awareness of how our own cognitive system works (Risko and Gilbert, 2016). Saving some information to a digital device, for example, could give people the opportunity to reallocate cognitive resources toward other information; when participants are told to forget an initial list of items, their memory is enhanced for a second list of items (Bjork and Woodward, 1973). Indeed, more recent work has shown that saving information to a computer enhances memory for information presented later (Storm and Stone, 2015). In fact, Hamilton and Benjamin (2019) suggest that a learner's offloading mechanism could be considered as an "extended organism" (p. 40). Using computers to save information can allow people to direct elsewhere the cognitive resources that would have been spent remembering. However, this kind of cognitive offloading may be associated with a cost: For example, saving valuable information to an untrustworthy source could lead to detrimental outcomes if that information is lost.

Using a digital device to offload is an interesting area of study among aging consumers, as there is thought to be a "digital divide" (p. 253) between younger and older adults (Charness and Boot, 2009). Stereotypes of older adults as incapable of using current-day technology are common (Broady, Chan, and Caputi, 2010), and older adults have been found to be less confident in their computer-related knowledge than younger adults are (Marquie, Jourdan-Boddaert, and Huet, 2002). While some older adults report experiencing negative outcomes associated with technology use, such as inconveniences and security issues, many older adults report more positive than negative outcomes (Mitzer et al., 2010). Perhaps decisions about how to use a digital device as a supplement to human memory is affected by both the characteristics of the participants (e.g., age, interest and confidence in using technology) as well as characteristics of the offloading device (e.g., the trustworthiness of the source, and whether it is designed in a way that is accessible to those with changes in visual or auditory acuity).

Stereotype Threat and Anxiety as Motivating Factors

As discussed above, the aging process is not all downhill—but it is often perceived to be (Levy, 2009). Stereotypes of older adults are often negative; for example, that they are unhappy, cognitively impaired, risk-avoidant, incompetent, and poor drivers (Chasteen, 2000; Coudin and Alexopolous, 2010; Cuddy, Norton, and Fiske, 2005; Lambert, Watson, Stefanucci, Ward, Bakdash, and Strayer, 2016; Okun, 1976). Younger individuals often hold these views about aging, but, importantly, stereotypes about aging can also be internalized and endorsed by older adults themselves (Kruse and Schmitt, 2006; Levy, 2009) and the people who care for them (e.g., Bleijenberg, 2012; Cowan, Fitzpatrick, Roberts, and While, 2004; Topaz and Doron, 2013).

Stereotype threat can occur when an individual is placed in an environment that may activate their negative stereotypes about the group to which they belong (e.g., an older adult's stereotypes about older adults), and this threat can impair performance on a number of tasks (e.g., driving, Lambert et al., 2016; see Barber,

2017 for a review). Of particular interest is how stereotype threat may impact older adults' memory performance, as forgetfulness is a pervasive age-related stereotype held by many, including older adults (Lineweaver and Hertzog, 1998; see also Beaudoin and Desrichard, 2011; Diehl and Wahl, 2009). Several studies indicate that conditions of stereotype threat lead to older adults' decreased cognitive performance on cognitive tasks, as compared to those who were not put under conditions of stereotype threat (Chasteen, Bhattacharayya, Horhota, Tam, and Hasher, 2005; Lemaire, Brun, and Régner, 2018; Nicolas, Lemaire, and Régner, 2019; see also Wong and Gallo, 2018).

Stereotype threat and anxiety about age-related deficits can detrimentally affect older adults' performance on cognitive tasks. However, such factors can also be considered as motivating cognition, similar to but different from factors such as socioemotional relevance and curiosity explored above. While relationship building and curiosity may drive older adults to pursue particular cognitive goals such as learning new information, stereotype threat and anxiety may influence goal pursuit in a negative way, such that certain activities are avoided or goals are modified to avoid reflecting age-related stereotypes. These factors influence younger and older adults differently, and these differences can have an impact on decision-making across the lifespan.

Some products use advertising to capitalize on the stereotype of older adults as forgetful. Advertisements for products that claim to treat memory loss, for example, may feature older people speaking about their use of this product and how it improved their forgetfulness. If an older adult who is susceptible to stereotype threat views advertisements like this, their discomfort about being perceived as incompetent and forgetful may influence them to purchase said item.

Some work suggests that the framing of a task can influence the effect of stereotype threat. Specifically, older adults tend to perform more accurately under conditions of stereotype threat when they are oriented to focus on preventing losses, as opposed to when they are oriented to maximize gains (Barber and Mather, 2013b; Barber, Mather, and Gatz, 2015). Older adults operating under stereotype threat may adopt a loss prevention strategy, which may actually improve motivation and performance on a task. Thus, if older adults do feel concern about their cognitive abilities, perhaps framing messaging to older consumers around loss prevention may decrease the impact of cognitive deficits associated with memory or decision-making.

Conclusion

Motivation, memory, and decision-making change across the lifespan. Many of these changes can be explained by peoples' priorities shifting from knowledge gathering in younger adulthood to relationship building in older adulthood (e.g., Carstensen et al., 1999); perhaps this explanation is compatible with a shift from primary to secondary control (e.g., Heckhausen and Schulz, 1995), or with a focus on avoiding losses (e.g., Freund, 2008). While overall curiosity may decrease with older age, it is still a powerful motivator of older adults' behavior and may even be a protective factor in old age (Sakaki et al., 2018). Brain training, for example, is a specific (and popular) way in which curiosity about how the brain works can be piqued, though being highly motivated to pursue information about anti-aging supplements may put older adults at risk for health issues or fraud. Variety-seeking behaviors tend to decrease as people get older, but older adults may focus their time, efforts, and cognitive abilities on behaviors that satisfy social and emotional goals rather than including variety for the sake of it. Age also affects perception of gains and losses. People across the lifespan may save important information to a computer or a smartphone application, but how and why we use such external offloading technologies may be affected by cognitive aging, memory abilities, and our perceptions about our own learning and about digital technology. Finally, emotional factors such as anxiety and stereotype threat can influence older adults' behavior, including their memory for information and their perceptions about products. Due to a focus on positive information, older adults may also be targets for financial fraud and scams, and future research and interventions are needed to address this growing concern.

In this chapter, we sought to investigate circumstances under which younger and older adults' behavior may differ with respect to motivated cognition. Future work may examine how different theories of motivation in cognitive aging may explain different facets of consumer behavior. In addition to socioemotional selectivity theory, lifespan theory of control, and selective optimization with compensation theory, we can also assess how value-directed remembering and selectivity affect motivation to learn and make decisions across the adult lifespan. While many older adults experience memory decline and possible onset of dementia, healthy older adults can use motivated cognition and continued curiosity to enhance cognitive function and maintain independence in older age.

Note

1 Author note: This work was supported in part by the National Institutes of Health (National Institute on Aging), Award Number R01AG044335.

References

Anguera, J. A., Boccanfuso, J., Rintoul, J. L., Al-Hashimi, O., Faraji, F., Janowich, J., Kong, Y., Larraburo, Y., Rolle, C., Johnstone, E., & Gazzaley, A. (2013). Video game training enhances cognitive control in older adults. *Nature*, *501*(7465), 97–101.

Arizona Daily Sun (2005, February 8). Arizonans accused of selling fake Botox to remain jailed. https://azdailysun.com/arizonans-accused-of-selling-fake-botox-to-remain-ja iled/article_518ebe73-1208-56ca-9a8b-3b98d236f7b4.html

Ball, K., Berch, D. B., Helmers, K. F., Jobe, J. B., Leveck, M. D., Marsiske, M., Morris, J., Rebok, G., Smith, D., Tennstedt, S., Unverzagt, F., Willis, S., & Advanced Cognitive

Training for Independent and Vital Elderly Study Group (2002). Effects of cognitive training interventions with older adults: A randomized controlled trial. *JAMA, 288*(18), 2271–2281.

Baltes, P. B., Sowarka, D., & Kliegl, R. (1989). Cognitive training research on fluid intelligence in old age: what can older adults achieve by themselves?. *Psychology and Aging, 4*(2), 217–221.

Baltes, P. B. (1997). On the incomplete architecture of human ontogeny: Selection, optimization, and compensation as foundation of developmental theory. *American Psychologist, 52*(4), 366–380.

Baltes, P. B., & Baltes, M. M. (1990). Psychological perspectives on successful aging: The model of selective optimization with compensation. In: P. B. Baltes & M. M. Baltes (Eds.), *Successful Aging: Perspectives from the Behavioral Sciences* (pp. 1–34). New York, NY: Cambridge University Press.

Baltes, P. B., Staudinger, U. M., & Lindenberger, U. (1999). Lifespan psychology: Theory and application to intellectual functioning. *Annual Review of Psychology, 50*(1), 471–507.

Barber, S. J. (2017). An examination of age-based stereotype threat about cognitive decline: Implications for stereotype-threat research and theory development. *Perspectives on Psychological Science, 12*(1), 62–90.

Barber, S. J., & Mather, M. (2013b). Stereotype threat can reduce older adults' memory errors. *The Quarterly Journal of Experimental Psychology, 66*(10), 1888–1895.

Barber, S. J., Mather, M., & Gatz, M. (2015). How stereotype threat affects healthy older adults' performance on clinical assessments of cognitive decline: The key role of regulatory fit. *The Journals of Gerontology, Series B: Psychological Sciences and Social Sciences, 70*(6), 891–900.

Beaudoin, M., & Desrichard, O. (2011). Are memory self-efficacy and memory performance related? A meta-analysis. *Psychological Bulletin, 137*(2), 211–241.

Benartzi, S., & Castel, A. (2016). The financial price of forgetting bad times. *The Wall Street Journal,* June 12, 2016 (print edition).

Bjork, R. A., & Woodward, A. E. (1973). Directed forgetting of individual words in free recall. *Journal of Experimental Psychology, 99*(1), 22–27.

Brehmer, Y., Westerberg, H., & Bäckman, L. (2012). Working-memory training in younger and older adults: training gains, transfer, and maintenance. *Frontiers in Human Neuroscience, 6*, 63.

Broady, T., Chan, A., & Caputi, P. (2010). Comparison of older and younger adults' attitudes towards and abilities with computers: Implications for training and learning. *British Journal of Educational Technology, 41*(3), 473–485.

Brouthers, K. D., Brouthers, L. E., & Werner, S. (2000). Influences on strategic decision-making in the Dutch financial services industry. *Journal of Management, 26*(5), 863–883.

Carstensen, L. L., Fung, H. H., & Charles, S. T. (2003). Socioemotional selectivity theory and the regulation of emotion in the second half of life. *Motivation and Emotion, 27*(2), 103–123.

Carstensen, L. L., Isaacowitz, D. M., & Charles, S. T. (1999). Taking time seriously: A theory of socioemotional selectivity. *American Psychologist, 54*(3), 165–181.

Cassidy, B. S., Hedden, T., Yoon, C., & Gutchess, A. (2014). Age differences in medial prefrontal activity for subsequent memory of truth value. *Frontiers in Psychology, 5*, 87.

Castel, A. D. (2008). The adaptive and strategic use of memory by older adults: Evaluative processing and value-directed remembering. In: A. S. Benjamin & B. H. Ross (Eds.), *Psychology of Learning and Motivation* (pp. 225–270). London: Academic Press.

Castel, A. D., Friedman, M. C., McGillivray, S., Flores, C. C., Murayama, K., Kerr, T., & Drolet, A. (2016). I owe you: Age-related similarities and differences in associative memory for gains and losses. *Aging, Neuropsychology, and Cognition, 23*(5), 549–565.

Castel, A. D., McGillivray, S., & Friedman, M. C. (2012). Metamemory and memory efficiency in older adults: Learning about the benefits of priority processing and value-directed remembering. In: M. Naveh-Benjamin & N. Ohta (Eds.), *Memory and Aging: Current Issues and Future Directions* (pp. 245–270). New York, NY: Psychology Press.

Chan, M. Y., Haber, S., Drew, L., & Park, D. C. (2016). Training older adults to use tablet computers: Does it enhance cognitive function? *Gerontologist, 56*(3), 475–484.

Charness, N., & Boot, W. R. (2009). Aging and information technology use: Potential and barriers. *Current Directions in Psychological Science, 18*(5), 253–258.

Chasteen, A. L. (2000). The role of age and age-related attitudes in perceptions of elderly individuals. *Basic and Applied Social Psychology, 22*(3), 147–156.

Chasteen, A. L., Bhattacharyya, S., Horhota, M., Tam, R., & Hasher, L. (2005). How feelings of stereotype threat influence older adults' memory performance. *Experimental Aging Research, 31*(3), 235–260.

Coudin, G., & Alexopoulos, T. (2010). 'Help me! I'm old!' How negative aging stereotypes create dependency among older adults. *Aging & Mental Health, 14*(5), 516–523.

Cuddy, A. J., Norton, M. I., & Fiske, S. T. (2005). This old stereotype: The pervasiveness and persistence of the elderly stereotype. *Journal of Social Issues, 61*(2), 267–285.

Deakin, J., Aitken, M., Robbins, T., & Sahakian, B. J. (2004). Risk taking during decision-making in normal volunteers changes with age. *Journal of the International Neuropsychological Society, 10*(4), 590–598.

Diehl, M. K., & Wahl, H. W. (2009). Awareness of age-related change: Examination of a (mostly) unexplored concept. *Journals of Gerontology. Series B: Psychological Sciences and Social Sciences, 65*, 340–350.

Drolet, A., Lau-Gesk, L., & Scott, C. (2011). The influence of aging on preferences for sequences of mixed affective events. *Journal of Behavioral Decision Making, 24*(3), 293–314.

Dror, I. E., Katona, M., & Mungur, K. (1998). Age differences in decision making: To take a risk or not? *Gerontology, 44*(2), 67–71.

Bleijenberg, N. (2012). Dutch nursing students' knowledge and attitudes towards older people—A longitudinal cohort study. *Journal of Nursing Education and Practice, 2*(2), 1–8.

East, R., Uncles, M. D., & Lomax, W. (2014). Hear nothing, do nothing: The role of word of mouth in the decision-making of older consumers. *Journal of Marketing Management, 30*(7–8), 786–801.

Engel, S. (2011). Children's need to know: Curiosity in schools. *Harvard educational review, 81*(4), 625–645.

Evanschitzky, H., & Woisetschläger, D. (2008). Too old to choose? The effects of age and age related constructs on consumer decision making. *Advances in Consumer Research, 35*, 630–636.

Farah, M. J. (2015). The unknowns of cognitive enhancement. *Science, 350*(6259), 379–380.

Freund, A. M. (2008). Successful aging as management of resources: The role of selection, optimization, and compensation. *Research in Human Development, 5*(2), 94–106.

Freund, A. M., & Baltes, P. B. (1998). Selection, optimization, and compensation as strategies of life management: Correlations with subjective indicators of successful aging. *Psychology and Aging, 13*(4), 531–543.

Fung, H. H., & Carstensen, L. L. (2003). Sending memorable messages to the old: Age differences in preferences and memory for advertisements. *Journal of Personality and Social Psychology, 85*(1), 163–178.

Gruber, M. J., Gelman, B. D., & Ranganath, C. (2014). States of curiosity modulate hippocampus-dependent learning via the dopaminergic circuit. *Neuron, 84*(2), 486–496.

Hamilton, K. A., & Benjamin, A. S. (2019). The human-machine extended organism: New roles and responsibilities of human cognition in a digital ecology. *Journal of Applied Research in Memory and Cognition, 8*, 40–45.

Han, S. D., Boyle, P. A., James, B. D., Yu, L., & Bennett, D. A. (2015). Mild cognitive impairment is associated with poorer decision-making in community-based older persons. *Journal of the American Geriatrics Society, 63*(4), 676–683.

Hargis, M. B., Siegel, A. L. M., & Castel, A. D. (2019). Motivated memory, learning, and decision making in older age: Shifts in priorities and goals. In G. Samanez-Larkin (Ed.), *The aging brain: Functional adaptation across adulthood*. Washington DC: American Psychological Association.

Heckhausen, J., & Schulz, R. (1995). A life-span theory of control. *Psychological Review, 102*(2), 284–304.

Hendricks, J., & Cutler, S. J. (2004). Volunteerism and socioemotional selectivity in later life. *The Journals of Gerontology Series B: Psychological Sciences and Social Sciences, 59*(5), 251–257.

Hess, T. M. (2014). Selective engagement of cognitive resources: Motivational influences on older adults' cognitive functioning. *Perspectives on Psychological Science, 9*(4), 388–407.

James, B. D., Boyle, P. A., & Bennett, D. A. (2014). Correlates of susceptibility to scams in older adults without dementia. *Journal of Elder Abuse & Neglect, 26*(2), 107–122.

Kashdan, T. B., Rose, P., & Fincham, F. D. (2004). Curiosity and exploration: Facilitating positive subjective experiences and personal growth opportunities. *Journal of Personality Assessment, 82*(3), 291–305.

Kashdan, T. B., Gallagher, M. W., Silvia, P. J., Winterstein, B. P., Breen, W. E., Terhar, D., & Steger, M. F. (2009). The curiosity and exploration inventory-II: Development, factor structure, and psychometrics. *Journal of Research in Personality, 43*(6), 987–998.

Kim, A., & Merriam, S. B. (2004). Motivations for learning among older adults in a learning in retirement institute. *Educational Gerontology, 30*(6), 441–455.

Knoll, M. A. Z. (2010). The role of behavioral economics and behavioral decision making in Americans' retirement savings decisions. *Social Security Bulletin, 70*(4), 1–24.

Kovalchik, S., Camerer, C. F., Grether, D. M., Plott, C. R., & Allman, J. M. (2005). Aging and decision making: A comparison between neurologically healthy elderly and young individuals. *Journal of Economic Behavior & Organization, 58*(1), 79–94.

Kruse, A., & Schmitt, E. (2006). A multidimensional scale for the measurement of agreement with age stereotypes and the salience of age in social interaction. *Ageing & Society, 26*(3), 393–411.

Lambert, A. E., Watson, J. M., Stefanucci, J. K., Ward, N., Bakdash, J. Z., & Strayer, D. L. (2016). Stereotype threat impairs older adult driving. *Applied Cognitive Psychology, 30*(1), 22–28.

Lambert-Pandraud, R., & Laurent, G. (2010). Why do older consumers buy older brands? The role of attachment and declining innovativeness. *Journal of Marketing, 74*(5), 104–121.

Lambert-Pandraud, R., Laurent, G., & Lapersonne, E. (2005). Repeat purchasing of new automobiles by older consumers: Empirical evidence and interpretations. *Journal of Marketing, 69*(2), 97–113.

Lemaire, P., Brun, F., & Régner, I. (2018). Negative aging stereotypes disrupt both the selection and execution of strategies in older adults. *Gerontology, 64*(4), 373–381.

Levy, B. (2009). Stereotype embodiment: A psychosocial approach to aging. *Current Directions in Psychological Science, 18*(6), 332–336.

Lichtenberg, P. A., Stickney, L., & Paulson, D. (2013). Is psychological vulnerability related to the experience of fraud in older adults? *Clinical Gerontologist, 36*(2), 132–146.

Lineweaver, T. T., & Hertzog, C. (1998). Adults' efficacy and control beliefs regarding memory and aging: Separating general from personal beliefs. *Aging, Neuropsychology, and Cognition, 5*(4), 264–296.

MacPherson, S. E., Phillips, L. H., & Della Sala, S. (2002). Age, executive function and social decision making: A dorsolateral prefrontal theory of cognitive aging. *Psychology and Aging, 17*(4), 598–609.

Marinac, J. S., Buchinger, C. L., Godfrey, L. A., Wooten, J. M., Sun, C., & Willsie, S. K. (2007). Herbal products and dietary supplements: a survey of use, attitudes, and knowledge among older adults. *The Journal of the American Osteopathic Association, 107*(1), 13–23.

Marquié, J. C., Jourdan-Boddaert, L., & Huet, N. (2002). Do older adults underestimate their actual computer knowledge? *Behaviour & Information Technology, 21*(4), 273–280.

Mata, R., & Nunes, L. (2010). When less is enough: Cognitive aging, information search, and decision quality in consumer choice. *Psychology and Aging, 25*(2), 289–298.

Mather, M. (2006). A review of decision making processes: Weighing the risks and benefits of aging. In: L. L. Carstensen & C. R. Hartel (Eds.), *When I'm 64* (pp. 145–173). Washington, DC: National Academies Press.

McDaniel, M. A., Waddill, P. J., Finstad, K., & Bourg, T. (2000). The effects of text-based interest on attention and recall. *Journal of Educational Psychology, 92*(3), 492–502.

McGillivray, S., Murayama, K., & Castel, A. D. (2015). Thirst for knowledge: The effects of curiosity and interest on memory in younger and older adults. *Psychology and Aging, 30*, 835–841.

Melby-Lervåg, M., & Hulme, C. (2013). Is working memory training effective? A meta-analytic review. *Developmental Psychology, 49*, 270–291.

Mikels, J. A., Reed, A. E., & Simon, K. I. (2009). Older adults place lower value on choice relative to young adults. *Journals of Gerontology Series B: Psychological Sciences and Social Sciences, 64*(4), 443–446.

Mitchell, K. J., & Hill, E. M. (2019). The impact of focusing on different features during encoding on young and older adults' source memory. *Open Psychology, 1*(1), 106–118.

Mitzner, T. L., Boron, J. B., Fausset, C. B., Adams, A. E., Charness, N., Czaja, S. J., Dijkstra, K., Fisk, A. D., Rogers, W. A., & Sharit, J. (2010). Older adults talk technology: Technology usage and attitudes. *Computers in Human Behavior, 26*(6), 1710–1721.

Nicolas, P., Lemaire, P., & Régner, I. (2019). When and how stereotype threat influences older adults' arithmetic performance: Insight from a strategy approach. *Journal of Experimental Psychology: General.*

Novak, D. L., & Mather, M. (2007). Aging and variety seeking. *Psychology and Aging, 22*(4), 728–738.

Okun, M. A. (1976). Adult age and cautiousness in decision. *Human Development, 19*(4), 220–233.

Park, D. C., Lodi-Smith, J., Drew, L., Haber, S., Hebrank, A., Bischof, G. N., & Aamodt, W. (2014). The impact of sustained engagement on cognitive function in older adults: The synapse project. *Psychological Science, 25*(1), 103–112.

Pinsker, D. M., McFarland, K., & Pachana, N. A. (2010). Exploitation in older adults: Social vulnerability and personal competence factors. *Journal of Applied Gerontology, 29*(6), 740–761.

Qato, D. M., Alexander, G. C., Conti, R. M., Johnson, M., Schumm, P., & Lindau, S. T. (2008). Use of prescription and over-the-counter medications and dietary supplements among older adults in the United States. *JAMA*, *300*(24), 2867–2878.

Rabipour, S., & Davidson, P. S. (2015). Do you believe in brain training? A questionnaire about expectations of computerised cognitive training. *Behavioural Brain Research*, *295*, 64–70.

Rabipour, S., Andringa, R., Boot, W. R., & Davidson, P. S. (2018). What do people expect of cognitive enhancement?. *Journal of Cognitive Enhancement*, *2*(1), 70–77.

Rahhal, T. A., May, C. P., & Hasher, L. (2002). Truth and character: Sources that older adults can remember. *Psychological Science*, *13*(2), 101–105.

Ratner, R., Kahn, B., & Kahneman, D. (1999). Choosing less-preferred experiences for the sake of variety. *Journal of Consumer Research*, *26*(1), 1–15.

Reed, A. E., Mikels, J. A., & Löckenhoff, C. E. (2013). Preferences for choice across adulthood: Age trajectories and potential mechanisms. *Psychology and Aging*, *28*(3), 625–632.

Risko, E. F., & Gilbert, S. J. (2016). Cognitive offloading. *Trends in Cognitive Sciences*, *20*, 676–688.

Sakaki, M., Yagi, A., & Murayama, K. (2018). Curiosity in old age: A possible key to achieving adaptive aging. *Neuroscience & Biobehavioral Reviews*, *88*, 106–116.

Schewe, C. D. (1984). Buying and consuming behavior of the elderly findings from behavioral research. *Advances in Consumer Research*, *11*, 558–562.

Schooley, D. K., & Worden, D. D. (1999). Investors' asset allocations versus life-cycle funds. *Financial Analysts Journal*, *55*(5), 37–43.

Schroeder, S. R., & Marian, V. (2012). A bilingual advantage for episodic memory in older adults. *Journal of Cognitive Psychology*, *24*(5), 591–601.

Shah, A. K., & Oppenheimer, D. M. (2008). Heuristics made easy: An effort-reduction framework. *Psychological Bulletin*, *134*(2), 207–222.

Shao, J., Zhang, Q., Ren, Y., Li, X., & Lin, T. (2019). Why are older adults victims of fraud? Current knowledge and prospects regarding older adults' vulnerability to fraud. *Journal of Elder Abuse and Neglect*, *31*(3), 225–243.

SharpBrains (2015, January). *The Digital Brain Health Market 2012–2020: Web-Based, Mobile and Biometrics-Based Technology to Assess, Monitor, and Enhance Cognition and Brain Functioning*. San Francisco, CA: SharpBrains.

Simons, D. J., Boot, W. R., Charness, N., Gathercole, S. E., Chabris, C. F., Hambrick, D. Z., & Stine-Morrow, E. A. (2016). Do "brain-training" programs work? *Psychological Science in the Public Interest*, *17*(3), 103–186.

Skinner, D. J., & Price, J. (2019). The roles of meaningfulness and prior knowledge in younger and older adults' memory performance. *Applied Cognitive Psychology*, *2019*, 1–10.

Smock, C. D., & Holt, B. G. (1962). Children's reactions to novelty: An experimental study of "curiosity motivation." *Child Development*, *33*, 631–642.

Storm, B. C., & Stone, S. M. (2015). Saving-enhanced memory: The benefits of saving on the learning and remembering of new information. *Psychological Science*, *26*, 182–188.

Swan, G. E., & Carmelli, D. (1996). Curiosity and mortality in aging adults: A 5-year follow-up of the Western Collaborative Group Study. *Psychology and Aging*, *11*(3), 449–453.

Topaz, M., & Doron, I. (2013). Nurses' attitudes toward older patients in acute care in Israel. *Online Journal of Issues in Nursing*, *18*(2), 46–60.

Uttl, B., & Graf, P. (2006). Age-related changes in the encoding and retrieval of emotional and non-emotional information. In: B. Uttl, N. Ohta & A. L. Siegenthaler (Eds.), *Memory and Emotion* (pp. 159–187). New York, NY: Blackwell Publishing.

Wong, J. T., & Gallo, D. A. (2018). Activating aging stereotypes increases source recollection confusions in older adults: Effect at encoding but not retrieval. *The Journals of Gerontology: Series B, 74*(4), 633–641.

Xiong, J., & Zuo, M. (2019). Older adults' learning motivations in massive open online courses. *Educational Gerontology, 45*(2), 82–93.

Yoon, C., Cole, C. A., & Lee, M. P. (2009). Consumer decision making and aging: Current knowledge and future directions. *Journal of Consumer Psychology, 19*(1), 2–16.

Yoon, C., Laurent, G., Fung, H. H., Gonzalez, R., Gutchess, A. H., Hedden, T., Lambert-Pandraud, R., Mather, M., Park, D. C., Peters, E., & Skurnik, I. (2005). Cognition, persuasion and decision making in older consumers. *Marketing Letters, 16*(3–4), 429–441.

Zacks, R., & Hasher, L. (2006). Aging and long-term memory: Deficits are not inevitable. In: E. Bialystok & F. I. Craik (Eds.), *Lifespan Cognition: Mechanisms of Change* (pp. 162–177). New York, NY: Oxford University Press.

Zuckerman, M., & Neeb, M. (1980). Demographic influences in sensation seeking and expressions of sensation seeking in religion, smoking and driving habits. *Personality and Individual Differences, 1*(3), 197–206.

PART II

Influence of Aging on Decision-Making

4

AGING-RELATED CHANGES IN DECISION-MAKING[1]

Pär Bjälkebring and Ellen Peters

While piloting a study of decision-making and cognition in older adults, a slightly annoyed participant told us that the memory test was "way too easy, but the math test was way too hard for people her age." She explained that she is good with math because she used to work at a bank before she retired. However, while she still uses math in her daily decisions, in most cases she "doesn't do any formal calculations, she just knows when a deal is a 'good deal' or not."

This example illustrates, first, that working with older adults is much more exciting than working with college students, as older adults are much more involved in studies. Second, we knew that the math test was not harder than the memory test; they were equally hard based on prior testing. However, this participant's memory score was exceptional not only for people her age, but for the average population, whereas her math ability was about average. The example illustrates that, even among older adults, heterogeneity exists within individuals (a person can score high on one ability but low on another) and between people (some people score below average and others above average). Lastly, the example suggests that good decisions can emerge from different processes. For example, it is possible that this participant used her previous experiences working at a bank to intuitively identify "good deals"; people with less experience may need to think and compare further to figure out the best deal.

Blanchard-Fields, Brannan, and Camp (1987) argued that wisdom can be operationalized as the ability to integrate cognition and affect. Thus, when understanding human decision-making, both logical/rational and affective/experiential ways of knowing may have positive effects on decision quality. Known as a dual-process approach, these two modes of thinking can be fruitfully extended to our understanding of adult age differences in judgment and decision-making. In particular, research supports the idea that decision-making changes as we age in complicated (and interesting) ways. Across the adult life span, aging is associated with robust declines in deliberative processing, examples of which include memory performance, the speed with which information is processed, and comprehension and use of numeric information. Such declines are predictive of a general decline in the quality of decisions as we age (Del Missier, Mäntylä, and Bruine de Bruin, 2012). However, people over 65 make many of our nation's most important decisions (think about the Supreme Court, governments, and corporations around the world), implying perhaps that deliberative decline does not and cannot fully explain adult age differences in decision-making. In fact, we review research demonstrating that at least three additional processes exist that compensate for age-related declines in deliberative ability: selective use of deliberative capacity (e.g., Hess, 2000), accumulated experience (Eberhardt, Bruine de Bruin, and Strough, 20192019), and changes in emotion processing (Reed, Chan, and Mikels, 2014). In many instances, age-related changes in these processes may compensate for age declines in deliberative processes, thus aiding decision-making in older age. Lastly, we briefly introduce methods based in these lower-level processes that might improve older adult decision-making in situations where they might be vulnerable.

Good Decision-Making is Fundamental to Maintenance of Independent Functioning

In 2017, the U.S. Census Bureau projected that by 2035 the number of people over 65 would exceed the number under the age of 18 in the United States; in 2018, they updated that projection to 2034 (U.S. Census Bureau, 2018). In other words, the older population is not only growing, it is growing faster than experts thought only a couple of years ago. Understanding how to help this growing population maintain independent decision-making will be important to their physical and psychological well-being. Moreover, from a societal perspective, the potential demands from this growing population will place increasing strain on already limited supports and resources. Thus, understanding the effects of aging on maintenance of independent functioning and facilitating such independent functioning becomes critical. The ability to make high quality decisions is one process that is key to independent functioning. For example, because health problems increase with aging, older adults are among the world's biggest users of (and decision makers about) health care. They make decisions about when to go to the doctor, whether to pay for a medication (because out-of-pocket expenditures rise rapidly with age, health care could be considered a luxury good, especially for the oldest-old; De Nardi, French, and Jones, 2006), which preventive measures to take, what to eat, and whether to exercise. Older adults also make many consequential financial decisions in terms of Social Security and other sources of wealth and retirement income. They have to decide when to stop driving, whether to continue living independently, whether to trust an individual asking for money, and so on. The quality of the decisions they make then will help determine their future life satisfaction.

To make good decisions, Hibbard and Peters (2003) suggested that a number of processes have to take place. First, the decision maker must have appropriate information; it has to be available, accurate, and timely. Policy makers sometimes think that this process suffices. In other words, if they provide all of the necessary information, an informed public will always make the choices that are right for them. However, decision makers have to be able to comprehend the given information and its meaning. They have to be able to determine meaningful differences between options and to weight factors to match their own needs and values. Decision makers also have to be able to make trade-offs that might be major (Would I prefer to pay my electricity bill or fill my prescription for my heart medicine?) or minor (Do I eat spaghetti or beef for dinner?). Further, in the lab, decision-making stimuli are often created to have normatively correct answers, but outside the lab, judging what option is objectively best is harder. Finally, the decision maker has to choose.

Barriers to using provided information to make good decisions also exist, and some of these barriers are related to age. For example, information may be available primarily on the Internet, and older adults may have less access to Internet-based information. The information may not be understood, and such comprehension problems may be larger for older adults than for younger adults, particularly if the information is unfamiliar and numeric (Hibbard, Slovic, Peters, Finucane, and Tusler, 2001). Older adults also may have more difficulty making trade-offs that are emotionally uncomfortable (Mather, 2006). Further, research has shown that, when making decisions with trade-offs, older adults prefer to defer or avoid making a choice (Chen, Ma, and Pethtel, 2011). These differences point toward the growing body of research that has found age differences in decision-making (e.g., Peters, Hess, Västfjäll, and Auman, 2007; Löckenhoff, 2018). The broader literature on the impact of dual information processes on judgments and decisions also provides a framework to understand and predict possible age differences in decision-making.

Dual Modes of Thinking and Their Impact on Decision-Making

Historically, human decision-making was seen as deliberative and rational, with emotions and intuitions perceived as simple disturbances to this deliberative process. However, since the 1990s, decision researchers increasingly realized that human emotions and intuitions are more complicated, with emotions having multiple functions in judgment and decision-making that can both help and hurt decision-making processes (Peters, Lipkus, and Diefenbach, 2006). Hence, many models now consider both experiential/emotional and deliberative ways of thinking and deciding (Epstein, 1994; Loewenstein, Weber, Hsee, and Welch, 2001;

Reyna, 2004; Sloman, 1996; these modes are sometimes called Systems 1 and 2, respectively; see Kahneman, 2003; Stanovich and West, 2002).

The experiential mode produces thoughts and feelings (often called "affect" in the decision literature) often in a relatively effortless and spontaneous manner. The operations of this mode are often thought to be implicit, intuitive, automatic, associative, and fast. Processing in the experiential mode is based on affective (emotional) feelings. As shown in a number of studies, affect provides information about the goodness or badness of an option that can be used heuristically, directly motivate a behavioral tendency in choice processes, or that might direct the decision maker to other congruent information that warrants further consideration (Damasio, 1994; Osgood, Suci, and Tannenbaum, 1957; Peters, Lipkus, and Diefenbach, 2006). The deliberative mode, in contrast, is conscious, analytical, reason-based, verbal, and relatively slow. It is the deliberative mode of thinking that is more flexible and provides effortful control over more spontaneous experiential processes. Kahneman (2003) and others have suggested that one of the functions of the deliberative mode is to monitor the quality of the information processing that emerges from the affective/experiential mode and its impact on behavior.

Both modes of thinking are important to forming decisions. Damasio (1994), for example, has claimed that good choices are most likely to emerge when affective and deliberative modes work in concert, and decision makers think as well as feel their way through judgments and decisions (see also Peters and Slovic, 2000). Additionally, affective and deliberative processes in decision-making are interdependent; in other words, our thoughts and feelings influence each other. The two modes also appear to be somewhat separable (e.g., Epstein, 1994; Petty and Wegener, 1999; Zajonc, 1980). The implicit assumption that good decision-making is a conscious, deliberative process has been one of the field's most enduring themes, but, in fact, deliberation about reasons for choice sometimes appears to have a negative impact on decision processes as deliberation might disrupt useful affect (e.g., Wilson, Dunn, Kraft, and Lisle, 1989). As a result, decision makers may attempt to "do the rational thing" instead of choosing what they feel to be experientially optimal. Such a process can result in people failing to choose what will make them happy (Hsee and Hastie, 2006).

Research also has demonstrated that affect may have a relatively greater influence when deliberative capacity is lower, suggesting that these two systems should not be seen as two totally separate processes without influence on each other, but rather as two aspects of a dynamic decision process (Hammond, 1996; Kruglanski et al., 2003; Peters and Slovic, 2007). Shiv and Fedorikhin (1999), for example, demonstrated that decision makers were more likely to choose an affect-rich option (and decide with their hearts) when deliberative capacity was diminished by cognitive load. Finucane, Alhakami, Slovic, and Johnson (2000) also found that the inverse relation between risks and benefits (linked to affect by Alhakami and Slovic, 1994) was enhanced under time pressure. Reducing the time for deliberation appeared to increase the use of affect and the affect heuristic. Hence, older adults might start relying more on experience-based processes because of two age-related changes: first, because of age declines in deliberation as suggested above and second, because they are more experienced (Hogarth, 2014).

Although these and other dual-process theories are only one means for understanding human thinking, we believe they are an effective way to understand current findings in human decision-making (De Neys and Pennycook, 2019). In subsequent sections, we discuss aging-related changes in both deliberative and experiential ways of thinking. Furthermore, we link these differences to various aspects of the decision-making process including strategy selection and decision-outcome evaluations.

Age Declines in Deliberative Processes

As previously mentioned, traditional decision research relies on the assumption that we deliberate in order to make our best decisions. Decision research developed from economic theory and, as a result of this rationalistic origin, has concentrated mostly on consequentialist explanations for how people make decisions and form judgments. The problem with this view, however, is that we have limited capacity to represent information, process it, and manipulate it; we are boundedly rational (Simon, 1955).

Research on age-related changes in cognition shows that cognitive abilities such as information-processing speed, novel problem solving, and reasoning ("fluid intelligence") generally decline with age (Baltes, Staudinger, and Lindenberger, 1999; Salthouse, 2012). Park et al. (2002), for example, demonstrated that a decline begins to occur in processes related to deliberation (e.g., speed of processing and working memory) among people in their 20s (see Figure 4.1). From a dual-process perspective, these processes are considered deliberative and slow. They are considered aspects of "fluid intelligence," and research has suggested that age declines in fluid intelligence negatively influence deliberate and active processing in decisions (Li et al., 2013). In contrast, knowledge that is acquired through experience ("crystallized intelligence") tends to be relatively stable or even increase with age (e.g., verbal and world knowledge). From a dual-process perspective, crystallized intelligence fits better in the intuitive, experiential, and affective mode. Hogarth (2014), for example, suggested that the intuition that comes with experience acts through affect, "a gut feeling." Further, when understanding cognitive decline, it is important to separate cognitive decline associated with "normal aging" from, for example, cognitive decline due to dementia (see, for example, Salthouse, 2019).

If good decisions depend on deliberation, the robust age-related declines in executive functioning suggest that the quality of judgments and decisions will suffer inevitably as we age. Several studies have identified biases in judgment processes that increase with age and were linked with deliberative processes such as working memory. For example, Mutter (2000) and Mutter and Pliske (1994) examined the impact of illusory correlation on performance. (In an illusory correlation, people

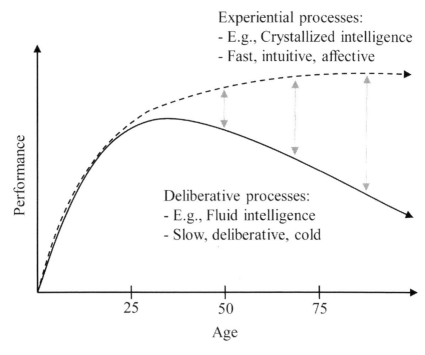

FIGURE 4.1 Development of deliberative and experiential processes over the life span. Whereas deliberative processes decrease in older age, experiential processes remain stable or increase. As a result, the difference between the deliberative and experiential processes is largest (gray arrows) in older age and may have consequences for decision-making in older age.

perceive that two variables covary consistently with their prior expectations even though no actual relation exists.) They found that older adults' judgments were more influenced by prior experiences than were those of younger adults, particularly under distraction conditions. Older adults were also less likely to correct their judgments when accurate information regarding the co-occurrence of events was made salient. Interestingly, Mutter found that age differences were more evident for memory-based judgments than for online judgments, suggesting that age differences in illusory-correlation biases may be based in part on the declining ability to encode and retrieve veridical information from episodic memory.

Such a conclusion was bolstered by other research that examined age differences in the ability to detect covariation between two events when there were no strong prior expectancies regarding contingencies between the events (Mutter and Pliske, 1996; Mutter and Williams, 2004). In this research, aging-related declines in the ability to accurately judge covariation were eliminated when performance was adjusted to take into account memory errors. The researchers also found that older adults tended to use simpler strategies in constructing judgments than did younger adults, and that younger adults used simpler strategies when the task demands were increased relative to situations with fewer cognitive demands. In another example, Chasseigne and colleagues found that older adults performed as well as young adults in probability-learning tasks when the cues had a direct relation with the criterion but performed less well when the cues had a more complex inverse or multiplicative relation with the criterion (Chasseigne, Grau, Mullet, and Cama, 1999; Chasseigne, Lafon, and Mullet, 2002; Chasseigne, Mullet, and Stewart, 1997). Such findings suggest that some declines in judgments and decisions in later adulthood may be tied to reductions in cognitive resources.

Research by Chen (2002, 2004; Chen and Blanchard-Fields, 2000) has also suggested that aging-related declines in deliberative processes have a negative impact on judgment processes. In these studies, participants were presented with information about an individual, some of which was identified as true and some as false (and thus to be ignored). Then, they were asked to make judgments based on this information. Chen found that the judgments of older adults were more likely to be influenced by the false information than were those of younger adults. In addition, younger adults in a divided-attention condition performed similarly to older adults under full attention. These findings suggested that older adults may have more difficulty controlling attention and monitoring the accuracy of information in memory, which in turn makes judgments more prone to error based on irrelevant information. In a related study, Skurnik, Yoon, Park, and Schwarz (2005) found that repeatedly identifying a (false) consumer claim as false assisted older adults' in the short term in remembering that it was false. Over longer term, however, the repetition caused them to misremember it as true.

A pragmatic implication of these studies is that information providers need to take care not to provide older adults with a "fact" and then state that it is a myth. This and similar tactics are surprisingly common (e.g., the U.S. Food and Drug Administration's (2017) "Question, Answers, and Facts About Generic Drugs" poses a question such as "'Are brand-name drugs made in better factories than generic drugs?" and then answers "No. All factories must meet the same high standards").

In general, evidence exists that, when making decisions, older adults use less complex strategies and consider fewer pieces of information than do younger adults. For example, Johnson and her colleagues (Johnson, 1990, 1993; Johnson and Drungle, 2000; Riggle and Johnson, 1996) examined decision-making strategies by different-aged adults using an information matrix that contained specific features (shown in rows) for different product choices (shown in columns). Participants were allowed to view only one cell of the matrix at a time, but they could view as many cells as they wished for as long as necessary before making a product decision. A relatively consistent finding in this research, across different types of products (e.g., cars, apartments, over-the-counter drugs), was that older adults spent a longer time studying each cell but sampled fewer pieces of information than did younger adults before making their decisions. Similar results were obtained by Streufert, Pogash, Piasecki, and Post (1990) in a study of decision-making in managers and by Hershey, Wal Read, and Chulef (1990) in a financial-planning task. The overall pattern of observed performance in these studies appears consistent with what might be expected with a decline in deliberative processes with aging.

In fact, research has demonstrated that, similar to covariation and other research reviewed above, younger adults adopt a strategy similar to that observed in older adults when task demands are increased. It may be that limited cognitive resources in later adulthood result in the adoption of strategies that minimize demands on deliberative processes. For example, to conserve resources, older adults may adopt a strategy of eliminating alternatives as soon as possible (Riggle and Johnson, 1996). Thus, as soon as an undesirable piece of information about a product is encountered, the alternative is eliminated from further consideration. Alternatively, a satisficing strategy may be employed. In it, information about a specific product is examined until a sufficient amount of information has been deemed acceptable. Consistent with such an explanation, Chen and Sun (2003) found that both older and younger adults adopted satisfying strategies in a simulated real-world task (i.e., maximizing profit at a yard sale), but the strategy adopted by older adults was less memory demanding than that adopted by younger adults. To mitigate these deficiencies, Sorce (1995) recommended that marketing strategies should attempt to segment older consumers to customize products and information to compensate for their cognitive decline.

Much research has confirmed that age-related lower levels of fluid intelligence are related to examples of worse decision competence among older adults (Eberhardt, Bruine de Bruin, and Strough, 2019; Missier et al., 2017). In a review of age-related differences in the effects of financial incentives on risky decisions, Samanez-Larkin and Knutson (2012) suggested that, although processing of reward information may be maintained in older adults, learning about new rewards may decline with age. Rosi, Bruine de Bruin, Missier, Cavallini, and Russo (2019) examined the independent roles of different types of fluid intelligence proxies (working memory, verbal fluency, semantic knowledge, and components of executive functioning). They found that age-related declines in the ability to apply provided rules in decision-making (e.g., equal weights, elimination by aspects, satisficing, and lexicographic rules) was mediated by age-related declines in working memory and verbal fluency.

Lastly, almost all studies on age-related differences in decision-making competence, are cross-sectional. Hence, age differences may reflect both cohort-related effects as well as age effects. Del Missier and colleagues (2020) presented a longitudinal study of age-related changes over five years in older adults (aged 60–85). In their study, they investigated three important aspects of decision-making competence: resistance to framing, applying decision rules, and resistance to sunk costs. Their finding indicated only a small, longitudinal decline with age in resistance to framing. No declines existed in applying decision rules or resistance to sunk costs. Their results also indicated that older adults' decision-making competence after five years was significantly related to their initial decision-making competence assessment. However, because no younger reference group was used, it remains possible that the stability should be interpreted in a negative light. Specifically, after five years of repeated testing, these older participants did not improve whereas younger participants might have improved with the same testing.

Numeracy and Decision-Making in Older Adults

Research has further suggested that an especially important deliberative factor for good decisions is numeracy (also called quantitative literacy; Cokely et al., 2016; Peters, Hess, et al., 2007; Peters, Västfjäll, et al., 2006; Reyna et al., 2009). Numeracy refers to the ability to understand and use mathematical and probabilistic concepts. Based on the National Adult Literacy Survey, almost half of the general population has difficulty with relatively simple numeric tasks such as calculating the difference between a regular price and sales price using a calculator or estimating the cost per ounce of a grocery item; scores on these tasks decline with age (Kirsch, Jungeblut, Jenkins, and Kolstad, 2002). Numeric information is important to many decisions because numbers instruct, inform, and give meaning to information, and those with greater numeracy generally understand more numeric information and make superior judgments and choices when numbers are involved (Peters et al., 2006). However, age declines in numeric ability have been demonstrated longitudinally (Schaie and Zanjani, 2006). Consistent with these declines, older adult research has linked worse decision performance on some tasks to older adults' lower numeracy (Chen et al., 2014).

Innumeracy in the general population appears to have an effect on risk perceptions and decision processes beyond simple comprehension of numbers. For example, Peters, Västfjäll, et al. (2006) pitted intuition against rational analysis by making an objectively worse choice more tempting. Subjects were offered a prize if they drew a colored jellybean from a bowl. Bowl A contained 9 colored and 91 white beans, and Bowl B contained 1 colored and 9 white beans. Consequently, the chance of picking a colored jellybean was objectively better if the subject picked from Bowl B (10 percent chance of winning) than if he or she picked from Bowl A (9 percent chance of winning). Despite this, 33 percent of less numerate subjects and 5 percent of more numerate subjects picked from Bowl A, which was clearly not the rational choice if one wanted to win a prize. Whereas highly numerate subjects appeared to perceive the probability of winning more clearly and selected Bowl B, the less numerate were drawn more to the number of winning beans than by the objective probability. These results combined with those of other studies imply that, compared to more numerate decision makers, the preferences expressed by the less numerate are likely to be more labile and influenced by extraneous cues, such as irrelevant sources of affect and emotion, and to be less influenced by objective numbers like probabilities.

Less numerate individuals, whether young or old, do not necessarily perceive themselves as "at risk" in their lives due to limited skills. However, inadequate numeracy may be an important barrier to individuals' understanding and use of health, financial, and other risks. In fact, in the United States and other developed nations, lower numeracy has been associated with a host of undesirable health outcomes, including self-reported poor health, health disparities, poor health knowledge and disease self-management skills, and choosing lower-quality health options (Baker, Parker, Williams, Clark, and Nurss, 1997; DeWalt, Berkman, Sheridan, Lohr, and Pignone, 2004; Hibbard, Peters, Dixon, and Tusler, 2007; Sentell and Halpin, 2006; Williams, Baker, Parker, and Nurss, 1998; Estrada, Martin-Hryniewicz, Peek, Collins, and Byrd, 2004; Apter et al., 2006; Rothman et al., 2006).

Because older adults, as a cohort, tend to be less numerate, they are likely to understand and use numeric information less well than younger adults in health, financial, and other consumer products. Results from health plan choice studies support these age declines in comprehension of numeric information and suggest that older decision makers do not always comprehend even fairly simple information. Hibbard, Peters, Slovic, Finucane, and Tusler (2001) presented employed-aged adults (18–64 years old; n = 239) and older adults (65–94 years old; n = 253) with 33 decision tasks that involved interpretation of numbers from tables and graphs. For example, participants were asked to identify the health insurance plan with the lowest copayment from a table that included four plans with information about monthly premiums and copayments. A comprehension index reflected the total number of errors made across the 33 tasks. The youngest participants (aged 18–35) averaged 8 percent errors; the oldest participants (aged 85–94) averaged 40 percent errors; the correlation between age and the number of errors was 0.31 (p < 0.001). Higher education was somewhat protective of these age declines, reducing the errors by about half in people aged 66–79 years. However, no education effect was seen in participants aged 80 or older.

These comprehension differences could indicate that older adults, in particular, should not be provided numeric information as it might undermine outcomes. Peters, Hart, Tusler, and Fraenkel (2014) examined evidence for these possible age differences in the processing of prescription drug information. Using a diverse sample of 905 adults (aged 18–89 years), participants were asked to imagine that they were prescribed drug for high cholesterol, were provided information about drug risks in either numeric or non-numeric terms, and were asked their likelihood of taking the drug. The results revealed that numeric information provided benefits across the numeracy spectrum. In particular, individuals higher and lower in numeracy were less likely to overestimate drug risks and more likely to use the drug when given numeric rather than non-numeric risk information. However, less numerate older adults did not appear to benefit as much from the provision of numeric information (neither were they harmed). Further study is required, however, to uncover numeric formats that facilitate processing even among less numerate older adults (Peters, Hibbard, Slovic, and Dieckmann, 2007).

Overall, the lower numeracy associated with older adulthood may exacerbate health and wealth disparities and potentially reduce the quality of older adults' lives. For example, in one study of older Italian adults, lower numeracy was related to higher levels of self-rated depression (Fastame, Manca, Penna, Lucangeli, and Hitchcott, 2019). Research has further suggested that lower numeracy is an important risk factor for older financial exploitation. Wood, Liu, Hanoch, and Estevez-Cores (2016) demonstrated that lower numeracy was an important predictor of being financially exploited in a sample of older adults; no evidence emerged of an influence of executive functioning or general cognitive functioning.

Numeracy and other deliberative processes also link formal schooling to older adult functioning. In particular, greater education as a child or adolescent may lead to greater numeracy and executive functioning, improved decision skills in situations that involve an understanding of numbers, and ultimately better choices about health and financial risks (Peters, Baker, et al., 2010; Bruine de Bruin, Parker, and Fischhoff, 2007; Goldman and Smith, 2002). It is unclear whether continued adult education may have similar effects among middle-aged and older adults as childhood education appears to have (although see Peters, Shoots-Reinhard, et al., 2017). Lastly, numeracy's relations with health and financial outcomes also appear to depend on numeric confidence (Peters, Tompkins, et al., 2019). Hence, objective ability and confidence interact to shape decision quality. It is possible that this interaction is especially important in older adults, as older adults might be unaware of age declines in deliberative processes and hence be overconfident, however, these relations remain unexplored.

Age-Related Compensatory Processes, Including Selectivity, Increased Experience, and Affective Processes

Age-related declines in deliberative abilities such as numeracy imply that older adults will inevitably make worse decisions and suffer their consequences. However, the vast majority of older adults appear to function effectively and independently in everyday life (Li et al., 2015). Further, many of the most influential and demanding positions in our society are held by late-middle-aged and older adults, suggesting that their ability to make decisions remains intact despite other declines (Carstensen, 2001; Salthouse, 1990). Hence, deliberative decline appears to be too simple an explanation of age differences in decision-making (Bruine de Bruin, Parker, and Fischhoff, 2020; Peters, Hess, Västfjäll, and Auman, 2007).

In fact, at least three reasons exist for why deliberative decline is too simple an explanation of age differences in decision-making. First, older adults appear to use their deliberative capacity selectively. For example, older adults seem to use strategies related to satisficing (vs maximizing) in decision-making, perhaps because finding an option that is good enough is less cognitively challenging compared to determining the best option (Bruine de Bruin, Parker, and Strough, 2016). Further, older adults appear to adapt to real or perceived declines in cognitive resources by becoming increasingly selective about where they spend effort (Hess, 2000). That is, the costs associated with resource-demanding deliberative processing result in older adults being more judicious than younger adults in their allocation of resources. Hess further hypothesized that this aging-related resource conservation should be most apparent in situations of low relevance or meaningfulness to the individual, with fewer age differences as relevance and meaningfulness increase. More generally, this theorizing suggests that older adults are more selective and adaptive than younger adults in how they process information and choose strategies in decisions (Hess et al., 2013).

The impact of this heightened selectivity on the involvement of deliberative and affective processes can be seen, for example, in a study that examined the extent to which attitudes toward proposed legislation were influenced by irrelevant affective information (i.e., the likeability of the lawmaker proposing the legislation; Hess, Germain, Rosenberg, Leclerc, and Hodges, 2005). When the personal relevance of the legislation was low, older adults exhibited attitudes that were consistent with how much they liked the lawmaker, whereas younger adults' attitudes were unaffected by this information. In contrast, when the legislation was rated high in personal relevance, neither the younger nor the older adults were influenced by the affective information. Related findings were reported by Chen (2004), who observed that increasing personal accountability benefited older adults' source memory relatively more than it did that of younger adults.

A second reason for why deliberative decline is too simple an explanation is that the experience individuals gain in life can compensate for some of the age-related declines in deliberative processes. One way of operationalizing experience is through measures of crystallized knowledge (e.g., vocabulary scores) that demonstrate robust increases across the adult life span (Park et al., 2002). Research has demonstrated that crystallized and fluid intelligence together influence decision-making (Toplak, Sorge, Benoit, West, and Stanovich, 2010). Thus, age-related increases in crystallized intelligence, especially in more familiar and practiced decisions, may compensate for age declines in fluid intelligence (Zaval, Li, Johnson, and Weber 2015). Crystallized intelligence therefore may represent a kind of decision-making capital that bypasses reduced levels of fluid intelligence. As a result, older adults may make decisions as good as or better than younger adults when the older adult can take advantage of their superior crystallized intelligence. Consistent with this thinking, Meyer, Russo, and Talbot (1995) found that older women behaved more like experts by seeking out less information, making decisions faster, and arriving at decision outcomes equivalent to younger women. Compared to the younger women, older individuals appeared to compensate for reductions in information seeking and bottom-up processing with a greater reliance on top-down processing, arriving at equivalent decisions. Of course, in other instances, when fluid intelligence is needed, older adults likely will be worse decision makers than younger adults.

A third reason for why deliberative decline cannot fully account for age differences in decision-making concerns the role of affect and emotion in decisions. Decision makers rely on affective meaning to guide judgments and decisions in everyday life (Bechara, Damasio, Damasio, and Anderson, 1994; Bechara, Damasio, Tranel, and Damasio, 1997; Bechara, Tranel, Damasio, and Damasio, 1996; Damasio, 1994; Peters and Slovic, 2000; Slovic, Finucane, Peters, and MacGregor, 2002). According to the "affect heuristic," all of the images in a person's mind are tagged or marked to varying degrees with affect. The "affect pool" contains all positive and negative markers that are consciously or unconsciously associated with the images. Using this overall, readily available affective impression can be easier and more efficient than weighing the pros and cons of a situation or retrieving relevant examples from memory. This reliance on affect may be especially true when the required judgment or decision is complex or when mental resources are limited, as in conditions of time pressure (Finucane et al., 2000).

Furthermore, decision makers rely on affect in at least four ways in the decision-making process (Peters, 2006; Peters, Lipkus, and Diefenbach, 2006). First, affect can act as information (as a substitute for other, sometimes more relevant, information; Kahneman, 2003) in judgments such as life satisfaction (Schwarz and Clore, 1983). Second, it can act as a common currency that allows people to integrate multiple pieces of information more effectively than when it is absent (Cabanac, 1992; Peters, 2006). Third, it can act as a spotlight to focus people's attention on different information (e.g., numerical cues), which may then be used in judgments instead of the affect itself. Fourth, affect can motivate people to take some action or process information. The use of affect is thought to generally improve judgments and decisions.

As a result, and consistent with age-related compensatory effects of crystallized knowledge, decision makers may learn over the life span to use affect as a particularly effective means of making decisions. Reyna (2004), for example, argued that affective and other related gist information processing is more advanced relative to the deliberative mode. In support of this idea, she provided evidence that people process less information and process it more qualitatively, in a more gist-like fashion, as development progresses both from childhood to adulthood and from less expertise to more.

Two dominant perspectives exist concerning the relationship between aging and affective influences on performance in a variety of cognitive domains (e.g., memory, judgment processes, decision-making). The first is a motivational perspective from socio-emotional selectivity theory (SST; Carstensen, 1993, 2006). It focuses on aging-related chronic activation of emotion regulation goals and an associated motivation to process affective information. This theory posits that changes in time perspective result in emotional goals becoming increasingly important as the end of life nears, which in turn results in greater monitoring of affective information. Because older adults are, by virtue of age, closer to the end of life, age therefore should be associated with an increased importance of emotional goals; increased attention to emotional content; and either an increased focus on positive information or a decreased focus on negative information to optimize emotional experience. These last predictions have potentially great relevance to the impact of affect and emotions in judgment and decision-making. In one study, for example, Fung and Carstensen (2003) found that, relative to younger adults, older adults exhibited greater preference and superior memory for emotional advertisements than for nonemotional ones.

However, SST also predicts a specific focus on positive information in later life as older adults seek to optimize emotional experiences. Bjälkebring, Västfjäll, and Johansson (2013), for example, asked participants to record one decision every day for a week. They found that older adults compared to younger adults regretted their reported decisions less and that they did so because they actively used strategies that reduced decision regret. Further, Charles, Mather, and Carstensen (2003) found that overall picture recall declined with age but that older adults recalled a greater proportion of positive images than negative images, whereas young and middle-aged adults recalled similar proportions of the positive and negative images (for a review, see Reed, Chan, and Mikels, 2014).

The motivational basis for SST (and the need to have resources available to attain one's goals) has received some support. Mather and Knight (2005) found that older adults who had more cognitive resources (due to better performance on tasks requiring cognitive control in one study and due to not being distracted by a divided-attention task in a second study) remembered relatively more positive than negative pictures compared to those with fewer cognitive resources; younger adults showed no such effect. This positivity effect in memory may be driven by effortful, resource-demanding regulatory functions and thus may be shown primarily by high-functioning older adults (Mather and Knight, 2005).

The second major perspective on the relation between aging and affect on performance is more cognitive in nature and focuses on the impact of changing cognitive skills on the relative influence of affective processes on performance. This perspective is typified by theories such as Labouvie-Vief's (2003, 2005) dynamic integration theory and by neuropsychological approaches that focus on the differential impact of aging on normative changes in cortical systems underlying affective and deliberative processes. In this alternative perspective on aging, affective processes take on increased importance as deliberative functions decline in later life.

One basis for this perspective is research suggesting that cortical structures associated with processing affect (e.g., the amygdala, the ventromedial prefrontal cortex) undergo less normative change with aging than those areas underlying executive or deliberative functions (e.g., the dorso-lateral prefrontal cortex; Bechara, 2005; Chow and Cummings, 2000; Good et al., 2001). This relative preservation view is supported by neuropsychological data demonstrating that adult age differences in performance were minimal on these tasks thought to be supported by affective-processing systems (e.g., Kensinger, Brierley, Medford, Growdon, and Corkin, 2002; MacPherson, Phillips, and Della Sala, 2002). These data contrast with the normative decline consistently observed on tasks associated with executive functions (for a review, see West, 1996).

This relative preservation view predicts that maintenance of basic mechanisms associated with processing affect would not lead to qualitative age differences such as positivity effects. In fact, researchers in this tradition have shown that, when participants are required to actively attend to emotional and neutral stimuli, younger and older adults exhibit similar patterns of memory for positive, negative, and neutral stimuli (Denburg, Buchanan, Tranel, and Adolphs, 2003; Kensinger et al., 2002).

The relative preservation view would not necessarily preclude the possibility of qualitative differences arising in cognitively later stages of processing, however. Kalenzaga, Lamidey, Ergis, Clarys, and Piolino (2016) attempted to answer this question by comparing younger adults to cognitively intact older adults as well as older adults who had cognitive decline. The results indicated that the positivity bias was most likely to occur in older individuals whose cognitive functions were preserved, after long retention delay, and in experimental conditions that did not constrain encoding. They concluded that the findings were more consistent with the motivational, rather than the relative preservation, perspective. Nonetheless, they did not fully support either theory because, in both younger and older adults, positive words were consolidated better and forgotten more slowly than negative and neutral words. Similarly, when investigating event-related brain potentials in the Iowa gambling task, Di Rosa and colleagues (2017) concluded that age-related changes in evaluating negative feedback were better interpreted as motivational in nature. Thus, although possible that age-related brain degradation could influence emotional processing, the data appear more consistent with a motivational pathway.

Lastly, research has focused on age's relation with both affective valence (positive - negative) and the level of experienced affective arousal (e.g., feeling satisfied and feeling excited are both positive feelings; however, they differ in the level of arousal; Scheibe, English, Tsai, and Carstensen, 2013; Bjälkebring, Västfjäll, and Johansson, 2015). Older adults, in particular, appear to prefer lower arousal levels, and this difference in preference for arousal might have consequences for decisions. For example, in a study by Sands and Isaacowitz (2016), older and younger participants freely selected from a set of affective videos using information about the valence and arousal of each video. Older adults selected more low-arousal videos whereas younger adults selected more high-arousal videos. Hence, both valence and arousal are important when understanding age differences in the preference for and processing of affect.

In sum, research has suggested that aging is associated with a greater focus on emotional content and on positive over negative information, although the latter effect appears moderated by situational goals and available cognitive resources. These processes are consistent with the model of selective optimization with compensation proposed by Baltes and colleagues (e.g., Baltes and Baltes, 1990), which postulates that the developmentally relevant goal of efficient use of processing resources results in older adults optimizing their best skills, in this case the processing of emotional information. A reasonable hypothesis at this point is that basic mechanisms underlying the processing of affect are relatively unchanged with age, but that variations may emerge at later stages of processing as goal-based factors (e.g., time perspective) or availability of cognitive resources influence the manner in which affective information is handled.

Implications for Judgment and Decision-Making

Deliberative declines predict that older adults will demonstrate lower comprehension and use of numeric information, less information seeking, and decision avoidance and delegation (to avoid negative emotions; see Mather, 2006). An increased focus on affect and emotion (whether a relative preference for positive information or increased use of affective information), however, suggests different age-related changes. Older adults who focus relatively more on positive information may process gain-versus-loss information in decisions differently from their younger counterparts who do not share this same focus. As a result, losses may not loom as large for older adults as they have been demonstrated to do for younger adults (Kahneman and Tversky, 1979). Older adults may be more likely to request and process information presented in a positive frame rather than a negative frame, so older adults may not demonstrate the well-known negativity bias shown by younger adults.

Some evidence exists already that is consistent with a lack of negativity bias among older adults (Mather and Knight, 2005; Wood, Busemeyer, Koling, Cox, and Davis, 2005). Strough, Mehta, McFall, and Schuller (2008), for example, demonstrated that older adults were less susceptible to the sunk-cost fallacy, an effect thought to be motivated by negativity biases in younger adults. The age difference remained after controlling for cognitive ability, providing possible support for the difference being due to emotional changes (see also Strough et al., 2016). Older adults also appear more likely to be in positive moods, states that have been associated with greater engagement in schema-based processing and less-specific, bottom-up processing (e.g., Fiedler, 2001). These age differences in the experience of incidental affect may be misattributed to aging-related deficits in deliberative processes.

Support for a possible positivity effect in decision processes comes from Löckenhoff and Carstensen (2007). In their study, older and younger adults selected information to examine about health choices by clicking on cues indicating information that was positive, negative, or neutral. As predicted, older adults selected and recalled a greater proportion of positive versus negative information compared to younger adults. In another study, older adults relied on their positive feelings more in donation decisions whereas younger adults relied on both negative and positive feelings (Bjälkebring, Västfjäll, Dickert, and Slovic, 2016). Further, in a second study, participants were asked to donate their earnings ($10) to children in need. A week later, the researchers followed up with the participants and asked how they felt about their decision (to donate or not to donate their earning). Those who donated felt happier compared to those who did not donate. More importantly, older adults who donated felt happier than younger adults who donated. This research indicates that older adults processed predecisional and postdecisional information in a manner different than younger adults.

Although this age-related difference could produce both positive and negative consequences for decisions, Eberhardt, Bruine de Bruin, and Strough (2019) demonstrated that older adults' lower negative emotions and higher experiential knowledge was significantly correlated with better scores on four financial decision-making measures (sunk cost, credit card payments, money management, and financial decision outcomes). However, the positivity bias has also been connected to worse decisions. For example, a link exists between certainty and positivity biases among older adults. In particular, older adults preferred certain lower gains over higher uncertain gains when compared to younger adults, suggesting that the positivity bias in older adults might be related to choosing certain over risky options even when the certain option is sub-optimal (Mather et al., 2012).

Alternatively, older adults may focus relatively more than younger adults on affective information overall (both positive and negative information). Several effects on judgments and decisions might be observed if this processing difference proves to be true. First, losses may loom equally large or larger for older adults than for younger adults if both positive and negative information are accentuated. In addition, more affective sources of information such as anecdotal or hedonic (not utilitarian) information may receive greater weight (Dhar and Wertenbroch, 2000; Strange and Leung, 1999). Consistent with this alternative hypothesis, Blanchard-Fields found that older adults focus more than younger adults on emotional aspects of everyday problems (Blanchard-Fields, Chen, and Norris, 1997). Evidence suggested that less numerate decision makers use explicit probabilities less and narrative information more than those who are more numerate (Dieckmann, Slovic, and Peters, 2009). Given that older adults are less numerate, it may well be the case that narratives, anecdotes, and other more verbal forms of information will have greater influence on their judgments and decisions. Finally, incidental sources of affect (positive and negative moods; positive and negative primes) may influence older adults' judgments and decisions more than those of younger adults.

In sum, research suggest that age differences exist in almost every part of the decision process from pre-decision identification of and engagement with options to post-decision evaluation and feedback (Löckenhoff, 2018).

A Life Span View of Judgment and Decision-Making

Thus far, we have mostly discussed age changes or age-related changes in decision-making processes as well as in the judgments and decisions themselves. However, when considering age differences, it is interesting to consider cumulative effects across the life span. Specifically, when examined in isolation, a single behavior often seems benign or even helpful in the moment. However, when viewed from a life-span perspective, a multiple of single behaviors may have detrimental cumulative effects (Johansson and Bjälkebring, 2015; Peters, 2020). For example, drinking one sugary soda with a meal has a miniscule impact on health. However, a failure to understand the risk associated with long-term consumption of sugary soda and drinking sugary soda with every meal for 45 years can have substantial detrimental health effects (Malik et al., 2010). Similar arguments can be made for economic decisions. One bad decision is often manageable and even inconsequential. However, poor decisions about retirement savings throughout one's life likely will lead to a less than optimal life in retirement.

In line with this thinking, more education has been linked to better health and lower mortality in older adults; however, little is known about exactly why this is the case (Lleras-Muney, 2005; Ross and Wu, 1995). Research has pointed toward potential causal links between more formal education leading to greater cognitive and decision-making abilities including numeracy, which relates, in turn, to healthier behaviors (Peters, Baker, et al., 2010). Additional research then has linked greater cognitive abilities to morbidity and mortality (Deary et al., 2008; Peters, Tompkins, et al., 2019). For example, older diabetic adults with lower levels of cognition (although still within normal ranges) were approximately 20 percent more likely to die and 13 percent more likely to become disabled over a two-year period than those with higher levels of cognitive functioning (McGuire, Ford, and Ajani, 2006).

We believe these health effects may be due to cumulative effects of having lower cognitive and decision abilities. Whereas most studies of decision-making skill evaluate this relationship at a single time point, we expect larger (cumulative) effects across time as one poor decision is followed by the next. An example consistent with our hypothesis comes from Estrada-Mejia, de Vries, and Zeelenberg (2016). They followed 1,000 adults for five years. At the start of their study, each additional correct answer on an 11-item numeracy questionnaire was related to 5 percent more personal wealth (controlling for education and risk preference). However, by the conclusion of the five years, more numerate people had accumulated wealth, while those lowest in numeracy decumulated wealth. As a result, numeracy-related wealth differences increased as people grew older.

Similarly, numeracy has been linked to better pension saving trajectories while controlling for education and other cognitive abilities (Banks, O'Dea, and Oldfield, 2011). Smith, McArdle, and Willis (2010) further compared the importance of different aspects of cognitive ability for financial success in the Health and Retirement Study (HRS; a nationally representative study of Americans who are at least 50 years old) and demonstrated that a three-item objective numeracy measure was the best predictor of financial success when compared to other cognitive measures and education. In the HRS sample, household wealth (owning a house, pension savings, bonds, stocks, etc.) averaged 1.7 million U.S. dollars when both spouses answered all three numeracy questions correctly; however, when neither spouse answered any question correctly, household wealth was about $200,000. With compounding interest, we would expect these differences to grow over time. With greater numeracy, we would further expect that those more numerate individuals who can better understand concepts such as risk, interest, and inflation, will grow even more wealthy, leaving the less numerate even further behind over time (Lusardi and Tufanorev, 2009; Sinayev and Peters, 2015).

Investigating longitudinal patterns in the effects of education, numeracy, and other cognitive factors on decision-making and decision outcomes would benefit our understanding of how to maintain and facilitate older adult functioning. In one early example, we used data from a diverse sample of 4,738 Americans in the Understanding America Study. We demonstrated that numeracy-related income satisfaction differences were larger among older than younger participants, controlling for education and verbal intelligence (see Figure 4.2; Bjälkebring and Peters, in preparation). This finding is in line with the hypothesis that the influence

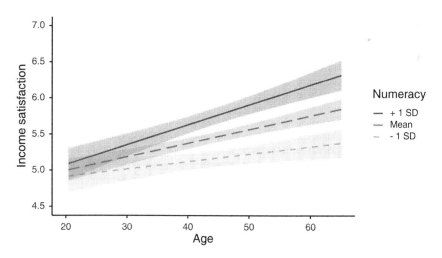

FIGURE 4.2 The relation of age with income satisfaction by numeracy (mean and 95 percent confidence interval indicated). Note that income satisfaction increases with age. However, in line with our hypothesis, the increase was markedly larger among those with higher objective numeracy, controlling for the influence of education and verbal intelligence (n = 4,738).

of decision competence (here numeracy) will accumulate over the life span. Of course, these findings are from a cross-sectional sample and must be replicated longitudinally to confirm these ideas. Nonetheless, they are consistent with the notion that being adept with numbers is particularly important for financial outcomes, and that this effect increases with older age.

Facilitating Better Decision-Making

Studying age differences in decision-making can reveal important psychological mechanisms that underlie how we judge and decide. They can further help us uncover methods to facilitate better decision-making among older adults (Strough, Bruine de Bruin, and Peters, 2015). However, it requires a focus on older adults, which does not currently exist to a large extent. For example, very few health decision aids have been developed specifically for older adults. In a review of 22 decision aids, only one aid was specifically designed for older adults (van Weert et al., 2016). In this section, we briefly review some possible ways to facilitate better decision-making based on the literature reviewed in this chapter.

One possibility comes directly from Tom Hess's (2000) work on older adults' selective use of deliberative capacity. Specifically, one could increase motivation to use capacity by increasing the relevance and meaningfulness of the decision to the older adult (e.g., increasing personal accountability; Chen, 2004).

A second possibility, based on older adults' increased reliance on affective information, is to increase the affective meaning of information through how that information is presented. Peters et al. (2009) were interested in the processes by which decision makers bring meaning to dry, cold facts. We attempted to influence the interpretation and comprehension of information about health plan attributes by providing information in a form that could be used easily to evaluate the overall goodness or badness of a health plan. For example, in one of the studies, older adult participants were presented with attribute information (quality of care and member satisfaction) about two health plans. The information was presented in bar chart format with the actual score displayed to the right of the bar chart (see Figure 4.3). The information for half of the subjects in each group was supplemented by the addition of evaluative categories (i.e., category lines plus labels that placed the health plans into categories of poor, fair, good, or excellent). The attribute information was designed such that Plan A was good on both attributes, while Plan B was good on quality of care but fair on member satisfaction. The specific scores for quality of care and member satisfaction were counterbalanced across subjects such that, for half of the subjects, the average quality-of-care scores were higher; for the other half, average member satisfaction scores were higher. We predicted and found that evaluative categories influenced the choices. Specifically, older adults preferred health Plan A more often when the categories were present (Plan A was always in the good evaluative category when the categories were present; see also Mikels et al., 2010).

Condition 1: Evaluative categories

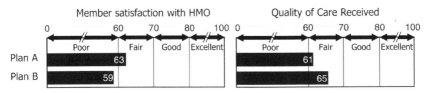

Condition 2: No evaluative categories

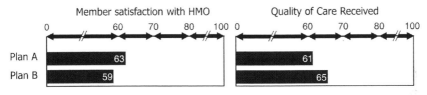

FIGURE 4.3 Example of evaluative categories in health-plan choices of older adults. The evaluative categories bring meaning to the numbers and facilitate more informed decisions.

A third possibility based on age declines in deliberative ability is to reduce the cognitive effort involved in processing information or doing some task. Studies have demonstrated, for example, that how information is presented may matter as much as what information is presented (Peters, Dieckmann, Dixon, Hibbard, and Mertz, 2007; Peters, Hibbard, et al., 2007). Showing only the most important information (or highlighting it), making key points easier to evaluate (order, summarize, interpret information), and generally requiring less cognitive effort and fewer inferences (e.g., do the math for them) can help older decision makers better understand and better use information.

Given that older adults demonstrate declines in deliberate efficiency and that comprehension and adherence to medical treatments is of great functional importance to them, efforts to aid their comprehension and decisions have focused in part, therefore, on how to support age-related declines in the efficiency of deliberative processes (Hibbard and Peters, 2003). Medication instructions that were well organized, explicit, and compatible with preexisting schemas about the task improved memory and were preferred over other formats, suggesting that they could improve medication adherence (Park, Willis, Morrow, Diehl, and Gaines, 1994). The use of external memory supports such as organizational charts and medication organizers have also been shown to be beneficial to older adults' adherence behaviors (Park, Morrell, Frieske, Blackburn, and Birchmore 1991; Park, Morrell, Frieske, and Kincaid, 1992). Older adults demonstrated effective use of memory aids. They appeared to spontaneously use them to summarize or check information at the end of information search, as if to verify forgotten information, whereas younger adults appeared to use these same aids in the middle of a search, as if for planning rather than memory purposes (Johnson, 1997).

Finally, rather than reducing the cognitive effort involved, some methods may actually increase flexibility in processing information in decisions. Isen (2000) has shown that individuals induced into more positive moods (compared to neutral moods) process information more systematically if it helps them maintain their positive mood. Positive mood inductions also tend to lead to more creative and efficient decisions (Forgas, 1995; Isen, 2000; Mano, 1992). Such methods also facilitate older adult decisions. In particular, Carpenter, Peters, Isen, and Västfjäll (2013) induced half of their older adult participants into a positive mood with a small gift; the rest received no gift. Subjects then completed a computer-based card task in which they won and lost money based on their choices. In the computer background, positive-mood subjects saw smiling suns; neutral-mood subjects saw control circles. Individuals in the positive-mood condition chose better from both gain and loss decks than did neutral-mood subjects, suggesting that positive mood facilitated processing overall rather than highlighting positive information only in a mood-congruency effect. Concurrently, the positive-mood manipulation was associated with an increase in cognitive capacity (working memory; see also Yang, Yang, and Isen, 2013).

Lastly, research has focused on why and how older adults make better decisions and how we can use older adults' "wisdom" to create interventions to improve decision-making. Strough and colleagues (2016) implemented an intervention to reduce the sunk-cost bias (in this case, sticking to a failing vacation plan because you already have driven halfway to a vacation destination). In the intervention, participants were asked to write about their thoughts and feelings about the failing vacation plan. The intervention successfully reduced the biased tendency to continue with the failing plan both compared to a control condition in which they did not write about anything and compared to a condition in which they wrote about all the things they could do to improve the situation. However, and more importantly, this intervention worked mainly in younger participants. Older adults, with or without the intervention, appeared to have implemented introspection processes that highlighted their feelings and the advantages of considering sunk costs. Thus, they largely avoided the sunk-cost bias and appropriately terminated the failing vacation plan.

Understanding how affective and cognitive processes interact in decisions across the life span may help researchers and policy makers improve how they present complex health, financial, and other important decisions to older adults. Of course, any choice of how to present information presents ethical issues (at what level of the quality indicator should a hospital be deemed "excellent" as opposed to "very good"; what attribute is "most important") and communicators need to choose thoughtfully. The future for research needs to be interdisciplinary, integrating not only cognition and affect, but also integrating views and theories from psychology, marketing, economics, and neuroscience (Yoon, Cole, and Lee, 2009; Samanez-Larkin and Knutson, 2015; Löckenhoff, 2018; Carstensen, 2019). Understanding when and how older adults make better and worse decisions should allow us insights into how to improve their decisions as well as those of younger adults.

Conclusion

In conclusion, older adults will process information in ways that are likely to be different from younger adults. Robust declines in deliberative capacity suggest that older adults will make worse decisions than younger adults in some situations. Deliberative decline is likely to be too simple a story, though, for three reasons. First, older adults appear to use their deliberative capacity selectively. Second, accumulated experience can compensate in part for age-related declines. And third, emotional focus appears to increase with age. As a result, older adults will make better decisions than younger adults in some situations. Older adults, however, are faced with more decisions about vital health, financial, and other personal issues. At the same time, their proportion of the consumer population is growing, but our nation's resources are not necessarily growing with them. As a result, understanding ways to facilitate decisions of those who have attained more advanced ages may not only provide individual advantages for the older adult but also ultimately may prove beneficial to the population at large. At present, however, most research results (and advice) are based primarily on younger adults, and older adults, in all of their complexity, have been largely ignored.

Note

1 Author note: This work was supported by a grant from the National Science Foundation (NSF) to Ellen Peters (1558230). The views expressed are those of the authors and do not represent the views of the NSF or United States. Portions of this research were done while the corresponding author was a postdoctoral researcher at The Ohio State University and a visitor in Dr. Peters' Cognitive and Affective Influences in Decision making (CAIDe) Lab supported by the Swedish Research Council (VR; DNR-2016-00507). Figures in this chapter are licensed under CC BY 4.0. This work is based in part on an earlier article (Peters, Hess, Västfjäll, and Auman, 2007). © 2007 John Wiley & Sons. Reprinted with permission.

References

Alhakami, A. S., & Slovic, P. (1994). A psychological study of the inverse relationship between perceived risk and perceived benefit. *Risk Analysis: An Official Publication of the Society for Risk Analysis, 14*(6), 1085–1096. doi:10.1111/j.1539-6924.1994.tb00080.x.

Apter, A. J., Cheng, J., Small, D., Bennett, I. M., Albert, C., Fein, D. G., George, M., & Horne, S. V. (2006). Asthma numeracy skill and health literacy. *Journal of Asthma, 43*(9), 705–710. doi:10.1080/02770900600925585.

Baker, D. W., Parker, R. M., Williams, M. V., Clark, W. S., & Nurss, J. (1997). The relationship of patient reading ability to self-reported health and use of health services. *American Journal of Public Health*, *87*(6), 1027–1030.

Baltes, P. B., & Baltes, M. M. (1990). Psychological perspectives on successful aging: The model of selective optimization with compensation. *Successful Aging: Perspectives from the Behavioral Sciences*, *1*, 1–34.

Baltes, Paul B., Staudinger, U. M., & Lindenberger, U. (1999). Lifespan psychology: Theory and application to intellectual functioning. *Annual Review of Psychology*, *50*(1), 471–507.

Banks, J., O'Dea, C., & Oldfield, Z. (2011). Cognitive function, numeracy and retirement saving trajectories. *Economic Journal (London, England)*, *120*(548), F381–F410.

Bechara, A. (2005). Neural basis of decision-making and implications for older adults. In: National Research Council (Ed.), *Papers from the Workshop on Decision Making by Older Adults*. Washington, DC: US: National Academy of Sciences. Retrieved June 13, 2006 from http:/ /www7.nationalacademies.org/csbd/ bechara_paper.pdf.

Bechara, A., Damasio, A. R., Damasio, H., & Anderson, S. W. (1994). Insensitivity to future consequences following damage to human prefrontal cortex. *Cognition*, *50*(1), 7–15. doi:10.1016/0010-0277(94)90018-3.

Bechara, A., Damasio, H., Tranel, D., & Damasio, A. R. (1997). Deciding advantageously Before knowing the advantageous strategy. *Science*, *275*(5304), 1293–1295. doi:10.1126/ science.275.5304.1293.

Bechara, A., Tranel, D., Damasio, H., & Damasio, A. R. (1996). Failure to respond autonomically to anticipated future outcomes following damage to prefrontal cortex. *Cerebral Cortex*, *6*(2), 215–225. doi:10.1093/cercor/6.2.215.

Bjälkebring, P., & Peters, E. (in preparation). *The Accumulating Effect of Numeracy Across the Lifespan*. Manuscript in preparation

Bjälkebring, P., Västfjäll, D., Dickert, S., & Slovic, P. (2016). Greater emotional gain from giving in older adults: Age-related positivity bias in charitable giving. *Frontiers in Psychology*, *7*. doi:10.3389/fpsyg.2016.00846.

Bjälkebring, P., Västfjäll, D., & Johansson, B. (2013). Regulation of experienced and anticipated regret for daily decisions in younger and older adults in a Swedish one-week diary study. *GeroPsych: The Journal of Gerontopsychology and Geriatric Psychiatry*, *26*(4), 233–241.

Bjälkebring, P., Västfjäll, D., & Johansson, B. E. A. (2015). Happiness and arousal: Framing happiness as arousing results in lower happiness ratings for older adults. *Frontiers in Psychology*, *6*. doi:10.3389/fpsyg.2015.00706.

Blanchard-Fields, F., Brannan, J. R., & Camp, C. J. (1987). Alternative conceptions of wisdom: An onion-peeling exercise. *Educational Gerontology*, *13*(6), 497–503. doi:10.1080/0360127870130605.

Blanchard-Fields, F., Chen, Y., & Norris, L. (1997). Everyday problem solving across the adult life span: Influence of domain specificity and cognitive appraisal. *Psychology and Aging*, *12*(4), 684–693. doi:10.1037/0882-7974.12.4.684.

Bruine de Bruin, Wändi, Parker, A. M., & Fischhoff, B. (2007). Individual differences in adult decision-making competence. *Journal of Personality and Social Psychology*, *92*(5), 938–956. doi:10.1037/0022-3514.92.5.938.

Bruine de Bruin, W., Parker, A. M., & Fischhoff, B. (2019). Decision-making competence: More than intelligence? *Current Directions in Psychological Science*, *29*(2), 186–192.

Bruine de Bruin, Wändi, Parker, A. M., & Strough, J. (2016). Choosing to be happy? Age differences in "maximizing" decision strategies and experienced emotional well-being. *Psychology and Aging*, *31*(3), 295–300. doi:10.1037/pag000007.

Cabanac, M. (1992). Pleasure: The common currency. *Journal of Theoretical Biology, 155*(2), 173–200. doi:10.1016/S0022-5193(05)80594-6.

Carpenter, S. M., Peters, E., Västfjäll, D., & Isen, A. M. (2013). Positive feelings facilitate working memory and complex decision making among older adults. *Cognition and Emotion, 27*(1), 184–192. doi:10.1080/02699931.2012.698251.

Carstensen, Laura L. (1993). Motivation for social contact across the life span: A theory of socioemotional selectivity. In: J. E. Jacobs (Ed.), *Current Theory and Research in Motivation, Vol. 40. Nebraska Symposium on Motivation, 1992: Developmental Perspectives on Motivation* (pp. 209–254). Lincoln, NE: University of Nebraska Press.

Carstensen, Laura L. (2001, January 2). Opinion | on the brink of a brand-new old age. *The New York Times.* Retrieved from https://www.nytimes.com/2001/01/02/opinion/on-the-brink-of-a-brand-new-old-age.html.

Carstensen, Laura L. (2006). The influence of a sense of time on human development. *Science (New York, NY), 312*(5782), 1913–1915. doi:10.1126/science.1127488.

Carstensen, Laura L. (2019). Integrating cognitive and emotion paradigms to address the paradox of aging. *Cognition and Emotion, 33*(1), 119–125. doi:10.1080/02699931.2018.1543181.

Charles, S. T., Mather, M., & Carstensen, L. L. (2003). Aging and emotional memory: The forgettable nature of negative images for older adults. *Journal of Experimental Psychology: General, 132*(2), 310–324. doi:10.1037/0096-3445.132.2.310.

Chasseigne, G., Grau, S., Mullet, E., & Cama, V. (1999). How well do elderly people cope with uncertainty in a learning task? *Acta Psychologica, 103*(1), 229–238. doi:10.1016/S0001-6918(99)00038-4.

Chasseigne, G., Lafon, P., & Mullet, É. (2002). Aging and rule learning: The case of the multiplicative law. *The American Journal of Psychology, 115*(3), 315–330. doi:10.2307/1423420.

Chasseigne, G., Mullet, E., & Stewart, T. R. (1997). Aging and multiple cue probability learning: The case of inverse relationships. *Acta Psychologica, 97*(3), 235–252. doi:10.1016/S0001-6918(97)00034-6.

Chen, Y. (2002). Unwanted beliefs: Age differences in beliefs of false information. *Aging, Neuropsychology, and Cognition, 9*(3), 217–230. doi:10.1076/anec.9.3.217.9613.

Chen, Y. (2004). Age differences in correction of context-induced biases: Source monitoring and timing of accountability. *Aging, Neuropsychology, and Cognition, 11*(1), 58–67. doi:10.1076/anec.11.1.58.29359.

Chen, Y., & Blanchard-Fields, F. (2000). Unwanted thought: Age differences in the correction of social judgments. *Psychology and Aging, 15*(3), 475–482. doi:10.1037/0882-7974.15.3.475.

Chen, Y., Ma, X., & Pethtel, O. (2011). Age differences in trade-off decisions: Older adults prefer choice deferral. *Psychology and Aging, 26*(2), 269–273. doi:10.1037/a0021582.

Chen, Y., Wang, J., Kirk, R. M., Pethtel, O. L., & Kiefner, A. E. (2014). Age differences in adaptive decision making: The role of numeracy. *Educational Gerontology, 40*(11), 825–833. doi:10.1080/03601277.2014.900263.

Chow, T. W., & Cummings, J. L. (2000). The amygdala and Alzheimer's disease. In JP Aggleton (Ed), *The Amygdala: A Functional Analysis* (pp. 656–680). Oxford: Oxford University Press.

Cokely, E. T., Feltz, A., Allan, J., Ghazal, S., Petrova, D., & Garcia-Retamero, R. (2016). Decision making skill: From intelligence to numeracy and expertise. In: K. A. Ericsson, R. R. Hoffman, A. Kozbelt, & A. M. Williams (Ed.), *Cambridge Handbook of Expertise and Expert Performance*, 2nd ed. New York: Cambridge University Press.

Damasio, A. R. (1994). *Descartes' Error*. New York: Putnam.

De Nardi, M., French, E., & Jones, J. B. (2006). *Differential Mortality, Uncertain Medical Expenses, and the Saving of Elderly Singles* (Working Paper No. 12554). doi:10.3386/w12554.

De Neys, W., & Pennycook, G. (2019). Logic, fast and slow: Advances in dual-process theorizing. *Current Directions in Psychological Science, 28*(5), 503–509. doi:10.1177/0963721419855658.

Deary, I. J., Batty, G. D., Pattie, A., & Gale, C. R. (2008). More intelligent, more dependable children live longer: A 55-year longitudinal study of a representative sample of the Scottish nation. *Psychological Science, 19*(9), 874–880. doi:10.1111/j.1467-9280.2008.02171.x.

Del Missier, F., Hansson, P., Parker, A. M., Bruine de Bruin, W., & Mäntylä, T. (2020). Decision-making competence in older adults: A rosy view from a longitudinal investigation. *Psychology and Aging*. [Epub ahead of print]. https://doi.org/10.1037/pag0000443

Del Missier, F., Mäntylä, T., & Bruine de Bruin, W. (2012). Decision-making competence, executive functioning, and general cognitive abilities. *Journal of Behavioral Decision Making, 25*(4), 331–351. doi:10.1002/bdm.731.

Denburg, N. L., Buchanan, T. W., Tranel, D., & Adolphs, R. (2003). Evidence for preserved emotional memory in normal older persons. *Emotion, 3*(3), 239–253. doi:10.1037/1528-3542.3.3.239.

DeWalt, D. A., Berkman, N. D., Sheridan, S., Lohr, K. N., & Pignone, M. P. (2004). Literacy and health outcomes. *Journal of General Internal Medicine, 19*(12), 1228–1239. doi:10.1111/j.1525-1497.2004.40153.x.

Dhar, R., & Wertenbroch, K. (2000). Consumer choice between hedonic and utilitarian goods. *Journal of Marketing Research, 37*(1), 60–71. doi:10.1509/jmkr.37.1.60.18718.

Di Rosa, E., Mapelli, D., Arcara, G., Amodio, P., Tamburin, S., & Schiff, S. (2017). Aging and risky decision-making: New ERP evidence from the Iowa Gambling Task. *Neuroscience Letters, 640*, 93–98. doi:10.1016/j.neulet.2017.01.021.

Dieckmann, N. F., Slovic, P., & Peters, E. (2009). The use of narrative evidence and explicit likelihood by decisionmakers varying in numeracy. *Risk Analysis: An Official Publication of the Society for Risk Analysis, 29*(10), 1473–1488. doi:10.1111/j.1539-6924.2009.01279.x.

Eberhardt, W., Bruine de Bruin, W., & Strough, J. (2019). Age differences in financial decision making: The benefits of more experience and less negative emotions. *Journal of Behavioral Decision Making, 32*(1), 79–93. doi:10.1002/bdm.2097.

Epstein, S. (1994). Integration of the cognitive and the psychodynamic unconscious. *The American Psychologist, 49*(8), 709. doi:10.1037/0003-066X.49.8.709.

Estrada, C. A., Martin-Hryniewicz, M., Collins, C., Byrd, J. C., & Peek, B. T. (2004). Literacy and numeracy skills and anticoagulation control. *The American Journal of the Medical Sciences, 328*(2), 88–93. doi:10.1097/00000441-200408000-00004.

Estrada-Mejia, C., de Vries, M., & Zeelenberg, M. (2016). Numeracy and wealth. *Journal of Economic Psychology, 54*, 53–63. doi:10.1016/j.joep.2016.02.011.

Fastame, M. C., Manca, C., Penna, M. P., Lucangeli, D., & Hitchcott, P. K. (2019). Numeracy skills and self-reported mental health in people aging well. *The Psychiatric Quarterly, 90*(3), 629–635. doi:10.1007/s11126-019-09655-y.

Fiedler, K. (2001). Affective influences on social information processing. In: J. P. Forgas (Ed.), *Handbook of Affect and Social Cognition* (pp. 163–185). Mahwah, NJ: Lawrence Erlbaum Associates Publishers.

Finucane, M. L., Alhakami, A., Slovic, P., & Johnson, S. M. (2000). The affect heuristic in judgments of risks and benefits. *Journal of Behavioral Decision Making, 13*(1), 1–17. doi:10.1002/(SICI)1099-0771(200001/03)13:1<1::AID-BDM333>3.0.CO;2-S.

Forgas, Joseph P. (1995). Mood and judgment: The affect infusion model (AIM). *Psychological Bulletin, 117*(1), 39–66. doi:10.1037/0033-2909.117.1.39.

Fung, H. H., & Carstensen, L. L. (2003). Sending memorable messages to the old: Age differences in preferences and memory for advertisements. *Journal of Personality and Social Psychology, 85*(1), 163–178. doi:10.1037/0022-3514.85.1.163.

Goldman, D. P., & Smith, J. P. (2002). Can patient self-management help explain the SES health gradient? *Proceedings of the National Academy of Sciences of the United States of America, 99*(16), 10929–10934. doi:10.1073/pnas.162086599.

Good, C. D., Johnsrude, I. S., Ashburner, J., Henson, R. N. A., Friston, K. J., & Frackowiak, R. S. J. (2001). A voxel-based morphometric study of ageing in 465 normal adult human brains. *NeuroImage, 14*(1), 21–36. doi:10.1006/nimg.2001.0786.

Hammond, K. R. (1996). *Human Judgment and Social Policy: Irreducible Uncertainty, Inevitable Error, Unavoidable Injustice*. New York: Oxford University Press.

Hershey, D. A., Walsh, D. A., Read, S. J., & Chulef, A. S. (1990). The effects of expertise on financial problem solving: Evidence for goal-directed, problem-solving scripts. *Organizational Behavior and Human Decision Processes, 46*(1), 77–101. doi:10.1016/0749-5978(90)90023-3.

Hess, T. M. (2000). Aging-related constraints and adaptations in social information processing. In U. von Hecker, S. Dutke, & G. Sedek (Eds.), *Generative Mental Processes and Cognitive Resources: Integrative Research on Adaptation and Control* (pp. 129–155). Springer Netherlands. https://doi.org/10.1007/978-94-011-4373-8_5

Hess, T. M., Germain, C. M., Rosenberg, D. C., Leclerc, C. M., & Hodges, E. A. (2005). Aging-related selectivity and susceptibility to irrelevant affective information in the construction of attitudes. *Aging, Neuropsychology, and Cognition, 12*(2), 149–174. doi:10.1080/13825580590925170.

Hess, T. M., Queen, T. L., & Ennis, G. E. (2013). Age and self-relevance effects on information search during decision making. *The Journals of Gerontology: Series B: Psychological Sciences and Social Sciences, 68*(5), 703–711. doi:10.1093/geronb/gbs108.

Hibbard, J. H., & Peters, E. (2003). Supporting informed consumer health care decisions: Data presentation approaches that facilitate the use of information in choice. *Annual Review of Public Health, 24*(1), 413–433. doi:10.1146/annurev.publhealth.24.100901.141005.

Hibbard, J. H., Peters, E., Dixon, A., & Tusler, M. (2007). Consumer competencies and the use of comparative quality information: It isn't just about literacy. *Medical Care Research and Review: MCRR, 64*(4), 379–394. doi:10.1177/1077558707301630.

Hibbard, J. H., Slovic, P., Peters, E., Finucane, M. L., & Tusler, M. (2001). Is the informed-choice policy approach appropriate for medicare beneficiaries? *Health Affairs, 20*(3), 199–203. doi:10.1377/hlthaff.20.3.199.

Hogarth, R. M. (2014). Deciding Analytically or Trusting Your Intuition? The Advantages and Disadvantages of Analytic and Intuitive Thought. In T. Betsch & S. Haberstroh (Eds.), *The Routines of Decision Making* (pp. 97–112). Psychology Press. https://doi.org/10.4324/9781410611826-11

Hsee, C. K., & Hastie, R. (2006). Decision and experience: Why don't we choose what makes us happy? *Trends in Cognitive Sciences, 10*(1), 31–37. doi:10.1016/j.tics.2005.11.007.

Isen, A. M. (2000). Some perspectives on positive affect and self-regulation. *Psychological Inquiry*, *11*(3), 184–187.

Johansson, B., & Bjälkebring, P. (2015). Psychology of longevity. In: A. N. Pachana (Ed.), *Encyclopedia of Geropsychology* (pp. 1–12). doi:10.1007/978-981-287-080-3_126-1.

Johnson, M. M. S. (1990). Age differences in decision making: A process methodology for examining strategic information processing. *Journal of Gerontology*, *45*(2), P75–P78. doi:10.1093/geronj/45.2.P75.

Johnson, M. M. S. (1993). Thinking about strategies during, before, and after making a decision. *Psychology and Aging*, *8*(2), 231–241. doi:10.1037/0882-7974.8.2.231.

Johnson, M. M. S. (1997). Individual differences in the voluntary use of a memory aid during decision making. *Experimental Aging Research*, *23*(1), 33–43. doi:10.1080/03610739708254025.

Johnson, M. M. S., & Drungle, S. (2000). Purchasing over-the-counter medications: The impact of age differences in information processing. *Experimental Aging Research*, *26*(3), 245–261.

Kahneman, D. (2003). A perspective on judgment and choice: Mapping bounded rationality. *The American Psychologist*, *58*(9), 697–720. doi:10.1037/0003-066X.58.9.697.

Kahneman, D., & Tversky, A. (1979). Prospect theory: An analysis of decision under risk. *Econometrica: Journal of the Econometric Society*, *47*(2), 263–291.

Kalenzaga, S., Lamidey, V., Ergis, A.-M., Clarys, D., & Piolino, P. (2016). The positivity bias in aging: Motivation or degradation? *Emotion*, *16*(5), 602–610. doi:10.1037/emo0000170.

Kensinger, E. A., Brierley, B., Medford, N., Growdon, J. H., & Corkin, S. (2002). Effects of normal aging and Alzheimer's disease on emotional memory. *Emotion*, *2*(2), 118–134. doi:10.1037/1528-3542.2.2.118.

Kirsch, I., Jungeblut, A., Jenkins, L., & Kolstad, A. (2002). *Adult Literacy in America: A First Look at the Findings of the National Adult Literacy Survey*, 3rd ed., Vol. *201*. Washington, DC: US Department of Education. National Center for Education.

Kruglanski, A. W., Chun, W. Y., Erb, H. P., Pierro, A., Mannetti, L., & Spiegel, S. (2003). A parametric unimodel of human judgment: Integrating dual-process frameworks in social cognition from a single-mode perspective. In: J. P. Forgas, K. D. Williams, & W. von Hippel (Eds.), *Social Judgments: Implicit and Explicit Processes* (pp. 137–161). New York: Cambridge University Press.

Labouvie-Vief, G. (2003). Dynamic integration: Affect, cognition, and the self in adulthood. *Current Directions in Psychological Science*, *12*(6), 201–206. doi:10.1046/j.0963-7214.2003.01262.x.

Labouvie-Vief, G. (2005). Self-with-other representations and the organization of the self. *Journal of Research in Personality*, *39*(1), 185–205. doi:10.1016/j.jrp.2004.09.007.

Li, Y., Baldassi, M., Johnson, E. J., & Weber, E. U. (2013). Complementary cognitive capabilities, economic decision making, and aging. *Psychology and Aging*, *28*(3), 595–613. doi:10.1037/a0034172.

Li, Y., Gao, J., Enkavi, A. Z., Zaval, L., Weber, E. U., & Johnson, E. J. (2015). Sound credit scores and financial decisions despite cognitive aging. *Proceedings of the National Academy of Sciences of the United States of America*, *112*(1), 65–69. doi:10.1073/pnas.1413570112.

Lleras-Muney, A. (2005). The relationship between education and adult mortality in the United States. *The Review of Economic Studies*, *72*(1), 189–221. doi:10.1111/0034-6527.00329.

Löckenhoff, C., & Carstensen, L. L. (2007). Aging, emotion, and health-related decision strategies: Motivational manipulations can reduce age differences. *Psychology and Aging*, *22*(1), 134.

Löckenhoff, C. E. (2018). Aging and decision-making: A conceptual framework for future research—A mini-review. *Gerontology, 64*(2), 140–148. doi:10.1159/000485247.

Loewenstein, G. F., Weber, E. U., Hsee, C. K., & Welch, N. (2001). Risk as feelings. *Psychological Bulletin, 127*(2), 267–286.

Lusardi, A., & Tufano, P. (2009). *Debt Literacy, Financial Experiences, and Overindebtedness* (Working Paper No. 14808). doi:10.3386/w14808.

MacPherson, S. E., Phillips, L. H., & Della Sala, S. (2002). Age, executive function and social decision making: A dorsolateral prefrontal theory of cognitive aging. *Psychology and Aging, 17*(4), 598–609.

Malik, V. S., Popkin, B. M., Bray, G. A., Després, J.-P., Willett, W. C., & Hu, F. B. (2010). Sugar-sweetened beverages and risk of metabolic syndrome and type 2 diabetes: A meta-analysis. *Diabetes Care, 33*(11), 2477–2483. doi:10.2337/dc10-1079.

Mano, H. (1992). Judgments under distress: Assessing the role of unpleasantness and arousal in judgment formation. *Organizational Behavior and Human Decision Processes, 52*(2), 216–245. doi:10.1016/0749-5978(92)90036-7.

Mather, M. (2006). A review of decision-making processes: Weighing the risks and benefits of aging. In: L. L. Carstensen & C. R. Hartel (Eds.), *When I'm 64* (pp. 145–173). Washington, DC: National Academies Press.

Mather, M., & Knight, M. (2005). Goal-directed memory: The role of cognitive control in older adults' emotional memory. *Psychology and Aging, 20*(4), 554–570.

Mather, M., Mazar, N., Gorlick, M. A., Lighthall, N. R., Burgeno, J., Schoeke, A., & Ariely, D. (2012). Risk preferences and aging: The "certainty effect" in older adults' decision making. *Psychology and Aging, 27*(4), 801–816. doi:10.1037/a0030174.

McGuire, L. C., Ford, E. S., & Ajani, U. A. (2006). The impact of cognitive functioning on mortality and the development of functional disability in older adults with diabetes: The second longitudinal study on aging. *BMC Geriatrics, 6*(1), 8. doi:10.1186/1471-2318-6-8.

Meyer, B. J. F., Russo, C., & Talbot, A. (1995). Discourse comprehension and problem solving: Decisions about the treatment of breast cancer by women across the life span. *Psychology and Aging, 10*(1), 84–103. doi:10.1037/0882-7974.10.1.84.

Mikels, J. A., Löckenhoff, C. E., Maglio, S. J., Goldstein, M. K., Garber, A., & Carstensen, L. L. (2010). Following your heart or your head: Focusing on emotions versus information differentially influences the decisions of younger and older adults. *Journal of Experimental Psychology: Applied, 16*(1), 87–95. doi:10.1037/a0018500.

Missier, F. D., Hansson, P., Parker, A. M., Bruine de Bruin, W., Nilsson, L.-G., & Mäntylä, T. (2017). Unraveling the aging skein: Disentangling sensory and cognitive predictors of age-related differences in decision making. *Journal of Behavioral Decision Making, 30*(1), 123–139. doi:10.1002/bdm.1926.

Mutter, S. A. (2000). Illusory correlation and group impression formation in young and older adults. *The Journals of Gerontology: Series B, 55*(4), P224–P237. doi:10.1093/geronb/55.4.P224.

Mutter, S. A., & Pliske, R. M. (1996). Judging event covariation: Effects of age and memory demand. *The Journals of Gerontology: Series B, 51B*(2), 70–P80. doi:10.1093/geronb/51B.2.P70.

Mutter, S. A., & Poliske, R. M. (1994). Aging and illusory correlation in judgments of co-occurrence. *Psychology and Aging, 9*(1), 53–63. doi:10.1037/0882-7974.9.1.53.

Mutter, S. A., & Williams, T. W. (2004). Aging and the detection of contingency in causal learning. *Psychology and Aging, 19*(1), 13–26. doi:10.1037/0882-7974.19.1.13.

Osgood, C. E., Suci, G. J., & Tannenbaum, P. H. (1957). *The Measurement of Meaning*. Urbana, IL: University of Illinois Press.

Park, D. C., Lautenschlager, G., Hedden, T., Davidson, N. S., Smith, A. D., & Smith, P. K. (2002). Models of visuospatial and verbal memory across the adult life span. *Psychology and Aging*, *17*(2), 299–320. doi:10.1037/0882-7974.17.2.299.

Park, D. C., Morrell, R. W., Frieske, D., Blackburn, A. B., & Birchmore, D. (1991). Cognitive factors and the use of over-the-counter medication organizers by arthritis patients. *Human Factors*, *33*(1), 57–67. doi:10.1177/001872089103300105.

Park, D. C., Morrell, R. W., Frieske, D., & Kincaid, D. (1992). Medication adherence behaviors in older adults: Effects of external cognitive supports. *Psychology and Aging*, *7*(2), 252–256. doi:10.1037/0882-7974.7.2.252.

Park, D. C., Willis, S. L., Morrow, D., Diehl, M., & Gaines, C. L. (1994). Cognitive function and medication usage in older adults. *Journal of Applied Gerontology*, *13*(1), 39–57. doi:10.1177/073346489401300104.

Peters, E. (2006). The functions of affect in the construction of preferences. In S. Lichtenstein & P. Slovic (Eds.), *The Construction of Preference* (pp. 454–463). New York: Cambridge University Press.

Peters, E. (2020). *Innumeracy in the Wild: Misunderstanding and Misusing Numbers*, 1st ed. Oxford/New York: Oxford University Press. Expected Publication May 27, 2020.

Peters, E., Baker, D. P., Dieckmann, N. F., Leon, J., & Collins, J. (2010). Explaining the effect of education on health: A field study in Ghana. *Psychological Science*, *21*(10), 1369–1376. doi:10.1177/0956797610381506.

Peters, E., Dieckmann, N., Dixon, A., Hibbard, J. H., & Mertz, C. K. (2007). Less is more in presenting quality information to consumers. *Medical Care Research and Review: MCRR*, *64*(2), 169–190. doi:10.1177/1077558707064002030.1.

Peters, E., Dieckmann, N. F., Västfjäll, D., Mertz, C., Slovic, P., & Hibbard, J. H. (2009). Bringing meaning to numbers: The impact of evaluative categories on decisions. *Journal of Experimental Psychology: Applied*, *15*(3), 213.

Peters, E., Hart, P. S., Tusler, M., & Fraenkel, L. (2014). Numbers matter to informed patient choices: A randomized design across age and numeracy levels. *Medical Decision Making: An International Journal of the Society for Medical Decision Making*, *34*(4), 430–442. doi:10.1177/0272989X13511705.

Peters, E., Hess, T. M., Västfjäll, D., & Auman, C. (2007). Adult age differences in dual information processes: Implications for the role of affective and deliberative processes in older adults' decision making. *Perspectives on Psychological Science: A Journal of the Association for Psychological Science*, *2*(1), 1–23.

Peters, E., Hibbard, J., Slovic, P., & Dieckmann, N. (2007). Numeracy skill and the communication, comprehension, and use of risk-benefit information. *Health Affairs*, *26*(3), 741–748. doi:10.1377/hlthaff.26.3.741.

Peters, E., Lipkus, I., & Diefenbach, M. A. (2006). The functions of affect in health communications and in the construction of health preferences. *Journal of Communication*, *56*(s1), S140–S162.

Peters, E., Shoots-Reinhard, B., Tompkins, M. K., Schley, D., Meilleur, L., Sinayev, A., Tusler, M., Wagner, L., & Crocker, J. (2017). Improving numeracy through values affirmation enhances decision and STEM outcomes. *PLoS One*, *12*(7), e0180674. doi:10.1371/journal.pone.0180674.

Peters, E., & Slovic, P. (2000). The springs of action: Affective and analytical information processing in choice. *Personality and Social Psychology Bulletin*, *26*(12), 1465–1475. doi:10.1177/01461672002612002.

Peters, E., & Slovic, P. (2007). Affective asynchrony and the measurement of the affective attitude component. *Cognition and Emotion, 21*(2), 300–329. doi:10.1080/02699930600911440.

Peters, E., Tompkins, M. K., Knoll, M. A. Z., Ardoin, S. P., Shoots-Reinhard, B., & Meara, A. S. (2019). Despite high objective numeracy, lower numeric confidence relates to worse financial and medical outcomes. *Proceedings of the National Academy of Sciences of the United States of America, 116*(39), 19386–19391. doi:10.1073/pnas.1903126116.

Peters, E., Västfjäll, D., Slovic, P., Mertz, C. K., Mazzocco, K., & Dickert, S. (2006). Numeracy and decision making. *Psychological Science, 17*(5), 407–413. doi:10.1111/j.1467-9280.2006.01720.x.

Petty, R. E., & Wegener, D. T. (1999). The elaboration likelihood model: Current status and controversies. In: S. Chaiken & Y. Trope (Eds.), *Dual-Process Theories in Social Psychology.* New York: Guilford Press.

Reed, A. E., Chan, L., & Mikels, J. A. (2014). Meta-analysis of the age-related positivity effect: Age differences in preferences for positive over negative information. *Psychology and Aging, 29*(1), 1–15. doi:10.1037/a0035194.

Reyna, V. F. (2004). How people make decisions that involve risk: A dual-processes approach. *Current Directions in Psychological Science, 13*(2), 60–66. doi:10.1111/j.0963-7214.2004.00275.x.

Reyna, V. F., Nelson, W. L., Han, P. K., & Dieckmann, N. F. (2009). How numeracy influences risk comprehension and medical decision making. *Psychological Bulletin, 135*(6), 943–973. doi:10.1037/a0017327.

Riggle, E. D. B., & Johnson, M. M. S. (1996). Age difference in political decision making: Strategies for evaluating political candidates. *Political Behavior, 18*(1), 99–118. doi:10.1007/BF01498661.

Rosi, A., Bruine de Bruin, W., Missier, F. D., Cavallini, E., & Russo, R. (2019). Decision-making competence in younger and older adults: Which cognitive abilities contribute to the application of decision rules? *Aging, Neuropsychology, and Cognition, 26*(2), 174–189. doi:10.1080/13825585.2017.1418283.

Ross, C. E., & Wu, C. (1995). The links between education and health. *American Sociological Review, 60*(5), 719–745. doi:10.2307/2096319.

Rothman, R. L., Housam, R., Weiss, H., Davis, D., Gregory, R., Gebretsadik, T., Shintani, A., & Elasy, T. A. (2006). Patient understanding of food labels: The role of literacy and numeracy. *American Journal of Preventive Medicine, 31*(5), 391–398. doi:10.1016/j.amepre.2006.07.025.

Salthouse, T. A. (1990). Cognitive competence and expertise in aging. In: *The Handbooks of Aging: Handbook of the Psychology of Aging*, 3rd ed. (pp. 310–319). doi:10.1016/B978-0-12-101280-9.50024-3.

Salthouse, T. A. (2012). Consequences of age-related cognitive declines. *Annual Review of Psychology, 63*(1), 201–226. doi:10.1146/annurev-psych-120710-100328.

Salthouse, T. A. (2019). Trajectories of normal cognitive aging. *Psychology and Aging, 34*(1), 17–24. doi:10.1037/pag0000288.

Samanez-Larkin, G. R., & Knutson, B. (2012). *Reward Processing and Risky Decision Making in the Aging Brain* (SSRN Scholarly Paper No. ID 2222681). Retrieved from Social Science Research Network website: https://papers.ssrn.com/abstract=2222681.

Samanez-Larkin, G. R., & Knutson, B. (2015). Decision making in the ageing brain: Changes in affective and motivational circuits. *Nature Reviews. Neuroscience, 16*(5), 278–289. doi:10.1038/nrn3917.

Sands, M., & Isaacowitz, D. M. (2016). Situation selection across adulthood: The role of arousal. *Cognition and Emotion*, 1–8. doi:10.1080/02699931.2016.1152954.

Schaie, K. W., & Zanjani, F. A. K. (2006). Intellectual development across adulthood. In: C. Hoare (Ed.), *Handbook of Adult Development and Learning* (pp. 99–122). New York: Oxford University Press.

Scheibe, S., English, T., Tsai, J. L., & Carstensen, L. L. (2013). Striving to feel good: Ideal affect, actual affect, and their correspondence across adulthood. *Psychology and Aging, 28*(1), 160–171. doi:10.1037/a0030561.

Schwarz, N., & Clore, G. L. (1983). Mood, misattribution, and judgments of well-being: Informative and directive functions of affective states. *Journal of Personality and Social Psychology, 45*(3), 513.

Sentell, T. L., & Halpin, H. A. (2006). Importance of adult literacy in understanding health disparities. *Journal of General Internal Medicine, 21*(8), 862–866. doi:10.1111/j.1525-1497.2006.00538.x.

Shiv, B., & Fedorikhin, A. (1999). Heart and mind in conflict: The interplay of affect and cognition in consumer decision making. *Journal of Consumer Research, 26*(3), 278–292. doi:10.1086/209563.

Simon, H. A. (1955). A behavioral model of rational choice. *The Quarterly Journal of Economics, 69*(1), 99–118. doi:10.2307/1884852.

Sinayev, A., & Peters, E. (2015). Cognitive reflection vs. calculation in decision making. *Frontiers in Psychology, 6*. doi:10.3389/fpsyg.2015.00532.

Skurnik, I., Yoon, C., Park, D. C., & Schwarz, N. (2005). How warnings about false claims become recommendations. *Journal of Consumer Research, 31*(4), 713–724. doi:10.1086/426605.

Sloman, S. A. (1996). The empirical case for two systems of reasoning. *Psychological Bulletin, 119*(1), 3–22. doi:10.1037/0033-2909.119.1.3.

Slovic, P., Finucane, M., Peters, E., & MacGregor, D. G. (2002, July). The affect heuristic. doi:10.1017/CBO9780511808098.025.

Smith, J. P., McArdle, J. J., & Willis, R. (2010). Financial decision making and cognition in a family context. *The Economic Journal, 120*(548), F363–F380. doi:10.1111/j.1468-0297.2010.02394.x.

Sorce, P. (1995). Cognitive competence of older consumers. *Psychology and Marketing, 12*(6), 467–480. doi:10.1002/mar.4220120603.

Stanovich, K. E., & West, R. F. (2002). Individual differences in reasoning: Implications for the rationality debate? In: T. Gilovich, D. Griffin, & D. Kahneman (Eds.), *Heuristics and Biases: The Psychology of Intuitive Judgment* (pp. 421–440). New York: Cambridge University Press.

Strange, J. J., & Leung, C. C. (1999). How anecdotal accounts in news and in fiction can influence judgments of a social problem's urgency, causes, and cures. *Personality and Social Psychology Bulletin, 25*(4), 436–449. doi:10.1177/0146167299025004004.

Streufert, S., Pogash, R., Piasecki, M., & Post, G. M. (1990). Age and management team performance. *Psychology and Aging, 5*(4), 551–559.

Strough, J., Bruine de Bruin, W., Parker, A. M., Karns, T., Lemaster, P., Pichayayothin, N., Delaney, R., & Stoiko, R. (2016). What were they thinking? Reducing sunk-cost bias in a life-span sample. *Psychology and Aging, 31*(7), 724–736. doi:10.1037/pag0000130.

Strough, J., Bruine de Bruin, W., & Peters, E. (2015). New perspectives for motivating better decisions in older adults. *Frontiers in Psychology, 6*. doi:10.3389/fpsyg.2015.00783.

Strough, J., Mehta, C. M., McFall, J. P., & Schuller, K. L. (2008). Are older adults less subject to the sunk-cost fallacy than younger adults? *Psychological Science, 19*(7), 650–652. doi:10.1111/j.1467-9280.2008.02138.x.

Toplak, M. E., Sorge, G. B., Benoit, A., West, R. F., & Stanovich, K. E. (2010). Decision-making and cognitive abilities: A review of associations between Iowa Gambling Task performance, executive functions, and intelligence. *Clinical Psychology Review, 30*(5), 562–581. doi:10.1016/j.cpr.2010.04.002.

U.S. Census Bureau (2018). The graying of America: More older adults than kids by 2035. Retrieved December 19, 2019, from The United States Census Bureau website: https://www.census.gov/library/stories/2018/03/graying-america.html.

U.S. Food and Drug Administration (2017, November 27). Questions, answers, and facts about generic drugs. Retrieved December 19, 2019, from FDA Website: http://www.fda.gov/drugs/resources-you-drugs/questions-answers-and-facts-about-generic-drugs.

van Weert, J. C. M., van Munster, B. C., Sanders, R., Spijker, R., Hooft, L., & Jansen, J. (2016). Decision aids to help older people make health decisions: A systematic review and meta-analysis. *BMC Medical Informatics and Decision Making, 16*(1), 45. https://doi.org/10.1186/s12911-016-0281-8

West, R. L. (1996). An application of prefrontal cortex function theory to cognitive aging. *Psychological Bulletin, 120*(2), 272–292.

Williams, M.V., Baker, D.W., Parker, R. M., & Nurss, J. R. (1998). Relationship of functional health literacy to patients' knowledge of their chronic disease: A study of patients with hypertension and diabetes. *Archives of Internal Medicine, 158*(2), 166–172. doi:10.1001/archinte.158.2.166.

Wilson, T. D., Dunn, D. S., Kraft, D., & Lisle, D. J. (1989). Introspection, attitude change, and attitude-behavior consistency: The disruptive effects of explaining why we feel the way we do. In: L. Berkowitz (Ed.), *Advances in Experimental Social Psychology*, Vol. *22*. (pp. 287–343). doi:10.1016/S0065-2601(08)60311-1.

Wood, S. A., Busemeyer, J., Koling, A., Cox, C. R., & Davis, H. (2005). Older adults as adaptive decision makers: Evidence from the Iowa Gambling Task. *Psychology and Aging, 20*(2), 220–225.

Wood, S. A., Liu, P.-J., Hanoch, Y., & Estevez-Cores, S. (2016). Importance of numeracy as a risk factor for elder financial exploitation in a community sample. *The Journals of Gerontology: Series B, 71*(6), 978–986. doi:10.1093/geronb/gbv041.

Yang, H., Yang, S., & Isen, A. M. (2013). Positive affect improves working memory: Implications for controlled cognitive processing. *Cognition and Emotion, 27*(3), 474–482. doi:10.1080/02699931.2012.713325.

Yoon, C., Cole, C. A., & Lee, M. P. (2009). Consumer decision making and aging: Current knowledge and future directions. *Journal of Consumer Psychology, 19*(1), 2–16. doi:10.1016/j.jcps.2008.12.002.

Zajonc, R. B. (1980). Feeling and thinking: Preferences need no inferences. *American Psychologist, 35*(2), 151–175. doi:10.1037/0003-066X.35.2.151.

Zaval, L., Li, Y., Johnson, E. J., & Weber, E. U. (2015). Chapter 8—Complementary contributions of fluid and crystallized intelligence to decision making across the life span. In: T. M. Hess, J. Strough, & C. E. Löckenhoff (Eds.), *Aging and Decision Making* (pp. 149–168). doi:10.1016/B978-0-12-417148-0.00008-X.

5

EFFECTS OF AGE ON RISKY AND INTERTEMPORAL CHOICES: DECISION STRATEGIES AND REAL-WORLD IMPLICATIONS

William H. Hampton and Vinod Venkatraman

General Introduction

The world population is graying at an increasingly rapid rate, with birth rates declining, and life expectancies increasing. This increased longevity is particularly prominent in more developed countries compared to less developed ones, due largely to increases in health expenditure (Mathers et al., 2003). Based on predictions that life expectancy will increase by three months every year, living to 100 years old in certain developed Western countries, such as the United States and Japan, may become relatively common for those born after the year 2000 (Christensen, Doblhammer, Rau, and Vaupel, 2009; Vaupel, 2010). This is a remarkable prospect, given that the average life expectancy in developed countries in 1900 was barely 45 years (Lim and Yu, 2015). This rapid aging of the world population is projected to continue over the next several decades (Lutz, Sanderson, and Scherbov, 2008). In the United States, in particular, the proportion of U.S. adults over 65 is projected to swell by 65 percent and top 79 million by 2035 (Social Security Administration, 2014). Although increased lifespan is a signature of improved human development (Anand and Sen, 1994), protracted longevity and an aging population also carry serious social and economic implications for society at large (Bloom, Canning, and Fink, 2010; Lloyd-Sherlock, 2000; Poterba, 2004; Schneider and Guralnik, 1990; Tinker, 2002).

Many of these societal implications stem from the decisions that older adults make and the ensuing consequences. As a cohort, older adults face a unique, complicated set of decision scenarios including when and how to decumulate their wealth, and how to manage their declining health. To make matters more difficult, such thorny decisions about finances and healthcare increase in frequency as we get older (Chen and Sun, 2003; Denburg, Tranel, and Bechara, 2005). Broadly, older adults are sometimes conceived to both take longer to make decisions, and to make generally poorer decisions, relative to younger adults (Deakin, Aitken, Robbins, and Sahakian, 2004). Perhaps unsurprisingly, older adult behavior is somewhat context-dependent: Their relative performance typically depends upon whether the decision or task relies more on their past experience or requires more of certain "fluid" cognitive capacities.

Although the scenarios that older adults encounter are diverse in nature, two types of decisions are particularly critical for older adults as they age. The first is risky choice, which is paramount for older adults given the heightened stakes of later-life personal finance and health decisions. Aging has been associated with elevated aversion to risk in certain decision domains, such as some gambling scenarios in which older adults fail to maximize expected value. Yet research using other kinds of risk measurement has found that older adults do not differ systematically or are even more risk-seeking than their younger counterparts (Mata, Josef, Samanez-Larkin, and Hertwig, 2011). In this chapter, we attempt to reconcile these apparent inconsistencies in age-related differences in risky choice.

The second type of decision that is crucial for older adults is intertemporal choice. Intertemporal choices are choices made across time, typically between larger later and smaller sooner rewards (Loewenstein, 1988). Older adults, like most people, exhibit *delay discounting*, in which they devalue future rewards according to how long they must wait (Read and Read, 2004a). This tension between present and future desires plays out every day, from the relatively trivial decision between enjoying the immediate comfort of sitting on the couch as opposed to going for a walk that will promote long-term health, to life-determining health decisions about when to take medication. Although discounting rates tend to decline with age, we discuss several key exceptions to this trend, as well as the extent to which discounting may be malleable.

We contend that any examination of age-related changes in decision-making should not just focus on the outcomes, but also the core mechanisms that drive older adults to behave differently. To this end, we discuss both changes in decision-making strategies with age, as well as the role that emotion, i.e., affect, may play in governing such age-related changes. Specifically, we consider how changes in information processing, and anticipation and integration of future rewards in older adults might underlie age-related differences in risky and intertemporal choice behavior.

We then examine how the findings of controlled laboratory studies have been, or could be, extended to real-world decisions made by older consumers. In the domain of risky choice, for example, we address whether differences in risk preferences in laboratory tasks necessarily translate into differences in preference for retirement investments or annuities, and the extent to which older adults use similar decision strategies in both decision scenarios. Similarly, intertemporal choices made by older adults in the lab studies also relate closely to many critical real-world scenarios, such as when to collect Social Security. We discuss the everyday implications of older adults' discounting and risky choices as well as some possible routes for interventions by which we might best support adaptive decision-making across the lifespan.

Finally, we address the corpus of cognitive neuroscience research in the last two decades that has begun to reveal the neural correlates and mechanisms underlying an array of decisions, as well as the effects of healthy aging on the brain. We discuss the latest pertinent neuroscience research, which hints at the importance of functional compensation, degradation of key brain structures, as well as aberrant neural connectivity in governing age-related changes in decision-making (also see Chapter 1 by Mukadam, Leger, and Gutchess, 2020).

Aging and Risk Preferences

Several studies have sought to understand how healthy aging affects decision-making across the lifespan (Drolet, Schwarz, and Yoon, 2011; Mata et al., 2011). In terms of risk preferences, aging is often associated with increased aversion to risk (Deakin et al., 2004; Tymula, Belmaker, Ruderman, Glimcher, and Levy, 2013). For example, in a computerized gambling task, aging was associated with reduced risk-taking, increased deliberation time, and overall poorer decisions (Deakin et al., 2004). Similarly, older adults tend to be more risk averse in a task called the Balloon Analog Risk Task (BART), making significantly fewer risky pumps relative to younger adults (Henninger, Madden, and Huettel, 2010). In a task using gain and loss gambles, older adults were again found to be risk averse, making decisions that resulted in lower expected monetary outcomes relative to their younger counterparts (Tymula et al., 2013). Critically, older adults violated stochastic dominance in more than 25 percent of the trials, indicating a heightened propensity for irrational decision-making. Finally, a recent large-scale smartphone study (with over 25,000 individuals) found that the number of risky options chosen in trials with potential gains decreased with age, consistent with risk-averse behavior (Rutledge et al., 2016).

In contrast to this evidence suggesting that older adults are uniformly more risk averse, a meta-analysis of several decades of research in this area found no systematic age differences in risk preferences (Mata et al., 2011). For example, the older adults who were risk *averse* in the BART were more risk-*seeking* in the Columbia Gambling Task (Henninger et al., 2010). In another similar gambling task called the Iowa Gambling Task, several studies have demonstrated that older adults make riskier, rather than risk-averse decisions (Beitz, Salthouse, and Davis, 2014; Nathalie L Denburg et al., 2005; Zamarian, Sinz, Bonatti, Gamboz, and Delazer, 2008). Therefore, it appears that the effect of aging on risk preferences varies significantly as a function of task and context, as well as learning requirements. Tasks that require participants to learn from recent experience like the Iowa Gambling Task and Columbia Gambling Task show differential patterns, relative to tasks where the performance does not depend on learning like the BART (Mata et al., 2011).

Some of the apparent discrepancies in findings across studies may be reconciled from an information processing perspective (Read and Read, 2004b). It is well known and recognized that humans are behaviorally heterogeneous. This is particularly important in the context of aging, where heterogeneity is relevant both in terms of cognitive capability and risk attitude. In terms of capability, individual differences in capabilities reflect the differential effects of aging on capacities such as executive function, processing speed, and working memory. Some individuals seem to age "better" than others, i.e., these cognitive capacities are better preserved. On the other hand, individuals may differ at a trait-level in their attitudes toward risk (Weber, Blais, and Betz, 2002). Therefore, the complex, task-dependent changes in decision preferences observed across studies may reflect the effect of aging on the ability to glean and process pertinent information, rather than the direct effects of age on risk attitudes. Consistent with this perspective, Henninger and colleagues found that cognitive capabilities like processing speed and memory fully mediated age-related changes in risk preferences across an array of tasks (Henninger et al., 2010).

Another framework by which these differences can be reconciled is through the differential effects of age on fluid and crystallized intelligence. It is known that fluid capabilities like attention, executive control, and working memory decline with age (Salthouse, 2000; Salthouse, 1996), while crystallized capabilities related to knowledge and experience are relatively spared (Park et al., 2002). The latter suggests that the accumulated experience over the lifespan should allow older adults to make better decisions and be less prone to biases in certain contexts (Korniotis and Kumar, 2011). Consistent with these predictions, in certain tasks where decision-making is known to decline with age, some older adults have relatively preserved functions (Denburg et al., 2005), while others exhibit notable deficits. Yet, it remains unclear if these differences are due to preserved fluid capabilities in these individuals, or due to deficits in motivation and cognition in other individuals (Denburg, Recknor, Bechara, and Tranel, 2006; Samanez-Larkin and Knutson, 2015). Li and colleagues demonstrated that older adults compensated for lower levels of fluid intelligence with their greater crystallized intelligence in a variety of tasks including temporal discounting, financial literacy, and debt literacy, rendering them better decision makers overall (Li, Baldassi, Johnson, and Weber, 2013). Similarly, using a unique dataset that combined measures of crystallized and fluid intelligence, the authors found that domain-specific knowledge and expertise provided an alternative route by which older adults could make sound financial decisions (Li et al., 2015).

More recently, Rutledge and colleagues demonstrated age-related decreases in risk-taking using a large cross-sectional sample from the general population. However, this effect was only robust in the gain domain, and not in the loss domain or for mixed gambles (Rutledge et al., 2016). The authors posited that the observed decreases in the gain domain are due to a decreased Pavlovian approach behavior in older adults rather than changes in subjective valuation or risk attitudes. The Pavlovian approach is a general propensity to choose higher rewards over a certain outcome, independent of the associated subjective value (Bossaerts and Murawski, 2016). The dopaminergic system is integral for the Pavlovian approach, with higher levels of dopamine positively associated with heightened preference for higher rewards (Rutledge, Skandali, Dayan, and Dolan, 2015). Notably, aging is associated with decreased expression of dopamine (Samanez-Larkin and Knutson, 2015), which in turn may cause older adults to be less likely to take risks than younger adults in the gain domain (Rutledge et al., 2016). Nonetheless, this explanation does not fully account for the variability in risk preferences observed in the loss domain, nor for the other contexts previously mentioned.

Effects of Age on Strategies

In a recent study, Venkatraman and colleagues sought to understand differences in risk preferences from an information processing and decision strategy perspective (Venkatraman, Yoon, and Vo, in press). In each trial, participants chose between three different mixed gambles, presented in a 4 × 4 grid format in fixed order with attributes rank ordered from gains to losses (see Figure 5.1). Each gamble proposition consisted of three outcomes, each with its own probability.

	0.33	0.33	0.33
G1 (Gmax)	$95	-$10	-$75
G2 (Pwin)	$75	$10	-$75
G3 (Lmin)	$75	-$10	-$55

	0.33	0.33	0.33
G1 (Gmax)	$75	-$20	-$70
G2 (Inter)	$65	-$10	-$70
G3 (Lmin)	$65	-$20	-$60

	0.33	0.33	0.33
G1 (Gmax)	-$10	-$75	$95
G2 (Inter)	$10	-$75	$75
G3 (Lmin)	-$10	-$55	$75

Pwin-Available (Fixed Order)	**Pwin-Unavailable** (Fixed Order)	**Pwin-Available** (Randomized Order)

FIGURE 5.1 An example of Pwin-available and Pwin-unavailable trial from the risky-choice task. All gambles had equal expected value in both trial types. In fixed order studies, attributes were presented in a rank-ordered format with gains in the first column and losses in the last column. In the study with randomized order, the order of attributes was randomized across trials. Participants indicated their preference by pressing an appropriate button on the keyboard. Labels for each of the alternatives are shown for display purposes only.

Specifically, participants chose one of the following three alternatives: (1) gain-maximizing (Gmax) alternative that was associated with the highest gain outcome; (2) loss-minimizing alternative associated with the lowest loss outcome and; (3) "intermediate" alternative associated with superior value for the intermediate outcome. The gambles were always constructed by improving one of the outcomes (gain, intermediate, or loss) from a three-outcome base gamble (Venkatraman, Payne, Bettman, Luce, and Huettel, 2009; Venkatraman, Payne, and Huettel, 2011, 2014). The magnitudes varied across trials, but probabilities and expected values were equal across the three gambles within a trial. Additionally, in some trials, the intermediate alternative had a greater overall probability of winning compared to the other alternatives (Pwin-available trials), while in others, there was no difference in the overall probability of winning across all alternatives (Pwin-unavailable trials). In addition to measuring preference across trials, the authors also used eye-tracking to quantify any differences in processing strategies.

Across trials, there was a significant effect of age, with younger adults strongly preferring the intermediate alternative, while older adults preferred the Gmax alternative. Critically, the preference for the intermediate alternative in younger adults was found only in Pwin-available trials, where the intermediate option was associated with a greater overall probability of winning. In other words, younger adults adapted their preferences in response to changing trial types. Older adults did not exhibit this trial-by-trial adaptation. Response time data also revealed a marginally significant interaction between group and trial type, with younger adults spending a longer time on Pwin-unavailable trials than Pwin-available trials, while older adults did differ in their trial-type reaction times. Together, these results show that younger adults were more adaptive in their decision strategies across trial types. In other words, older adults were more rigid and less likely than younger adults to adapt their choices to changes in the decision context.

The pattern of increased preference for Gmax choices in older adults is consistent with optimistic and risk-seeking behavior, and more broadly with socio-economic selectivity theory (SST; Carstensen, 1991). SST contends that older adults place greater priority on goals related to well-being, and comparatively less emphasis on emotionally riskier goals, leading to a positivity bias (Carstensen and Mikels, 2005). A similar positivity bias in older adults in this task could, therefore, lead to a preference for alternatives that maximize the highest gain. Alternatively, it is possible that older adults merely use simpler decision strategies and hence overweight the information presented in the earlier column (i.e., first column). Since the leftmost column always contained gain attributes, this could have led older adults to overweight this information when making choices.

In a follow-up study, Venkatraman and colleagues (Venkatraman, Yoon, and Vo, in press) tested whether older adults were more strongly influenced by the information presented in the earlier columns by randomizing the order of attributes across trials (see Figure 5.1, right column). In other words, despite an insensitivity to systematic changes in a decision context, are older adults influenced by task-irrelevant factors such as the order in which information is presented? This was indeed the case, with older adults choosing the gain alternatives more when they were presented in the earlier columns. These findings were further corroborated by eye-tracking data. Older adults exhibited heightened processing of gain outcomes, compared to intermediate outcomes, only when the gain attributes were displayed in the first column. They also exhibited increased processing of intermediate outcomes, compared to gain outcomes, when the intermediate outcomes were presented in the first column. In contrast, younger adults were less influenced by changes in information presentation format in the same task.

In summary, in contrast to younger adults who preferred maximizing the overall probability of winning in an adaptive manner, older adults tended to prefer options that maximized gains and were also influenced by the order in which the attributes were presented. This difference between age cohorts may be driven by alterations in information processing and decision-making strategies.

Aging and Intertemporal Choice

A person's desire for immediate rewards is often at odds with the desire to improve upon one's current situation, which typically requires waiting. Such choices, known as intertemporal choices, are frequently between smaller, sooner, and larger later rewards. One striking characteristic of intertemporal decisions is that people discount the value of future rewards as a function of the delay in receiving them. This phenomenon is known as delay discounting, or temporal discounting (Odum, 2011). A person's discount rate, often denoted their k score, can be calculated based upon how much they discount future rewards relative to immediate ones. Critically, k scores derived from lab-based studies using hypothetical monetary rewards are not systematically different from those using real money, suggesting experimental results are likely valid proxies for decisions involving real money (Johnson and Bickel, 2002). Individual differences in discounting rates predict an array of real-world outcomes, with lower discount rates robustly predicting a slew of positive outcomes such as collegiate academic performance (Kirby, Winston, and Santiesteban, 2005) and higher-income (Hampton, Asadi, and Olson, 2018). Conversely, higher discount rates have been associated with deleterious behaviors such as smoking (Bickel, Odum, and Madden, 1999), drug abuse (Perry, Larson, German, Madden, and Carroll, 2005), and texting while driving (Hayashi, Russo, and Wirth, 2015).

While nearly all individuals discount the value of future rewards, there is significant inter-individual variability in k values. Although numerous factors have been proposed to explain this variability, one of the most extensive literatures relates to the role of age in delay discounting. Several studies have reported reduced discounting with age in humans (Eppinger, Nystrom, and Cohen, 2012; Löckenhoff, O'Donoghue, and Dunning, 2011; Myerson and Green, 1995). However, other studies have not found significant changes in discounting between age groups (Chao,

Szrek, Pereira, and Pauly, 2009; Rieger and Mata, 2015; Roalf, Mitchell, Harbaugh, and Janowsky, 2012; Samanez-Larkin et al., 2011; Whelan and Mchugh, 2009). One study even found discounting to increase with age (Read and Read, 2004a).

There are many possible explanations for the aforementioned inconsistency in the relationship between age and delay discounting. First, as a cohort, older adults also tend to be more variable in the extent to which they discount future rewards (Green, Myerson, and Ostaszewski, 1999). Second, previous studies have varied significantly in their methodological approach and decision-making domain (Best and Charness, 2015; Mata et al., 2011). Further, many prior studies were deficient or completely lacked middle-aged adult participants, who make up over one fourth of the population (U.S. Census Bureau, 2019). Perhaps because of this gap, very few studies examine age-related decision-making differences continuously and instead have examined only group differences. This is a limiting approach, as many cognitive changes evolve in a continuous, nonlinear fashion across the lifespan (Piper et al., 2011; Samanez-Larkin and Knutson, 2015).

One particularly weighty intertemporal choice that older adults must face is the decision of when to start collecting Social Security income. Many older adults depend heavily on their Social Security for income to maintain their quality of life. Specifically, over a fifth of married Social Security recipients and nearly half of single recipients over the age of 65 depend on Social Security for 90 percent or more of their income (Social Security Administration, 2014). Given the importance of this income, it is perhaps not surprising that more than a third of older adults claim Social Security as soon as they are eligible, at age 62 (Munnell, Webb, and Hou, 2014). This decision often proves to be a serious mistake, as many older adults find themselves without the necessary funds to maintain their quality of life. In comparison, older adults who delay collecting Social Security until age 70 received a 76 percent higher monthly benefit (Social Security Administration, 2014).

As they age, older adults also face daily intertemporal choices that are increasingly consequential to their health. For instance, older adults must frequently choose between the immediate gratification of being sedentary and preventive health measures such as exercise that result in future good health. Delay discounting has also been connected with addictive behaviors. For instance, cigarette smoking, which is increasingly dangerous with age, involves the rapid loss of subjective value for delayed outcomes (LaCroix, Guralnik, Berkman, Wallace, and Satterfield, 1993). Similarly, higher discounting rates have been associated with overeating and obesity (Rasmussen, Lawyer, and Reilly, 2010), which in turn increase the likelihood of deadly heart disease and certain types of cancer (Calle and Thun, 2004). Finally, older adults are known to discount when making medical decisions. For example, older adults are more likely than younger adults to discount the temporally delayed health benefits from hypothetical drugs (Seaman et al., 2016). Each of these situations is, in essence, a delay discounting scenario, in which many older adults opt for the immediately preferable, yet ultimately less beneficial option.

The Role of Affect on Decision-Making across the Lifespan

In examining age-related changes in decision-making, it is important to consider not just outcomes, but also the underlying mechanisms that drive older adults to behave differently. Until relatively recently, the role of *affect*, i.e., emotion, in decision-making received little attention from researchers—even less so regarding its role in age-related changes in decision-making. Although affect is now thought to be of critical importance, decision-making was previously conceived of as a cognitive process in which agents actively (and more or less rationally) selected among alternatives based on their respective outcome (Loewenstein and Lerner, 2003). Converging evidence now suggests that a person's affective state influences decision-making (Naqvi, Shiv, and Bechara, 2006).

Emotional experience can be conceptualized as consisting of two primary dimensions: valence and arousal (Russell, 1980). Positive arousal is thought to increase approach *motivation*, while negative arousal is thought to increase *avoidance* (Watson, Wiese, Vaidya, and Tellegen, 1999). In consumption contexts, approach motivation is associated with greater likelihood to purchase and higher willingness to pay (Bellizzi and Hite, 1992; Penz and Hogg, 2011). Scholarly research on affective decision-making has been extended to include additional mechanisms that might *integrate* their influences to promote an appropriate behavioral response. Together, these components of affect, integration, and motivation have recently been combined into a decision-making framework to explain age-related changes in risky and intertemporal choice (Samanez-Larkin and Knutson, 2015).

Theoretically, the affect–integration–motivation (AIM) framework builds upon previous academic research and models that have associated these factors with valuation by assigning each factor a different, albeit connected, function that starts with affect and concludes with motivation; beginning with activity in the affective components, which is then transmitted to motivational components. Notably, affective components are proposed to receive some degree of input from motivational components, while motivational components *require* input from affective components. In this way, the framework retains flexibility to account for choice through different combinations of AIM components, as well as an input from additional components. In other words, the AIM framework is hierarchical, sequential, and fairly flexible.

Looking at intertemporal choice from an AIM framework, there are several possible explanations as to why older adults tend to more optimally balance future and present rewards (recall that older adults tend to discount future rewards less than their young counterparts). The first interpretation is that older adults discount future rewards less due to reduced anticipation of gains from immediate rewards, as has been shown in related research (Samanez-Larkin et al., 2007). It is also possible that older adults have increased anticipation of gain of future rewards, or that they have elevated integration of future rewards into their overall value assessment (Samanez-Larkin and Knutson, 2015).

Alterations in risky choice across the lifespan may also be explained by the AIM framework. Recall that older adults tended to avoid risk when risk taking has the potential to increase earnings but are more risk prone when risk taking decreased earnings. Older adults also show reduced loss anticipation during value assessment (Samanez-Larkin et al., 2007). Together, these findings suggest that older adults may not necessarily be more prone to financial risk taking. Instead, age-related cognitive decline and associated deterioration of value integration might more conspicuously affect financial risk taking in older adults.

Although the general importance of affect in determining decision-making outcomes is well-established, these AIM-based explanations of age-related changes in decision-making are still being formally tested. The results of these and related studies will help elucidate the robustness of the AIM model to predict age-related differences in intertemporal choice.

Real-World Applications of Lab-Based Aging Decision Science

Despite the popular belief that older adults are easily susceptible to scams and make poor decisions in life, the evidence is mixed. For example, studies involving real-world investment choices have found that older adults are less effective in applying their investment knowledge, and generally make poorer financial decisions (Agarwal, Driscoll, Gabaix, and Laibson, 2009; Korniotis and Kumar, 2011). However, there are a number of other studies that demonstrate that older adults perform just as well, or even better than younger adults (Castel, 2005; Nobahar Ahari, Nejati, and Hosseini, 2010; Samanez-Larkin et al., 2011). The parallels between findings from lab studies and actual real-world decisions are striking. Yet, these are largely based on independent cross-sectional studies, and very little is known about how aging impacts decision-making within the same individual across tasks and contexts. Therefore, it is critical to understand whether risk-averse behavior in a simulated gambling task generalizes to poorer and maladaptive real-world decisions like healthcare and finances. Otherwise, findings from lab-based studies may have very little relevance for actual decisions made by the individuals. Addressing this issue will have very important implications for the development of interventions and public policies.

In the study described earlier by Venkatraman and colleagues (Venkatraman et al., in press), participants also completed a financial decision-making task in the same session, in which they chose between multiple annuities that varied on different attributes. Several studies have sought to examine the mechanisms underlying this annuity puzzle (Payne, Sagara, Shu, Appelt, and Johnson, 2013; Shu, Zeithammer, and Payne, 2016). In each trial, participants had to choose between three different annuities, based on information about four different attributes (CR: company rating, PC: period certainty, AI: annual increment, MP: monthly payment). The authors also varied the presentation order of attributes similar to the risky-choice task. While there were no age-related differences in the purchase rates of annuities, there was a significant interaction between group and presentation order ($b = 0.08$, $SE = 0.04$, $z = 2.13$, $p = 0.033$). Eye-tracking revealed that though both younger and older adults spent longer time processing attributes presented in earlier columns relative to later columns, this pattern was stronger for younger adults, unlike the risky-choice task. Therefore, the susceptibility of older adults to task-irrelevant features did not generalize across tasks. These findings suggest that motivation and engagement at the task level can play an important role in influencing age-related changes in decision strategies.

Similarly, given the gravity of the intertemporal choices that older adults make, there has been growing interest in developing interventions to reduce discounting in older adults. Previous research has shown that discounting rates within-individual are relatively stable for time periods on the order of weeks to a year, assuming the consistent methodological approach (Jimura et al., 2011; Kirby, 2009; Ohmura, Takahashi, Kitamura, and Wehr, 2006). However, nascent evidence suggests that intertemporal choice is, in fact, plastic, such that an individual's discount rate can be influenced by state and context (For review, see Lempert and Phelps, 2016).

One simple intervention involves the use of framing to "nudge" a person toward the delayed option. In the canonical delay discounting task, participants make a series of binary choices between an immediate smaller reward and a larger delayed reward. Though there is much evidence that people hyperbolically discount delayed rewards, the extent to which an individual's discounting rate is a product of this particular way of framing the options is still debated. That is, could the discounting rate be altered by reframing the choice options? Magen and colleagues conducted one such experiment (Magen, Dweck, and Gross, 2008), in which they altered choice presentation to include explicit zero information that was previously implicit (e.g., "Would you prefer (1) $500 today and $0 in 1 month OR (1) $0 today and $1,000 in 1 month?"). Interestingly, they found that for both hypothetical and real money conditions, participants in the explicit-zero condition exhibited significantly lower discount rates than those in the traditional frame condition. Could similar framing be leveraged to influence older adults' behavior in important intertemporal choices such as Social Security?

As previously noted, many older adults claim Social Security too early and find themselves in a difficult financial situation as a result. There is preliminary evidence that a framing approach could be issued to improve Social Security claiming decisions. A recent quasi-experiment using the 1983 Social Security reform found that framing a reform as benefit cut diminishes response, whereas framing a reform as a change in the reference point magnifies impact (Behaghel and Blau, 2012). Similarly, a recent randomized, controlled experiment found a "breakeven analysis" encourages early Social Security claiming, and that older adults were more likely to wait to claim when it was framed as a gain (Brown, Kapteyn, and Mitchell, 2016).

An ongoing study provides a more direct test of the effects of value framing on intertemporal choices across the life span (Hampton, 2018). In their value framing study, the authors examine whether reframing a traditional delay discounting task as either (1) a loss or (2) a bonus can attenuate delay discounting. They also examined the degree to which individual susceptibility to value framing varies with age and whether such framing might apply in a Social Security context.

The loss-framed version of the delay discounting task proceeded in a similar manner as a traditional delay task, i.e., by presenting a series of choices between immediate and future rewards of varying magnitudes and temporal distances. However, an additional line was added to each choice option that made explicit the loss information that was previously implicit. That is, it reminded participants that by taking a $600 reward now instead of $1000 in one month, for example, they would effectively be "forfeiting" $400. On the future reward side, an additional line was added to indicate that choosing the future reward would result in $0 forfeited. As predicted, they found that loss frame k scores were significantly lower than gain frame k scores. They also found that susceptibility to framing decreased approximately linearly with age. They speculate that loss framing might reduce intertemporal choice due to *loss aversion*. Loss aversion is a component of Prospect Theory, which is supported by empirical data showing that people are asymmetrically averse to losses relative to gains of equal magnitude (Loewenstein, 1988; Tversky and Kahneman, 1992).

In the bonus-framed version of the task, Hampton and colleagues also divided the future reward into two lines. The first line matched the immediate reward; the second line presented the remainder of the total future reward as a "bonus." For instance, in the canonical task, a participant might select between a future reward of $1,100 and the immediate reward of $800. In the bonus frame, the participant would see the immediate reward as $800 with a bonus of $0, and the future reward as $800 plus a bonus of $300. Bonus framing also reduced delay discounting behavior, although the effects were not as strong or consistent as loss framing. The authors posit this effect may be the result of "mental accounting," in which money is categorized and handled differently according to category. This explanation is consistent with research on mental accounting, showing that people create budgets and subsequently expend money in ways that are counter to fungibility (Prelec and Loewenstein, 1998). For instance, a $1,000 lottery windfall is more likely to be coded as "income" and subsequently spent, than a $1,000 bonus from work, which is more likely to be coded as "wealth" and saved (Shefrin and Thaler, 1988).

Finally, to examine the possible efficacy of a value framing intervention for older adults, Hampton and colleagues created two delay discounting tasks in the context of Social Security. The Social Security discounting tasks asked participants to make an initial choice between claiming Social Security immediately for a smaller monthly amount and waiting to claim a larger monthly amount. This was done in both loss and gain frames, similar to the other versions of the delay discounting tasks previously discussed. They found that discounting scores in the loss frame were significantly lower than in the traditional frame, across all ages. Looking only at older adults, the effect held, with older adults exhibiting significantly lower Social Security discounting in the loss compared with traditional frame. Together, these findings evince the importance of framing on intertemporal choice and open the door for similar framing-based interventions to support decision-making in older adults.

Neuroscience of Aging

Over the past several decades, there has been significant progress toward characterizing the impact of healthy aging on the brain. Only more recently, however, have researchers begun to delineate how age-related alterations in brain structure and function affect decision-making (Grady, 2012; Hedden and Gabrieli, 2004). Multiple psychological and neural factors underlie decision-making outcomes. Cognitive and affective capacities are integral in governing decision-making because they connect sensory information to motor outputs. These capacities are particularly important when individuals must do real-world cost-benefit analyses.

Regarding cognition, research suggests that although aging compromises certain cognitive capacities, others remain relatively preserved. As alluded to earlier, fluid cognitive abilities (e.g., working memory, executive control, and attention) tend to decline with age, while crystallized intelligence and cognitive capacities (e.g., domain-specific knowledge) are better conserved (Park and Schwarz, 2012). These differential cognitive changes mean that older adults tend to perform more poorly in decision environments that require fluid cognitive abilities (see Figure 5.2). For example, older adults perform poorly if a decision requires that they consider and compare multiple attributes or choose among several options simultaneously (Samanez-Larkin and Knutson, 2015). This cognitive account predicts that middle-aged adults may make the most optimal decisions across a broad range of contexts, which is consistent with a recent suggestion that financial reasoning peaks in middle age (Agarwal et al., 2009).

In functional MRI studies, older adults tend to show greater neural activity across the entire brain than younger adults. Contrary to a lay misconception that "more brain activity is better," and the related ten-percent myth (Higbee and Clay, 1998), such elevated activity is better understood as a cognitive coping mechanism. Often observed in the prefrontal cortex, this increased activity is typically interpreted as representing functional compensation, in which areas of the brain not strictly "required" for a behavior are nonetheless recruited in older adults (Cabeza, Anderson, Locantore, and McIntosh, 2002; Park and Reuter-Lorenz, 2009). Older adults also tend to exhibit heightened variability in their neural activity in reward areas such as the nucleus accumbens. It is thought that this variability contributes to the suboptimal financial decision-making sometimes observed in older adults (Samanez-Larkin, Kuhnen, Yoo, and Knutson, 2010).

a Cognitive change across adulthood

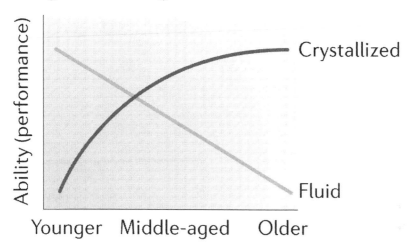

b Context-dependent performance peaks

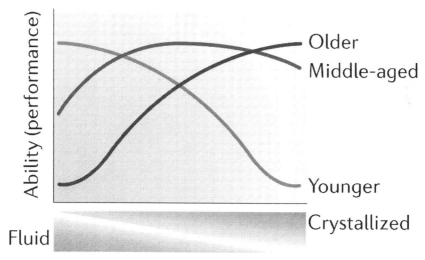

FIGURE 5.2   Changes in (a) cognitive ability and (b) decision-making performance across the lifespan. Reproduced from Samanez-Larkin and Knutson, 2015.

Another important neural factor in age-related changes in decision-making is brain structure. With age comes a generally steady degradation of both neural gray matter across many areas of the brain, and more acutely in the hippocampus for those developing Alzheimer's (Giorgio et al., 2010; Raji, Lopez, Kuller, Carmichael, and Becker, 2009). Although previously overlooked, interconnective white matter of the brain also appears to suffer with age (Daselaar et al., 2013; Giorgio et al., 2010). Although such structural alteration explains certain detriments in older adult decision-making, it remains unclear exactly how and why certain cognitive functions are more robust to the aging process than are others.

In terms of intertemporal choice, there are several preliminary studies that highlight the importance of neural connectivity, particularly connectivity of the striatum and the ventromedial prefrontal cortex. Specifically, connectivity between the striatum and hippocampus may be important in determining whether older adults can exert the cognitive control necessary to delay gratification (Sasse, Peters, and Brassen, 2017). Similarly, functional connectivity of the ventromedial prefrontal cortex has also been associated with delay discounting preferences among older adults (Han et al., 2013). Finally, there is converging evidence that differences in connectivity of the striatum to various regions of the frontal lobe (i.e., frontostriatal connectivity) may govern discounting behavior across a range of ages (Hampton, Alm, Venkatraman, Nugiel, and Olson, 2017; Peper et al., 2013; van den Bos, Rodriguez, Schweitzer, and McClure, 2015). As mentioned, however, some behavioral studies indicate that intertemporal preferences are relatively stable with age; therefore, these neuroimaging studies should be treated as preliminary evidence in an ongoing investigation.

Conclusion

The world population is projected to age rapidly over the next several decades (Lutz et al., 2008). Although a longer average lifespan is often greeted as a welcome signal of improved human development (Anand and Sen, 1994), extended lifespans and an older population also carry serious economic and social implications (Bloom et al., 2010; Lloyd-Sherlock, 2000; Poterba, 2004; Schneider and Guralnik, 1990; Tinker, 2002). Many of these societal implications are the downstream consequences of the increasingly complex and weighty decisions made by older adults. Although diverse in nature, two types of decisions are particularly critical for older adults as they age: risky choices and intertemporal choices.

Risky choice outcomes are paramount for older adults, given the heightened stakes of later-life personal finance. Although not uniformly the case, aging is often associated with increased aversion to risk (Deakin et al., 2004; Tymula et al., 2013). Such aversion can manifest as the rational avoidance of superfluous risk in certain cases, or as a maladaptive failure to maximize expected value in others. A review of the current literature suggests not that there are systematic age differences in risk preferences, but rather that older adults are risk-seeking in certain environments and risk-averse in others (Mata et al., 2011). Some of the apparent discrepancies in findings across studies may be explained by differences in information processing, a perspective that is supported by recent eye-tracking evidence. Overall, one interpretation of the current evidence is that some of the age-related differences in risk preferences may be related to cognitive decline and associated deterioration of value integration.

In addition to risk-related decisions, older adults also face many critical real-world intertemporal choices. These intertemporal decisions include when to collect Social Security and how to manage their long-term health. Among older adults, higher discounting of future rewards has been associated with a host of negative outcomes, including lower wealth, fewer investments in health, and less planning for end-of-life care. Although still an area of active research, studies suggest that several interventions might be effective in reducing discounting in older adults, including strategic reframing of information. Looking at intertemporal choice through the perspective offered by the AIM framework, it is possible that older adults discount future rewards less due to reduced anticipation of gain from immediate rewards, increased anticipation of gain of future rewards, or elevated integration of future rewards into their overall value assessment (Samanez-Larkin and Knutson, 2015). This framework is one of many explanations that are increasingly predicated on how shifting affective responses might explain age-related changes in decision-making. Broadly, such affective accounts have tended to find that older adults have a "rosier" view of the future and to make more accurate affective forecasts of the experience of these rewards over various delays.

Although the current literature provides an important starting point for our understanding of decision-making in older adults, there are several limitations that we hope will be addressed by future research. First, while examining these factors in isolation has been critical for our understanding of aging and decision-making, research on the interplay of these factors is needed to clarify the mechanisms that underlie changes in decision-making behavior across the lifespan. Second, most studies to date have focused on differences between older and younger adults or other group differences. This is a limiting approach, as many cognitive changes evolve in a continuous, nonlinear fashion across the lifespan (Piper et al., 2011; Samanez-Larkin and Knutson, 2015). Therefore, we also recommend that future studies include a continuous age sample that includes middle-aged adults. Finally, we encourage future cognitive neuroscience research of older adults to take into account both activity and connectivity, so as to best encapsulate the complex structural and functional neural changes that occur with healthy aging.

References

Agarwal, S., Driscoll, J. C., Gabaix, X., & Laibson, D. (2009). The age of reason: Financial decisions over the life cycle and implications for regulation. *Brookings Papers on Economic Activity, 2009* (2), 51–117.

Anand, S., & Sen, A. (1994). Human Development Index: Methodology and Measurement. *Human Development Report Office.*

Behaghel, L., & Blau, D. M. (2012). Framing social security reform: Behavioral responses to changes in the full retirement age. *American Economic Journal: Economic Policy, 4*(4), 41–67.

Beitz, K. M., Salthouse, T. A., & Davis, H. P. (2014). Performance on the Iowa gambling task: From 5 to 89 years of age. *Journal of Experimental Psychology: General, 143*(4), 1677.

Bellizzi, J. A., & Hite, R. E. (1992). Environmental color, consumer feelings, and purchase likelihood. *Psychology and Marketing, 9*(5), 347–363.

Best, R., & Charness, N. (2015). Age differences in the effect of framing on risky choice: A meta-analysis. *Psychology and Aging, 30*(3), 688–698. doi:10.1037/a0039447.

Bickel, W. K., Odum, A. L., & Madden, G. J. (1999). Impulsivity and cigarette smoking: Delay discounting in current, never, and ex-smokers. *Psychopharmacology, 146*(4), 447–454. doi:10.1007/PL00005490.

Bloom, D. E., Canning, D., & Fink, G. (2010). Implications of population ageing for economic growth. *Oxford Review of Economic Policy, 26*(4), 583–612.

Bossaerts, P., & Murawski, C. (2016). Decision neuroscience: Why we become more cautious with age. *Current Biology, 26*(12), R495–R497.

Brown, J. R., Kapteyn, A., & Mitchell, O. S. (2016). Framing and claiming: How information-F raming affects expected social security claiming behavior. *Journal of Risk and Insurance, 83*(1), 139–162.

Cabeza, R., Anderson, N. D., Locantore, J. K., & McIntosh, A. R. (2002). Aging gracefully: Compensatory brain activity in high-performing older adults. *Neuroimage, 17*(3), 1394–1402.

Calle, E. E., & Thun, M. J. (2004). Obesity and cancer. *Oncogene, 23*(38), 6365.

Carstensen, L. L. (1991). Selectivity theory: Social activity in life-span context. *Annual Review of Gerontology and Geriatrics, 11*(1), 195–217.

Carstensen, L. L., & Mikels, J. A. (2005). At the intersection of emotion and cognition: Aging and the positivity effect. *Current Directions in Psychological Science, 14*(3), 117–121.

Castel, A. D. (2005). Memory for grocery prices in younger and older adults: The role of schematic support. *Psychology and Aging, 20*(4), 718.

Chao, L.-W., Szrek, H., Pereira, N. S., & Pauly, M. V. (2009). Time preference and its relationship with age, health, and survival probability. *Judgment and Decision Making, 4*(1), 1–19. doi:10.1111/j.1746-1561.2010.00542.x.

Chen, Y., & Sun, Y. (2003). Age differences in financial decision-making: Using simple heuristics. *Educational Gerontology, 29*(7), 627–635.

Christensen, K., Doblhammer, G., Rau, R., & Vaupel, J. W. (2009). Ageing populations: The challenges ahead. *The Lancet, 374*(9696), 1196–1208.

Daselaar, S. M., Iyengar, V., Davis, S. W., Eklund, K., Hayes, S. M., & Cabeza, R. E. (2013). Less wiring, more firing: Low-performing older adults compensate for impaired white matter with greater neural activity. *Cerebral Cortex, 25*(4), 983–990.

Deakin, J., Aitken, M., Robbins, T., & Sahakian, B. J. (2004). Risk taking during decision-making in normal volunteers changes with age. *Journal of the International Neuropsychological Society: JINS, 10*(4), 590–598.

Denburg, Natalie L., Recknor, E. C., Bechara, A., & Tranel, D. (2006). Psychophysiological anticipation of positive outcomes promotes advantageous decision-making in normal older persons. *International Journal of Psychophysiology: Official Journal of the International Organization of Psychophysiology, 61*(1), 19–25.

Denburg, Nathalie L., Tranel, D., & Bechara, A. (2005). The ability to decide advantageously declines prematurely in some normal older persons. *Neuropsychologia*, *43*(7), 1099–1106.

Drolet, A., Schwarz, N., & Yoon, C. (2011). *The Aging Consumer: Perspectives from Psychology and Economics*. Routledge.

Eppinger, B., Nystrom, L. E., & Cohen, J. D. (2012). Reduced sensitivity to immediate reward during decision-making in older than younger adults. *PLoS One*, *7*(5), e36953. doi:10.1371/journal.pone.0036953.

Giorgio, A., Santelli, L., Tomassini, V., Bosnell, R., Smith, S., De Stefano, N., & Johansen-Berg, H. (2010). Age-related changes in grey and white matter structure throughout adulthood. *Neuroimage*, *51*(3), 943–951.

Grady, C. (2012). The cognitive neuroscience of ageing. *Nature Reviews Neuroscience*, *13*(7), 491.

Green, L., Myerson, J., & Ostaszewski, P. (1999). Discounting of delayed rewards across the life span: Age differences in individual discounting functions. *Behavioural Processes*, *46*(1), 89–96. doi:10.1016/S0376-6357(99)00021-2.

Hampton, W. (2018). *To Wait or to Lose? Framing Attenuates Delay Discounting Across the Lifespan*. Temple University Libraries.

Hampton, W. H., Alm, K. H., Venkatraman, V., Nugiel, T., & Olson, I. R. (2017). Dissociable frontostriatal white matter connectivity underlies reward and motor impulsivity. *NeuroImage*, *150*, 336–343. doi:10.1016/j.neuroimage.2017.02.021.

Hampton, W. H., Asadi, N., & Olson, I. R. (2018). Good things for those who wait: Predictive modeling highlights importance of delay discounting for income attainment. *Frontiers in Psychology*, *9*, 1545.

Han, S. D., Boyle, P. A., Yu, L., Fleischman, D. A., Arfanakis, K., & Bennett, D. A. (2013). Ventromedial PFC, parahippocampal, and cerebellar connectivity are associated with temporal discounting in old age. *Experimental Gerontology*, *48*(12), 1489–1498.

Hayashi, Y., Russo, C. T., & Wirth, O. (2015). Texting while driving as impulsive choice: A behavioral economic analysis. *Accident Analysis and Prevention*, *83*, 182–189. doi:10.1016/j.aap.2015.07.025.

Hedden, T., & Gabrieli, J. D. E. (2004). Insights into the ageing mind: A view from cognitive neuroscience. *Nature Reviews Neuroscience*, *5*(2), 87.

Henninger, D. E., Madden, D. J., & Huettel, S. A. (2010). Processing speed and memory mediate age-related differences in decision making. *Psychology and Aging*, *25*(2), 262.

Higbee, K. L., & Clay, S. L. (1998). College students' beliefs in the ten-percent myth. *The Journal of Psychology*, *132*(5), 469–476.

Jimura, K., Myerson, J., Hilgard, J., Keighley, J., Braver, T. S., & Green, L. (2011). Domain independence and stability in young and older adults' discounting of delayed rewards. *Behavioural Processes*, *87*(3), 253–259. doi:10.1016/j.beproc.2011.04.006.

Johnson, Matthew W., & Bickel, Warren K. (2002). Within-subject comparison of real and hypothetical money rewards in delay discounting. *Journal of the Experimental Analysis of Behavior*, *77*(2), 129–146.

Kirby, K. N. (2009). One-year temporal stability of delay-discount rates. *Psychonomic Bulletin and Review*, *16*(3), 457–462. doi:10.3758/PBR.16.3.457.

Kirby, K. N., Winston, G. C., & Santiesteban, M. (2005). Impatience and grades: Delay-discount rates correlate negatively with college GPA. *Learning and Individual Differences*, *15*(3), 213–222. doi:10.1016/j.lindif.2005.01.003.

Korniotis, G. M., & Kumar, A. (2011). Do older investors make better investment decisions? *The Review of Economics and Statistics*, *93*(1), 244–265.

LaCroix, A. Z., Guralnik, J. M., Berkman, L. F., Wallace, R. B., & Satterfield, S. (1993). Maintaining mobility in late life. II. Smoking, alcohol consumption, physical activity, and body mass index. *American Journal of Epidemiology, 137*(8), 858–869.

Lempert, K. M., & Phelps, E. A. (2016). The malleability of intertemporal choice. *Trends in Cognitive Sciences, 20*(1), 64–74. doi:10.1016/j.tics.2015.09.005.

Li, Y., Baldassi, M., Johnson, E. J., & Weber, E. U. (2013). Complementary cognitive capabilities, economic decision making, and aging. *Psychology and Aging, 28*(3), 595.

Li, Y., Gao, J., Enkavi, A. Z., Zaval, L., Weber, E. U., & Johnson, E. J. (2015). Sound credit scores and financial decisions despite cognitive aging. *Proceedings of the National Academy of Sciences of the United States of America, 112*(1), 65–69.

Lim, K. T. K., & Yu, R. (2015). Aging and wisdom: Age-related changes in economic and social decision making. *Frontiers in Aging Neuroscience, 7*, 120.

Lloyd-Sherlock, P. (2000). Population ageing in developed and developing regions: Implications for health policy. *Social Science and Medicine, 51*(6), 887–895.

Löckenhoff, C. E., O'Donoghue, T., & Dunning, D. (2011). Age differences in temporal discounting: The role of dispositional affect and anticipated emotions. *Psychology and Aging, 26*(2), 274–284. doi:10.1037/a0023280.

Loewenstein, G. F. (1988). Frames of mind in intertemporal choice. *Management Science, 34*(2), 200–214.

Loewenstein, G., & Lerner, J. S. (2003). The role of affect in decision making. *Handbook of Affective Science, 619*(642), 3.

Lutz, W., Sanderson, W., & Scherbov, S. (2008). The coming acceleration of global population ageing. *Nature, 451*(7179), 716.

Magen, E., Dweck, C. S., & Gross, J. J. (2008). The hidden-zero effect: Representing a single choice as an extended sequence reduces impulsive choice: Short report. *Psychological Science, 19*(7), 648–649. doi:10.1111/j.1467-9280.2008.02137.x.

Mata, R., Josef, A. K., Samanez-Larkin, G. R., & Hertwig, R. (2011). Age differences in risky choice: A meta-analysis. *Annals of the New York Academy of Sciences, 1235*(1), 18–29. doi:10.1111/j.1749-6632.2011.06200.x.

Mathers, C. D., Murray, C. J. L., Salomon, J. A., Sadana, R., Tandon, A., Lopez, A. D., Ustün, B., & Chatterji, S. (2003). Healthy life expectancy: Comparison of OECD countries in 2001. *Australian and New Zealand Journal of Public Health, 27*(1), 5–11.

Munnell, B. A. H., Webb, A., & Hou, W. (2014). How much should people save ? *Center for Retirement Research at Boston College*, (14), 1–8. Retrieved from http://crr.bc.edu/wp-content/uploads/2014/07/IB_14-111.pdf.

Myerson, J., & Green, L. (1995). Discounting of delayed rewards: Models of individual choice. *Journal of the Experimental Analysis of Behavior, 64*(3), 263–276. doi:10.1901/jeab.1995.64-263.

Naqvi, N., Shiv, B., & Bechara, A. (2006). The role of emotion in decision making: A cognitive neuroscience perspective. *Current Directions in Psychological Science, 15*(5), 260–264.

Nobahar Ahari, M., Nejati, V., & Hosseini, A. (2010). Comparing age-ralated changes of balance performance in youth and older adults. *Iranian Journal of Ageing, 5*(1), 0.

Odum, A. L. (2011). Delay discounting: I'm a k, you're a k. *Journal of the Experimental Analysis of Behavior, 96*(3), 427–439. doi:10.1901/jeab.2011.96-423.

Ohmura, Y., Takahashi, T., Kitamura, N., & Wehr, P. (2006). Three-month stability of delay and probability discounting measures. *Experimental and Clinical Psychopharmacology, 14*(3), 318–328. doi:10.1037/1064-1297.14.3.318.

Park, D. C., Lautenschlager, G., Hedden, T., Davidson, N. S., Smith, A. D., & Smith, P. K. (2002). Models of visuospatial and verbal memory across the adult life span. *Psychology and Aging, 17*(2), 299.

Park, D. C., & Reuter-Lorenz, P. (2009). The adaptive brain: Aging and neurocognitive scaffolding. *Annual Review of Psychology, 60*, 173–196.

Park, D., & Schwarz, N. (2012). *Cognitive Aging: A Primer.* Psychology Press.

Payne, J. W., Sagara, N., Shu, S. B., Appelt, K. C., & Johnson, E. J. (2013). Life expectancy as a constructed belief: Evidence of a live-to or die-by framing effect. *Journal of Risk and Uncertainty, 46*(1), 27–50. doi:10.1007/s11166-012-9158-0.

Penz, E., & Hogg, M. K. (2011). The role of mixed emotions in consumer behaviour: Investigating ambivalence in consumers' experiences of approach-avoidance conflicts in online and offline settings. *European Journal of Marketing, 45*(1/2), 104–132.

Peper, J. S., Mandl, R. C. W., Braams, B. R., De Water, E., Heijboer, A. C., Koolschijn, P. C. M. P., & Crone, E. A. (2013). Delay discounting and frontostriatal fiber tracts: A combined DTI and MTR study on impulsive choices in healthy young adults. *Cerebral Cortex, 23*(7), 1695–1702. doi:10.1093/cercor/bhs163.

Perry, J. L., Larson, E. B., German, J. P., Madden, G. J., & Carroll, M. E. (2005). Impulsivity (delay discounting) as a predictor of acquisition of IV cocaine self-administration in female rats. *Psychopharmacology, 178*(2–3), 193–201. doi:10.1007/s00213-004-1994-4.

Piper, B. J., Acevedo, S. F., Edwards, K. R., Curtiss, A. B., McGinnis, G. J., & Raber, J. (2011). Age, sex, and handedness differentially contribute to neurospatial function on the Memory Island and Novel-Image Novel-Location tests. *Physiology and Behavior, 103*(5), 513–522. doi:10.1016/j.physbeh.2011.03.024.

Poterba, J. (2004). *The Impact of Population Aging on Financial Markets.* National Bureau of Economic Research.

Prelec, D., & Loewenstein, G. (1998). The red and the black: Mental accounting of savings and debt. *Marketing Science, 17*(1), 4–28. doi:10.1287/mksc.17.1.4.

Raji, C. A., Lopez, O. L., Kuller, L. H., Carmichael, O. T., & Becker, J. T. (2009). Age, Alzheimer disease, and brain structure. *Neurology, 73*(22), 1899–1905.

Rasmussen, E. B., Lawyer, S. R., & Reilly, W. (2010). Percent body fat is related to delay and probability discounting for food in humans. *Behavioural Processes, 83*(1), 23–30. doi:10.1016/j.beproc.2009.09.001.

Read, D., & Read, N. L. (2004a). Time discounting over the lifespan. *Organizational Behavior and Human Decision Processes, 94*(1), 22–32. doi:10.1016/j.obhdp.2004.01.002.

Read, D., & Read, N. L. (2004b). Time discounting over the lifespan. *Organizational Behavior and Human Decision Processes, 94*(1), 22–32. doi:10.1016/j.obhdp.2004.01.002.

Rieger, M., & Mata, R. (2015). On the generality of age differences in social and nonsocial decision making. *The Journals of Gerontology: Series B, Psychological Sciences and Social Sciences, 70*(2), 202–214. doi:10.1093/geronb/gbt088.

Roalf, D. R., Mitchell, S. H., Harbaugh, W. T., & Janowsky, J. S. (2012). Risk, reward, and economic decision making in aging. *Journals of Gerontology—Series B—Psychological Sciences and Social Sciences, 67 B*(3), 289–298. doi:10.1093/geronb/gbr099.

Russell, J. A. (1980). A circumplex model of affect. *Journal of Personality and Social Psychology, 39*(6), 1161.

Rutledge, R. B., Skandali, N., Dayan, P., & Dolan, R. J. (2015). Dopaminergic modulation of decision making and subjective well-being. *Journal of Neuroscience, 35*(27), 9811–9822.

Rutledge, R. B., Smittenaar, P., Zeidman, P., Brown, H. R., Adams, R. A., Lindenberger, U., Dayan, P., & Dolan, R. J. (2016). Risk taking for potential reward decreases across the lifespan. *Current Biology, 26*(12), 1634–1639.

Salthouse, T. (2000). *A Theory of Cognitive Aging* (Vol. *28*). Elsevier.

Salthouse, T. A. (1996). The processing-speed theory of adult age differences in cognition. *Psychological Review, 103*(3), 403.

Samanez-Larkin, G. R., Gibbs, S. E. B., Khanna, K., Nielsen, L., Carstensen, L. L., & Knutson, B. (2007). Anticipation of monetary gain but not loss in healthy older adults. *Nature Neuroscience, 10*(6), 787.

Samanez-Larkin, G. R., & Knutson, B. (2015). Decision making in the ageing brain: Changes in affective and motivational circuits. *Nature Reviews Neuroscience, 16*(5), 278–289. doi:10.1038/nrn3917.

Samanez-Larkin, G. R., Kuhnen, C. M., Yoo, D. J., & Knutson, B. (2010). Variability in nucleus accumbens activity mediates age-related suboptimal financial risk taking. *Journal of Neuroscience, 30*(4), 1426–1434.

Samanez-Larkin, G. R., Mata, R., Radu, P. T., Ballard, I. C., Carstensen, L. L., & McClure, S. M. (2011). Age differences in striatal delay sensitivity during intertemporal choice in healthy adults. *Frontiers in Neuroscience, 5*(NOV), 126. doi:10.3389/fnins.2011.00126.

Sasse, L. K., Peters, J., & Brassen, S. (2017). Cognitive control modulates effects of episodic simulation on delay discounting in aging. *Frontiers in Aging Neuroscience, 9*, 58.

Schneider, E. L., & Guralnik, J. M. (1990). The aging of America: Impact on health care costs. *JAMA, 263*(17), 2335–2340.

Seaman, K. L., Gorlick, M. A., Vekaria, K. M., Hsu, M., Zald, D. H., & Samanez-Larkin, G. R. (2016). Adult age differences in decision making across domains: Increased discounting of social and health-related rewards. *Psychology and Aging, 31*(7), 737–746. doi:10.1037/pag0000131.

Shefrin, H. M., & Thaler, R. H. (1988). The behavioral life-cycle hypthesis. *Economic Inquiry, 26*(4), 609–643.

Shu, S. B., Zeithammer, R., & Payne, J. W. (2016). Consumer preferences for annuity attributes: Beyond net present value. *Journal of Marketing Research, 53*(2), 240–262.

Social Security Administration (2014). Social security basic facts.

Tinker, A. (2002). *The Social Implications of an Ageing Population.* Elsevier.

Tversky, A., & Kahneman, D. (1992). Advances in prospect theory: Cumulative representation of uncertainty. *Journal of Risk and Uncertainty, 5*(4), 297–323. doi:10.1007/BF00122574.

Tymula, A., Belmaker, L. A. R., Ruderman, L., Glimcher, P. W., & Levy, I. (2013). Like cognitive function, decision making across the life span shows profound age-related changes. *Proceedings of the National Academy of Sciences of the United States of America, 110*(42), 17143–17148.

U.S. Census Bureau (2019). Age and Sex Composition in the United States: 2019. Retrieved from https://www.census.gov/data/tables/2019/demo/age-and-sex/2019-age-sex-composition.html.

van den Bos, W., Rodriguez, C. A., Schweitzer, J. B., & McClure, S. M. (2015). Adolescent impatience decreases with increased frontostriatal connectivity. *Proceedings of the National Academy of Sciences of the United States of America, 112*(29), E3765–E3774. doi:10.1073/pnas.1423095112.

Vaupel, J. W. (2010). Biodemography of human ageing. *Nature, 464*(7288), 536.

Venkatraman, V., Payne, J. W., Bettman, J. R., Luce, M. F., & Huettel, S. A. (2009). Separate neural mechanisms underlie choices and strategic preferences in risky decision making. *Neuron, 62*(4), 593–602.

Venkatraman, V., Payne, J. W., & Huettel, S. A. (2011). 7 Neuroeconomics of risky decisions: From variables to strategies. *Attention and Performance, 23*, 153.

Venkatraman, V., Payne, J. W., & Huettel, S. A. (2014). An overall probability of winning heuristic for complex risky decisions: Choice and eye fixation evidence. *Organizational Behavior and Human Decision Processes, 125*(2), 73–87.

Venkatraman, V., Yoon, S., & Vo, K. (n.d.). Adaptivity in decision-making strategies across age: Process insights and implications. *The Journal of Marketing Behavior.*

Watson, D., Wiese, D., Vaidya, J., & Tellegen, A. (1999). The two general activation systems of affect: Structural findings, evolutionary considerations, and psychobiological evidence. *Journal of Personality and Social Psychology, 76*(5), 820.

Weber, E. U., Blais, A., & Betz, N. E. (2002). A domain-specific risk-attitude scale: Measuring risk perceptions and risk behaviors. *Journal of Behavioral Decision Making, 15*(4), 263–290.

Whelan, R., & Mchugh, L. A. (2009). Temporal discounting of hypothetical monetary rewards by adolescents, adults, and older adults. Retrieved May 8, 2018, from The Psychological Record website: https://search.proquest.com/docview/722352373?pq-origsite=gscholar.

Zamarian, L., Sinz, H., Bonatti, E., Gamboz, N., & Delazer, M. (2008). Normal aging affects decisions under ambiguity, but not decisions under risk. *Neuropsychology, 22*(5), 645.

6

EFFECTS OF AGE ON SHOPPING BEHAVIOR FOR CONSUMER PACKAGED GOODS

Anand V. Bodapati and Aimee Drolet

Introduction

It is important for marketers to understand the effects of age on consumer decision-making because the usefulness of different marketing strategies depends on it. One large effect due to increasing age is the shift in consumer demand for different types of products. In the previous volume of *The Aging Consumer*, Hurd and Rohwedder (2010) found large differences in how older adults versus young adults spend their money. They found that older adults spend relatively more of their income in the domains of health care and charitable giving and relatively less in the domains of clothing and travel. Hurd and Rohwedder link these age-related changes in spending to life-stage factors, such as the presence of children in the home and whether the consumer is working versus retired.

Hurd and Rohwedder's (2010) study is among the few studies that have documented age-related differences in consumer spending across major consumption domains, such as health care and travel. Even fewer studies have investigated age-related differences in spending behavior specifically for consumer package goods (CPG), which are products that consumers use up and replace on a frequent basis, such as grocery products. This is surprising given that scanner data on grocery store expenditures is increasingly available to academics. Indeed, we could find only one paper by Boatwright, Dhar, and Rossi (2004) that explicitly investigated the effect of age on consumer spending in the domain of CPG. However, their investigation was limited in several important ways. First, they examined only one CPG category, coffee. Second, their unit of analysis was at the store chain level and market level rather than at the individual consumer level. As a result, their analysis did not test for the effect of age per se but instead compared aggregate sales response across markets whose median age differed; for example, they compared the Cleveland market which has a median age of 37 to the Atlanta market which has a median age of 33). Third, their analysis also did not control for individual household income. Instead, the researchers relied on a measure of wealth derived from geospatial data.

In the present chapter, we report the results of an analysis of age effects on spending behavior in a total of 29 different CPG categories. Our analysis was confined to single-person households and controlled for individual-level household income. Specifically, we analyzed spending for food staples (coffee, cold cereal, margarine and butter, mayonnaise, milk, soup, yogurt, ketchup and mustard, peanut butter, and spaghetti sauce) and household staples (i.e., laundry detergent, toilet paper, facial tissue, paper towels, and household cleaner). Further, we analyzed spending in categories where changes in buying behavior should be related to life-stage changes. For example, we examined the diapers category where one would expect expenditures to decline with age due to the absence of young children in the household.

Our analysis also included categories related to participation (or lack of participation) in the workforce. In particular, we examined the effect of age on expenditures for food items such as frozen dinner entrees and frozen pizza. Briefly, we expected that age would have a decreasing effect on expenditures in these categories due to an increase in the amount of time older consumers have available to prepare meals. We also examined age-related differences in spending in categories related to personal grooming such as toothbrush, toothpaste, razor blades, and deodorant. We note that spending in these categories might decline upon retiring from the workforce but also due to the onset of age-related diseases, such as Alzheimer's and Parkinson's, that are associated with a decline in personal grooming. Finally, given the increasing effect of age on consumers' health and health concerns, we also included in our analysis several categories related to dietary health: sugar substitutes, salty snacks, carbonated soda, beer, and cigarettes.

We investigated the effect of age on a variety of buying behaviors that one might expect to vary by age and CPG category. In particular, we focused on age-related differences in buying volume, brand loyalty, unit size, mean volume per shopping occasion, and size loyalty. We also examined the effect of age on other shopping-behavior metrics, in particular shopping trip frequency, inter-trip gap stability, time of day, day of week, store loyalty, and preferred store size.

Last, in addition to investigating the effect of age on spending behaviors across the 29 CPG categories, we investigated the effect of age on consumer response to marketers' promotional activities, including feature advertising, in-store displays, and price promotions. The present chapter is the first research we are aware of that tests for age differences in consumer responsiveness to marketing efforts in the CPG context.

Method

Some past studies, including Hurd and Rohwedder (2010), have examined the effect of age on grocery shopping behavior (Goodwin and MxElwee, 1999; Hare,

2003; Meneely, Strugnell, and Burns 2009; Hurd and Rohwedder, 2010; Angell et al., 2012). The studies that have examined age differences in grocery shopping behavior rely on survey data. There are several potential problems with statistical analyses based on surveys in which consumers were polled about their preferences and behaviors. First, the target population may not be properly represented by the survey population. Second, survey respondents may not accurately report their behavior or do so in insufficient detail and with inadequate temporal coverage. Indeed, human respondents are frequently inaccurate in their reports of the relative frequencies of their behaviors, such as how often they buy their most favorite brand versus their second-most favorite brand or shop in two stores. A notable exception occurs when virtually all behavior is concentrated exclusively on shopping for one brand or in one store.

These concerns are mitigated if one uses behavioral data from balanced, carefully constructed samples. Such behavioral data exist in the United States and some parts of Europe and are widely available because these regions have highly developed market research industries with some providers having invested heavily in data recording infrastructures. However, for a proper behavioral analysis, one needs data on what a consumer buys and *also* data on what is offered to the consumer by the retailers. Datasets that recorded data on both the consumer and the retailer in a coherent consistent manner are called "singe source datasets."[1]

Information Resources, Incorporated (IRI) Data

For the present study, we use a dataset that Information Resources, Incorporated released to academics in 2008 (see Bronnenberg, Kruger, and Mela, 2008). The panel dataset contained in this release was from two "BehaviorScan markets": Eau Claire, Wisconsin and Pittsfield, Massachusetts. A BehaviorScan market is an unusual infrastructural setup that requires some explanation. A primary goal of IRI in creating these market setups was to be able to determine how television advertising influences grocery shopping behavior. Accordingly, it needed to be able to record television viewing of households and the advertisements that the households were exposed to. IRI found that cable television viewing was much easier to capture via electronic devices IRI connected to the cable boxes than with over-the-air television watching, where the transmission could not be similarly trapped and observed. As a result, IRI decided to locate panels in small towns that are too far from the major metros to receive over-the-air TV signals and thus depended on the local cable companies for TV programming. IRI then connected the electronic devices to the cable boxes to be able to observe which consumers were exposed to which TV advertisements.

IRI also partnered with grocery stores and drugstores to install scanners to record which products the panelists purchased. Panel members were incentivized to participate by being eligible for prizes in drawings. Each panelist was provided with an IRI panelist membership card that he/she presented at checkout on every store visit. Therefore, IRI had records of exactly what each panelist purchased at each participating store. Not all stores in these cities participated in the IRI's data collection infrastructure. To capture purchasing made by the panelists outside of the infrastructurally-connected stores, panelists scanned those purchases with handheld scanners and recorded where the product was purchased, and the quantity and price.

IRI recognized that the exposure rate of many TV advertisements can be small and that to get enough a sufficiently large sample of panelists who are exposed to a certain category of TV advertisements, it would need a moderately large sample size in each city. The number of panelists is approximately 5100 in the Pittsfield market and 5800 in the Eau Claire market. Samples of such large sizes are unusual in panel datasets. Having a large sample size is meritorious because it allows us to select smaller segments and still retain a sample of substantial size. This is particularly important for our study because we focus on single-person households. Using multi-person households is problematic in that we do not know who has made the purchase decision and who is the target of the purchase. Therefore, we use only single-person households which comprise approximately 13 percent of all households. Even after sampling down to such a small segment, we are left with 656 households in the Pittsfield market, still a large enough sample size for substantial analysis. However, Eau Claire has significantly fewer single-person households and so we did not work with that market.

To ensure that its sampling was balanced and representative, IRI recorded a set of demographic variables for each of its panelists, including the householder's age, income, education, ethnicity, and marital status. Across our sub-sample of 656 single-person households, the median income interval is $35000–$45000, with the 25th percentile interval being $20000–$25000 and the 75th percentile interval being $45000–$55000. Almost 60 percent of the households are age 65 or over, consistent with the fact that in the United States the majority of single-person households consist of older adults. In this sub-sample, only about 2 percent of the households are Hispanic; this is well below the 6 percent that Hispanics currently occupy in Pittsfield and the roughly 15 percent for the United States as a whole. This does not, however, necessarily point to non-representativeness of our sample among single-person households because Hispanics tend to live in multi-person households and are therefore in lower occurrence in even a representative sample of single-person households. The median level of education in the sample corresponds to high-school graduation and attendance at a technical school but not attendance at college.

Grocery Store and Drug Store Spending Behaviors

The IRI dataset reports the following raw data for each panelist trip during which at least one item was purchased: store ID, panelist ID, shopping date, hour of the day, and total purchase amount. We also have a data file that provides basic information about the store, specifically whether it is a grocery store or a drug store, its size in terms of total sales volume, its geographical region, and the masked name of the store chain that it belongs to. This store data file allowed us to construct groupings or subsets of stores as grocery store, drug store, or all stores combined. Based on the raw data for each consumer, we computed 42 measures for each of the three groupings of stores Across these three groupings, these 42 measures total to $42 \times 3 = 126$ measures.

Table 6.1 reports the age effect sizes and statistical significances for each of the 42 measures in each of the three store groupings. For any one grouping of stores, the 42 measures that are computed are listed in the first column of Table 6.1 with conceptually similar measures collected together in the same block. The distinct blocks of measures correspond conceptually to the following behavioral aspects:

1. Volume of shopping by dollar expenditure and occurrence frequency per unit time
2. Distribution of trip occasions over day-parts and days of the week
3. Distribution of dollar expenditure over day-parts and days of the week
4. Degree of store loyalty in terms of concentration of trip occasions in a small subset of stores
5. Degree of store loyalty in terms of concentration of dollar expenditure in a small subset of stores
6. Size of the most patronized store, by volume or number of trip occasions
7. Two characterizations of the distribution of the number of hours between two successive store visits, i.e. the median and the interquartile (IQR) range
8. Two characterizations of the distribution of the dollar expenditure on a store visit, i.e. the median and the IQR
9. An aggregation of measures 2 through 5 at the level of the weekday vs. weekend-day or the day of week or day-part where the most shopping happens

Within-Category Purchase Behaviors

For each product category it covers, the IRI data set reports the following raw data for each panelist for each purchase: universal product code (UPC) for the product being purchased, number of units purchased, price paid, store ID of the store where the purchase happened, week (but not the exact date or time) when the purchase happened. There is a separate data file that lists, for each store-UPC-week tuple, the price of the product, whether it was on sale, and whether it was featured in the store flyer or was on special display. Based on these raw data, we computed 15 measures that characterize each consumer's purchase behaviors in each of the 29 CPG categories. This yields a total of $29 \times 15 = 435$ measures across all the categories. We list the 15 measures below, noting as before that conceptually similar measures were collected together in the same block.

TABLE 6.1 Age Effect Sizes on Store Visitation Characteristics and Their Significance Levels

	Characteristic	All Stores		Drug Stores		Grocery Stores	
		Store Subset Considered					
Block 1	Number of trips	0.10	★	0.15	★★★	0.05	
	Expenditure	−0.05		0.10	★	−0.07	
Block 2	% of trips 12am−6am	−0.10	★	NA		−0.10	★
	% of trips 6am−12pm	0.26	★★★	0.08		0.25	★★★
	% of trips 12pm−6pm	0.10	★	0.08		0.10	★
	% of trips 6pm−12am	−0.52	★★★	−0.32	★★★	−0.50	★★★
	% of trips Mon	0.04		0.16	★★	0.04	
	% of trips Tue	0.00		−0.02		0.01	
	% of trips Wed	0.03		−0.07		0.03	
	% of trips Thur	0.06		−0.04		0.07	
	% of trips Fri	0.12	★★	0.04		0.12	★★
	% of trips Sat	−0.02		−0.07		−0.01	
	% of trips Sun	−0.23	★★★	−0.01		−0.25	★★★
Block 3	% of spend 12am−6am	−0.05		NA		−0.05	
	% of spend 6am−12pm	0.24	★★★	0.08		0.24	★★★
	% of spend 12pm−6pm	0.09	★	0.07		0.10	★
	% of spend 12pm−6pm	−0.50	★★★	−0.32	★★★	−0.49	★★★
	% of spend Mon	0.05		0.13	★	0.06	
	% of spend Tue	0.04		0.00		0.04	
	% of spend Wed	0.00		−0.05		0.00	
	% of spend Thur	0.07		−0.06		0.07	
	% of spend Fri	0.11	★★	0.05		0.10	★
	% of spend Sat	−0.01		−0.08		−0.01	
	% of spend Sun	−0.24	★★★	−0.01		−0.24	★★★
Block 4	% of trips in the most visited store	−0.07		−0.11	★	−0.02	
	% of trips in the 2 most visited stores	−0.10	★	−0.07		−0.03	
	% of trips in the 3 most visited stores	−0.10	★	−0.07		−0.01	
Block 5	% of spend in the most spent-at store	−0.04		−0.10	★	−0.01	
	% of spend in the 2 most spent-at stores	−0.06		−0.08		−0.02	
	% of spend in the 3 most spent-at stores	−0.08		−0.04		−0.02	
Block 6	Size of the most visited store	−0.15	★★★	−0.06		−0.15	★★★
	Size of the most spent-at store	−0.15	★★★	−0.05		−0.16	★★★

(*Continued*)

TABLE 6.1 Continued

		Store Subset Considered					
	Characteristic	All Stores		Drug Stores		Grocery Stores	
Block 7	Median of inter-trip time	−0.07		−0.15	★	−0.06	
	IQR (std.dev) of inter-trip times	−0.15	★★★	−0.25	★★★	−0.10	★
Block 8	Median spend across trips	−0.05		−0.07		−0.03	
	IQR (std.dev) spend of across trips	−0.13	★★	0.03		−0.13	★★
Block 9	% of spend on weekdays	0.16	★★★	0.06		0.16	★★★
	% of visits on weekdays	0.16	★★★	0.05		0.16	★★★
	% of spend on most spent-at day of week	0.08	★	−0.21	★★★	0.09	★
	% of trips on most shopped-at day-part	0.20	★★★	−0.09		0.21	★★★

Key: ★ = p-value < 0.05; ★★ = p-value < 0.01; ★★★ = p-value < 0.001.

The distinct blocks of measures correspond conceptually to the following behavioral aspects:

1. Level of purchase participation in the category
2. Extent of concentration of purchasing with respect to only one or two brands, either in terms of the number of purchase occasions or in the dollar expenditure
3. Two characterizations of the distribution of product sizes across purchase occasions, the median and the IQR. We also consider the expenditure-weighted version of the distribution
4. Promotion responsiveness
5. Typical amount purchased per occasion when a purchase was made in the category

The 29 categories recorded in IRI's academic data set span a wide range of spending measures: average annual household expenditure, fraction of households buying in that category, purchase frequency, perishability, and promotion intensity.[2] In total, we examined the following CPG categories: (1) toilet paper; (2) toothbrush; (3) toothpaste; (4) beer; (5) razor blades; (6) carbonated beverages; (7) cigarettes;

(8) coffee; (9) cold cereal; (10) facial tissues; (11) margarine and butter; (12) mayonnaise; (13) milk; (14) salty snacks; (15) shampoo; (16) soup; (17) yogurt; (18) deodorant; (19) diapers; (20) frozen pizza; (21) household cleaner; (22) frozen dinner entrees; (23) hot dogs; (24) laundry detergent; (25) mustard and ketchup; (26) paper towels; (27) peanut butter; (28) spaghetti sauce; and (29) sugar substitute.

Approach to Statistical Analysis

Pooling across the two broad categories of behaviors listed above, we computed a total of 435 + 126 = 562 metrics for each consumer. For each of these 561 metrics, we fit a regression model predicting that metric as a function of the age bucket provided by IRI. We estimated standardized regressions where the predictor variable is standardized to mean 0 and variance 1 so that the regression coefficient is scale independent and can be interpreted as an effect size. If, for a particular metric, the regression coefficient is statistically insignificant or if the effect size is small, it would indicate that older consumers are no different from younger consumers on that metric. If, on the other hand, the regression coefficient is significant and the effect size large, it would suggest that older consumers are higher or lower than younger consumers on that metric, depending on the sign of the regression coefficient.

Because income is an important driver of many of these behavioral metrics and income is correlated with age, we needed to understand the age effect apart from the income effect. Accordingly, we also included in our regression models the household's income bucket as provided by IRI in addition to age bucket.

On the whole, we did not have strong predictions, largely because there is little to no relevant past research to go on. We had very general expectations that, for example, age would have a negative effect on spending in the diapers category due to the decreased presence of children in the house. We would also expect that age would have a negative effect on spending in categories related to employment status, such as quick-serve foods (e.g., frozen dinners) and personal grooming. With respect to the latter, one might expect that age would have a decreasing effect on spending in personal grooming categories. Age is associated with a lower rate of work force participation and a higher rate of diseases like Alzheimer's that interfere with older adults' ability to engage in personal grooming.

In contrast, we generally expected that age would have a positive effect on dieting behavior. For example, older adults may spend relatively more than young adults on sugar substitutes due to age-related medical conditions such as diabetes and obesity. We also generally expected, based on past findings, that older (vs. younger) consumers might be more brand loyal and more store loyal (Lambert-Pandraud, Laurent, and Lapersonne, 2005; Lapersonne, Laurent, and Le Goff, 1995). Next, we describe the results of our analysis, and review our expectations with respect to the different relationships between age and each behavior measure.

Results

Age and Shopping Trip Behavior

Trip Frequency and Expenditure

There is a positive effect of age on purchase trips per unit time for grocery store and drug store trips combined. Older adults make more purchase trips per unit time. However, this effect is driven by older consumers making more trips to drug stores. Age does not have a significant effect on grocery store trip frequency. Age also had no effect on grocery store expenditures but did have a significant effect on drug store expenditures. See Table 6.2.

TABLE 6.2 Standardized Beta for Variable Age

Category	# Purchase Occasions	Total Spend in Category	# Units Bought	Total Volume in Category
Beer	−0.14***	−0.13***	−0.14***	−0.12**
Carbonated beverages	−0.20***	−0.20***	−0.16***	−0.19***
Cigarettes	−0.08	−0.10**	−0.10**	−0.10**
Coffee	+0.06ˢ	+0.02	+0.07	+0.02
Cold cereal	−0.14***	−0.15***	−0.14***	−0.15***
Deodorant	−0.05 ᴺˢ	−0.06	−0.05	−0.05
Diapers	−0.13***	−0.14***	−0.13**	−0.14***
Facial tissue	+0.16***	+0.11**	+0.12**	+0.12**
Frozen dinners	+0.08*	+0.05	+0.05	+0.05
Frozen pizza	−0.09*	−0.13***	−0.10**	−0.16***
Household cleaner	+0.02 ᴺˢ	+0.03	+0.02	+0.02
Hot dogs	−0.04	−0.04	−0.07	−0.08
Laundry detergent	−0.02	−0.09*	−0.08	−0.13***
Margarine/butter	+0.06	+0.04	+0.02	−0.02
Mayonnaise	−0.06	−0.08*	−0.08*	−0.09*
Milk	+0.04	−0.01*	+0.01	−0.14***
Mustard/ketchup	−0.12**	−0.15***	−0.13***	−0.18***
Paper Towels	+0.08*	+0.08*	+0.06	+0.07
Peanut butter	−0.02	−0.07	−0.03	−0.05
Razor blades	−0.09*	−0.12**	−0.08*	−0.19***
Salty snacks	−0.19***	−0.18***	−0.15***	−0.18***
Shampoo	−0.15***	−0.18***	−0.16***	−0.17***
Soup	+0.14***	+0.08*	+0.12**	+0.10**
Spaghetti sauce	−0.16***	−0.18***	−0.16***	−0.17***
Sugar substitute	+0.09*	+0.09*	+0.09*	+0.10*
Toilet tissue	+0.05	+0.03	+0.01	+0.01
Toothbrush	−0.09*	−0.11**	−0.10**	−0.10**
Toothpaste	+0.03	+0.02	+0.03	−0.01
Yogurt	−0.08*	−0.10**	−0.08*	−0.10*

Key: * = p-value < 0.05; ** = p-value < 0.01; *** = p-value < 0.001.

Inter-Trip Gap Stability

Analysis finds that the inter-trip gap is more stable among older (vs. younger) consumers. Older consumers are more regular in their trip timing. This finding holds for both grocery stores and drug stores. See Table 6.1.

Time of Day

Age has an enormous influence on what time of day consumers chose to shop at. Specifically, compared to younger consumers, older consumers are much more likely to shop between 6 am and 12 noon, somewhat more likely to shop from between 12 noon and 6 pm, and much less likely to shop between 6 pm and 6 am. These results make sense insofar as work force participation is lower among older adults. See Table 6.1.

Day of Week

With respect to grocery stores, older consumers were much more likely than their younger counterparts to shop on Fridays and much less likely to shop on the weekends. Further, older consumers are much more likely than are younger consumers to shop in drug stores on Mondays. See Table 6.1.

Time of Day Loyalty and Day of Week Loyalty

Compared to younger consumers, older consumers are more likely to shop in the same time-of-day slot and on the same day of the week repeatedly. See Table 6.1. This result accords with past research showing that older adults are generally more habit driven compared to young adults (e.g., Drolet, Bodapati, Suppes, Rossi, and Hochwarter, 2016).

Store Loyalty

We created a store loyalty measure which is the fraction of trips or purchases accounted for by the first, second, or third most-frequented stores by an individual consumer. Against strong expectation, we found that older consumers were less store loyal, especially with respect to drug stores (see Table 6.1). This unexpected result might be due to an increase in free time among older consumers (e.g., retirees).

Preferred Store Size

We created a proxy measure of store size by examining sales in dollars (per store), with larger sales indicating a larger-sized store and smaller sales indicating a smaller-sized store. Analysis found that the size of the most-frequented grocery store is smaller for older consumers than for younger consumers. See Table 6.1. It may be that older consumers prefer shopping in stores that are physically smaller. Of course, further analysis is needed to determine what factors account for this particular finding.

Age and Category-Wise Buying Behavior

Buying Volume

We found large differences across categories with respect to whether age had a significant increasing or decreasing effect on buying volume. Older consumers in our sample spent more in the following categories: (1) facial tissue; (2) paper towels; (3) soup; and (4) sugar substitutes. They spent less in the following categories: (1) beer; (2) razor blades; (3) carbonated beverages; (4) cold cereal; (5) diapers; (6) frozen pizza; (7) mustard and ketchup; (8) salty snacks; (9) shampoo; (10) spaghetti sauce; (11) toothbrushes; and (12) yogurt. See Table 6.2.

Brand Loyalty

Consistent with past research showing an increasing effect of age on brand loyalty (e.g., Lambert-Pandraud, Laurent, and Lapersonne, 2005; Lapersonne, Laurent, and Le Goff, 1995), there were no categories in which older consumers are less loyal compared to younger consumers. Moreover, older consumers were more brand loyal compared to younger consumers in the following categories: (1) razor blades; (2) carbonated beverages; (3) cold cereal; (4) mayonnaise; (5) salty snacks; (6) shampoo; and (7) spaghetti sauce. See Table 6.3.

Unit Size

Looking that the across-shopping-occasion median unit size, we see that except for the category of razor blades, there are no categories where older consumers typically bought larger unit sizes. Moreover, compared to young adults, older adults buy significantly more smaller units in the following categories: (1) frozen pizza; (2) laundry detergent; (3) margarine and butter; (4) milk; (5) mustard and ketchup; (6) salty snacks; and (7) toothpaste. See Table 6.4.

Mean Volume per Shopping Occasion

In none of the 29 categories did older (vs. younger) consumers buy more volume of product per shopping occasion. In fact, they buy less volume of product per shopping occasion in many categories, including: (1) frozen dinner entrees; (2) frozen pizza; (3) hot dogs; (4) laundry detergent; (5) margarine and butter; (6) milk; (7) mustard and ketchup; (8) shampoo; (9) soup; (10) spaghetti sauce; and (11) toothpaste. See Table 6.4.

TABLE 6.3 Standardized Beta for Variable Age

Category	Occasions w/ Top Brand	Occasions w/ Top 2 Brands	Spend w/ Top Brand	Spend w/Top 2 Brands
Beer	+0.09	+0.03	+0.10	+0.03
Carbonated beverages	+0.11**	+0.15***	+0.08*	+0.13**
Cigarettes	+0.04	+0.08	+0.03	+0.05
Coffee	0.00	+0.02	+0.01	0.00
Cold cereal	+0.17***	+0.20***	+0.16***	+0.21***
Deodorant	+0.05	+0.02	+0.05	−0.01
Diapers	+0.16	0.00	+0.14	0.00
Facial tissue	−0.03	−0.05	−0.02	−0.06
Frozen dinners	−0.02	−0.10*	−0.04	−0.10*
Frozen pizza	+0.09	+0.06	0.10*	+0.09
Household cleaner	+0.06	+0.09	+0.05	+0.10
Hot dogs	+0.07	+0.07	+0.08	+0.07
Laundry detergent	+0.03	+0.04	+0.02	+0.05
Margarine/butter	−0.02	−0.05	−0.04	−0.04
Mayonnaise	+0.10*	+0.11**	0.10*	+0.10*
Milk	+0.01	+0.02	0.00	+0.01
Mustard/ketchup	0.00	+0.02	+0.01	+0.04
Paper towels	−0.05	−0.04	−0.01	−0.04
Peanut butter	−0.02	0.00	−0.05	−0.01
Razor blades	+0.18**	+0.15*	+0.19**	+0.12
Salty snacks	+0.14***	+0.17***	+0.15***	0.20***
Shampoo	+0.21***	+0.17**	+0.20***	0.19***
Soup	−0.06	−0.08	−0.05	−0.08*
Spaghetti sauce	+0.06	+0.09*	+0.09	+0.10*
Sugar substitute	+0.03	−0.06	−0.03	−0.04
Toilet tissue	−0.04	−0.06	−0.05	−0.04
Toothbrush	+0.12	+0.08	+0.12	+0.09
Toothpaste	+0.07	+0.09	+0.08	+0.09
Yogurt	−0.04	+0.03	−0.04	0.00

Key: * = p-value < 0.05; ** = p-value < 0.01; *** = p-value < 0.001.

Product Size Loyalty

To study the effect of age on consumer loyalty to size of per unit product, we examined the "spread" of sizes bought by each consumer. There are no categories for which older (vs. younger) consumers are less size loyal. They are more size loyal in the following nine categories: (1) coffee; (2) frozen pizza; (3) margarine and butter; (4) milk; (5) mustard and ketchup; (6) peanut butter; (7) salty snacks; (8) shampoo; and (9) spaghetti sauce. See Table 6.4.

TABLE 6.4 Standardized Beta for Variable Age

Category	Median Size across Occasions	Variation of Size across Occasions	Median Size Weighted by Spend	Variation of Size Weighted by Spend
Beer	+0.05	+0.01	+0.08	−0.02
Carbonated beverages	−0.02	0.00	−0.07	−0.05
Cigarettes	+0.04	+0.06	+0.05	+0.06
Coffee	−0.09	−0.13*	−0.09	−0.14*
Cold cereal	−0.03	+0.06	−0.03	+0.04
Deodorant	NA	NA	NA	NA
Diapers	−0.24*	−0.27*	−0.24*	−0.29**
Facial tissue	−0.03	+0.01	+0.06	+0.01
Frozen dinners	−0.02	+0.03	−0.03	+0.03
Frozen pizza	−0.13**	−0.10*	−0.13**	−0.14**
Household cleaner	+0.07	0.00	+0.06	0.00
Hot dogs	−0.01	+0.07	+0.08	+0.07
Laundry detergent	−0.22***	−0.08	−0.22***	−0.05
Margarine/butter	−0.18***	−0.13**	−0.18***	−0.06
Mayonnaise	−0.04	−0.08	−0.05	−0.05
Milk	−0.22***	−0.15***	−0.21***	−0.12**
Mustard/ketchup	−0.15***	−0.14**	−0.18***	−0.16***
Paper towels	0.00	+0.02	+0.03	−0.02
Peanut butter	−0.06	−0.14**	−0.09	−0.13**
Razor blades	+0.15*	−0.05	+0.18**	−0.04
Salty snacks	−0.18***	−0.18***	−0.16***	−0.11**
Shampoo	−0.08	−0.22***	−0.01	−0.22***
Soup	−0.06	−0.06	−0.02	−0.03
Spaghetti sauce	−0.10*	−0.06	−0.07	−0.12**
Sugar substitute	+0.18*	+0.13	+0.14	+0.11
Toilet tissue	−0.04	0.00	−0.05	+0.02
Toothbrush	NA	NA	NA	NA
Toothpaste	−0.20***	−0.01	−0.19***	−0.05
Yogurt	0.00	−0.05	+0.01	−0.07

Key: * = p-value < 0.05; ** = p-value < 0.01; *** = p-value < 0.001.

Aging and Response to Marketers' Promotion Efforts

As mentioned above, a novel aspect of our study is its examination of the effect of age on consumer response to marketers' promotional activities. Controlling for income, we tested for age differences in consumer response to: (1) feature advertising; (2) in-store displays; and (3) price promotions. On the whole, analysis found relatively few significant age differences in consumers' response to promotional efforts.

Feature-Advertising Response

There is no category where feature-advertising response is more for older consumers than for younger consumers. Given the paucity of significant results, one might conclude that older consumers are not reviewing store flyers more or less so compared to younger consumers. Indeed, feature-advertising response is actually less for older consumers in the following categories: (1) coffee; (2) frozen dinner entrees; (3) peanut butter; and (4) toilet tissue. See Table 6.5.

TABLE 6.5 Standardized Beta for Variable Age

Category	Product Featured in Flyer	Product on Display	Product Discounted
Beer	−0.02	−0.08	−0.01
Carbonated beverages	+0.03	−0.01	−0.03
Cigarettes	−0.07	NA	+0.07
Coffee	−0.15**	+0.11*	+0.12*
Cold cereal	−0.02	0.00	+0.03
Deodorant	0.00	−0.07	+0.05
Diapers	−0.06	+0.04	0.00
Facial tissue	−0.02	−0.01	+0.08
Frozen dinners	−0.15**	+0.11*	+0.10*
Frozen pizza	−0.08	−0.09	+0.07
Household cleaner	+0.06	0.00	−0.03
Hot dogs	+0.03	−0.09	−0.05
Laundry detergent	+0.02	−0.05	0.00
Margarine/butter	−0.04	−0.12**	+0.04
Mayonnaise	−0.04	+0.06	+0.02
Milk	+0.06	−0.05	−0.12**
Mustard/ketchup	+0.01	0.00	−0.01
Paper towels	0.00	0.00	+0.07
Peanut butter	−0.12**	+0.05	+0.11*
Razor blades	−0.09	−0.04	−0.02
Salty snacks	−0.02	−0.03	+0.07
Shampoo	−0.03	−0.02	+0.02
Soup	−0.05	+0.08*	+0.03
Spaghetti sauce	−0.08	+0.04	+0.08
Sugar substitute	−0.06	+0.01	+0.04
Toilet tissue	−0.10*	+0.01	+0.10*
Toothbrush	−0.05	−0.04	+0.14
Toothpaste	+0.08	−0.07	−0.01
Yogurt	+0.02	+0.03	0.00

Key: * = p-value < 0.05; ** = p-value <0 .01; *** = p-value < 0.001.

Response to In-Store Displayed Products

Consumer response to in-store displayed products was higher among older consumers in only the following categories: (1) coffee; (2) frozen dinner entrees; and (3) soup. Consumer response is lower in the category of margarine and butter. See Table 6.5.

Response to Price Promotions

Last, our analysis showed a positive effect of age on consumer response to price promotions in the categories of: (1) coffee; (2) frozen dinner entrees; (3) peanut butter; and (4) toilet tissue. However, their response to price promotions is lower in the category of milk. See Table 6.5.

Discussion

In the present chapter, we report the results of an analysis of age effects on consumer spending behavior across a total of 29 different CPG categories. We confined our analysis to single-person households and controlled for household income. We investigated the effect of age on buying behaviors that one would expect to change with age and CPG category. Specifically, we tested for the effect of age on spending for numerous food and household staples, as well in CPG categories related to workforce participation. In terms of spending behaviors, we studied buying volume, brand loyalty, unit size, mean volume per shopping occasion, size loyalty, shopping trip frequency, inter-trip gap stability, time of day, day of week, store loyalty, and preferred store size.

Our results reveal large differences across categories in terms of whether age had a significant increasing or decreasing effect on buying volume. Older consumers in our sample spent more in four categories, including sugar substitutes (dietary health), but less in 12 categories, including in four workforce-related categories and four food categories antagonistic to dietary health. Further, we found that older (vs. younger) consumers are more size loyal and brand loyal but (surprisingly) not store loyal. On the whole, older consumers preferred smaller volumes of products, smaller unit sizes, and smaller-sized stores.

In addition to investigating the effect of age on spending behaviors across the 29 CPG categories, we investigated the effect of age on consumer response (and responsiveness) to marketers' promotional activities, including feature advertising, in-store displays, and price promotions. This is another novel aspect of our study. Taken together, the results reveal few differences in consumer response due to age. There is no category where response to feature-advertising is larger among older consumers. Moreover, there are few age-related differences in response to in-store displays (three categories) or price promotions (four categories).

In conclusion, the present study is among the first to focus on the (pure) effect of age on spending on CPG. We examined the effect of age on actual consumer behaviors in 29 categories. We not only examined expenditures but a host of other buying behaviors, including loyalty behaviors (e.g., store loyalty, product size loyalty, and brand loyalty) and habit-driven behaviors (e.g., when people shop). Moreover, this is the first study to investigate the effect of age on consumer response to marketing promotions. By and large, there were few significant effects of age. This particular pattern of mostly null findings suggests that older consumers may not be more likely than young consumers are to notice and respond to marketers' promotional activities.

Notes

1 In the United States, the leading-source data providers for a few decades were Information Resources, Inc. (IRI) and AC Nielsen (CAN). Each firm maintained a distinct consumer panel which it tried to ensure was representative of the U.S. population. There were some important differences in the recording technology. Given the high cost of managing the panelists, the retail partners and the single-source data collection technology, it is not surprising that in 2009 the two firms decided to combine their efforts and maintain only a single dataset and group of panelists.
2 Bronnenberg et al. (2008) describes how the 29 categories vary along these important characteristics.

References

Angell, Robert, P. Megicks, J. Memery, T. Heffernan, and K. Howell. "Understanding the older shopper: A behavioural typology." *Journal of Retailing and Consumer Services 19*(2) (2012): 259–269.

Boatwright, Peter, Sanjay Dhar, and Peter E. Rossi. "The role of retail competition, demographics and account retail strategy as drivers of promotional sensitivity." *Quantitative Marketing and Economics 2*(2) (2004): 169–190.

Bronnenberg, Bart J., Michael W. Kruger, and Carl F. Mela. "Database paper: The IRI marketing data set." *Marketing Science 27*(4) (2008): 745–748.

Drolet, Aimee, Anand V. Bodapati, Patrick Suppes, Benjamin Rossi, and Harrison Hochwarter. "Habits and free associations: Free your mind and mind your habits." *Journal of the Association for Consumer Research 2*(3) (2016): 293–305.

Goodwin, David R., and Rachel E. McElwee. "Grocery shopping and an ageing population: Research note." *The International Review of Retail, Distribution and Consumer Research 9*(4) (1999): 403–409.

Hare, Caroline. "The food-shopping experience: A satisfaction survey of older Scottish consumers." *International Journal of Retail and Distribution Management 31*(5) (2003): 244–255.

Hurd, Michael D., and Susann Rohwedder. "Spending patterns in the older population," In Drolet, Aimee, Norbert Schwarz, and Carolyn Yoon (editors) *The Aging Consumer: Perspectives from Psychology and Economics* (2010) 25–50. Routledge.

Lambert-Pandraud, Raphaëlle, Gilles Laurent, and Eric Lapersonne. "Repeat purchasing of new automobiles by older consumers: Empirical evidence and interpretations." *Journal of Marketing 69*(2) (2005): 97–113.

Lapersonne, Eric, Gilles Laurent, and Jean-Jacques Le Goff. "Consideration sets of size one: An empirical investigation of automobile purchases." *International Journal of Research in Marketing 12*(1) (1995): 55–66.

Meneely, Lisa, Chris Strugnell, and Amy Burns. "Elderly consumers and their food store experiences." *Journal of Retailing and Consumer Services 16*(6) (2009): 458–465.

PART III

Implications of Aging on Consumer Behavior

7

SUCCESSFUL RETIREMENT: FROM RETIRING TO REWIRING

Jill Steinberg

Introduction

When thinking about "successful retirement," most people and the research literature have a limited scope, a scope that this chapter will expand. Often, researchers, writers, and the lay public consider having enough money and having more free time as the primary issues of retirement, without much thought as to what retirement will actually look like. They ignore such significant concerns as how to spend one's time and money, finding purpose, the importance of friendships and social connections, and couple issues that may arise. This chapter will address those often-overlooked quality of life factors that are so important to a successful retirement.

Until recently, many thought of 65 as the age of retirement. Sixty-five was the age legislated by the Social Security Act of 1935 as a time when individuals could start collecting "an old age benefit" (Social Security Administration, Social Security Act of 1935). In 1935, life expectancy was 61. Currently, the average life expectancy is in the 80s (Social Security Administration, Benefits Planner/Life Expectancy). Life in retirement has the potential to be over 20 years.

Retirement is a stage of life (Horner, 2014) where one can arrive having earned and gained invaluable resources along the way. Goals change across the life span. With age, although memory might not be what it used to be, research supports the important conclusion that emotional stability improves, knowledge has grown and expertise deepened (Carstensen, 2014; Carstensen, Mikels and Mahers, 2006). In important ways, older people can contribute more than younger people.

The research literature finds significant individual differences among retirees in satisfaction and happiness, but that for most retirees, life in retirement is better or the same as it was before (Blendon et al., 2011; Carstensen, 2014; Carstensen,

2011; and Carstensen et al., 2006). More specifically, the research finds that retirement can start with a great honeymoon phase, may proceed to a steep decline in happiness, and then usually stabilizes (Horner, 2014) with as much happiness as one had while working. In contrast with the general finding of a honeymoon period, there is an initial decline in satisfaction for those who retired earlier than expected (Hershey and Henkens, 2013). Depending on the survey, up to 25 percent experience difficulty adjusting (van Solinge, 2013, p. 319), 10 percent are not at all satisfied, and retirement satisfaction tends to decrease as people age (Banerjee, 2016). This is true regardless of the age the person retires. Retirees with higher net worth and better health report higher retirement satisfaction (Banerjee, 2016).

What Is Retirement?

The literature tends to define and discuss retirement as a discrete point in time (Blendon et al., 2011; Kubicek, Korunka, Raymo, and Hoonakker, 2011). It tends to be seen as a clear point when the person stops working. That was true and typical of how retirement was historically but is no longer the case. For many, the boundary between work and retirement has become unclear. Retirement is now an evolving process and for many, it takes the form of being self-employed or working for someone else, for purpose or to give back rather than accumulate more wealth (Brown, Aumann, Pitt-Catsouphes, Galinsky, and Bond, 2010; Freedman, 2011; Lawrence-Lightfoot, 2009). More older people are working longer (Hayutin, Beals, and Borges, 2013). Of those who do stop working completely, about 30 percent unretire within six years of retiring (Cahill, Giandria, and Quinn, 2015).

University of California (UC) emeriti faculty are a good example. The Council of the University of California Emeriti Associations reports

> viewed in aggregate, the teaching, the scholarship and the community work of UC emeriti during this period (2015–2018) is equivalent to that of a major university. Their contributions to the mission of the University of California amount to a virtual eleventh campus.
> *(Council of University of California Emeriti Associations (CUCEA), 2018, p. 1)*

"After twenty years or more of retirement, half of the responders are still making contributions" (CUCEA, 2018, p. 4). Retirees of many other occupations and professions would probably point to comparable contributions in their own realms.

Changes in how people retire are changing the demographics of the U.S. workforce. According to employment statistics, the older workforce is growing more rapidly than the younger workforce (Drake, 2014) including an aging of the Science and Engineering labor force (National Science Board, 2014). Fifty-five and older is the only age group where workforce participation rates have been rising which is in contrast to past decades of decline (Cahill, Giandrea, and Quinn, 2013). Those with more education are likely to work longer. (Health and Retirement Study, 2018, p. 22). The Sloan Center on Aging and Work at Boston College (Brown et al., 2010), reports that in the general population, one in five workers aged 50 and older has a retirement job; the mean age of those working in retirement is 63.

For those in the Science and Engineering sector, in spite of the perceived and actual pressure for older workers to retire (Brooke, 2009) there is a trend toward a rising median age. In 2010, the median age of scientists and engineers in the labor force was 44 years compared to 41 in 1993. In 2010, one in three science and engineering workers was over 50 compared to one in five in 1993.

Research supports (Brooke, 2009) that there can be pressure for older computer scientists to go into management or retire because of the assumption that older engineers' minds aren't as quick as younger ones. However, Brooke's 2009 research suggests that the real issue with age is that one's priorities change. People may no longer be willing to work the intense hours they once did.

Working in retirement used to be an oxymoron and is now becoming the new normal (Brown et al., 2010).

Sense of Control: The Decision of When and How to Retire

Having a sense of control over the decision to retire (Calvo, Haverstick, and Sass, 2009: Wolinsky, Wyrwich, Babu, Kroenke, and Tierney, 2003), including how and when to retire, can affect the person's ability to plan, and is correlated with higher levels of self-efficacy, mental well-being, and how well people take care of their health (Novak, 2011; Wolinsky et al., 2003) as well as with higher levels of income (Calvo et al., 2009). In terms of finances and sense of control, research finds that having a pension helps people make the decision to retire, and helps retirees feel more in control of their lives and more secure and happy with being retired (Blendon, et al., 2011; Calvo et al., 2009). Forced retirement, on the other hand, is a predictor of adjustment problems and can have negative effects on the retired worker and their spouse or partner (van Solinger and Henkens, 2005).

A significant factor associated with stopping work is self-reported poor health. (Aaron and Callan, 2011). Personal growth and gaining self-knowledge, on the other hand, are correlated with being less likely to engage in post-retirement employment (Fasbender, Deller, Wang, and Wiernik, 2014). Some of the literature supports the finding that transitioning into retirement with bridge employment is associated with better physical and mental health in comparison with full retirement (Kubicek et al., 2011). Other research finds no significant difference between bridge and full retirement.

Overall, the literature is consistent in the finding that what matters most for successful retirement is whether the person perceives the retirement decision as chosen or forced (Calvo et al., 2009). Perceived control increases with education, wealth, and socioeconomic status (Calvo and Sarkisian, 2011; Mitchell, Ailshire, Brown, Levine, and Crimmins, 2016). Advantaged individuals accumulate more opportunities for controlling their transitions through life (Mirowsky and Ross, 2007).

Planning and Goal-Directedness

Another consistent research finding is that retirement tends to be easier for people who are goal oriented and therefore able to plan what to do once they have retired (Kubicek et al., 2011). Planning is correlated with higher retirement satisfaction and better adjustment (Kubicek et al., 2011; Taylor and Doverspike, 2003). People who are conscientious are associated with the positive life outcomes of earning more, having more positive emotions and life satisfaction (Duckworth, Weir, Tsukayama, and Kwok, 2012); people who are more agreeable correlate with lower income, fewer financial resources, and lower life satisfaction (Duckworth et al., 2012).

In addition to being goal oriented and able to plan, some other consistent predictors of well-being include flexibility in goal adjustment and tenacity in goal pursuit as well as the ability to deal with failure/loss (Kubicek et al., 2011). My qualitative research with 125 highly educated, above-average-income retirees living in Santa Cruz, CA, a university town or in Silicon Valley, supports these findings (Steinberg, 2019). My sample was comprised of 60 males and 65 females from a wide range of professions, e.g., engineers, university professors, psychologists, teachers, medical doctors, private business owners. The youngest responder was 47 and the oldest was 95. The time in retirement ranged from three months to over 30 years. One of my responders, Elliot Aronson, Ph.D., a social psychologist known especially for his work on cognitive dissonance, talked about his experience with retirement and what he did when he had learned he was going blind. Soon after hearing his diagnosis, while still sighted and working, Elliot proactively obtained training to walk with a white cane, training to live with and work with a service dog, prepared his computer to be able to read text to him, and moved to downtown Santa Cruz with his wife so that he could walk everywhere. Elliot has been able to continue doing his research as well as stay in touch with his colleagues. After many years of giving up teaching because he could no longer see his students, at age 81, Elliot began teaching again. He started co-teaching his social influence course with a fully sighted colleague and then continued to teach by himself.

My research also finds that *implementing anything before* retiring correlates with higher satisfaction. Those 20 percent who self-reported being most satisfied all implemented some activities before they retired. It does not matter what the person implements (e.g., taking classes at the university, volunteering) or whether the person continues with that particular activity after retiring, it is the process of planning and implementing that helps the retiree approach their new found time with meaning and structure. Implementing engages the person in actively doing something to figure out how to make the transitions and subsequent time in retirement more successful (Steinberg, 2019).

Arthur, one of my responders, is a software engineer who was responsible for developing text messaging while working at Google. He retired at age 47 and is very happy with his life. Arthur told me a story during our interview that he said made him realize he had to carefully plan if he was going to retire. The story involved a 103-year-old woman who retired at age 50 and advised:

> Before you retire, make sure you know what you are going to do. Don't just jump off a cliff so to speak and try to figure it out after you've left. It doesn't mean that what you are going to do is what you planned to do, but have a plan or it can be very disorienting not to have one.

Arthur took her advice and started thinking about retirement many years before he retired. Two years before retirement, Arthur started planning. He wrote down three categories: projects he wanted to work on; goals he wanted to achieve; and descriptions of what he wanted a typical day to be like. He knew being concrete and specific was important. He identified smaller steps to achieving the goals. Arthur put the conditions in place to work on his own projects before he retired. Creating a routine continues to help and guide his day.

It may be that planning and implementing before retiring increase the sense of control that is associated with a successful retirement. However, according to current social security information, future retirees do not plan for the decision for very long (Knoll, 2011). According to the 2008 Employee Benefit Research Institute report (MacDonald, 2008), 22 percent of survey respondents first began to think about the retirement decision six months before they left their jobs. Another 22 percent spent only a year thinking about the retirement decision. Abraham and Houseman (2004), using data from the 1992–2000 Health and Retirement Survey (HRS), found the most common response (38 percent) regarding planning for retirement, was—"not much thought or had no plans" (p. 9). Pre-retirees may underestimate the challenges of retirement (Blendon et al., 2011); most retirees, especially women, wish they had planned ahead more for retirement (Moen, Erickson, Agarwal, Fields, and Todd, 2000).

High-achieving retirees like Arthur can be focused and self-driven and make excellent decisions and plans. The research supports the generalization that these people will use the same approach of dealing with the "problem situation" of retirement that they used with other problems to be solved in their careers (Martin and Lee, 2015).

However, the literature on behavioral economics finds that people are not good at accurately predicting their future happiness and behavior, which can lead to less than optimal retirement decisions (Knoll, 2011). For example, results from the Employee Benefit Research Institute (EBRI) Retirement Confidence Surveys

(Helman Greenwald, Copeland, and VanDerhei, 2010; Retirement Confidence Survey, 2019) indicate that 41 percent of people retire earlier than expected (only 5 percent later). The majority of workers plan to work after age 65, while only 27 percent actually do (Helman et al., 2010). The median expected age of retirement is 65 while the median actual age is 62.

Staying Connected to Social Networks and the Internet

Having social networks (Kubicek et al., 2011) as well as Internet connectedness (Cardale and Brady, 2010; Novak, 2011) is vital at any time in life and definitely in retirement. Carstensen's socioemotional selectivity theory posits that older adults shift priorities to stronger, emotionally rewarding ties vs. cultivating new relationships, and that one's perspective and sense of time changes to how much time one has left (Carstensen, 2014; Carstensen et al., 2006). "Spending time with other adults enhances older adults capabilities, life satisfaction, general well-being, health" (Sayer, Feldman, and Bianchi, 2016, p. 217) and sense of mattering (Froidevaux, Hirschi, and Wang, 2016). Perceptions of positive social relationships are associated with greater involvement in leisure activities; and greater involvement in leisure activities is correlated with better health in old age (Chang, Wray, and Lin, 2014). Those with higher education have more leisure and enjoy it more.

This is a time in life when people can experience many losses. The retirees' world can shrink—from ending work, declining health, death of loved ones including pets, and moves (Cornwell, Laumann, and Schumm, 2008; Novak, 2011). Consequently, social robotics including robotic pets is a growing field (Klinenberg, 2012).

Communication online can also help. One report by economists at the Phoenix Center for Advanced Legal and Economic Policy Studies finds that older people using the Internet experienced a 20 percent reduction in depression (Klinenberg, 2012). Older people tend to use the Internet to disseminate information, meet people, and strengthen ties (Xie, Huang, and Watkins, 2013). Therefore, being open to others and staying connected in person, by email, or video chats are especially important at this stage (Chang et al., 2014; Novak, 2011).

Sense of Purpose

The experience of mattering (Froidevaux, Hirschi, and& Wang, 2016) and having a sense of purpose (Strecher, 2016) have important roles for physical health, well-being, and decreased mortality in retirement (Alimujiang et al., 2019; Kim, Hershner, and Strecher, 2015; Kim, Sun, Park, Kubzansky, and Peterson, 2013; Seligman, 2011; Kim, Victor, and Ryff, 2014; Windsor, Curtis, and Luszcz, 2015). Purpose is defined in the research as "a self-organizing life aim that stimulates goals, promotes healthy behaviors, and gives meaning to life" (Alimujiang et al., 2019, p. 2). The research on purpose in life finds that lack of purpose contributes at least as much to disease and death as do lifestyle factors such as tobacco use, poor diet, inactivity, and stress (Strecher, 2016, p. 13). With strong purpose in life, individuals seem to do better psychologically, socially, at sleeping, sexually, are less likely to become depressed, and are more relaxed (Hamblin, 2014; Hill and Turiano, 2014; Kim, Hershner, and Strecher, 2015; Kim, Sun, Park, Kubzansky, and Peterson, 2013; Kim, Sun, Park, and Peterson, 2013; Strecher, 2016). A strong sense of "ikigai," which means a joy and sense of well-being from being alive and realizing the value of being alive, is associated with a lower risk of incident functional disability (Mori et al., 2017; Sone et al., 2008). Elizabeth Blackburn, the 2009 Nobel Prize winner in medicine, and her colleagues found that having a purpose in life was associated with telomere (the ends of chromosomes) length and therefore better health and less risk of dying (Blackburn and Epel, 2017; Strecher, 2016).

Purpose in life can determine goals and thus influence daily decisions regarding the use of one's resources (Irving, Davis, and Collier, 2017, p. 2). As one researcher put it, purpose can foster "efficiency of action" (Irving et al., 2017, p. 27). Individuals with a high sense of purpose may adapt more effectively through changing environmental and life conditions (Hill, Turiano, Spiro, and Mroczek, 2015).

> Purpose can be derived from relationships, societal, work or familial roles, pursuit of personal goals, maintaining independence, generativity, community engagement, or participation in activities that are individually meaningful and relevant. (Irving et al., 2017, p. 2)

Two of my responders support the research. Arthur says

> "Purpose is paramount … having a basic purpose clearly in mind has been absolutely essential to my mental well-being. There's almost nothing worse than feeling adrift."

Leslie did not have to find purpose, she merely shifted it. Leslie, a clinical psychologist, retired as Director of Mental Health when she was in her 60s. Plans for her retirement with her husband were ended abruptly as he suddenly died. Not long after, her dog died. In spite of these difficult losses, purpose continues to help Leslie structure her day and enjoy her life. Leslie says she reordered her thinking. Instead of planning for months and years, she now plans each day by including the following "elements:" physical activity, social connection, meditation, creativity (e.g. writing, cooking, going to a musical activity), and service to others. For example, she finds meaning in providing support and mentoring to a younger generation, the staff of an organization instead of working directly with clients. She also teaches mindfulness classes to people living in assisted living, staff working in non-profits, and lawyers. Leslie says "Bringing one's gifts to meet the needs of the world, joy is felt."

However, the literature shows that purpose declines with age (Irving et al., 2017; Pinquart, 2002). The literature suggests that age is not the significant factor, but rather age-related losses (e.g. death of partner, retirement) and decreased opportunities for meaningful engagement (Irving et al., 2017).

Health Issues Related to Neurocognitive Disorders

Health issues, a significant factor for enjoying life at any age, affect retirement decisions and life in retirement. It is not possible to cover all the health issues of aging in this one short chapter. However, because of the widespread concerns related to neurocognitive disorders (e.g. Alzheimer's dementia) and aging, including the emotional, physical, and financial costs, a few points will be covered here.

Factors associated with education and school success appear to have relevance in a discussion of retirement. Although higher educational levels correlate with protection against cognitive decline in older age, once a person does get dementia, the speed of decline is the same as those with less education. (Alley, Suthers, and Crimmins, 2007; Health & Retirement Study, 2018). The benefits of education for dementia risk appear to span generations. For example, those with a mother with less than an 8th grade education have an increased risk of dementia (Rogers et al., 2009). More recently, it has been found that educational quality may be even more important in establishing and maintaining cognitive abilities (Mehta et al., 2009). People who report doing well in school, regardless of level completed, are associated with a much lower risk of being diagnosed with Alzheimers dementia. At this stage of research, our understanding of dementia and who is susceptible is limited.

Some Differences in the Experience of Retirement between Men and Women

In some aspects, retirement affects men and women differently (Kubicek et al., 2011). For women, there is a negative effect of a lifetime of household and caretaking on planning for retirement, earnings, and retirement income (Sayer, Freedman, and Bianchi, 2016). Consequently, economic insecurity in old age is particularly acute among single, divorced, and widowed women even though women tend to retire later than men (Sayer et al., 2016).

For many women, retirement isn't as satisfactory as it is for their male partners/ spouse because retirement may not relieve the burdens of family life. Women often continue to do the household and caretaking work for their spouse/partner/elderly parents/adult children/grandchildren (Coursolle, Sweeney, Rayno, and Ho, 2010; Sayer et al., 2016; Suitor, Gilligan, and Pillemer, 2016; Wink and James, 2013). Work may have been the women's source of emotional support and limited the amount of time they could spend dealing with family responsibilities and conflicts (Courselle et al., 2010). Lyu and Burr (2016) found that for women, the birth of a new grandchild correlates with more than an 8 percent increase in the chances of retiring. However, some research finds that women enjoy being grandmothers more when they worked than in retirement (Calvo, et al., 2009). Caring for a spouse has a significant impact on the time of retiring; a woman with an ill husband is five times more likely to retire; a man with a sick wife is 50 percent slower to retire (Griffin, Loh, and Hesketh, 2013). Clearly, domestic responsibilities continue and often increase for women during retirement.

For men, leaving a job that was very satisfactory is associated with more difficult retirement adjustments than for women (Kubicek et al., 2011). After retirement, men are generally not as good as women at substituting the social involvements they had when they were working (Kubicek et al., 2011). Men can end up feeling as if they do not have enough friends. On the other hand, research suggests that in retirement males report higher levels of purpose than females (Irving et al., 2017; Pinquart, 2002). This may be due to men's greater tendency to have bridge employment and leisure activity.

As a result of a lifetime of gender roles and expectations, once retired, women tend to do more housework, volunteer more than men, and spend more time with others, while men are more likely to have bridge employment, leisure activities (Griffin et al., 2013), and rely on their partners for social connection.

Couples' Issues

In terms of couples' issues, Google's past CFO Patrick Pichette expressed it best upon giving his leaving notice, when he said

> Tamar and I will be celebrating our 25th anniversary. When our kids are asked by their friends about the success of the longevity of our marriage, they simply joke that Tamar and I have spent so little time together that it's really too early to tell if our marriage will in fact succeed.
>
> *(Interview with Larry Page, March 10, 2015)*

The transition to retirement can be difficult for couples (Coursolle, Sweeney, Raymor, and Ho, 2010; Calvo, Haverstick, and Sass, 2009; van Solinge and Henkens, 2005; Moen et al., 2000). The early transition period is associated with conflict and declines in marital quality (Moen et al., 2000). Although married retirees usually have better psychological well-being than single or widowed retirees (Wang and Shi, 2014; MetLife Study, 2010), this beneficial effect disappears if one of the spouses is still working—with the most dissatisfied couple situation being when the wife is still working and the husband has retired (Griffin et al., 2013). After the adjustment period, being married and retired with some joint leisure activities correlates with happiness (Calvo et al., 2009). Interestingly, although over three-quarters of partners expect to engage in more activities together, less than half do (Matthews and Fisher, 2013, p. 362).

Having both people at home all the time creates problems for some couples. Sixty-eight percent of my research participants, especially women, expressed what the research found (van Solinge and Henkens, 2005): Space/togetherness can be an issue and wives tend to encourage their husbands/male partners to get involved with something meaningful outside of the house. These women felt as if their home environment changed in a way that curtailed some of their freedoms. Among non-employed women at least 65, living with a spouse increases household and care work by one hour per day with most of the time spent cooking and cleaning (Sayer et al., 2016).

Partners who take care of partners with dementia may be at risk for cognitive decline, more so than partners who take care of partners with other problems (Dassel, Carr, and Vitaliano, 2015). Women with dementia are much less likely to receive informal care at home (Katz, Kabeto, and Langa, 2000); of those women and men receiving informal care at home, children are the most likely to provide care for their mothers and wives provide care for their husbands.

"Going Solo"

In contrast with the standard "couples" model, living alone is a growing phenomenon (Klinenberg, 2012). Currently, 28 percent of all U.S. households are made up of people living alone "which means that they are now tied with childless couples as the most prominent residential type—more common than the nuclear family, the multigenerational family, the roommate or group home" (Klinenberg, 2012, p. 5). A greater proportion of individuals reaching retirement are unmarried. One in three Baby Boomers is unmarried and lives alone. (Klinenberg, 2012, pp. 157, 16). Women tend to live longer, marry older men, and consequently, can live their last 15–20 years as widows (HRS, 2018).

Even though being unmarried makes one more vulnerable to social isolation, loneliness, health problems, and being economically disadvantaged, those living alone are healthier than those living with adults other than a spouse, or even, in some cases, than those living with a spouse (Klinenberg, 2012, p. 17). In recent decades, older people have demonstrated a clear preference for living alone rather than moving in with family or friends, having "intimacy at a distance" (Klinenberg, 2012, p. 162). Today, only 20 percent of elderly widows live with a child vs. up to 70 percent in the past (Klinenberg, 2012, p. 162). In terms of coupling, one woman expressed the research that "she's more interested in having someone to go out with than someone to come home to" (Klinenberg, 2012, p. 163). Consequently, compared to people who live with partners, people who live alone become more socially active and involved in their community (Klinenberg, 2012, p. 163). The picture is complex and defies simple description.

Using One's Money/Financial Resources

Many older people come into retirement financially under-prepared; they have little savings (Diamond and Hausman, 1984) and are not correctly informed about their pensions and Social Security Benefits (Gustman and Steinmeier, 2004) even though older consumers are identified as having larger household assets and more disposable income than younger consumers (Yoon and Cole, 2008).

How retirees spend money changes. As people age, spending increases for health care services, donations, and gifts and decreases for transportation, vacations, and trips (Hurd and Rohwedder, 2010). In the beginning of retirement, for those more fortunate, with increased finances and time, travel increases (Hurd and Rohwedder, 2010). Americans over 50 account for 45 percent of all leisure trips in the U.S. and 70 percent of all cruise passengers (Moody and Sood, 2010). Spending steadily decreases with age (Banerjee, 2012) with declines in spending appearing to diminish through the first years.

Entertainment/leisure spending is the only type of expenditure positively related to happiness, due in part from an increase in social connections (DeLaire and Kalil, 2010). Older consumers report being more satisfied with their purchases (Yoon, Feinberg, and Schwarz, 2010).

Individuals spend differently than couples (Hurd and Rohwedder, 2010). Couples, in general, have more money to spend and spend proportionately less on goods such as housing. However, decision-making about how to use one's resources is more complicated for couples. Research discussing who in the couple makes the final say in terms of financial decisions, finds that 44 percent report both individuals and 35 percent disagree about who makes the final say (Barbiarz, Robb, and Woodyard, 2012). For various reasons, older people report increasing their financial help to their adult children and others, including siblings.

Satisfaction with life increases for those who report having discussed retirement with their partners and had some type of tax-deferred retirement plan (Noone, Stephens, and Alpass, 2009).

Using One's Time

Working on how to spend the day can be an ongoing issue. The research says that people need strategies to support achieving their goals as well as strategies to cope with failure of not achieving goals (Kubicek, 2011; Schaie and Willis, 2010). Exercise continues to be an important component of mental and physical well-being (Simone and Haas, 2009).

The literature says volunteering can be especially beneficial at this stage (Moen et al., 2000) and is cited as one of the things that make people happy (Cornwell, Laumann, and Schumm, 2008). However, finding volunteer work that is fulfilling isn't always easy. There may be a lot of volunteer opportunities, but not necessarily at the level of responsibility the person is used to. The literature finds that when volunteering, women tend to assume the role of helping and men assume administrative roles (Dorfman, 2013). People with more social capital are the ones most likely to volunteer. The literature on managers says that they find mentoring deeply satisfying, especially those situations with more long-term ongoing relationships (Martin and Lee, 2015). Further, retirees involved for generative reasons, working for teaching and sharing knowledge with the younger generation, experience improved psychological well-being (Wang and Shi, 2014). "Innovators" who start new activities have an even higher rate of satisfaction (Dorfman, 2013).

Retirees are involved in a wide variety of activities, some continuing with extensions of their previous work like Elliot Aronson and others finding involvements outside of their careers. For example, some are taking courses not related to their previous work, others are learning piano and a foreign language. Some are gaining new skills working with international students helping them with their English while others are working with children who have been abused and or as docents teaching about ocean life. One of my research responders, Eric, earned his degree in Art and Architecture from MIT and ended up spending his career working in early childhood education. Upon retiring, he is using both of his interests, designing and making wooden toys for all ages and writing children's books. One married couple in my research, Jim and Paula, both in their 90s, met at MGM in Hollywood working on *Tom and Jerry* cartoons. After retiring from a career as a film editor, Jim, along with four others, started University of California, Santa Cruz's Osher Life Long Learners (OLLI) 30 years ago when they first retired and moved to Santa Cruz. Additionally, Jim and Paula started and kept up a film group they ran in their home for over 25 years until one week before Jim died (Steinberg, 2019*).

The Environment

One's environment is important for a successful retirement (Blendon et al., 2011). How older people feel about their neighborhood is important for positive mental health; neighborhood socioeconomic status (SES) has a strong and consistent relationship with a range of health outcomes for older people (Aneshensel, Harig, and Wight, 2016, pp. 321, 323). Environments that allow older people to feel safe, to walk, to exercise, or go to favorite destinations, contribute to greater physical activity and lower rates of obesity, depression, and alcohol abuse (Aneshensel et al., 2016, p. 326). Not surprisingly, what appears to be important throughout one's life, is important for retirees.

Limitations in the Current Findings and Suggestions for Future Research

Simply stated, although this chapter covers a diverse and large body of well-done research, the research on successful retirement in terms of quality of life factors is a relatively new field, problems exist, and there is much more to investigate.

Retirement has become an evolving process, not a discrete point in time. Much of the existing data rely on studies that investigate individuals at one point in time in their life; individuals whose expectations and reactions about retirement are based on outdated ideas/concepts of what retirement actually is. More large-scale comprehensive ongoing studies like the longitudinal HRS study (2018) need to be done to systematically understand the process of how individuals, couples, and society can better prepare and deal with this stage of life.

Concepts like "successful" retirement need to be clearly defined with testable, reliable, and valid variables. What is considered "satisfaction" no doubt has wide individual differences and may be age/stage dependent. Significant findings on adjusting to retirement, like those of Horner (2014) and Wang, Henkens, and van Solinge (2011), need to be quantified to give a better idea of the time and expectations involved in the various stages of transition. Developmental goals, milestones, norms, and how to prepare for retirement could be quantified and concretized. My research finding that implementing something before retiring correlates with the most successful retirements comes from exploratory qualitative research and needs to be experimentally researched and tested over time. Topics like the more recent phenomena of living alone (Klinenberg, 2012) and "recoupling" during retirement need more thorough investigation.

Older people in general, retirees to be specific, have become an increasingly larger part of the population. Samples of "retirees" being studied need to be expanded and diversified to address specific needs and concerns. For example, my research involves those retirees who are privileged enough to choose to retire vs. those people who have barely earned enough money to live, let alone consider, plan for, and experience a successful retirement. Additionally, research needs to focus on specific subpopulations so that a more nuanced picture of retirement can emerge. The retirement process, key issues, and successful strategies are possibly quite different, depending on ethnic and other group characteristics. Two examples of such studies are the MetLife Study (2010) and Cohler and Hostetler's (2006) research which investigated gay, lLesbian, bisexual, and transgendered individuals to understand their particular experience of retirement.

The body of research needs to be expanded from focusing mostly on individuals to including more about how retirement impacts communities and society in general. Additionally, the research needs to become more expansive and address policy concerns. There is a potential paradigm shift. People spend a lifetime preparing and doing what they need to do to earn enough money to survive, support their family, etc. and now there is the potential for the person to do what they want, to find meaning, and contribute/give back with their newly found large amounts of "free" time. Retirees can be a source of invaluable resources for society with their increased experience, emotional stability, and knowledge (Carstensen, 2014; Carstensen et al., 2006). The retirees' potential contributions, the real resources of society, are often ignored or lost and not fully realized for the individual or society. Finding ways and establishing policies to utilize the retiree is good for the individual and good for society.

Conclusion

Most retirees are largely satisfied with this stage of life (Horner, 2014) even with satisfaction decreasing over time. Having sufficient financial resources, a sense of control, being goal-directed, planning for retirement, implementing some projects and involvements before retiring, having concrete strategies to deal with goals and losses, and having supportive social and tech connections are all factors associated with having a more purposeful and successful retirement, including better health and being better prepared for dealing with changes in their finances, time, health, and relationships. Retirement, like other developmental stages, takes adequate financial resources, planning and reflection, and is an ongoing process of multiple and cumulative transitions (Calvo and Sarksisian, 2011; Wang et al., 2011).

References

Aaron, H. J. & Callan, J. M. (2011). *Who Retires Early?* CRR Working Paper No. 2011-10. Boston, MA: Center for Retirement Research at Boston College.

Abraham, K. G. & Houseman, S. N. (2004). *Work and Retirement Plans Among Older Americans.* Upjohn Institute Working Paper No. 04-105. Kalamazoo, MI: W.E. Upjohn Institute for Employment Research. Retrieved from: http://research.upjohn.org/up_workingpapers/105.

Alimujiang, A., Wiensch, A., Boss, J., Fleischer, N. L., Mondul, A. M., McLean, K., Mukherjee, B., & Pearce, C. L. (2019). Association between life purpose and mortality among US adults older than 50 years. *JAMA Network Open, 2*(5), e194270. DOI:10.1001/jamanetworkopen.2019,4270.

Alley, D., Suthers, K., & Crimmins, E. (2007). Education and cognitive decline in older Americans: Results from the AHEAD sample. *Research on Aging, 29*(1), 73–94.

Aneshensel, C. S., Harig, F., & Wight, R. G. (2016). Aging, neighborhoods, and the built environment. In: L. K. George & K. F. Ferraro (Eds.), *Handbook of Aging and the Social Sciences, 8th Edition* (pp 315–335). Amsterdam, Netherlands: Academic Press/Elsevier.

Babiarz, P., Robb, C. A., & Woodyard, A. (2012). Family decision making and resource protection adequacy. *Journal of Consumer Affairs, 46*(1), 1–36.

Banerjee, S. (2012, February). *Expenditure Patterns of older Americans, 2001–2009.* EBRI (Employee Benefits Research Institute) Issue Brief, 368. Washington, DC, 1–25. Retrieved from https://www.ncbi.nlm.nih.gov/pubmed/22397080.

Banerjee, S. (2016, April). *Trends in Retirement Satisfaction in the United States: Fewer Having a Great Time.* EBRI (Employee Benefits Research Institute) Notes, 37, 4. Washington, DC, 1–12. Retrieved from https://www.ebri.org/docs/default-source/ebri-notes/ebri_notes_04_apr16.pdf?sfvrsn=cbcb292f_0.

Blackburn, E. & Epel, E. (2017). *The Telomere Effect: A Revolutionary Approach to Living Younger, Healthier, Longer.* New York, NY: Grand Central Publishing.

Blendon, R. J., SteelFisher, G. K., Mailhot, J., Ben-Porath, E., Mann, F., Sullivan, H. K., Colby, D., Neel, J., Gudenkauf, A., & Drummond, S. (Released 2011, September). Poll: Retirement and health summary and chart pack. NPR/Robert Wood Johnson Foundation/Harvard School of Public Health.

Brooke, L. (2009). Prolonging the careers of older information technology workers: Continuity, exit or retirement transitions? *Ageing and Society 29*(2), 237–256. Cambridge Univ. Press. DOI:10.1017/S0144686X0800768X.

Brown, M., Aumann, K., Pitt-Catsouphes, M., Galinsky, E., & Bond, J. (2010, July). *Working in Retirement: A 21st Century Phenomenon.* Chesnut Hill, MA: Families and Work Institue. The Sloan Center on Aging & Work at Boston College.

Cahill, K. E., Giandrea, M. D., & Quinn, J. F. (2013). Bridge employment. In: M. Wang (Ed.), *Oxford Library of Psychology. The Oxford Handbook of Retirement* (pp. 293–310). New York, NY: Oxford University Press.

Cahill, K. E., Giandrea, M. D., & Quinn, J. F. (2015). Retirement patterns and the macroeconomy, 1992–2010. The prevalence and determinants of bridge jobs, phased retirement, and reentry among three recent cohorts of older Americans. *The Gerontologist, 55*(3), 384–403.

Calvo, E., Haverstick, K., & Sass, S. A. (2009, January). Gradual retirement, sense of control, and retirees' happiness. *Research on Aging, 31*(1), 112–135. © 2009 Sage Publications. Center for Retirement Research at Boston College. DOI:10.1177/0164027508324704. Retrieved from http://roa.sagepub.com hosted at http://online.sagepub.com.

Calvo, E. & Sarkisian, N. (2011, April). Documento de Trabajo No2, Retirement and well-being: Examining the characteristics of life course transitions, under review. *American Sociological Review.* Working Paper #2, Public Policy Institute at Universidad Diego Portales

Cardale, A. & Brady, E. M. (2010, Fall). To talk or to text—Is that the question? *LLI Review, the Annual Journal of the Osher Lifelong Learning Institute: Explorations by and About Older Learners, 5,* 15–28.

Carstensen, L. (2011, December). Older people are happier. *TEDxWomen 2011,* 5 15–28. Retrieved from https://www.ted.com/talks/laura_carstensen_older_people_are_happier?language=en.

Carstensen, L. (2014). Our aging population—It may just save us all. In: P. Irving (Ed.), *The Upside of Aging: How Long Life Is Changing the World of Health, Work, Innovation, Policy, and Purpose* (pp. 1–18). Hoboken, NJ: John Wiley.

Carstensen, L., Mikels, J. A., & Mather, M. (2006). Aging and the intersection of cognition, motivation, and emotion. In: J. E. Birren & K. W. Schaire (Eds.), *Handbook of the Psychology of Aging* (pp. 343–362). Amsterdam, Netherlands: Elsevier. DOI:10.1016/B978-012101264-9/50018-5.

Chang, P., Wray, L., & Lin, Y. (2014). Social relationships, leisure activity and health in older adults. *Health Psychology, 33*(6), 516–523.

Cohler, B. J. & Hostetler, A. J. (2006). Gay lives in the third age: Possibilities and paradoxes. *Annual Review of Gerontology and Geriatrics, 26,* 263–281.

Cornwell, B., Laumann, E. O., & Schumm, L. P. (2008, April). The social connectedness of older adults: A national profile. *American Sociological Review, 73*(2), 185–203. Special Issue: Happiness and Older Americans.

Council of University of California Emeriti Associations (CUCEA). (2018). *A Virtual Eleventh Campus: The Ninth Inventory of University of California Emeriti Activity 2015–2018* (pp. 1–9). Retrieved from https://cucea.ucsd.edu.

Coursolle, K. M., Sweeney, M. M., Raymo, J. M., & Ho, J. (2010). The association between retirement and emotional well-being: Does prior work–family conflict matter? *The Journals of Gerontology. Series B—Psychological Sciences and Social Sciences, 65*(5), 609–620. Oxford University Press. DOI:10.1093/geronb/gbp116 PubMed: 20064839. Available from www.pubmedcentral.nih.gov.

Dassel, K. B., Carr, D. C., & Vitaliano, P. (2017, April 1). Does caring for a spouse with dementia accelerate cognitive decline? Findings from the Health and Retirement Study. *The Gerontologist, 57*(2), 319–328. Doi:10.1093/geront/gnv148. Advance online publication.

DeLeire, T. & Kalil, A. (2010). Does consumption buy happiness? Evidence from the United States. *International Review of Economics, 57*(2), 163–173.

Diamond, P. A. & Hausman, J. A. (1984). Individual retirement and savings behavior. *Journal of Public Economics, 23*(1–2), 81–114.

Dorfman, L. T. (2013). Leisure activities in retirement. In: M. Wang (Ed.), *The Oxford Handbook of Retirement* (pp. 339–353). Oxford, England: Oxford University Press.

Drake, B. (2014, January 7). *Number of Older Americans in the Workforce is on the Rise*. Pew Research Center. Retrieved from https://www.pewresearch.org/fact-tank/2014/01/07/number-of-older-americans-in-the-workforce-is-on-the-rise/.

Duckworth, A. L., Weir, D., Tsukayama, E., & Kwok, D. (2012). Who does well in Life? Conscientious adults excel in both objective and subjective success. *Frontiers in Psychology, 3*, 1–8.

Fasbender, U., Deller, J., Wang, M., & Wiernik, B. (2014). Deciding whether to work after retirement. The role of the psychological experience of aging. *Journal of Vocational Behavior, 84*(3), 2915–2224.

Freedman, M. (2011). *The Big Shift: Navigating the New Stage beyond Midlife*. New York, NY: Public Affairs.

Froidevaux, A., Hirschi, A., & Wang, M. (2016). The role of mattering as an overlooked key challenge in retirement planning and adjustment. *Journal of Vocational Behavior,* (94), 57–69.

Griffin, B., Loh, V., & Hesketh, B. (2013). Age, gender and the retirement process. In: M. Wang (Ed.), *The Oxford Handbook of Retirement* (pp. 202–214). New York: Oxford Univ Press.

Gustman, A. L. & Steinmeier, T. L. (2004). What people don't know about their pensions and social security: An analysis using linked data from the health and retirement study. In: W. G. Gale, J. B. Shoven, & M. J. Warshawsky (Eds.), *Private Pensions and Public Policies* (pp. 57–119). Washington, DC: Brookings Institutions.

Hamblin, J. (2014, November 3). Health tip: Find purpose in life. The growing science on how a body imbued with meaning becomes healthier. *The Atlantic*. Retrieved from https://www.theatlantic.com/health/archive/2014/11/live-on-purpose/382252/.

Hayutin, A., Beals, M., & Borges, E. (2013). *The Aging US Workforce: A Chartbook of Demographic Shifts*. Stanford Center on Longevity. Retrieved from http://longevity.stanford.edu/2013/04/18/the-aging-u-s-workforce-a-chartbook-of-demographic-shifts/.

The Health and Retirement Study (HRS) (2018). Aging in the 21st century, challenges and opportunities for Americans. (pp. 1–102). Survey Research Center, Institute for Social Research, University of Michigan. Retrieved from http://hrsonline.isr.umich.edu/sitedocs/databook/inc/pdf/HRS-Aging-in-the-21St-Century.pdf?_ga=2.30406719.1670850385.1564678742-723814463.1499458963.

Helman, R., Greenwald, M., Copeland, C., & VanDerhei, J. (2010). *The 2010 Retirement Confidence Survey: Confidence Stabilizing, but Preparations Continue to Erode*. Issue Brief No. 340. Washington, DC: Employee Benefit Research Institute. Retrieved from http://www.ebri.org/pdf/briefspdf/ EBRI_IB_03-2010_No340_RCS.pdf.

Hershey, D. & Henkens, K. (2013). Impact of different types of retirement transitions on perceived satisfaction with life. *The Gerontologist*, 13. Oxford University Press,. DOI:10.1093/geront/gnt006.

Hill, P. L. & Turiano, N. A. (2014, May 8). Purpose in life as a predictor of mortality across adulthood. *SAGE Journals*, *25*(7), 1482–1486. DOI:10.1177/095679761453 1799.

Hill, P. L., Turiano, N. A., Spiro, A., & Mroczek, D. K. (2015). Understanding inter-individual variability in purpose: Longitudinal findings from the VA Normative Aging Study. *Psychology and Aging*, *30*(3), 529–533.

Horner, E. M. (2014, February). Subjective well-being and retirement: Analysis and policy recommendations. *Journal of Happiness Studies*, *15*(1). DOI:10.1007/s10902-012-9399-2. Published online. Springer Science & Business Media, Dordrecht.

Hurd, M. & Rohwedder, S. (2010). Spending patterns in the older population. In: A. Drolet, N. Schwarz, & C. Yoon (Eds.), *The Aging Consumer: Perspectives from Psychology and Economics* (pp. 25–50). New York: Routledge.

Irving, J., Davis, S., & Collier, A. (2017). Aging with purpose: Systematic search and review of literature pertaining to older adults and purpose. *The International Journal of Aging and Human Development*, 1–35. Retrieved from Sagepub.com/journalsPermission.nav DOI:10.1177/0091415017702908.

Katz, S. J., Kabeto, M., & Langa, K. M. (2000). Gender disparities in the receipt of home care for elderly people with disability in the United States. *Journal of the American Medical Association*, *284*(23), 3022–2027.

Kim, E. S., Hershner, S. D., & Strecher, V. (2015). Purpose in life and incidence of sleep disturbances. *Journal of Behavioral Medicine*, *38*(3), 590–597. DOI:10.1007/s10865-015-9635-4. Epub 2015 March 31.

Kim, E., Sun, J., Park, N., Kubzansky, L., & Peterson, C. (2013). Purpose in life and reduced risk of myocardial infarction among older U.S. adults with coronary heart disease: A two year follow-up. *Journal of Behavioral Medicine*, *36*(2), 124–133.

Kim, E., Sun, J., Park, N., & Peterson, C. (2013, May). Purpose in life and reduced incidence of stroke in older adults. *The Health and Retirement Study*, *74*(5), 427–432.

Kim, E., Victor, S. J., & Ryff, C. D. (2014, August 2). Purpose in life and use of preventive health care services. *PNAS*, *111*(46), 16331–16336. DOI:10.1073/pnas.141482611.

Klinenberg, E. (2012). *Going Solo: The Extraordinary Rise and Surprising Appeal of Living Alone*. London: Penguin Books.

Knoll, M. A. Z. (2011). Behavioral and psychological aspects of the retirement decision. *Social Security Bulletin*, *71*(4). Retrieved from https://www.ssa.gov/policy/docs/ssb/v71n4/v71n4p15.html.

Kubicek, B., Korunka, C., Raymo, J. M., & Hoonakker, P. (2011). Psychological well-being in retirement: The effects of personal and gendered contextual resources. *Journal of Occupational Health Psychology*, *16*(2), 1076–8998.

Lawrence-Lightfoot, S. (2009). *The Third Chapter: Passion, Risk and Adventure in the 25 Years After 50*. New York, NY: Sarah Crichton Books.

Lyu, J. & Burr, J. (2016). Socioeconomic status across the lifecourse and cognitive function among older adults: An examination of the latency, pathways, and accumulation hypotheses. *Journal of Aging and Health*, *28*(1), 40–67.

MacDonald, J. (2008, July 16). *How Long Do Workers Consider Retirement Decision?* EBRI (Employee Benefit Research Institute), Fast Facts from EBRI, FFE #91. Retrieved from https://www.ebri.org/docs/default-source/fast-facts/fastfact_91_retdec-16ju ly08.pdf?sfvrsn=dac7372f_2.

Martin, B. & Lee, M. D. (2015, July 3). Managers' work and retirement: Understanding the Connections. *Work, Employment and Society*, *30*(1), 21–39. DOI:10.1177/095001701558364.

Matthews, R. A. & Fisher, G. G. (2013). Family, work and the retirement process: A review and new directions. In: M. Wang (Ed.), *The Oxford Handbook of Retirement* (pp. 354–370). Oxford, England: Oxford University Press.

Mehta, K. M., Stewart, A. L., Langa, K. M., Yaffe, K., Moody-Ayers, S., Williams, B. A., & Covinsky, K. E. (2009). "Below average" self-assessed school performance and Alzheimers disease in the aging. Demographics and memory study. *Alzheimer's and Dementia, 5*(5), 380–387.

Metlife Mature Market Institute 2 & The Lesbian and Gay Aging Issues Network of the American Society on Aging. (2010.) Out and aging: The MetLife study of lesbian and gay baby boomers. *Journal of GLBT Family Studies, 6*(1), 40–57. DOI:10.1080/15504280903472949.

Mirowsky, J. & Ross, C. E. (2007). Life course trajectories of perceived control and their relationship to education. *American Journal of Sociology, 112*(5), 1339–1382.

Mitchell, U. A., Ailshire, J. A., Brown, L. L., Levine, M. E., & Crimmins, E. M. (2018). Education and psychosocial functioning among older adults: 4-year change in sense of control and hopelessness. *The Journals of Gerontology: Series B*, 73 (5), 849–859. Advances online publication.

Moen, P., Erickson, W. A., Agarwal, M., Fields, V., & Todd, L. (2000). *The Cornell Retirement and Well-Being Study*. Final Report 2000.

Moody, H. & Sood, S. (2010). Age branding. In: A. Drolet, N. Schwarz, & C. Yoon (Eds.), *The Aging Consumer: Perspectives from Psychology and Economics* (pp. 229–247). New York: Routledge.

Mori, K., Kaiho, Y., Tomata, Y., Narita, M., Tanji, F., Sugiyama, K., Sugawara, Y., & Tsuji, I. (2017). Sense of life worth living (*ikigai*) and incident functional disability in elderly Japanese: The Tsurugaya Project. *Journal of Psychosomatic Research, 95*, 62–67.

National Science Board. (2014). *Science and Engineering Indicators 2014*. Arlington VA: National Science Foundation (NSB 14-01). Retrieved from https://www.nsf.gov/stati stics/seind14/index.cfm/front/f3.htm#s2.

Noone, J. H., Stephens, C., & Alpass, F. M. (2009). Preretirement planning and well-being in later life a prospective study. *Research on Aging, 31*(3), 295–317.

Novak, Mark (2011). *Issues in Aging, 3rd Edition*. New York, NY: Pearson Education, Inc.

Page, L. Co-founder of Google. (2015, March 10). *Interview with Patrick Pichette*. Retrieved from https://plus.google.com/+LarryPage/posts/THXDPTgTFcb.

Pinquart, Martin (2002, Spring). Creating and maintaining purpose in life in old age: A meta-analysis. *Ageing International, 27*(2), 90–114.

Retirement Confidence Survey Summary Report—2019 (2019, April 23) Employee Benefit Research Institute (EBRI). Washington, DC. ©2019 EBRI/Greenwald Retirement Confidence Survey, 1–37. Retrieved from https://www.ebri.org/docs/default-source/ rcs/2019-rcs/2019-rcs-short-report.pdf.

Rogers, M. A. M., Plassman, B. L., Kabeto, M., Fisher, G. G., McArdle, J. J., Llewellyn, D. J., Potter, G. G., & Laga, K. M. (2009). Parental education and late-life dementia in the United States. *Journal of Geriatric Psychiatry and Neurology, 22*(1), 71–80.

Sayer, L. C., Freedman, Vicki A., & Bianchi, S. M. (2016). Gender, time use, and aging. In: L. K. George & K. F. Ferraro (Eds.), *Handbook of Aging and the Social Sciences* (pp. 163–180). Academic Press.

Schaie, K. W. & Willis, S. L. (2010). *Handbook of the Psychology of Aging, 7th Edition*. San Diego, CA: Academic Press.

Seligman, M. (2011). *Flourish: A Visionary New Understanding of Happiness and Well-Being*. New York: Free Press.

Simone, P. M. & Haas, A. L. (2009, Fall). Cognition and leisure time activities of older adults. *LLI Review, the Annual Journal of the Osher Lifelong Learning Institute: Explorations by and About Older Learners, 4*, 22–28.

Social Security Administration. *Benefits Planner/Life Expectancy*. Retrieved from https://www.ssa.gov/planners/lifeexpectancy.html.

Social Security Administration. *Social Security Act of 1935*. Retrieved from https://www.ssa.gov/history/35act.html.

Sone, T., Nakaya, N., Ohmiri, K., Shimazu, T., Higashiguchi, M., Kakizaki, M., Kikuchi, N., Kuriyama, S., Tsujii, & Ichiro, M. (2008, July/August). Sense of life worth living (Ikigai) and mortality in Japan: Ohsaki Study. *Psychosomatic Medicine, 70*(6), 709–715.

Strecher, V. J. (2016). *Life on Purpose: How Living for What Matters Most Changes Everything*. New York, NY: HarperOne.

Steinberg, J. (2019). *MyRetirementWorks.com—From Retiring to Rewiring*. Retrieved from http://myretirementworks.com.

Suitor, J., Gilligan, M., & Pillemer, K. (2016). Stability, change and complexity in later-life families. In: L. K. George & K. F. Ferraro (Eds.), *Handbook of Aging and the Social Sciences* (pp. 206–226). Amsterdam, Netherlands and New York, NY: Academic Press.

Taylor, M. & Doverspike, D. (2003). Retirement planning and preparation. In: G. A. Adams & T. A. Beehr (Eds.), *Retirement: Reasons, Processes, and Results* (pp. 53–82). New York, NY: Springer.

van Solinge, H. (2013). Adjustment to retirement. In: M. Wang (Ed.), *The Oxford Handbook of Retirement* (pp. 311–324). New York, NY: Oxford University Press.

van Solinge, H. & Henkens, K. (2005, February). Couples' adjustment to retirement: A multi-actor panel study. *The Journals of Gerontology Series B Psychological Sciences and Social Sciences, 60*(1), S11–20. DOI:10.1093/geronb/60.1.S11.

Wang, M., Henkens, K., & van Solinge, H. (2011, April). Retirement adjustment: A review of theoretical and empirical advancements. *The American Psychologist, 66*(3), 204–213. DOI:10.1037/a0022414.

Wang, M. & Shi, J. (2014). Psychological research on retirement. *Annual Review of Psychology, 65*, 209–233.

Windsor, T. D., Curtis, R. G., & Luszoz, M. A. (2015, July). Sense of purpose as a psychological resource for aging well. *Developmental Psychology, 51*(7), 975–986.

Wink, P. & James, J. B. (2013). The life course perspective on life in the post-retirement period. In: M. Wang (Ed.), *The Oxford Handbook of Retirement* (pp. 59–72). New York, NY: Oxford Univ.

Wolinsky, F. D., Wyrwich, K. W., Babu, A. N., Kroenke, K., & Tierney, W. M. (2003). Age, aging, and the sense of control among older adults: A longitudinal reconsideration. *Journal of Gerontology: Social Sciences, 58B*(4), S212–220.

Xie, B., Huang, M., & Watkins, I. (2013). Technology and retirement life: A systematic review of the literature on older adults and media. In: M. Wang (Ed.), *The Oxford Handbook of Retirement* (pp. 493–509). New York, NY: Oxford Univ. Press.

Yoon, C. & Cole, C. (2008). Aging and consumer behavior. In: C. P. Haugtvedt & P. M. Herr, & F. R. Kardes (Eds.), *Handbook of Consumer Psychology* (pp. 247–270). New York: Lawrence Erlbaum Associates.

Yoon, C., Feinberg, F., & Schwarz, N. (2010). Why do older consumers tell us they are more satisfied? In: A. Drolet, N. Schwarz, & C. Yoon (Eds.), *The Aging Consumer: Perspectives from Psychology and Economics* (pp. 209–228). New York: Routledge.

8

IMPACT OF AGE ON BRAND CHOICE

Raphaëlle Lambert-Pandraud and Gilles Laurent

Brand choice processes and actual brand choices differ importantly across consumers belonging to different age groups. In this chapter, we consider the effects of chronological age (defined by a consumer's date of birth) rather than the effects of subjective age (how young a consumer feels) or of a consumer's perception of the gap between her subjective and chronological age (see chapter 12; Amatulli, Peluso, Guido & Yoon, 2018). Interest in the impact of a consumer's age on brand choice goes well beyond its short-term managerial implications for marketing action. It illustrates the importance, when analyzing consumers' choices among alternatives, of taking into account the decision makers' previous experiences with the available alternatives. In many categories, the competing brands among which one can choose became known to consumers starting at different times in their lives. For example, whereas one of the leading perfumes worldwide was introduced almost 100 years ago, dozens of new perfumes are launched every year. Thus, a consumer typically encounters different brands for the first time at different periods of her life (e.g., one brand at 15 years old and another brand at 60 years). Conversely, when a new brand is launched, potential consumers vary in the periods they are in their lives: some are coming of age while others are retired.

Consumer memory plays an important role. Which brands are known or come to mind spontaneously? Brand recognition depends on both the consumer's age and personal history with the brand. Different facets of memory critically impact brand consideration and choice. Investigating real-world brand choice offers insights that cannot be obtained in experimental laboratory studies using brand stimuli, which are equally new to the respondents.

Several theoretical explanations of the underlying mechanisms have been advanced to explain how these differences in consumer age and brand launch dates may create observed differences in brand choice and brand choice processes. Some mechanisms have to do with affective factors, whereas others pertain to changes in cognitive abilities, even within the same product category. Consider cars as an example. A consumer may have developed an affective attachment to a specific car brand over several decades, perhaps since she first started driving, while the attachment to a new car brand has to be developed from scratch. At the same time, another consumer may have several car brands stored in long-term memory from when she was younger, while it is a struggle to encode many of the new car brands.

In this chapter, we present results regarding brand choice and brand memory, including findings that have emerged in the last ten years. We review a variety of mechanisms that may account for the results and identify potential questions for further research.

Selected Results for Brand Choice and Choice Processes

Previous literature indicates that older consumers are more likely to prefer longer-established brands, maintain a smaller consideration set (and more generally, a shrinking purchase process), and engage in repeat purchase of the brands they have owned in the past. In terms of memory, older consumers are not impaired when recalling long-established brands, but they struggle to recall recent brands. These tendencies create notable market share differences across different consumer age ranges.

Preference for Long-Established Brands

Older car buyers tend to favor longer-established brands (Furse, Punj, and Stewart, 1984; Lambert-Pandraud, Laurent, and Lapersonne, 2005). To compare older and younger consumers, we often follow Schaie's (1996) age categorization, distinguishing 60–74 years as the "young-old," from over 74 years "old-old," and comparing both groups with middle-aged (40–59 years) and the young (under 40 years) age groups. For example, older French buyers purchase one of the three leading, long-established, national brands (Peugeot, Renault, or Citroën) at higher rates: 49 percent among buyers under 40 years, 56 percent for those aged 40–59, 69 percent for those aged 60–74, and 74 percent for those over 74 years. Similarly, perfumes introduced before 1982 enjoy a 54 percent share among French consumers aged 60 years and older, compared with only 20 percent among those 30 years and younger, according to a 2002 survey (Axciom-Consodata, 2002). In the radio market, stations created before 1981 have a market share of 58 percent among older audiences versus 12 percent among the younger audiences, according to 2007 data (Médiamétrie, Audience study, Jan. 2008).

Older and Smaller Awareness Set

Age impacts the brands a consumer knows, i.e., the "awareness set," which greatly determines brand consideration and choice. When persons aged 18 to 92 were questioned about the radio stations they know if only by name, we observed a turning point in brand knowledge in consumers in their early 60s: For long-established brands, age has a direct positive impact up to the turning point but no significant impact afterward. For recent brands, the pattern is the opposite: There is no direct impact before the turning point and a significant negative impact afterward. For example, respondents recall at age 20 about 2.6 long-established stations versus 9.1 recent ones; at age 60, 3.9 versus 5.7; and at age 80, 3.5 versus 2.7. Thus, recent stations represent a large majority of the recalled stations (78 percent) at age 20, a small majority (60 percent) at age 60, and a minority (43 percent) at age 80. Declining cognitive ability measured by slower processing speed mediates the impact of age on the number of radio stations spontaneously recalled (Lambert-Pandraud et al., 2017). Indeed, in a second survey about awareness of radio stations, 76-year-old respondents could spontaneously retrieve 11 percent of the brands they knew versus 52 percent for 21-year-olds, with an overall average of 38 percent (Lambert-Pandraud et al., 2018).

Smaller Consideration Set, Shrinking Purchase Process

Before making a purchase, older consumers tend to consider fewer brands (Cole and Balasubramanian, 1993; Johnson, 1990; Lambert-Pandraud et al., 2005; Lapersonne, Laurent, and Le Goff, 1995; Uncles and Ehrenberg, 1990; Uncles and Lee, 2006). Similarly, Deshpandé and Zaltman (1978) and Deshpandé and Krishnan (1981) find that older consumers tend to make fewer price comparisons and collect less information before they purchase. Uncles and Ehrenberg (1990) observe that, on average, households in which members are 55 years and older buy fewer brands of frequently purchased consumer goods, partly because of their lower purchase rates. Cole and Balasubramanian (1993) also find that older people consider fewer brands and varieties of cereals before a purchase. Similarly, Aurier and Jean (1996) report that the number of drinks considered during specific purchase occasions decreases with age. In contrast, neither Gruca (1989) nor Campbell (1969) observes a significant relationship between consumer age and the size of the consideration set for coffee and grocery products, respectively.

Prior results converge more for new car purchases: Both Johnson (1990) and Srinivasan and Ratchford (1991) observe that older consumers search for less information before they make a decision. Maddox, Gronhaug, Homans, and May (1978) find that, with increased age of consumers, there is a decrease in the number of car brands considered. From another perspective, Cattin and Punj (1983) reveal that car buyers who consider a single dealer are significantly older, a finding they attribute to the higher psychological cost of information search. Lapersonne and colleagues (1995, p. 55) indicate that being older than 60 years significantly increases the probability that the consumer will have a "consideration set of size one" before purchasing a new car, which in four of five cases leads to repeat purchase. Furthermore, Lambert-Pandraud and colleagues (2005) find that age significantly reduces the average number of car brands considered. Older buyers of new cars are much less likely to consider three or more brands and much more likely to consider only a single brand. They are also more likely to simplify the purchase process by considering a single dealer or a single model (see Table 8.1).

Overall, these studies describe the "shrinkage" of the decision process with age—fewer brands considered and bought, fewer price comparisons made, fewer drinks considered, less information sought, fewer dealers and fewer models considered—which means that older consumers consider fewer options on the basis of the more limited information they attain.

Higher Tendency to Repeat Purchase

Not surprisingly, smaller consideration sets lead older consumers to exhibit a higher tendency to repeat purchase their previous car brand (Lambert-Pandraud et al., 2005), at levels of 42 percent among those 39 years or younger, 54 percent among those aged 40–59, 66 percent among those aged 60–74, and 72 percent among those 75 years and older (see Figure 8.1).

Similarly, the extent to which consumers purchase a new car from the same dealer increases (21 percent, 34 percent, 44 percent , and 49 percent for the same age categories, respectively). We observe comparable results in the context of voting intentions during the 2007 presidential election in France: The older the person, the more likely she planned to vote for the same party as she had during the 2002 presidential election. Across six categories of fast-moving consumer goods, Singh et al. (2012) find the observed rate of sole brand buying to be more frequent (at 37 percent) among consumers aged 60–74 than in younger age groups, although buying patterns (category penetration and frequency) and double jeopardy (smaller penetration and frequency for smaller brands) do not differ across age groups.

TABLE 8.1 Older Buyers Consider Fewer Brands, Dealers, and Models before Buying a New Car

Age group	18–39	40–59	60–74	75 and over
Average number of car brands considered before buying	2.24	2.16	1.92	1.77
Percent considering three and more brands	24	22	14	7
Percent considering a single brand	11	15	26	33
Percent considering a single dealer	47	53	66	79
Percent considering a single model	6	11	20	28

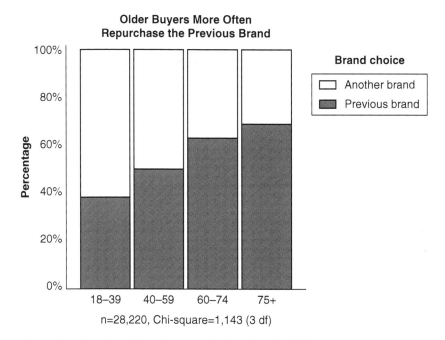

FIGURE 8.1   Reprinted from Lambert-Pandraud et al., 2005.

Market Shares Depend on Consumer Age and Brand Age

Perfumes launched around the same date tend to have similar profiles in terms of their consumers' ages. Consider two perfumes launched six years prior to a 2002 survey of French consumers, both of which experience the same pattern of lower sales with increasing age: The older the consumers, the lower the perfume's success. Shares of choice equal 5 percent (a high score for a perfume) for both perfumes among users around 20 years of age; these shares drop to 3 percent among consumers aged 40 years, to 1 percent among consumers aged 60 years; and finally to 0 percent and 1 percent among consumers aged 80 years. For two perfumes launched in the 1920s, more than 80 years before the survey, the older the consumers, the greater their success. Finally, two mature perfumes launched about 30 years before the survey reveal an inverted U-shaped consumer age profile in terms of shares: increasing between 20 and 40 years of age, reaching maximum share among consumers age 40 years, then declining for those older than 40.

These results imply sizable differences in market shares for consumers across the age ranges. In the perfume survey, those scents launched in the preceding 10 years together earned a choice share of greater than 60 percent among consumers in the 20-year-old age group but of less than 20 percent among consumers older than 70. In contrast, the perfumes launched more than 30 years ago together

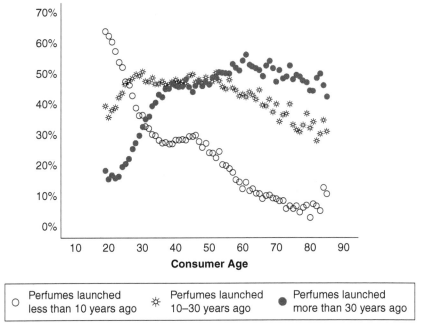

FIGURE 8.2 Reprinted from Lambert-Pandraud and Laurent, 2010.

achieved a share of approximately 10 percent among younger consumers but more than 40 percent among older consumers. Finally, the perfumes launched between 10 and 30 years prior to the survey attained their maximum share among mature consumers (Lambert-Pandraud and Laurent, 2010, see Figure 8.2). This finding is consistent with the results pertaining to both new car purchases and radio audiences, as reported previously.

What explains older consumers' preference for long-established options, shrinking purchase process, and tendency to repeat purchase? Research suggests various mechanisms. Some mechanisms are linked to aging itself (cognitive decline, biological aging, increased aversion to change, declining innovativeness), while others are linked to a reduced temporal horizon (Socioemotional Selectivity). Some mechanisms develop over time (attachment, expertise, habits), and some are related to the period during which one has lived (nostalgia, cohort effects).

Possible Mechanisms

Cognitive Decline

Robust findings from psychology associate aging with reliable declines in higher-order cognitive resources such as memory (Salthouse and Ferrer-Caja, 2003).

These declines seem closely related and share a high proportion of age-related variance, which suggests that a general, common factor may underlie the performance decrements associated with aging, as observed in studies conducted by various research teams using different materials (Birren and Schaie, 2006). One of the most promising of these general factors is processing speed (Salthouse, 1996). Specifically, a central slowdown may reduce older people's processing speed, which prompts consumers to simplify their purchase processes by considering fewer options or repeating their previous choice (Bryan and Luszcz, 1996; Zelinski and Burnight, 1997). The decrease in processing speed is highly correlated with performance in other resources, such as working memory (Gutchess, 2009). Similarly, a decline in working memory capacity, associated with reduced processing speed, may lower a person's ability to encode information about new brands and to retrieve previously stored information (Gutchess, 2009, Park and Gutchess, 2004).

Biological Aging

The results from previous research also document the decline of physical capacities that occurs because of biological aging, or "the array of modifications happening in the organism with age" that leads to "lowering of resistance and adaptability to the pressures of the environment" (Barrère, 1992, p. 16). For example, older persons with serious physical problems may have problems driving a car, or even walking, which could prevent them from visiting multiple car dealers or car dealers located far from home. They may also experience loss in hearing or vision, which makes it difficult for older people to learn or attend to new information about brands.

Aversion to Change

An aversion by older adults to the risks linked to change, even if the present solution is far from ideal, is a well-documented phenomenon in gerontology. Wallach and Kogan (1961) and Botwinick (1966) asked subjects to choose between two options: staying in a secure but mediocre occupation with limited prospects for a pay increase or changing to an occupation that will lead, with probability p, to a salary increase or, with probability $1 - p$, to financial disaster. Older subjects are markedly more likely to choose staying, whatever the value of p (Botwinick, 1978). Botwinick (1978) suggests two hypotheses to explain this resistance to change. First, due to their intellectual decline, older people may avoid making decisions. Second, older people may avoid the risk associated with a bad decision, especially one that may lead to financial risk. Thus, the purchase behavior of older persons could be the consequence of change aversion, which would lead them to repeat their previous choice; staying with the same brand, same model, and the same dealer provides ways to avoid the complexity of a new decision.

Innovativeness

Innovativeness here refers to the "propensity of consumers to adopt novel products" (Hirschman, 1980, p. 283). Lesser and Kunkle (1991) describe exploratory behavior as a central feature of younger respondents (18–39 years). Applying this finding to consumer behavior, and specifically to brand choice, younger persons should be more likely to try new brands that may or may not prove satisfactory. In contrast, older people prefer to stick to well-known brands, even if they are not entirely satisfying, because their knowledge about these products reduces perceived risk. Consumer behavior studies related to this topic are limited, with most of the research having been aimed at finding a relationship between age and the adoption of new product categories (rather than the adoption of new brands in an existing category). They also do not offer a consensus. In an oft-quoted classical review, Rogers and Shoemaker (1971) mention that 76 studies report a positive correlation between age and time of adoption, 44 studies have negative correlations, and 108 studies find no correlation. Thirty-two years later, Rogers (2003, p. 288) confirmed that

> Earlier adopters are no different from later adopters in age. There is inconsistent evidence about the relationship between age and innovativeness. About half of the many diffusion studies on this subject show no relationship, a few found that earlier adopters are younger, and some indicate they are older.

These variations may reflect differences in the products under study. Hauser, Tellis, and Griffin (2006, p. 689) conclude that "While some studies have shown that innovators are better educated, wealthier, more mobile, and younger, other studies have failed to validate these findings." In fact, a negative relationship might exist between age and innovativeness, according to Tellis, Yin, and Bell (2005, p. 21) who claim that lower innovativeness measured by "reluctance is best explained by age and income, closely followed by mobility, education, and gender." Given these conflicting results, there is a need for more empirical investigations to test whether younger consumers' proneness to exploration, variety, and change stimulate their choice of newer brands.

Socioemotional Selectivity

According to socioemotional selectivity theory (Carstensen, Isaacowitz, and Charles, 1999; Isaacowitz, Charles, and Carstensen, 2000), older adults perceive their temporal horizon as limited and therefore emphasize emotional goals over knowledge-related goals. This shift occurs as persons "become increasingly aware that time is in some sense 'running out'" (Carstensen et al., 1999, p. 165). More generally, persons of all ages feeling a limited time horizon seek "intimacy and affective gain in their social interactions" (Drolet et al., 2009a, p. 5). Older adults select more easily familiar social partners over new informative contacts (Fredrickson and Carstensen, 1990), which reduces their social network to their closest ties. Compared with younger respondents, they selectively remember more positive than negative attributes of the options they have chosen in the past (Mather and Johnson, 2000). As a correlate of their reduced social network, consumers aged 65 years and over receive significantly less word of mouth about consumption in the repertoire and subscription markets (East, Uncles and Lomax, 2014). These effects could lead older adults to prefer longer-established brands that they have known for an extended period rather than new brands.

Attachment

Older consumers may develop strong bonds on the basis of their longer interactions with certain brands. These may form outside the "sensitive period" hypothesized by Holbrook and Schindler (1994). Thomson, MacInnis, and Park (2005, p. 77) extend the parent-infant relationship (Bowlby, 1979) to their definition of attachment as "an emotion-laden target-specific bond between a person and a specific object." Kleine and Baker (2004) also find that attachments to objects mirror those to other people, such that continuous activities undertaken with the object (e.g., cleaning, displaying, discussing) imbue it with greater meaning. According to Thomson and colleagues (2005), strong attachments require time, repeated interactions, and memories that pertain specifically to the object and thereby encourage the person to invest in the object with greater meaning. Price, Arnould, and Curasi (2000, p. 188), analyzing the "cherished possessions" of respondents aged 65 years and older, cite one of them verbatim with the following: "It's almost like a history of our life." Attachment evolves according to self-meaning, such that brand choices made during the coming-of-age period may not satisfy the goals of a mature adult. The mature adult may make new brand choices and form new attachments.

Expertise

Previous research often suggests that expertise (Alba and Hutchinson, 1987) is a key reason for older consumers' consideration of fewer brands or their greater likelihood of making a repeat purchase. Through prolonged usage experience, older consumers would be expected to have developed expertise, identified the brands that suit them best, and thus would no longer need to investigate other options. This line of reasoning could be used to explain the reduced consideration sets, higher repeat purchase rates, and preference for longer-established brands among older consumers. However, this rationale also assumes, in some sense, that the market and the available options remain identical over time, so that expertise once acquired, remains valid (as it might for, say, chess or piano playing or knowledge of classical literature). Consider the contrast between the automobile market and frequently purchased goods. Car purchases occur at long time intervals, during which the models change markedly, so even experienced purchasers cannot rely solely on the knowledge they have accumulated from past purchases to choose among current models. Many markets for durables change rapidly, such as for high-tech consumer electronics. In contrast, for frequently purchased categories, the offerings change minimally, or not at all, between purchase occasions; thus, accumulated expertise is much less subject to obsolescence. Lambert-Pandraud and colleagues (2005) find that self-reported expertise with cars leads respondents to search for more, rather than less, information before purchasing a new car.

Habits

The repeat purchase of a brand could be driven by habit, developed through a history of repeatedly purchasing that brand, which then leads to an automatic propensity to repeat the behavior. "As people age, the relationships between associations and stimuli and those between associations and behaviors become increasingly reinforced. Therefore, the elderly are more likely to activate (through external stimuli) and rely on habits to make decisions" (Drolet, Suppes, and Bodapati, 2009b, p.21). Hence "the average stated likelihood of buying the same item on the next shopping occasion was higher for the elderly versus young" (p.23). This adaptation may be a useful way to compensate for age-related declines in cognitive and other abilities. However, there should be differences across product categories. For example, such routinization should be more likely for brands sold in supermarkets, where the frequency of purchases by definition is much higher, which creates more opportunities for developing associations in memory, especially if the available options remain identical across successive purchase occasions. However, routinization should be less likely for new products or durable goods, whose infrequent purchase occasions do not afford consumers with opportunities to develop associations and habits, especially if the options change markedly between successive purchase occasions (Labrecque et al., 2017; Drolet et al., 2017).

Nostalgia

Although the word "nostalgia" was originally coined to describe a longing for a native country, Holbrook and Schindler (1991, p. 330) define it as "a preference … toward objects (people, places, or things) that were more common (popular, fashionable, or widely circulated) when one was younger (during early adulthood, adolescence, childhood, or even before birth)." Psychologists contend that a person has an early critical period in terms of her psychological development (Schindler and Holbrook, 2003, p. 277). Holbrook and Schindler (1994, p. 414) further explain that "consumers form enduring aesthetic preferences during a sensitive period," specifically their "late adolescence or early adulthood" (Holbrook and Schindler, 1989, p. 119) or "late teens and early twenties" (Schindler and Holbrook, 1993, p. 551). They further suggest that consumers maintain these early imprinted preferences for the rest of their lives. Note that this claim is similar to the results of the famous Bennington study (Alwin, Cohen, and Newcomb, 1991) that noted the persistence of political preferences people acquire during their college years. The specific limits of this formative period are, however, somewhat uncertain. Consumers like most the pop songs introduced when they were about 23 years of age (Holbrook and Schindler, 1989), fashion styles that emerged when they were 33 (Schindler and Holbrook, 1993), movie stars from when they were about 14 (Holbrook and Schindler, 1994), motion pictures awarded an Oscar when they were about 27 (Holbrook and Schindler, 1996), and automobiles from when they were about 26 (scored by male subjects; Schindler and Holbrook, 2003). Although this stream of research by Holbrook and colleagues considers salient but unbranded items such as pop songs, movie stars, motion pictures, and car models, the findings likely extend as well to nostalgic preferences for brands encountered by consumers during their youth.

Cohort Effects

For the mechanisms described previously, consumers change their behavior as they age. However, an alternative explanation may be that these differences are due to cohort effects: That is, consumers from different cohorts behave differently. A cohort is typically defined as "the aggregate of individuals who experienced the same event within the same time interval" (Rentz, Reynolds, and Stout, 1983, p.12; based on Ryder, 1965). For the present focus on brand choice, the cohort experience to consider should not be major events that occurred when persons came of age, such as the Vietnam War (as in Meredith and Schewe, 2002), but rather the brand situation at a particular time. In the French car market, for example, why would older cohorts be expected to have a higher rate of repeat purchases, favor longer-established brands, and consider fewer models? This could be linked to the market structure that existed in France when each cohort came of age and became interested in cars. When older people came of age, the market belonged almost entirely to a few French brands, including the three that still remain as market leaders (Renault, Peugeot, and Citroën), and each of these offered only a few models. Breakdowns were frequent and largely regarded as normal. But when younger cohorts came of age, dozens of foreign brands had appeared in the French marketplace with a large number of models, and breakdowns were rare, such that consumers who faced a breakdown opt to switch to another brand.

We suggest that it is likely that multiple mechanisms underlie the phenomena associated with brand choice. Some mechanisms predict only some of these phenomena. This gap leaves multiple research questions that we consider in the next section.

Questions for Further Research

Testing the Impact of Cognitive Variables

Previous marketing literature mostly offers an affective mechanism, mainly nostalgia, to explain preferences for long-known options. The impact of cognitive factors provides an alternative avenue for interesting research. As indicated previously, slower processing speed mediates the negative impact of age on the number of spontaneously recalled recent brands. Reduced cognitive resources may lead consumers to simplify their purchase processes by considering fewer options or repeating their previous choices. Thus, our first question pertains to how cognitive factors can explain why older consumers focus more on longer-established brands, repeat purchase more, and so forth. If they do, what cognitive factors are at play? Are the observed differences in brand choices due to memory problems, or do slowdowns in processing speed and declines in short-term memory capacity lead older consumers to resort to simplifying heuristics, such as repeat purchases? Cognitive factors also may influence specific stages of the choice process, such as information search or consideration, and additional research should attempt to identify these effects.

Moreover, assuming that memory is important, is it that consumers encode brand information more easily when they are younger, so that longer-established brands, or information about them, are more likely to be encoded in long-term memory than more recent brands? Or is it that all brands are equally well encoded, but that among older persons, retrieval is easier when it comes to information encoded at a younger age, which usually means information about longer-established brands? Finally, do cognitive factors play a role in purchasing products in a context relying primarily on recognition, such as fast-moving consumer goods displayed on a supermarket shelf?

Specific Measures of Affective and Cognitive Variables

Previous marketing literature mostly uses age as the operational explanatory variable. For example, Holbrook and Schindler (1989, 1994, 1996) statistically analyze the impact of age on option preferences to support their theory about nostalgia. This reliance on age may result from the operational constraints of using secondary data (e.g., panel data) about brand choice, which rarely include information about psychological variables, either affective or cognitive. However, it would be interesting to develop specific measures of such variables, in addition to measuring age itself. For example, to assess the possible impact of cognitive decline on brand choice, researchers need to measure cognitive ability, separately from age, to assess whether cognitive decline mediates, totally or partially, the impact of age on brand choice (i.e., preference for older brands, repeat purchase, reduced consideration sets).

Expertise

Expertise should, on average, increase with experience and, therefore with age. However, these variables are also required as separate measures to conduct analyses of the relationship between expertise and age and to assess their impact on brand choice phenomena. Involvement in a product category and frequent usage may account for expertise better than age. Certain categories evolve very quickly, such as those that rely on technological innovations and constant introduction of new models, in which case expertise may be uncorrelated or negatively correlated with experience. Brand choice may also occur in a very dynamic setting for the impact of expertise compared with an immutable setting like a chess game. In addition, experts may be able to collect more complete information and deal with greater complexity. They are thereby capable of exercising greater informed judgment. That is, expertise may lead to consideration of larger choice sets or more complex choice processes.

Research Across Adulthood

Should we focus on studying changes in consumers that occur after mature adulthood, i.e., at 60 or 70 years old? Or should the change processes be deemed continuous, beginning as early as in one's 20s? In most brand choice studies, observed variables change in a continuous and often linear manner over adulthood. This trend also emerges for fundamental psychological variables, such as processing speed and working memory capacity. Therefore, to answer the new research questions posited in this chapter, researchers should go beyond a simple contrast between respondents of college-age and those 65 years and older; they should study age-related changes in brand choice processes (and more generally, consumer behavior) over a broad range of ages within adulthood.

Impact on Consumer Satisfaction in Daily Life

Research showing that older consumers have different choice processes, which lead to different brand choices, leaves open the question of the practical consequences of these differences on consumer satisfaction. For example, according to socioemotional selectivity theory, older persons give more weight to affective factors, which logically leads them to prefer long-known options that become the most satisfying solutions for them. At the same time, we would expect there is some difference between the level of satisfaction resulting from a brand choice that derives from a smaller consideration set consisting of the previously purchased brand, and a theoretically "optimal" brand choice based on a sophisticated analysis that takes into consideration all available information about all brands. Yet this difference may have only marginal value, such that the consumer, at the end of the simplified purchase process, may be reasonably satisfied with the product choice. As discussed previously, relying on habits may be an efficient way for consumers with reduced cognitive ability to make satisfying choices. Therefore, research should again distinguish among stable and mature markets and those that change rapidly, in which older buyers may routinely choose options that have grown obsolete.

Public Policy

Depending on the mechanisms at work, the public policy implications of this research are very different. If older consumers are handicapped mostly by cognitive declines, they may benefit from external guidance and support, which would give them easier, more complete access to all market opportunities, especially in fast-changing categories such as consumer electronics. However, such public policy guidance and support must be carefully designed, because source memory weakens in older consumers (Law, Hawkins, and Craik, 1998), which may create confusion between commercial and consumerist sources (Skurnik, Yoon, Park, and Schwarz, 2006). In addition, any adopted policies should be careful not to interfere with heuristics or habits that consumers may have developed to compensate for age-related declines in cognitive and other abilities. For an older car buyer, limiting the consideration set to a small number of well-known brands may be a useful process to avoid the consequences of a reduced ability to encode and analyze complex data about many new brands.

Age–Cohort–Period

As discussed previously, differences uncovered in a cross-sectional data set between older and younger consumers might be due to an aging effect or to a cohort effect. To separate the two, as Rentz and colleagues (1983) demonstrate, researchers need to analyze similar data at different dates. However, with such data, a third effect may be at work, namely, a period effect: Consumers tend to behave similarly on the same date but differently on different dates. These potential effects create a major statistical problem because perfect collinearity exists among the three variables. That is, if a cohort is defined by the person's birth year and the period equals the year of observation, by definition, age = period − cohort. In a regression approach, the matrix of explanatory variables does not achieve full rank, and the ordinary least squares estimate cannot be computed, because the same predicted values (and errors) would be obtained by different combinations of the age, period, and cohort coefficients. Despite the proposals of several solutions to address this difficulty, all of them pose problems, and there remains room for the development of better statistical methods.

Other Data Issues

Age is obviously an exogenous variable and can be easily measured, but existing analyses often bear on underlying mechanisms, and therefore on the hypothesized roles of mediating variables influenced by age (or birth date) that reportedly influence the dependent variables related to brand choice. Some variables, though strongly influenced by age, are conceptually different and should be measured separately. A typical example includes measures of the current cognitive ability of each respondent (e.g., processing speed, working memory capacity). A more difficult case pertains to the value of the same variables at a particular point in the past, such as the cognitive ability that an 80-year-old person had when the specific brand launched 20 years prior. This variable seems impossible to measure. A third case entails past values of certain variables that may be measured by retrospective questions, such as the brand of a person's first car. The degree of reliability of the answer likely varies according to the topic: A respondent is more likely to remember the brand of his or her first car than the brand of initial purchase in a frequently purchased category such as coffee. In addition, the quality of the retrospective data may be jeopardized by a respondent's level of cognitive decline.

Some of the mechanisms discussed previously attempt to predict differences across cohorts (e.g., Holbrook and Schindler's (1989) analysis of preferences for music styles as a function of birth year). In contrast, others predict differences within cohorts (e.g., persons with different degrees of cognitive decline or different perceived time horizons may behave differently). The latter approach requires individual-level data, whereas the former can employ data aggregated at the cohort level. For analyses that are not of actual panel data (i.e., repeated observations of the same subjects), researchers might use pseudo-panels (i.e., same cohorts observed repeatedly, using different individuals for each observation date).

Some brand choice phenomena appear difficult to reproduce or simulate in a lab through the use of new, artificial material and relatively young subjects, such as college students. In most categories, competing brands are introduced on different dates. A consumer, therefore, has multiple opportunities to encounter and encode them, including at different ages (a brand introduced when she was 15 years of age versus one introduced when she was 60) and over different lengths of time (if she is now 61, she had the opportunity to encounter the first brand for 46 years versus just one year for the second brand). Such differences in encoding opportunities may be a cause of the brand choice differences observed today.

Conclusion

The proportion of older people in the worldwide population has been increasing, even in new leading economies such as China. A psychological perspective on older consumers' choice processes is needed to avoid drawing potentially misleading inferences and conclusions. For example, older buyers have more free time after retiring, but they tend to consider fewer brands when buying a new car. Or, one might assume that older buyers consider fewer brands because they are more experienced when, in fact, older buyers who are experts consider more brands before buying. Research focusing on older people's choices has important implications for the academic and managerial community, as well as for public policy. As product and service technology evolve rapidly, further research is needed to generate a more nuanced understanding of how biological aging and cognitive decline affect older consumers' brand choice and brand choice processes.

References

Alba, J.W. & Hutchinson, J.W. (1987), Dimensions of consumer expertise, *Journal of Consumer Research*, *13*(4), 411–455.

Alwin, D.F., Cohen, R.L., & Newcomb, T.M. (1991), *Political Attitudes over the Lifespan: The Bennington Women After Fifty Years*. Madison, WI: University of Wisconsin Press.

Amatulli, C., Peluso, A.M., Guido, G., & Yoon, C. (2018), When feeling younger depends on others: The effects of social cues on older consumers, *Journal of Consumer Research*, *45*(4), 691–709.

Aurier, P. & Jean, S. (1996), L'ensemble de considération du consommateur: Une approche "personne*objet*situation,". In: J.-M. Aurifeille (Ed.), *Actes du 12° Congrès Annuel de l'Association Française du Marketing* (pp. 599–614). Pascal-Francis (France). https://pascal-francis.inist.fr/vibad/index.php?action=getRecordDetail&idt=6289650

Barrère, Hélène, ed. (1992), *La relation psychosociale avec les personnes âgées*. Toulouse, France: Privat.

Birren, James E. & Schaie, K. Warner (2006), *Handbook of the Psychology of Aging*, 6th ed. Amsterdam: Elsevier.

Botwinick, J. (1966), Cautiousness in advanced age, *Journal of Gerontology*, *21*(July), 347–353.

Botwinick, J. (1978), *Cautiousness in Decision, Aging and Behavior* (pp. 128–141). New York: Springer Publishing Company.

Bowlby, J. (1979), *The Making and Breaking of Affectional Bonds*. London: Tavistock.

Bryan, J. & Luszcz, Mary A. (1996), Speed of information processing as a mediator between age and free-recall performance, *Psychology and Aging*, *11*(1), 3–9.

Campbell, B.M. (1969), The existence and determinants of evoked set in brand choice behavior, Doctoral dissertation. Columbia University.

Carstensen, L.L., Isaacowitz, D.M., & Charles, S.T. (1999), Taking time seriously. A theory of socioemotional selectivity, *The American Psychologist*, *54*(March), 165–181.

Cattin, P. & Girish, P. (1983), Identifying the characteristics of single retail (dealer) visit new automobile buyers, *Advances in Consumer Research*, *10*, 383–388.

Cole, C.A. & Balasubramanian, S.K. (1993), Age differences in consumers' search for information: Public policy implications, *Journal of Consumer Research*, *20*(June), 157–169.

Deshpandé, R. & Krishnan, S. (1981), Correlates of deficient consumer information environments: The case of the elderly, *Advances in Consumer Research*, *9*, 515–519.

Deshpandé, R. & Zaltman, G. (1978), The impact of elderly consumer dissatisfaction and buying experience on information search: A path-analytic approach. In: R.L. Day & H.K. Hunt (Eds.), *Third Annual Conference on Consumer Satisfaction, Dissatisfaction and Complaining Behavior* (pp. 145–152). Bloomington, IN: Indiana University.

Drolet, A., Bodapati, A.V., Suppes, P., Rossi, B., & Hochwarter, H. (2017), Habits and free associations: Free your mind but mind your habits, *Journal of the Association for Consumer Research*, 2(3), 293–305.

Drolet, A., Lau-Gesk, L., Williams, P., & Jeong, H. Genevieve (2009a), Socioemotional Selectivity theory: Implications for consumer research, Chapter XX in this book.

Drolet, A., Suppes, P., & Bodapati, A.V. (2009b), Habits and free associations: Free your mind and mind your habits. Working Paper. University of California, Los Angeles.

East, R., Uncles, M., & Lomax, W. (2014), Hear nothing, do nothing: The role of word of mouth in the decision-making of older consumers, *Journal of Marketing Management*, 30(7–8), 7–8, 786–801.

Fredrickson, B.L. & Carstensen, L.L. (1990), Choosing social partners: How old age and anticipated endings make people more selective, *Psychology and Aging*, 5(September), 335–347.

Furse, D.H., Punj, G.N., & Stewart, D.W. (1984), A typology of individual search strategies among purchasers of new automobiles, *Journal of Consumer Research*, 10(March), 417–431.

Gruca, T.S. (1989), Determinants of choice set size: An alternative method for measuring evoked sets, *Advances in Consumer Research*, 16, 515–521.

Gutchess, A.H. (2009), Cognitive psychology and neuroscience of aging, Chapter XX in this book.

Hauser, J., Tellis, G.J., & Griffin, A. (2006), Research on innovation: A review and agenda for marketing science, *Marketing Science*, 25(6), 687–717.

Hirschman, E. (1980), Innovativeness, novelty seeking and consumer creativity, *Journal of Consumer Research*, 7(December), 283–295.

Holbrook Morris, B. & Schindler, R.M. (1989), Some exploratory findings on the development of musical tastes, *Journal of Consumer Research*, 16(June), 119–124.

Holbrook Morris, B. & Schindler, R.M. (1991), Echoes of the dear past: Some work in progress on nostalgia, *Advances in Consumer Research*, 18, 330–333.

Holbrook Morris, B. & Schindler, R.M. (1994), Age, sex, and attitude towards the past as predictors of consumers' aesthetic tastes for cultural products, *Journal of Marketing Research*, 31(8), 412–422.

Holbrook Morris, B. & Schindler, R.M. (1996), Market segmentation based on age and attitude toward the past: Concepts, methods and findings concerning nostalgic influences on customer tastes, *Journal of Business Research*, 37(1), 27–39.

Isaacowitz, D.M., Charles, S.T., & Carstensen, L.L. (2000), Emotion and cognition. In: F.I.M. Craik & T.A. Salthouse (Eds.), *The Handbook of Aging and Cognition*, 2nd ed. (pp. 593–631). London: Lawrence Erlbaum Associates.

Johnson, Mitzi M.S. (1990), Age differences in decision making: A process methodology for examining strategic information processing, *Journal of Gerontology: Psychological Sciences*, 45(March), 75–78.

Kleine, Susan Schultz & Baker, S.M. (2004), An integrative review of material possession attachment, *Academy of Marketing Science Review* [Online], 2004(1), 1–36. Available at http://www.amsreview.org/articles/kleine01-2004.pdf.

Labrecque, J.S., Wood, W., Neal, D.T., & Harrington, N. (2017), Habit split: When consumers unintentionally resist new products, *Journal of the Academy of Marketing Science*, 45(1), 119–133. DOI:10.1007/s11747-016-0482-9.

Lambert-Pandraud, R. & Laurent, G. (2010), Why do older consumers buy older brands: The role of attachment and declining innovativeness, *Journal of Marketing*, 74(July), 104–121.

Lambert-Pandraud, R., Laurent, G., & Gourvennec, B. (2018), Investigating Brand Verbal Fluency: When known brands do not come to mind, *International Journal of Market Research, 60*(3), 304–315.

Lambert-Pandraud, R., Laurent, G., & Lapersonne, E. (2005), Repeat purchasing of new automobiles by older consumers: Empirical evidence and interpretations, *Journal of Marketing, 69*(April), 97–103.

Lambert-Pandraud, R., Laurent, G., Mullet, E., & Yoon, C. (2017), Impact of age on brand awareness sets: A turning point in consumers' early 60s, *Marketing Letters, 28*(2), 205–218. DOI:10.1007/s11002-016-9407-0.

Lapersonne, Eric, Laurent, G., & Le Goff, J.-J. (1995), Consideration sets of size one: An empirical investigation of automobile purchases, *International Journal of Research in Marketing, 12*(1), 55–66.

Law, S., Hawkins, S.A., & Craik, F.I.M. (1998), Repetition induced belief in the elderly: Rehabilitating age-related memory deficits, *Journal of Consumer Research, 25*(2), 91–107.

Lesser, Jack A. & Kunkel, S.R. (1991), Exploratory and problem-solving consumer behavior across the life span, *Journal of Gerontology: Psychological Sciences, 46*(5), 259–269.

Maddox, Neil R., Gronhaug, K., Homans, R.E., & May, F.E. (1978), Correlates of information gathering and evoked set size for new automobile purchasers in Norway and in the U.S., *Advances in Consumer Research, 5*, 167–170.

Mather, M. & Johnson, M.K. (2000), Choice-supportive source monitoring: Do our decisions seem better to us as we age? *Psychology and Aging, 15*(December), 596–606.

Médiamétrie (2008), '126000' study, Jan.–Feb. 2007 & Sept.–Oct. 2007.

Meredith, G. & Schewe, C.D. (2002), *Defining Markets, Defining Moments: America's 7 Generational Cohorts, Their Shared Experiences and Why Business Should Care.* New York: John Wiley & Sons.

Park, D.C. & Gutchess, A.H. (2004), Long-term memory and aging: A cognitive neuroscience perspective. In: R. Cabeza, L. Nyberg, & D.C. Park (Eds.), *Cognitive Neuroscience of Aging: Linking Cognitive and Cerebral Aging* (pp. 218–245). New York: Oxford Press.

Price, L.L., Arnould, E.J., & Curasi, C.F. (2000), Older consumers' disposition of special possessions, *Journal of Consumer Research, 27*(September), 179–201.

Rentz, O. Joseph, Reynolds, F.D., & Stout, R.G. (1983), Analyzing changing consumption patterns with cohort analysis, *Journal of Marketing Research, 20*(February), 12–20.

Rogers, E.M. (2003), *Diffusion of Innovations*, 5th ed. New York: The Free Press.

Rogers, E.M., & Shoemaker, F.F. (1971), *Communication of Innovations.* New York: The Free Press.

Ryder, Norman B. (1965), The cohort as a concept in the study of social change, *American Sociological Review, 30*(6), 843–861.

Salthouse, T.A. (1996), The processing-speed theory of adult age differences in cognition, *Psychological Review, 103*(3), 403–428.

Salthouse, T.A., & Ferrer-Caja, E. (2003), What needs to be explained to account for age-related effects on multiple cognitive variables?, *Psychology and Aging, 18*(1), 91–110.

Schaie, K. Warner (1996), Intellectual development in adulthood. In: J.E. Birren & K.W. Schaie (Eds.), *Handbook of the Psychology of Aging* (pp. 266–281). San Diego, CA: Academic Press.

Schindler, R.M. & Holbrook, M.B. (1993), Critical periods in the development of men's and women's tastes in personal appearance, *Psychology and Marketing, 10*(6), 549–564.

Schindler, R.M. & Holbrook, M.B. (2003), Nostalgia for early experience as a determinant of consumer preferences, *Psychology and Marketing, 20*(April), 275–302.

Singh, J., Dall'Omo Riley, F., & Hand, C. (2012), Measuring brand choice in the older customer segment in Japan, *International Journal of Market Research, 54*(3), 347–368.

Skurnik, I., Yoon, C., Park, D., & Schwarz, N. (2006), How warnings become recommendations: Paradoxical effects of warnings on beliefs of older consumers, *Journal of Consumer Research, 31*, 713–724.

Srinivasan, N. & Ratchford, B.T. (1991), An empirical test of a model of external search for automobiles, *Journal of Consumer Research, 18*(September), 233–242.

Thomson, M., MacInnis, D.J., & Park, C.W. (2005), The ties that bind: Measuring the strength of consumers' emotional attachments to brands, *Journal of Consumer Psychology, 15*(1), 77–91.

Tellis, G.J., Yin, E., & Bell, S. (2005), Global consumer innovativeness: Country differences and individual commonalities. Working Paper. University of Southern California.

Uncles, M.D. & Ehrenberg, A.S.C. (1990), Brand choice among older consumers, *Journal of Advertising Research, 30*(August), 19–22.

Uncles, M.D. & Lee, D. (2006), Brand purchasing by older consumers: An investigation using the Juster scale and the Dirichlet model, *Marketing Letters, 17*(1), 17–29.

Wallach, M.A. & Kogan, N. (1961), Aspects of judgment and decision making: Interrelationships and changes with age, *Behavioral Science, 6*, 23–36.

Zelinski, E. M. & Burnight, K. P. (1997), Sixteen-year longitudinal and time lag changes in memory and cognition in older adults, *Psychology and Aging, 12* (September), 503–13.

9

COMPREHENSION OF AND VULNERABILITY TO PERSUASIVE MARKETING COMMUNICATIONS AMONG OLDER CONSUMERS

Carolyn M. Bonifield and Catherine A. Cole

According to the U.S. Census Bureau, the most recent Census, taken in 2010, indicated that over 40.2 million Americans were aged 65 and older (Werner, 2011). The Census Bureau projects that by 2050, the number of Americans aged 65 and older will be 88.5 million (Vincent and Velkoff, 2010). Both new products and advertising directed toward this age group have increased over the past few years, as companies such as Whirlpool, GE, Sony, L'Oreal, and Microsoft have shifted their product development and advertising strategies to target older consumers more aggressively (Glader, 2008; Schechner and Kumar, 2009). As older consumers increasingly use smartphones for email and text messaging, marketers are using this technology to reach the growing segment. For example, healthcare providers are experimenting with medication reminders and health tracking apps for older consumers (Barrett, 2011). Both researchers and practitioners are interested in better understanding this rapidly growing older market.

In this chapter, we identify the individual, task, and contextual characteristics that influence older consumers' comprehension of marketing communications (see Bonifield and Cole, 2007; Yoon et al., 2009 for more general reviews). We present these as research propositions in Table 9.1. We draw primarily on applications for marketing communications, but also discuss applications for product warnings, where a warning is "designed to alert people about potential dangers related to a particular object or environment" (Rousseau et al., 1998). Finally, we discuss how and when these characteristics interact to increase older adults' vulnerability to persuasive marketing communications. Based on our literature review, we outline hypotheses to be tested in the context of age differences in vulnerability to persuasive marketing communications (see Table 9.2 below).

Comprehension is an important topic for several reasons. First, prior research estimates that miscomprehension is fairly high in the general population. According to Jacoby and Hoyer (1989), consumers miscomprehend approximately one-third of all mass media messages. Rogers et al. (2000) review literature on warnings and conclude that even a good warning may not be understood and complied with by many perceivers. Second, comprehension is vital because it affects persuasion (Bradley and Meeds, 2004). In fact, the multiplicative comprehension elaboration model, discussed in Wyer (2002), suggests that the probability that someone will be persuaded by a message is a multiplicative function of the probability of comprehending and the probability of generating positive elaborations (Wyer, 2002). In this model, as comprehension decreases, persuasion decreases.

Background

To better inform decisions about how to design messages that are easily comprehended, we review the growing body of literature in marketing and psychology which examines how individual, task, and contextual characteristics affect older consumers' comprehension from an information processing perspective (Cole and Gaeth, 1990; Cole and Houston, 1987; Gaeth and Heath, 1987; Law et al., 1998; Rousseau et al., 1998; Skurnik et al., 2005; Yoon, 1997; Yoon et al., 2007). Underlying this review are models of comprehension and aging, which are discussed next.

Models of Comprehension and Aging

Current models of text processing recognize that text must be processed by individuals using a cognitive system with limited capacity. To comprehend text, the perceiver must perceptually encode the input, identify lexical elements such as nouns and verbs, determine syntactic and semantic relationships between these elements, and develop an understanding. The perceiver uses linguistic context and world knowledge to frame and interpret the input (Stine and Wingfield, 1987; Was and Woltz, 2007). Recently, Stine-Morrow et al. (2006) have presented a model of self-regulated language processing (SRLP) which argues that the receiver plays an active role in the comprehension process by explicitly or implicitly allocating resources to construct meaning from language, depending on the receiver's processing capacity, knowledge, and goals, as well as the characteristics of the task and the context.

When processing text, the receiver constructs three basic levels of comprehension: the surface form, the propositional textbase, and the situation model. All three levels have been studied in advertising research. The surface form corresponds to comprehension of the actual words and syntax that are employed in the text. Bradley and Meeds (2004), for example, investigate the effects of using defined or undefined technical language in an advertisement on comprehension and persuasion. The propositional textbase level is an abstract representation of the information explicitly conveyed in the text. Advertising and product warning research on claim comprehension have been conducted at the textbase level (e.g.,

Cowley, 2006). The situation model is a global understanding of what the text is about (Radvansky et al., 2001). Recent research on how advertising characteristics affect comprehension of a story that spans several ads in a campaign is research done at the situation model level (e.g., Luna, 2005).

A good example of the three levels in marketing communications is found by dissecting a 30-second Twitter ad aired during the 2015 World Series. In this ad, called "Post-Season," Twitter intended to promote their new "Moments" section, which focuses on trending content. During the ad, printed words, hashtag statements, and images rolled across the screen very quickly, hampering comprehension at the surface level. The propositional abstract representation of the information conveyed in the text was summarized in the last four seconds of the commercial "A new way to get the best of Twitter" but viewers were unsure of what the new way to get the best of Twitter was. Viewers even failed to understand the situation model: what the 30-second ad was about. All these problems led Business Insider to rate the ad as one of the ten worst ads of 2015 (O'Reilly, 2015).

Age differences in text-based processing are most likely to occur at the propositional text-based and the situation levels (Radvansky et al., 2001; Stine-Morrow et al., 1996). In the Radvansky et al. (2001) study, after reading a text passage (length of 58–85 sentences), younger participants (ages 18–26), when compared to older participants (ages 61–96), were significantly more accurate on recognition tasks requiring use of propositional text-based information, but significantly less accurate on tasks requiring use of the situation model. In other words, younger adults are often better at remembering what the text said, but older adults are often better at remembering what the text is about.

Age differences that emerge in text-based processing are at least in part attributable to age-related declines in cognitive mechanics; however, there is considerable heterogeneity in the rate of change in these mechanics (Stine-Morrow et al., 2006). The implicated cognitive mechanics include changes in processes such as working memory capacity or processing speed (Beese et al., 2019), reductions in attentional resources (Craik and Byrd, 1982), failure to inhibit irrelevant information (Hasher et al., 1999), and reduced ability to spontaneously generate associations between pieces of information (Naveh-Benjamin, 2000). For example, age differences in comprehension of spoken material may arise because older adults have trouble remembering earlier presented material to keep communication in context (Light and Capps, 1986).

Age differences in text-based processing may be also attributable to age-related changes in motivation (Fung and Carstensen, 2003; Williams and Drolet, 2005); Adams et al., 1997). Adams et al. (1997) suggest that because older adults may be motivated to understand the interpretive meaning of text, they may devote more processing resources to the situation level of text than younger adults. However, because younger adults may be motivated to acquire the facts from the text, they may devote a larger proportion of their processing resources to the propositional text base than older adults (Adams et al., 1997).

TABLE 9.1 Summary of Propositions

P1   Age differences in comprehension of marketing materials will depend on the level of text comprehension being assessed, such that there will be minimal age differences in surface level comprehension, younger adults will demonstrate better propositional text-based comprehension than older adults and older adults will demonstrate better situation level comprehension than younger adults. .

P2   Age differences in comprehension of marketing communications material will be larger for externally paced than self-paced media.

P3   Age differences in claim comprehension will be smaller for simple explicit claims and larger for implicit complex claims or for claims with pragmatic implications.

P4   Age differences in comprehension of marketing communications material will be larger for factual than for emotional information.

P5   Age differences in comprehension of visual images such as symbols in signs can be reduced with training and/or the addition of text.

P6   Age differences in comprehension will be smaller when the information is clearly presented in a consistent location or without competing visual/auditory information, but age differences in comprehension will increase when the information is inconspicuous or surrounded with distracting information.

P7   The effects of repetition may depend on the level of comprehension being assessed: Increased repetition of visual elements and story elements across an ad series will reduce age differences in comprehension at the situation level, but increased repetition of specific claims will make older adults more vulnerable to the truth effect than younger adults and will increase age differences in comprehension at the text-based level.

P8   Age differences in comprehension will be smaller for familiar domains where consumers possess knowledge and when consumers can easily access this knowledge, but larger for unfamiliar domains and in situations where knowledge is difficult to access.

P9   Age differences in comprehension will be smaller when all adults are able and motivated to use systematic processing.

The research on comprehension models and aging provides evidence for our first proposition (P1) listed in Table 9.1: Age differences in comprehension of marketing materials will depend on the level of text comprehension being assessed, such that there will be minimal age differences in surface level comprehension, younger adults will demonstrate better propositional text-based comprehension than older adults, and older adults will demonstrate better situation level comprehension than younger adults.

Task Characteristics Affecting Comprehension

Mode of Message Transmission

The mode of message transmission (e.g., radio, television, social media, telephone, or print) is important because some forms of communication tax processing resources and physical abilities more than others (Charness and Holley, 2004). For example, an auditory message puts demands on the older listener who may have experienced some hearing loss (e.g., after about age 70, most adults experience a moderate hearing loss, particularly in the higher frequency range) and because they must devote resources to keep pace with the rate of speech input (Charness and Holley, 2004). Additionally, unlike written messages, speech messages are physically present only transiently.

Regarding television, several studies have investigated age differences in comprehension of television ads (Cole and Houston, 1987, O'Donoghue et al., 2019). O'Donoghue et al. (2019) studied age differences in responses to direct-to-consumer (DTC) prescription drug television ads. They exposed consumers to one of eight DTC ads, manipulating characteristics of the major voiceover, which contained warnings. They did not find age differences in claim recognition, but age was related to the main message recall, risk recall, and ad comprehension, such that younger groups tended to recall more information compared with the oldest group.

In contrast, when the information is in print form, the reader can control both the rate of input and also reread sections as needed. For example, Abernathy and Adams-Price (2006) find no age differences in younger and older adults' comprehension of complex drug information when it was presented within print advertisements. Accordingly, our second proposition (P2) is: Age differences in comprehension of marketing communications material will be larger for externally paced than for self-paced media.

Claim Format

Marketers use a variety of claims in order to inform consumers about their brands and to issue warnings. However, consumers can misinterpret these claims by incorrectly accepting as true pragmatic implications of claims, by making incorrect inferences from comparative statements with missing referents (Shimp, 1978), and by changing how they evaluate brands after exposure to puffery claims (Cowley, 2006). Older and younger adults tend to perform comparably on comprehension questions about claims that are present during the test phase and that require automatic or very simple inferential processing (Gaeth and Heath, 1987). However, older adults may encounter problems with comprehension of claims and warnings that were recently heard or read but are no longer available, and with claims that are potentially misleading due to the presence of a pragmatic implication or that require complex relational or inferential reasoning (Gaeth and Heath, 1987; Rousseau et al., 1998; Todd et al., 2019; Uekermann et al., 2008). Several well-known cereal brands have marketed their products as "natural," when in fact, their products contain artificial ingredients. The word "natural" is one example of a product claim that can cause consumers to make incorrect inferences about a product.

Hancock et al. (2005) report two experiments to determine if age affects comprehension for explicit and implied warning information. Across the two studies, they found that as memory demands decreased, warning inference accuracy increased. Overall, younger adults were better at recognizing true inferences and rejecting incorrect inferences. Additionally, when consumers were not able to use existing product and warning knowledge to aid inferences, older adults' inferencing ability was negatively affected. Understanding of medication and household product warnings is an important topic, especially because older consumers tend to be heavy users of medications and health devices.

Recently, Uekermann et al. (2008) studied age differences in comprehension of proverbs. To understand a proverb, one must take the limited, very concrete information and infer a more general lesson or moral. Uekermann et al. (2008) compared 105 (ages 20–39, 40–59, and over 60) participants' ability to select the correct figurative non-literal meaning of 32 proverbs (e.g., barking dogs seldom bite.) The older participants selected significantly fewer correct interpretations, even though they reported more familiarity with each proverb. The authors speculate that older adults' relative impairments on a variety of cognitive mechanisms may have contributed to their proverb interpretation problems.

Taken together, these results suggest that age differences in comprehension of claims depend on the types of claims. Age differences may be small for simple explicit sentences that limit the inferences the consumer must make. For example, "use in a well-ventilated room," is simple, but not explicit because the user must infer what well-ventilated means. In contrast, "use in a room with at least one window open," is simple and explicit (Rousseau et al., 1998). This leads to the following proposition (P3): Age differences in comprehension will be smaller for simple explicit claims and larger for complex implicit claims or for claims with pragmatic implications.

Emotional Content

Several studies suggest that comprehension of everyday interpersonal issues increases with age so that older adults make more accurate, complex inferences about social situations than younger adults (Blanchard-Fields et al., 1995; Hess et al., 2005). Mares (2007) reports results consistent with the idea that age differences in comprehension are minimized for emotional content. In her study, three groups of adults (ages 19–30, 65–70, and 71–78) watched two TV dramas. After each program, she assessed memory for characters' emotions and relationships, recognition, recall, and chronology of main events, and ability to make inferences about the content. In general, the size of age difference in comprehension varied based on how comprehension was measured, so that age differences were smaller for socioemotional content but larger for chronological sequencing and inference measures.

In marketing and psychology, researchers have found similar results for recall with older adults remembering emotionally relevant content or preferring emotional ads, perhaps because older adults devote more attentional resources toward affective than factual information (Drolet et al., 2007; Fung and Carstensen, 2003; Uttl and Graf, 2006; Williams and Drolet, 2005). Uttl and Graf (2006) reported a meta-analysis of age-related changes in encoding and retrieval of emotional versus non-emotional information. They also reported the results of an experiment indicating that memory for emotional information shows no age declines. The pattern of results indicated that the presence or absence of age declines occurs during memory encoding rather than retrieval. Our next proposition (P4) thus relates to age differences in comprehension of factual versus emotional information: Age differences in comprehension of marketing communications material will be larger for factual than for emotional information.

Visual Information

Because much marketing communications and many warnings combine both verbal and visual information, it is essential to consider whether age differences will emerge in the process of integrating and comprehending communications with both verbal and visual information (Wyer et al., 2008). Wyer et al. (2008) present evidence that incompatibility between visual and verbal information harms product evaluations, especially for people who are inherently visualizers. An interesting study suggests that older adults spontaneously generate visual images consistent with their global comprehension of the text, while younger adults spontaneously generate visual images consistent with the surface form or actual words in the text (Dijkstra et al., 2004). These results suggest that older and younger visualizers may spontaneously generate different visual information after exposure to text and that there may be age differences in judgments about the consistency of visual and verbal information.

Symbols are considered an effective way of visually conveying warning information. For example, symbols may communicate safety information to populations with different languages, backgrounds, and reading skills (Rousseau et al., 1998). However, recent studies suggest that older adults are slower to respond to and less likely to understand road signs with symbols, regardless of whether the signs are presented in context (with a driving surrounding) or on a white background (Ben-Bassat and Shinar, 2015). Scialfa et al. (2019) found that healthy older adults comprehend driving (e.g., merging) and warnings signs (e.g., deer crossing) as well as younger adults, but have trouble with way-finding signs (e.g., stairwell). However, Lesch et al. (2011) show that training can reduce age effects on comprehension, confidence, and speed of responding to warning symbols, and Scialfa et al. (2019) report that adding text to signs with symbols reduced age effects. This leads to the proposition (P5) that age differences in comprehension of visual images such as symbols in signs can be reduced with training and/or the addition of text.

Context

Clutter and Noise

Noise and clutter may increase age differences in comprehension. For example, age differences in performance on speech perception tests tend to be greater in noisy conditions than in less noisy conditions (Hutchinson, 1989). Hutchinson speculates that this may occur because background babble has a masking effect on acoustic cues that aid in understanding. Gorn et al. (1991) extend this research by predicting and finding that background music in television commercials impairs learning among older consumers. In their study, recall of product claims was lower for older adults exposed to the commercials with background music than when compared to older adults exposed to the same commercials without background music.

When printed information is very detailed with similar information mixed together, such as that found on a nutritional label, older and younger adults differ in their ability to use the printed information correctly. Cole and Gaeth (1990) examined how age differences in selective attention might affect older adults' ability to use the printed nutritional information contained on product labels, and found that while both older and younger adults benefited from the use of a perception aid that encouraged them to focus on the relevant information, older adults were worse at using the information to make good nutritional choices than younger adults. In a follow-up study, the relevant information was boxed and placed in a separate location on the label; the only older adults to be helped were those who scored moderately well (but not those who scored poorly) on an Embedded Figures Test (a test to measure one's ability to detect simple objects embedded in larger, more elaborate figures). This study by Cole and Gaeth (1990) indicates that the interplay between individual characteristics (disembedding ability) and copy characteristics (information complexity and placement) affect the use of printed material.

In general, older adults who are poor inhibitors may be more susceptible to interference from distracting and irrelevant information than younger adults (Lustig et al., 2001). The distractions may arise from external sources (e.g., from background noise) or internal sources (e.g., personal concerns), and the inability to inhibit them might interfere with comprehension. The bottom line is summarized in the next proposition (P6): Age differences in comprehension will be smaller when the information is clearly presented in a consistent location or without competing visual/ auditory information, but age differences will be greater when the information is inconspicuous or surrounded with distracting information.

Repetition

Another characteristic that affects age differences in comprehension is the repetition of the information. Luna (2005) investigated how consumers' comprehension evolves across multiple ads for a brand. He showed that advertisers could facilitate comprehension if an ad series possess referential continuity (each of the parts explicitly or implicitly refers to an entity introduced in the previous parts). Consequently, we predict that for ad series with high levels of referential continuity, age differences in comprehension will be low, but for ad series with low levels of referential continuity, age differences in comprehension will be larger. This finding may generalize to the literature on warnings such that multiple ads showing the proper use of a product may minimize age differences in comprehension if referential continuity is high across ads.

Older adults are more vulnerable to the truth effect (the tendency to believe repeated information as more true than new information) because older adults have relatively poor context or source memory, but relatively intact familiarity with repeated claims (Law et al., 1998). Interestingly, Skurnik et al. (2005) found that repeatedly identifying a claim as false helped older adults remember it as false in the short term, but made them more likely to remember it as true after a three-day delay. In contrast, younger adults' memories for truth benefited from repeated warnings after both short and long delays. For the older adults, this unintended effect of repetition was due to increased familiarity with the claim itself but decreased recollection of the claim's original context.

These findings lead to the proposition (P7) that the effects of repetition may depend on the level of comprehension assessed: Increased repetition of visual elements and story elements across an ad series will reduce age differences in comprehension at the situation model level, but increased repetition of specific claims will make older adults more vulnerable to the truth effect than younger adults and will increase age differences in comprehension at the text-based level.

Individual Differences

Knowledge

Research indicates that crystallized intelligence may remain stable or increase across the adult life span (Cattell, 1987; Park and Gutchess, 2006). Crystallized intelligence refers to individuals' knowledge bases such as vocabulary, understanding about how people operate, and how to access and use media. Several studies support the assertion that being able to access one's knowledge base minimizes age differences in comprehension (Harris et al., 1990; Mares, 2007; Yoon et al., 2015). In the study by Mares (2007), half the adults within each age group were familiar with the characters and typical storylines in a television program that they watched. In general, the size of age differences in comprehension was greater for unfamiliar than familiar programs. Results from a study by Yoon et al. (2015) report that when older adults were presented with implausible sentences, they were more likely to experience declines in comprehension and greater susceptibility to interference than when presented with plausible sentences.

This leads to our next proposition (P8): Age differences in comprehension will be smaller in familiar domains in which consumers possess knowledge and can easily access this knowledge, but larger in unfamiliar domains where knowledge is difficult to access.

Processing Strategies

Individual differences in processing strategies may also explain age differences in comprehension and subsequent decision making. Henninger et al. (2010) suggest that differences between age groups in decision quality reflect age-related differences including processing speed and that older adults' decisions may be highly sensitive to how information is represented. They posit that changing how information is presented, such as enabling heuristic strategies that reduce processing or memory demands, may help with age-related changes in decision making.

Besedeš et al. (2012), in an experiment using a series of choice tasks, found that the use of heuristics differs with age and that older individuals discard information on the relative importance of attributes, instead selecting options with the largest number of attributes. Older subjects were less likely to make optimal decisions from larger choice sets, i.e., when the number of options increased and were more easily manipulated through presentation and design of options.

Yoon (1997) initially examined schema-based versus detailed processing strategies between older and younger adults and found that although older adults generally exhibit greater use of schema-based processing, specific task conditions had a significant effect. Older adults were able to engage in levels of detailed processing when exposed to high-incongruity cues during their optimal time of day (morning), but during their non-optimal time of day, the presence of any level of incongruity led to the use of schema-based processing. To explain an age-associated decrease in systematic processing, Hess et al. (2001) propose a resource allocation hypothesis, which states that, as people age, they learn to allocate and conserve their mental energy better, so that they rely on heuristic processing unless explicitly motivated to use detailed processing. However, even given proper instructions or context, not all older adults are able to engage in systematic processing. Age-related changes in prefrontal brain regions may limit some, although not all, older adults' abilities to process in a detailed manner (Denburg et al., 2005; Hedden and Gabrieli, 2004). These findings lead to our final proposition (P9): Age differences in comprehension will be smaller when all adults are able and motivated to use systematic processing.

Vulnerability to Persuasive Communications

Consumer vulnerability continues to be an important, but poorly defined, issue in public policy and macro-marketing. Baker et al. (2005, p.134) point out that vulnerability arises from the "interaction of individual states, individual characteristics, and external conditions within a context where consumption goals may be hindered and the experience affects personal and social perceptions of self." This state-based view of vulnerability fits with our review of the age differences in comprehension literature, which recognizes that task characteristics, context factors, and individual differences can interact to create age differences in comprehension. In this section, we adopt this conceptualization of vulnerability because it shifts the focus away from vulnerability as an inherent characteristic of older adults to vulnerability as a state which can arise as a result of various interactions. We present in Table 9.2, a series of testable hypotheses with respect to these external conditions.

TABLE 9.2 Hypotheses Related to Older Consumer Vulnerability to Persuasive Messages

H1	There will be larger age differences in comprehension of specific risk information and smaller age differences in comprehension of the benefit information in advertising. Media pace will moderate this relationship such that age differences will be smaller in self-paced media such as print and larger in externally paced media such as television and social media.
H2	Age differences in comprehension of fraudulent scams will be larger in externally paced media than in self-paced media.
H3	Age differences in accessibility of persuasion knowledge may lead to age differences in comprehension of fraudulent scams.
H4	Age differences in accuracy of persuasion knowledge may lead to age differences in comprehension of fraudulent scams.

We analyze two situations where miscomprehension may increase consumer vulnerability. These include direct-to-consumer prescription drug advertising and telephone scams because they both target older adults. Direct-to-consumer prescription drug advertising on television and in social media inform consumers about health conditions, prescription treatments, and risk information. Older adults are targeted by DTC prescription drug advertising more often because medication use increases with age (DeLorme, Hug and Reid 2016; Ball et al., 2011). A prescription drug commercial typically provides benefit information with images, music, and actors, and risk information as an audio message as required by the FDA. More recently, some commercials are moving to both audio and superimposed risk test (dual modality) (Sullivan et al., 2017). One possible hypothesis based on P1, P2, and P4 is that in product advertising, there will be larger age differences in comprehension of specific risk information and smaller age differences in comprehension of the benefit information. Media pace will moderate this relationship such that age differences will be smaller in self-paced media such as print and larger in externally paced media such as television and social media (H1). Consistent with this hypothesis, one analysis of a large commercial advertising research database found that older consumers tended to recall different executional elements than their younger counterparts (Phillips and Stanton, 2004).

Regarding the proposition that age differences in comprehension will be larger for externally paced rather than self-paced media (P2), this suggests that older adults will be particularly vulnerable to externally paced telemarketing/phone scams, such as the grandparent scam, which cost consumers $41 million in the 12 months ending October 31, 2018 (American Association of Retired Persons (AARP), 2018). According to the National Council on Aging, in this scam, scammers place a call to an older person. When the target picks up the phone, the scammer will say something like, "Hi Grandma, do you know who this is?" The "fake" grandchild then asks for money (National Council on Aging, n.d.). We predict that age differences in comprehension of fraudulent scams will be larger in externally paced media than in self-paced media (H2).

While a host of individual characteristics may increase vulnerability including living alone, mild cognitive impairment, lack of familiarity with financial management, and loneliness (Cohen, 2006), we focus on an important individual characteristic, persuasion knowledge, which like other forms of accessible knowledge may reduce vulnerability (P8).

Persuasion Knowledge

Like younger consumers, older consumers may protect themselves from marketing scams with persuasion knowledge, which is knowledge about persuasion tactics and methods of resisting persuasion attempts. Scheibe et al. (2014) conducted a field experiment to test whether forewarning could protect older consumers' susceptibility to telemarketing fraud. They tested two types of scam warnings—same scam and different scam warnings among previous victims of mail fraud. They found that both warnings reduced unequivocal acceptance of a mock scam pitched two or four weeks later. But outright refusals to participate were more frequent with the same scam warning than the different scam warning.

The Scheibe et al. (2014) study is evidence of the effectiveness of consumer education. However, there are several reasons why older adults may have trouble using their persuasion knowledge to reduce vulnerability. When cognitive capacity is constrained, consumers are less likely to recruit persuasion knowledge to resist selling efforts. This suggests that older adults may encounter problems accessing their rich knowledge bases to accurately comprehend the nature of scams when faced with a scam on an externally paced media (H3) (Campbell and Kirmani, 2000).

Additionally, rapid changes in technology may mean that some older consumers' persuasion knowledge is outdated (H4). An AARP survey suggests that older adults lack knowledge in important areas such as their rights as consumers. For example, older consumers (those over the age of 65) are much less likely than consumers under the age of 65 to know that individuals have several days to cancel purchases made from door-to-door salespeople (36 percent vs. 53 percent) and that consumers are not able to cancel purchases made by credit card over the telephone (19 percent vs. 28 percent) (cited in Lee and Geistfeld, 1999).

A question arises about older adults' willingness to use their persuasion knowledge (Langenderfer and Shimp, 2001). Since the early 1970s, marketing research has reported that older consumers are often reluctant to complain about salespeople or to be rude to them (LaForge, 1989). LaForge (1989) offers as an explanation the theory of "learned helplessness," which suggests that after repeated punishment or failure, people become more passive and continue to remain so even after the environment changes to make success possible. In the case of older adults, they may learn this helplessness from prior experiences in eras when businesses tended not to respond to customers' complaints. Also, their feelings of helplessness may increase as physical disabilities make them aware of their limitations. However, it is unclear how much of this learned helplessness is a cohort effect. For example, the aging Baby Boomers who are accustomed to getting results by complaining may not experience the same hesitation to complain as earlier elderly cohorts.

General Discussion

On the one hand, some firms and organizations have straightforward global messages that they want understood by both older and younger consumers. Such messages—such as getting a flu shot or trying a new restaurant—will likely be readily comprehended by all age groups. As we have seen, there are minimal age differences in consumers' ability to construct situation models.

On the other hand, organizations concerned about comprehension of specific claims in a message or warnings need to account for the information processing skills of target consumers. For example, the health clinic may want consumers to know that they should come in before November 1 to get their flu shot. As a result, marketers may want to adapt the format, content, location, and timing of marketing communications, including warnings, to the comprehension abilities of the target market.

Marketers may initiate such adaptations by pilot testing the comprehensibility of claims and warnings on older adults. They may want to experiment with providing information at the time it is needed (e.g., during product use), not just prior to purchase, or with making information easily accessible to consumers, either with product handouts or through online Web pages. Firms and industry associations may also develop internal sets of guidelines as a proactive way of preventing potential litigation and negative publicity, as well as enhancing a firm's or industry's reputation for socially responsible behavior. Involving key individuals from influential groups such as AARP in company decision-making in the area of marketing to older adults is another avenue to consider. Additionally, industries and non-profit organizations may introduce training programs to help increase and update older adults' knowledge about claims and symbols. Gaeth and Heath (1987), for example, developed an interactive training program to reduce susceptibility to misleading claims in advertising and found that the training reduced susceptibility to misleading statements among older adults.

And finally, given increased media attention to unfair advertising practices or lack of adequate warning signs and labels, lawmakers may be inclined to become more involved in preventing unfair or deceptive practices through increased legislation. For example, the Consumer Product Safety Commission and the U.S. Congress have been in an ongoing tug of war to set new labeling rules for toys (Trottman, 2008). The Federal Trade Commission (FTC), which considers how advertising practices affect the targeted consumer in judging unfairness and deception, may order offending firms to produce corrective advertising. For example, the FTC ordered Novartis to spend $8 million on corrective advertisements regarding claims it made about Doan's back medication (Darke et al., 2008). In terms of public policy, simply making accurate information available will not necessarily ensure that older consumers will comprehend it; further empirical evidence needs to be provided for the propositions we have identified in Table 9.1.

References

AARP. (2018, December 31). *Grandparent Scam*. https://www.aarp.org/money/scams-fr aud/info-2019/grandparent.html?CMP=KNC-DSO-Adobe-Google-FRD-Elder -Scams-Grandparent-scam&ef_id=EAIaIQobChMInda28sWt4wIVQvbjBx1ELw jFEAAYASAAEgIgvfD_BwE:G:s&s_kwcid=AL!4520!3!275695377242!e!!g!!grandpar ent scams.

Abernathy, L. T., & Adams-Price, C. E. (2006). Memory and comprehension of magazine-based prescription drug advertisements among young and old adults. *Journal of Current Issues and Research in Advertising*, *28*(Fall), 1–13.

Adams, C., Smith, M. C., Nyquist, L., & Perlmutter, M. (1997). Adults age-group differences in recall of the literal and interpretive meanings of narrative text. *Journal of Gerontology: Psychological Sciences*, *52B*, 187–195.

Baker, S. M., Gentry, J., & Rittenburg, T. (2005). Building understanding of the domain of consumer vulnerability. *Journal of Macromarketing*, *25*(December), 128–139.

Ball, J. G., Manika, D., & Stout, P. (2011). Consumers young and old: Segmenting the target markets for direct-to-consumer prescription drug advertising. *Health Marketing Quarterly*, *28*(4), 337–353.

Barrett, L. L. (2011, January). *Health and Caregiving Among the 50+: Ownership, Use and Interest in Mobile Technology*. AARP. https://www.aarp.org/technology/innovations/info -01-2011/health-caregiving-mobile-technology.html.

Beese, C., Vassileiou, B., Friederici, A. D., & Meyer, L. (2019). Age differences in encoding-related alpha power reflect sentence comprehension difficulties. *Frontiers in Aging Neuroscience*, *11*(July), 1–14.

Ben-Bassat, T., & Shinar, D. (2015). The effect of context and drivers' age on highway traffic signs comprehension. *Transportation Research Part F: Traffic Psychology and Behaviour*, *33*(August), 117–112.

Besedeš, T., Deck, C., Sarangi, S., & Shor, M. (2012). Age effects and heuristics in decision making. *The Review of Economics and Statistics*, *94*(2), 580–595.

Blanchard-Fields, F., Jahnke, H. C., & Camp, C. (1995). Age differences in problem-solving style: The role of emotional salience. *Psychology and Aging*, *10*(2), 173–180.

Bonifield, C., & Cole, C. (2007). Advertising to vulnerable segments. In: *The Sage Handbook of Advertising*, Tellis, G. J., & Ambler, T. (Eds.). London, England: Sage Publications, 430–444.

Bradley, S., & Meeds, R. (2004). The effects of sentence-level context, prior word knowledge and need for cognition on information processing of technical language in print ads. *Journal of Consumer Psychology*, *14*(3), 292–302.

Campbell, M. C., & Kirmani, A. (2000). Consumers' use of persuasion knowledge: The effects of accessibility and cognitive capacity on perceptions of an influence agent. *Journal of Consumer Research*, *10*(1), 69–83.

Cattell, R. B. (1987). *Intelligence: Its Structure, Growth and Action*. New York: Elsevier.

Charness, N.,& Holley, P. (2004). The new media and older adults: Usable and useful? *The American Behavioral Scientist*, *48*(4), 371–376.

Cohen, C. (2006). Consumer fraud and the elderly: A review of Canadian challenges and initiatives. *Journal of Gerontological Social Work*, *46*(3–4), 137–144.

Cole, C. A., & Gaeth, G. J. (1990). Cognitive and age-related differences in the ability to use nutritional information in a complex environment. *Journal of Marketing Research*, *27*(2), 175–184.

Cole, C. A., & Houston, M. J. (1987). Encoding and media effects on consumer learning deficiences in the elderly. *Journal of Marketing Research*, *24*(February), 55–63.

Cowley, E. (2006). Processing exaggerated advertising claims. *Journal of Business Research*, *59*(6), 728–734.

Craik, F., & Byrd, M. (1982). Aging and cognitive deficits: The role of attentional resources. In: *Aging and Cognitive Processes: Advances in the Study of Communication and Affect*, Craik, F., & Trehub, S. (Eds.). New York: Plenum, 191–211.

Darke, P., Ashworth, L., & Ritchie, R. J. (2008, November). Damage from corrective advertising: Causes and cures. *Journal of Marketing*, *72*, 81–97.

DeLorme, D. E., Huh, J., & Reid, L. N. (2006). Perceived effects of direct-to-consumer (DTC) prescription drug advertising on self and others: A third-person effect study of older consumers. *Journal of Advertising*, *35*(3), 47–65.

Denburg, N., Tranel, L. D., & Bechara, A. (2005). The ability to decide advantageously declines prematurely in some normal older persons. *Neuropsychologica*, *43*(7), 1099–1106.

Dijkstra, K., Yaxley, R. H., Madden, C. J., & Zwaan, R. A. (2004, June). The role of age and perceptual symbols in language comprehension. *Psychology and Aging*, *19*(2), 352–356.

Drolet, A., Williams, P., & Lau-Gesk, L. (2007). Age-related differences in responses to affective vs. rational ads for hedonic vs. utilitarian products. *Marketing Letters*, *18*(4), 211–221.

Fung, H. H., & Carstensen, L. (2003). Sending memorable messages to the old: Age differences in preferences and memory for advertisements. *Journal of Personality and Social Psychology*, *85*(1), 163–178.

Gaeth, G. J., & Heath, T. B. (1987). The cognitive processing of misleading advertising in young and old adults: Assessment and training. *Journal of Consumer Research*, *14*(June), 43–54.

Glader, P. (2008, December 3). Home appliances to soothe the aches of aging boomers. *Wall Street Journal*, D1.

Gorn, G., Goldberg, M., Chattopadhyay, A., & Litvack, D. (1991). Music and information in commercials: Their effects with an elderly sample. *Journal of Advertising*, *31*(Oct/Nov), 23–32.

Hancock, H. E., Fisk, A. D., & Rogers, W. A. (2005). Comprehending product warning information: Age-related effects and the roles of memory, inferencing, and knowledge. *Human Factors*, *47*(2), 219–234.

Harris, J. F., Durso, F. T., Mergler, N. L., & Jones, S. K. (1990). Knowledge base influences on judgments of frequency of occurrence. *Cognitive Development*, *5*(2), 223–233.

Hasher, L., Zacks, R. T., & May, C. P. (1999). Inhibitory control, circadian arousal, and age. In: *Attention and Performance, XVII, Cognitive Regulation of Performance: Interaction of Theory and Application*, Gopher, D. & Koriat, A. (Eds.). Cambridge, MA: MIT Press, 653–657.

Hedden, T., & Gabrieli, J. D. E. (2004). Insights into the ageing mind: A view from cognitive neuroscience. *Nature Reviews: Neuroscience*, *5*(February), 87–96.

Henninger, D. E., Madden, D. J., & Huettel, S. A. (2010). Processing speed and memory mediate age-related differences in decision making. *Psychology and Aging, 25*(2), 262–270.

Hess, T., Rosenberg, D. C., & Waters, S. J. (2001). Motivation and representational processes in adulthood: The effects of social accountability and information relevance. *Psychology and Aging, 16*(4), 629–642.

Hess, T. M., Osowski, N. L., & Leclerc, C. M. (2005). Age and experience influences on the complexity of social inferences. *Psychology and Aging, 20*(3), 447–510.

Hutchinson, K. (1989). Influence of sentence context on speech perception in young and older adults. *Journal of Gerontology: Psychological Sciences, 44*(2), 36–44.

Jacoby, J., & Hoyer, W. D. (1989). The comprehension/miscomprehension of print communication: Selected findings. *Journal of Consumer Research, 15*(4), 434–443.

LaForge, M. C. (1989). Learned helplessness as an explanation of elderly consumer complaint behavior. *Journal of Business Ethics, 8*(5), 359–366.

Langenderfer, J., & Shimp, T. A. (2001). Consumer vulnerability to scams, swindles, and fraud: A new theory of visceral influences on persuasion. *Psychology and Marketing, 18*(7), 763–783.

Law, S., Hawkins, S. A., & Craik, F. I. M. (1998, September). Repetition-induced belief in the elderly: Rehabilitating age-related memory deficits. *Journal of Consumer Research, 25*(2), 91–107.

Lee, J., & Geistfeld, L. V. (1999). Elderly consumers' receptiveness to telemarketing fraud. *Journal of Public Policy and Marketing, 18*(2), 208–217.

Lesch, M. F., Horrey, W. J., Wogalter, M. S., & Powell, W. R. (2011). Age-related differences in warning symbol comprehension and training effectiveness: Effects of familiarity, complexity, and comprehensibility. *Journal of Ergonomics, 54*(10), 879–890.

Light, L., & Capps, J. (1986). Comprehension of pronouns in young and older adults. *Developmental Psychology, 22*(4), 580–585.

Luna, D. (2005). Integrating ad information: A text processing perspective. *Journal of Consumer Psychology, 15*(1), 38–51.

Lustig, C., May, C. P., & Hasher, L. (2001). Working memory span and the role of proactive interference. *Journal of Experimental Psychology: General, 130*(2), 199–207.

Mares, M. (2007). Developmental changes in adult comprehension of a television program are modified by being a fan. *Communication Monographs, 74*(March), 55–77.

National Council on Aging. (n.d.). *Top 10 Financial Scams Targeting Seniors.* https://www.ncoa.org/economic-security/money-management/scams-security/top-10-scams-targeting-seniors/#intraPageNav4.

Naveh-Benjamin, M. (2000). Adult age differences in memory performance: Tests of an associative deficit hypothesis. *Journal of Experimental Psychology: Learning, Memory, and Cognition, 26*(5), 1170–1187.

O'Donoghue, A. C., Johnson, M., Sullivan, H. W., Parvanta, S., Ray, S., & Southwell, B. G. (2019). Aging and direct-to-consumer prescription drug television ads: The effects of individual differences and risk presentation. *Journal of Health Communication.* Advance online publication.

O'Reilly, Lara (2015, December 2). The 10 worst ads of 2015. *Business Insider.* https://www.businessinsider.com/the-10-worst-ads-of-2015-12.

Park, D., & Gutchess, A. (2006). The cognitive neuroscience of aging and culture. *Current Directions in Psychological Science, 15*(3), 105–108.

Phillips, D. M., & Stanton, J. L. (2004). Age-related differences in advertising: Recall and persuasion. *Journal of Targeting, Measurement and Analysis for Marketing, 13*(1), 7–20.

Radvansky, G., Zwaan, R. A., Curiel, J. M., & Copeland, D. E. (2001). Situation models and aging. *Psychology and Aging, 16*(1), 145–160.

Rogers, W. A., Lamson, N., & Rousseau, G. K. (2000). Warning research: An integrative perspective. *Human Factors, 42*(1), 102–139.

Rousseau, G., Lamson, N., & Rogers, W. (1998). Designing warnings to compensate for age-related changes in perceptual and cognitive abilities. *Psychology and Marketing, 15*(7), 643–662.

Schechner, S., & Kumar, V. (2009, January 16). Retirement living TV gets boost: Comcast deal will expand audience as more marketers pursue older crowd. *The Wall Street Journal,* B9.

Scheibe, S., Notthof, N., Menkin, J., Ross, L., Shadel, D., Deevy, M., & Carstensen, L. L. (2014). Forewarning reduces fraud susceptibility in vulnerable consumers. *Basic and Applied Social Psychology, 36*(3), 272–279.

Scialfa, C., Spadafora, P., Klein, M., Lesnik, A., Dial, L., & Heinrich, A. (2019). Iconic sign comprehension in older adults: The role of cognitive impairment and text enhancement. *Canadian Journal on Aging / La Revue Canadienne du Vieillissement, 27*(3), 253–265.

Shimp, T. A. (1978). Do incomplete comparisons mislead? *Journal of Advertising Research, 18*(December), 21–28.

Skurnik, I., Yoon, C., Park, D. C., & Schwarz, N. (2005, March). How warnings about false claims become recommendations. *Journal of Consumer Research, 31*(4), 713–724.

Stine, E., & Wingfield, A. (1987). Process and strategy in memory for speech among younger and older adults. *Psychology and Aging, 2*(3), 272–279.

Stine-Morrow, E., Loveless, M., & Soederberg, L. M. (1996). Resource allocation in on-line reading by younger and older adults. *Psychology and Aging, 11*(3), 475–486.

Stine-Morrow, E., Miller, L., & Hertzog, C. (2006). Aging and self-regulated language processing. *Psychological Bulletin, 132*(4), 582–606.

Sullivan, H. W., Boudewyns, V., O'Donoghue, A., Marshall, S., & Williams, P. A. (2017). Attention to and distraction from risk information in prescription drug advertising: An eye-tracking study. *Journal of Public Policy and Marketing, 36*(2), 236–245.

Todd, J.-A. M., Andrews, G., & Conlon, E. G. (2019). Relational thinking in later adulthood. *Psychology and Aging, 34*(4), 486–501.

Trottman, M. (2008, August 29). U.S. News: Consumer-products agency faces looming deadlines on rules. *The Wall Street Journal,* A4.

Uekermann, J., Thoma, P., & Daum, I. (2008). Proverb interpretation changes in aging. *Brain and Cognition, 67*(1), 51–57.

Uttl, B., & Graf, P. (2006). Age-related changes in the encoding and retrieval of emotional and non-emotional information. In: *Memory and Emotion: Interdisciplinary Perspectives,* B. Uttl, N. Ohta, & A. L. Siegenthaler (Eds.). Oxford, UK: Blackwell Publishing.

Vincent, G. K., & Velkoff, V. A. (2010, May). *The Next Four Decades. The Older Population in the United States: 2010 to 2050.* Census.Gov. https://www.census.gov/prod/2010pubs /p25-1138.pdf.

Was, C., & Woltz, D. (2007). Reexamining the relationship between working memory and comprehension: The role of available long-term memory. *Journal of Memory and Language, 56*(1), 86–102.

Werner, C. A. (2011, November). *The Older Population: 2010.* Census.Gov. https://www .census.gov/content/dam/Census/library/publications/2011/dec/c2010br-09.pdf.

Williams, P., & Drolet, A. (2005). Age-related differences in responses to emotional advertisements. *Journal of Consumer Research, 32*(December), 343–354.

Wyer, R. S. (2002). Language and advertising effectiveness: Mediating influences on comprehension and cognitive elaboration. *Psychology and Marketing, 19*(7–8), 693–712.

Wyer, R., Hung, I., & Jiang, Y. (2008). Visual and verbal processing strategies in comprehension and judgement. *Journal of Consumer Psychology, 18*(4), 244–257.

Yoon, C. (1997). Age differences in consumers' processing strategies: An investigation of moderating influences. *Journal of Consumer Research, 24*(December), 329–342.

Yoon, C., Cole, C., & Lee, M. P. (2009). Consumer decision making and aging: Current knowledge and future directions. *Journal of Consumer Psychology, 19*(1), 2–16.

Yoon, C., Lee, M. P., & Danziger, S. (2007). The effects of optimal time of day on persuasion processes in older adults. *Psychology and Marketing, 24*(5), 475–495.

Yoon, J., Campanelli, L., Goral, M., Marton, K., Eichorn, N., & Obler, L. K. (2015). The effect of plausibility on sentence comprehension among older adults and its relation to cognitive functions. *Experimental Aging Research, 41*(3), 272–302.

10

AGE BRANDING

Sanjay Sood and Harry R. Moody

Introduction

Age branding continues to grow in importance as the demographics in the United States shift toward an increasingly large number of seniors. Although marketers still covet younger consumers, especially millennials, there has been an evolution in age branding due to the sheer amount of spending power of the older consumer segment. Baby boomers, defined as people born between 1946 and 1964, are a very large segment comprising approximately 79 million consumers. Boomers outnumber Generation X by almost 50 percent, 79 million to 55 million people. Combined with the fact that Boomers are postponing retirement, they represent a huge opportunity.

In this chapter, we update how the four different families of age branding have evolved over the last decade. The four families are (1) age-denial brands ("I don't have to get old"); (2) age-adaptive brands ("Age presents problems but I can deal with them"); (3) age-irrelevant brands ("Mind over matter; if you don't mind, it doesn't matter"); and (4) age-affirmative brands ("The best is yet to be").

Age-Denial Brands

Age-denial brands focus on marketing techniques that help older consumers feel young. These brands rely on self-enhancement to compete. Self-enhancement is defined as the need to perceive oneself favorably (Greenwald, 1980; Greenwald, Bellezza, and Banaji, 1988). As age-denial branding has evolved, marketers have focused on downward comparisons portraying one group of seniors who use a product as better off relative to another group of seniors that does not use a product. Capitalizing on this technique, so-called "anti-aging medicine" has quickly become the great merchandising success of age branding in our time. From a distant corner of quackery in the medical world a few decades ago, anti-aging medicine has now grown into a multi-billion-dollar business. The facts about so-called "anti-aging" medicine are clear enough and not encouraging. First and foremost, there are no interventions ever shown to slow or reverse the biological process of aging. There is one curious exception: caloric restriction, or eating less, a lot less. This drastic approach has long been proven to work with every lower organism on which it has been tried. Experiments on caloric restriction with primates are underway, but the long lifespan of higher primates means the jury is still out on this experiment. Yet even before our current epidemic of obesity, caloric restriction has never been popular with Americans. Other so-called "remedies" for aging will hit the pocketbook, and perhaps damage health with side-effects (cancer, carpal tunnel syndrome, etc.), yet fail to do what anti-aging promoters promise. Perhaps most emblematic of age-denial, plastic surgery continues to grow in popularity in the United States. and Asia.

The "Magna Carta" of the anti-aging movement is the book by co-founders of the American Academy of Anti-Aging Medicine, Ronald Klatz and Robert Goldman. The book's title itself is an extravagant promise of the things to come, *Stopping the Clock: Why Many of Us Will Live Past 100—and Enjoy Every Minute!*[1] The book touches all the bases of contemporary anti-aging treatments, including hormone replacement therapy, human growth hormone, thyroid supplements, vitamins and minerals, and much more. While many of these treatments lack a solid scientific research basis, the book does contain some sound advice—for example, in favor of exercise and stress reduction, and other interventions that meet with the approval of America's leading guru of alternative medicine, Dr. Andrew Weil—who is otherwise a harsh critic of anti-aging medicine.

What are the prospects for age-denial brands as the cohort of Boomers rapidly enters old age? In *10 Things about Baby Boomers*, the Yankelovich survey group concludes: "Whether it's more Botox or usurping cars originally targeted to young adults, Boomers will continue to appreciate products, services and experiences that reinforce their conviction that age is purely a state of mind."[2] Aging Boomers are highly resistant to brands associated with aging:

> Boomers recognize that they are aging, but they do not see themselves getting old. In fact, the defining attitude for Baby Boomers continues to be about youthfulness. Boomers have long understood that getting what you want in life comes from having a youthful spirit—being engaged with life in a way that is active and spirited. Think of it this way: For Boomers, being old means closure, while youthfulness involves continuous exploration and reinvention. Being old means deceleration, while youthfulness involves energy. Being old means convention, while youthfulness involves transformation.[3]

The Yankelovich report cites its own survey data where Boomers responded favorably to the following items: "I will be healthy and active until age 70 at least" (79 percent agreed) and "Medical advances will enable me to stay active and vigorous well into my 80s" (64 percent agreed). Clearly, Boomers are expecting to grow old and hence age-denial branding will likely continue to be effective.

Age-Adaptive Brands

In contrast to age-denial brands that refute the effects of aging, age-adaptive brands help seniors accept and adjust to the inevitable effects of aging. In essence, age-adaptive brands are problem solvers for seniors. Over time age-adaptive brands have made the process of aging less stigmatized in society. Rather than portraying aging as a negative that needs to be avoided as in age-denial branding, age-adaptive branding focuses on how the product or service can help seniors achieve their personal goals.

Age-adaptive branding continues to be fundamental to public health campaigns and health promotion. The problem is getting people to pay attention. Aging typically involves habituation, or "getting used to" changes that come on slowly. This inertia can create a challenge for age-adaptive branding because instilling behavior change is so difficult. In later life, it is not too late for so-called secondary and tertiary prevention: that is, early diagnosis and better disease management as people grow older.

Prevention, then, becomes the strategy for age-adaptive branding in public health campaigns as well as consumer marketing. To reach consumers in this way, it becomes important to convey the message "it's not too late" for better health. Age-adaptive brands, such as hypertension drugs, can position themselves to convey that message, but the message will only be heard to the extent that denial is reduced. Age-adaptive branding, therefore, needs to be linked to age-affirmative images that lodge in the minds of consumers. An age-adaptive strategy need not frighten people about the risk of stroke for untreated hypertension. Instead, the age-adaptive message could be packaged in terms of "the good life" in the later years, without dwelling on age or disability at all.

One of the most successful recent age-adaptive ad campaigns is "Thrive" by Kaiser Permanente. The key to the thrive campaign is a recognition that all consumers, especially seniors, don't want to be sick. The mere thought of going to a doctor can create anxiety instantaneously in many people. Thrive focuses on prevention as the solution to staying away from the doctor's office. While the competitors' positioned themselves on price of their health insurance plans, Kaiser distinguished itself by positioning on how good life could be if people adopted a lifestyle that included exercise and healthy diets. A unique aspect of the Thrive campaign was the absence of any doctors in the ads. Instead of showing a doctor treating a patient, the campaign focused on healthy foods, exercise, and other positive adaptive behaviors. This is evident from the voiceover of the initial launch ad of the Thrive campaign:

> We stand for Broccoli.
> For Pilates. And dental floss.
> We believe in the treadmill and its sibling the elliptical.
> In SPF 30 we trust.
> We believe in seatbelts and stopping HIV.
> And that fruit makes a wonderful dessert.
> We have faith in optimism, in laughter as medicine as well as penicillin.
> All hail cold turkey, the gum and the patch.
> We're anti addiction and pro anti-oxidant.
> We believe there is art to medicine as well as science.
> And that health isn't an industry, it's a cause.
> We're Kaiser Permanente, and we stand for health.
> May you live long and Thrive.

Another striking example of an age-adaptive brand in the clothing industry is Chico's, a store that has appealed to older Boomer women. Chico's is an age-adaptive brand because it helps consumers fulfill their practical needs, while also appealing to values of self-esteem and individual identity. As David Weigelt and Jonathan Boehman observe, Chico's has focused on midlife women who may be self-conscious about their clothing size. Chico's made an innovation by changing the conventional size chart to an easy-to-remember 0, 1, 2, and 3, with half-sizes included. This shift to a new sizing chart bypasses stigma that might be associated with traditional sizes that midlife women remember from their youth. Instead of the depressing experience of discovering that you can no longer fit your old size, Chico's size numbers offer a more positive approach: "it's all about how the clothes make a woman feel," Weigelt and Boehman note.[4] They quote Chico's own website:

> Focus on comfort is the reason for our unique sizing. There are many characteristics incorporated into each and every product we make, but top on our list is comfort. Chico's clothing is made to wear how you like it to fit. If you like a little room, go for a bigger size.

Thus, instead of focusing on an unpleasant attribute ("overweight"), Chico's shifts the focus to comfort and feeling. Chico's has carried this philosophy over into the retail store experience. Store managers encourage sales personnel to share their own sizes and experiences with clothing. Chico's stores avoid mirrors in the dressing room. Product descriptions retain the comfort theme, but also add references to color, style, and sexiness. A tagline message says it all: "Finally … Pants that fit your body—not the other way around."

Hearing aids are an obvious age-adaptive product to correct the problem. But denial of hearing problems is a big barrier to the purchase of an age-adaptive product that offers many benefits. Approximately one-third of those between the ages of 65 and 74 have hearing problems, a figure that rises to half of those 85 and older.[5] Hearing problems can be modest, such as missing sounds or being unable to hear voices in a social setting. Or problems can be severe, up to the point of deafness. Hearing problems are complex, and recent research suggests that deficits may be caused as much by information processing in the brain as by defects in the ear. But hearing aids can often provide some measure of assistance. Recent "high-tech" hearing aids have given consumers multiple choices that were not available in the past.[6]

Despite these needs and the benefits of the product, the hearing aid industry has long suffered from a marketing challenge, mainly because hearing aids were perceived as ugly and were presumed to be purchased only by the elderly. By some estimates, fewer than a quarter of those who needed hearing aids ended up buying them. Moreover, hearing aids still remained an age-segregated product: the average age of a first-time hearing aid buyer for all manufacturers has been 69. As a result, aging Boomers, especially, have been reluctant to admit to hearing losses which carry the stigma of old age. Any product linked to an image of people who are "frail" and "weak" is a hard sell.

In the post-Second World War period, marketers used a variety of approaches to confront this problem. One was a celebrity endorsement approach, where actors like Lorne Greene and Nanette Fabray were featured in ad campaigns to promote hearing aids. Bob Hope also became a spokesman: "It is gratifying to know that with Paravox hearing aids, the hard of hearing everywhere may now enjoy my radio and moving picture shows." After Ronald Reagan appeared in public in 1983 wearing an in-the-ear hearing aid, sales rose.

Another approach was technological innovation permitting ever-more miniaturization of these devices so that hearing aids could become nearly invisible to others.[7] Integrated circuits, directional microphones, and new types of batteries were all part of the marketing appeal during the closing decades of the twentieth century. Manufacturers launched marketing campaigns with claims such as the following tag lines: "Invisible Hearing Aids," "Cannot Be Seen," or "Hides Deafness." Another solution was using a cell phone earpiece as a delivery vehicle for the hearing aid, so that this age-adaptive brand becomes invisible once again. All these approaches involved a traditional marketing appeal to "features and benefits." But the deep problem of stigma still remained unaddressed and customer resistance did not disappear.

One recent creative approach has been to rebrand ear pieces not as "hearing aids" at all but as, "personal communication aids" (PCAs). Phonak is one company that has taken this approach, pushing the PCA as the "ultimate high-tech accessory."[8] One consumer, responding enthusiastically to this brand strategy said, "Phonak's marketing is right on. When you visit Phonak's websites, you feel like you're buying a Lexus, not a watch or a hearing aid. The models have names like Audéo, Salia, Una, and Valea."

Another approach was taken by Oticon, based in Somerset, New Jersey.[9] Before 2006, Oticon's sales were in the doldrums like its competitors. A more dramatic branding approach was called for: "We realized that the stigma (surrounding hearing aids) was more deeply felt than we had allowed ourselves to believe," said Gordon Wilson, Oticon's vice-president of marketing.

> Some people felt that wearing a hearing aid was like wearing a glaring sign that said I am broken, I am not ideal. For some, a hearing aid had a very negative product connotation—and as a result, they would only get them when they were desperate to hear.

Oticon responded to this challenge with ads featuring middle-aged, attractive models wearing its new hearing device. Their ad campaign broke out of stereotyped approaches. Like Phonak, they called their product, named Delta, a "personal hearing device." Oticon maintained an appeal based on features and benefits and grounded in technological advances, such as small size and signal-processing electronics. But it created an innovative age-adaptive brand that succeeded in doubling the percentage of sales to coveted first-time buyers.

Current hearing aid marketers are moving in a similar direction, by shrinking and streamlining the aids, adding new patterns and colors, and linking hearing aids for use with MP3 players, mobile phones, and even global positioning systems. Yet the problems remain. Despite rising rates of hearing loss, "companies have been unable to persuade a larger portion of people with hearing loss to buy hearing aids," said Valentin Chapero Rueda, chief executive officer of Sonova, the world's third-largest maker of the products.[10]

The success of the Oticon strategy illustrates the complexity of age-adaptive products in a consumer marketplace that resists aging. Some elements of the strategy sound like age-denial, while others seem like ageless marketing, to be discussed shortly. But the basic message remains one of problem-solving. Recent research on health promotion has attempted to disentangle some of these elements.[11] Researchers have looked at purchase of age-adaptive brands, such as hearing aids or erectile medication, in comparison to age-denial products such as plastic surgery or wrinkle-removing cosmetics. They specifically examined the validity of the newly developed Health Behavior Inventory (HBI). It turns out that "young old" respondents (those aged 55–76) have a different consumer profile compared with older respondents (over age 76). Differences appear with respect to dieting and use of diet supplements as well as hearing aids and Viagra-like medications. The young old group is significantly more likely to use age-denial than the older respondents, which may suggest that the Oticon sales strategy was simply more effective in reaching middle-aged people with hearing problems.

Age-adaptive brands respond to some level of anxiety that leads to problem-solving behavior, a point confirmed by research. Silverstein and Abramson have conducted important research on age-related marketing through data from a national sample of Baby Boomers, drawn from the "Images of Aging" study sponsored by the American Association of Retired Persons (AARP). A particular focus of interest was on different types of anxiety associated with aging. The big sources of worry they found were anxiety over loss of autonomy, followed by uneasiness around physical manifestation of age, and attitudes of optimism or pessimism with respect to contentment in later life.

Silverstein and Abramson put their finger on the distinctive style of age-denial branding as reflected in positive images of age in mass media: "Positive images of aging have emerged in advertisements and have tended to emphasize the use of products that resist or even reverse the physical and mental changes that accompany aging."[12] They argue that such images are, ultimately, unrealistic, and contribute to diminished credibility of both advertising and so-called scientific findings purporting to support anti-aging interventions. When it comes to aging, the "power of positive thinking" is a two-edged sword. On the other hand, they argue, aging anxiety can actually be useful if worries about age reflect realistic concerns which could motive preventive activities: precisely what age-adaptive brands seek to do.

Silverstein and Abramson note that advertising has often been effective in defusing stigma associated with an embarrassing condition, such as incontinence, constipation, or erectile dysfunction: "To do this, advertisers have positioned products to appeal to a desirable identity as much as to 'fix' an external problem."[13] As we have seen, age-adaptive brands often combine a mixture of messages and values, both problem-solving promises and aspirational values.

We have seen that age-denial branding explicitly appeals to magical thinking and denial of reality. By contrast, age-adaptive branding can accept reality while at the same time offering a positive alternative. Silverstein and Abramson give an example of this point in the case of ads for cosmetic products that diminish signs of aging of the skin: "These ads let middle-aged and other adults know that it is acceptable that their bodies have changed, and suggest almost second-handedly that the product will make them look younger."[14] They make the important point that age-adaptive brands succeed when they avoid identifying consumers in negative terms ("old" or "frail"), instead offering a more complex message that solves a problem while providing positive and aspirational images which transcend age.

Silverstein and Abramson argue that fear of age-related dependency is a powerful motivator. In their study,

> Anxiety over financial and social dependence emerged as the most powerful factor. Products and services, such as long-term care insurance, congregate housing, and investment counseling, may find a welcome reception

among the now near-elderly baby-boomers who are concerned about their continued autonomy.[15]

Age-Irrelevant Brands

Age-irrelevant brands have become much smarter about evolving their traditional campaigns to be more inclusive and appealing to seniors. They have realized that seniors are an important segment of the market that should not be ignored. Instead of emphasizing how aging can introduce problems in need of a solution like age-adaptive brands, age-irrelevant brands take their main positioning and specifically focus on seniors as a core segment.

Age-irrelevant brands rely on traditional branding concepts for success. Following the seminal paper on branding by Keller (1993), age-irrelevant brands adapt the brand image to show the relevance to seniors. According to Keller's framework, a brand is a knowledge structure in memory with links to various attributes, benefits, and image associations. The key to this strategy is to recognize which associations are salient in consumer memory and leverage the strongest ones in a context that includes seniors.

The key here is in the marketing concept of positioning. Charles Schewe believes that positioning is all-important in developing successful age brands and positioning presents a distinctive challenge.[16] Schewe argues that positioning means putting a brand in a particular framework in the consumer's mind: that is, in relationship to competing brands or product characteristics. There is no brand "in itself" except in relationship to the entire field of the marketplace and in the minds of consumers. Schewe also argues that chronological age, like sociological, economic, and demographic attributes, is a poor way to reach the aging consumer's mind. The reason is that with increasing age, we become more and more different, indeed more and more distinctive as individuals. In that respect, age is the opposite of youth. Chronological age might make sense in positioning products for young people. For young children, for instance, we can generalize about the "terrible twos." But for elders, we can't make such generalizations about, say, "typical" 80-year olds. Here, in Schewe's words, is the logic for age-irrelevant branding:

> Savvy marketers bypass direct reference to age and age-related problems in their marketing; instead, they create subtle associations to underlying consumption problems. By focusing on a concern, perhaps, or an issue involving the basic age-related need, the marketer can catch the awareness and interest of older buyers and avoid an overt confrontation with age itself.[17]

Another important voice on behalf of age-irrelevant branding is Dick Stroud, author of *50-Plus Market*, who makes a strong argument that what he calls age-neutral marketing is essential for reaching the emerging market of aging

Boomers.[18] Paralleling what David Wolfe showed for the U.S. market, Stroud's work draws on international research in Australia, the Czech Republic, France, and the United Kingdom. Wolfe has argued consistently that direct appeals to age are generally wrong for marketing. Wolfe, instead, favors what he calls "ageless marketing," a strategy which parallels the key ideas of age-irrelevant branding.[19] Here we consider a few examples to make the point clear.

Nike is one brand that has successfully broadened its positioning to include old and young alike. The Just Do It campaign began in 1988 by highlighting athletes as the pinnacle of athletic performance. Nike recognized that there was a pyramid of influence starting with professional athletes that ultimately influenced the purchase decisions of non-professional semi-athletes as well as average consumers. The enormously successful strategy spanned a myriad of sports. Michael Jordan in basketball, Tiger Woods in golf, Roger Federer in tennis, and Bo Jackson in football (and baseball) were a few of the example athlete endorsers that skyrocketed Nike to domination of the athletic shoe category.

Initially focused on teens and young adults, Nike has since evolved the Just Do It campaign to include other segments. One critical ingredient to the success of this evolution is that the brand has managed to adapt to different geographies and consumer segments while maintaining its laser focus on performance. For example, Nike has taken a similar strategy in global markets where American sports are not popular. Whether it's soccer in Europe or cricket in India, Nike's focus on performance has been translated to the sport that is popular in the local country.

More recently, Nike has gone beyond professional athletes to highlight the athlete in all of us. This strategy has been effectively broadened to seniors as well. For example, Nike created a campaign that focused on the so-called "Iron Nun," Sister Madonna Buder. The ad shows seniors in an unexpected light, one that makes age irrelevant. Specifically, the ad features an 86-year-old Sister Buder who has broken Ironman race records well into her eighties. Sister Buder completed her first race at age 55 and has run over 45 Ironman races in total. This remarkable lady definitely puts a new meaning on what it means to be a senior athlete and the ad has gone viral online.

One of the most successful forms of age-irrelevant branding is a strategy known as "universal design."[20] Universal design is a creative approach to housing and living environments that aims to provide greater access for people with disabilities without stereotyping or stigmatizing them. For example, instead of a separate ramp to a building for those who are disabled, universal design aims for an environment that is accessible to all. Universal design evidently has enormous importance for age-related marketing. Instead of age-targeted products, universal design is consistent with a strategy of age-irrelevant branding.

The concept of universal design, also called "ageless design," has been summarized in seven principles by the Center for Universal Design[21] as follows:

1. Equitable use appealing to all users and their needs
2. Flexibility in use (e.g., adjustable work counters and stair-ramp combinations)

3. Simple and intuitive application (e.g., design allowing easy entrance)
4. Perceptive information about a building's circulation and focal points
5. Tolerance for error (e.g., electrical grounding to avoid electrocution)
6. Low physical effort (e.g., places for people to sit or rest)
7. Size and space for approach use (e.g., wide doorways and hallways).

In housing for older people, principles of universal design have stimulated many creative examples of age-irrelevant branding.[22] For example, the strategy of universal design has prompted developing new types of shower grab bars and replacing toggle light switches with knobs that are easier to use. In the home, universal design elements include no-step entrances, location of the master bedroom on the ground floor, and walk-in showers. Homes inspired by principles of universal design will have beneficial features affecting interior circulation, bathroom and kitchen design, home automation, electrical switches, and appliance controls, among other elements. These elements can have great appeal to older consumers. The call for "barrier-free," "accessible design," or "assistive technology" is likely to lead to significant product innovation in the aging society.

Universal design is not limited to housing. It is also, perhaps surprisingly, at work in consumer products, such as Folgers coffee. For example, Folgers' "AromaSeal" coffee canister features an easy-grip handle endorsed by the American Arthritis Foundation. This is an age-adaptive feature couched in an age-irrelevant brand format. Different age-branding strategies can coexist and reinforce each other. As Boomers grow older, such a strategic approach could flourish because as the Yankelovich group advises:

> Boomers are skittish about anything associated with old age, even if it is a useful fix. So finesse it with a 'universal design' strategy of simplicity, flexibility and ease of use—designs with a youthful vibe that are intentionally inclusive of all age groups.[23]

In years to come, the strategy of age-irrelevant branding is likely to make many products available to consumers without the stigma associated with age and disability.

Age-Affirmative Brands

Positive aging is what age-affirmative branding is all about. But positive aging has not exactly been a prominent American tradition. On the contrary, as a nation, the United States was founded in a spirit of youthful enthusiasm, a country defining itself as a "New Order of the Ages" and rejecting age and tradition. But the picture of age in America is more complicated than it seems. Noted historian David Hacket Fischer has recounted the complex history of aging in America.[24] Fischer describes colonial America as an era very different from our own "youth culture." In Colonial times, elders were typically regarded with honor and awe, though sometimes also with fear and resentment linked to their power in holding property. Of course, there were far fewer people over 65 in the population than there are today. But those who did reach the later years were rewarded with a measure of respect more far-reaching than today's "senior discounts." In the 18th century, it was common even for younger people to wear wigs with white hair, just as British jurists do today. In other words, it was the opposite of our contemporary world where gray-haired people dye their hair in order to look young. So we wonder: In our contemporary world, is it possible to imagine that products could be branded and marketed with a positive image of age? The answer is "yes," because age-affirmative branding has already proved successful, at least in certain cases. Analyzing those successful cases can give us clues about how marketing and branding can become a more positive force in our aging society in the future.

Age-affirmative branding often relies on development of a relevant brand personality in order to make a connection with seniors. Aaker (1997), in a study that included 37 brands and over 100 personality traits, found evidence for five brand personality dimensions: sincerity, excitement, competence, sophistication, and ruggedness. When the brand personality matches the consumer's personality, then purchase likelihood increases.

How can we find a picture of age-affirmative branding? A visual definition actually appeared in an issue of *More* magazine, with a full-page photo, presenting a two-piece black outfit displaying layers of fat, or "love handles," on the waist of film actress Jamie Lee Curtis, then age 43. The photo was a big surprise. Commenting on the picture, Jamie Lee Curtis acknowledged, "I don't have great thighs. I have very big breasts and a soft fatty little tummy. Glam Jamie, the perfect Jamie … it's such a fraud." She added "The more I like me, the less I want to be other people."[25] Jamie Lee Curtis later appeared on the cover of *AARP The Magazine* at the time of her 50th birthday, the year that she became eligible to be an AARP member.

The Jamie Lee Curtis story may be a sign of things to come. David Wolfe cites this ad as a dramatic example of a changing attitude toward aging.[26] Jamie Lee is not an isolated instance. Over four million Americans share the same year as her birth, and Wolfe adds, "Many have no doubt come to terms with themselves in much the way that Jamie has." Of course, acceptance is only part of the picture. The key idea is actually conveyed in Curtis's last comment: "The more I like me, the less I want to be other people," which is a perfect illustration of Carl Jung's concept of the whole purpose of the second half of life: namely, individuation, or becoming more truly myself, the person I was meant to be. Here lies the foundation for age-affirmative branding.

Wolfe's own book on "ageless marketing" includes many examples and case studies of what I call age-affirmative branding. Successful age-affirmative branding has to be something more than sentimentality or wishful thinking. It demands authenticity, which is priceless at any age. Authenticity is evident in Jamie Lee

Curtis and in her *More* photo. She does not ignore the signs of age; she flaunts them, since her vision is trained on something else. As Wolfe puts it,

> By integrating the unchangeable fact of her aging into her worldview and comfortably adjusting to the idea that the blush of her youth is fading, Jamie has clearly caught on to the idea that after adulthood comes a higher and more complex state that offers more.[27]

This "higher and more complex state" is not ageless, but age-affirmative. It has also been called "conscious aging."

Age-affirmative branding is a form of conscious aging:[28] that is, becoming intentionally aware of age. In this respect, it is fundamentally counter-cultural and it goes against the grain of everything in our youth-oriented society. To make this point, Professor Toni Calasanti[29] tells the story of asking her college students to assume that a beloved relative is clearly old and then to imagine what their response should be. The answer from the students is always the same: "No, you're not!" they say. Calasanti then points out that if we posit the reverse, for example, a student telling the grandparent, "Grandma, you know, I'm young," in that case no one would ever imagine that the reply would be "No, you're not." In other words, youth is accepted, and affirmed, in a way that age is not. Being young doesn't mean being carefree. It has its pains. We understand the limits of youth, but we also acknowledge its positive dimensions. Above all, we have hope for the future. As Molly Andrews has noted, there is no such positive content or hope attached to being old in our society.[30] As a traditional saying has it, everyone wants to live long, but no one wants to grow old.

Molly Andrews' critique of "agelessness" underscores the limits of "ageless marketing." It also points to the limits of the quest for an "age-irrelevant society" promoted by Bernice Neugarten. Why are we so insistent on agelessness or age-irrelevance? There are ways in which age-irrelevance can be a form of denial or evasion. Not explicitly so, perhaps, as we see in age-denial branding, but unconsciously so. As we try to define the meaning of "age-affirmative" branding, therefore, we need to ask difficult questions, such as "how does age resistance differ from age denial?"[31] Margaret Cruikshank answers this question by saying that with age resistance, "I deliberately step out of the box provided for me by deeply-ingrained cultural messages." With age-denial branding, on the other hand, "I claim to be ageless or exceptional."[32] Age resistance, then, is the core of messaging for age-affirmative branding.

Another wonderful example of age-affirmative branding comes from the fashion industry. In fashion it had been typical to focus on models in their twenties and thirties, anything above that age group was unusual. However, nowadays celebrities are starting to show off their looks well into their fifties, sixties, and beyond. Fashion brands have followed suit. Saint Laurent featured Joni Mitchell in a recent campaign, Celine featured Joan Didion, and Givenchy featured a campaign with Julia Roberts. One fashion brand leading the charge toward an age-affirmative strategy is Barney's department store. In 2012, Barney's campaign included the 63-year-old model Penelope Tree. In 2014, Barney's highlighted transgender men and women. A year later the brand featured a campaign of older supermodels including Christie Brinkley, Brooke Shields, and Stepanie Seymour.

Age-affirmative branding, as shown by these examples, is evidently a proven strategy for targeting older consumers. But it remains an uncommon strategy and there may be many explanations for that fact. One explanation is perhaps that creative departments in advertising agencies typically have an average age under 30. Given the power of ageism, it is hard for young people to have much imagination or empathy for positive aging, even though recent psychological research has convincingly demonstrated its reality.[33] Then too, television advertising still favors the classic "18 to 49" demographic and advertisers tend to ignore those over age 50. Perhaps for these reasons, the greatest success in brand communication for age-affirmative brands has come mostly through viral marketing (word of mouth), not through paid ads.

Age-affirmative brands are ultimately based on aspirational values: an image of who we want to be as we grow older. Age-affirmative brands are about values, identity, and hope. Age-affirmative brands can take their cue here from other aspirational brands. For example, consider L'Oreal's Preference hair color, with its tagline, "Because you're worth it." L'Oreal's campaign sought to put attractive, but realistic women in ads where consumers could imagine themselves, not as icons of unattainable beauty, but as images of aspiration and self-confidence. Aspiration plus authenticity is an unbeatable combination. Another aspirational brand is the famous diamond company De Beers, with its familiar slogan, "Diamonds are forever." Now there's an aspiration: Who wouldn't pay for love that lasts? Self-esteem and immortality are strong aspirational values, which become powerful brand messages remaining in the minds of audiences for years.

The same principles apply to age branding. Age-affirmative brands offer a similar kind of affirmation and sense of identity: a version of aging quite different from decline or as a problem to be solved. Age-affirmative brands are ultimately about hope and positive aging and, when successful, they evoke strong emotional response and brand loyalty.

Conclusion

One challenge for positioning age brands is that we cannot simply ask customers what they want. Two giants of advertising and market research, Kevin Clancy and Robert Shulman, summed up the problem by noting that "Because consumers don't choose rationally, any research that forces rational answers has to be flawed." Behavioral economics has amply confirmed their point.[34] So, how then do we listen to our customers? Clancy and Shulman again: "[Brand] positioning cannot be developed from what people say they want."[35] So much for focus groups, interviewing, and survey research in this context.

Yet positioning is crucial for age branding. When it comes to age branding, the key question is: How to overcome a profound customer resistance based on negative feelings about aging itself? Age-denial brands do this by appealing to magical thinking: "Buy my product and you won't grow old!" Age-adaptive brands take a different tack. They overcome resistance by promising a solution to genuine problems associated with age. Age-irrelevant brands make subliminal appeal to age-related needs and desires, but without mentioning age itself. And age-affirmative brands are a kind of "aspirational positioning" that promises a future better than the past. In short, age-affirmative brands appeal to hope instead of fear.

In the 1968 film *The Graduate*, there is a memorable scene where Dustin Hoffman's character is talking with an older man who gives him advice about the future. What is his advice? In a single word, the older man whispers, "Plastics." Plastics, he believes, will be the growth sector of the future. In the same way, we could easily predict that, in years to come, the U.S. economy will be driven increasingly by population aging. It takes no genius to do this; we just look at the demography. To our Dustin Hoffman-like students and graduates today, we can whisper in their ears that "aging" is the new "plastics."

Notes

1 Ronald Klatz and Robert Goldman, *Stopping the Clock: Why Many of Us Will Live Past 100—and Enjoy Every Minute!* Keats Publishing Company, 1996.
2 *10 Things about Baby Boomers*, Yankelovich Monitor Think Tank (December, 2008), p. 20.
3 *Ibid.*, p. 5.
4 *Ibid.*
5 Kathleen M. Cienkowski, "Auditory Aging: A Look at Hearing Loss in Older Adults," *Hearing Loss*, 24 (May–June, 2003), pp. 12–15.
6 Cathie Gandel, "Now Hear This," *AARP The Magazine,* 49:2C (March–April, 2006), pp. 42–43.
7 "Marketing of Hearing Devices," at: http://beckerexhibits.wustl.edu/did/advert/part4 .htm.
8 "Hearing Aids Just Got Cool and Sexy," *Inventor Spot*, at: http://inventorspot.com/articles/how_get_boomer_wear_hearing_aid_6247.
9 Laurie Lande, "How a Hearing Aid Company Doubled the Percentage of Sales to Valuable First-Time Buyers," at: http://www.marketingprofs.com/casestudy/55.
10 Frances Schwartzkopff, "Hearing Aid Makers Look to De-stigmatize Hearing Aids," *Bloomberg News* (September 26, 2008).
11 Erdman B. Palmore, "Healthy Behaviors or Age Denials?" *Educational Gerontology*, 33:12 (December, 2007), pp. 1087–1097.
12 Merril Silverstein and Alexis Abramson, "How Baby-Boomers in the United States Anticipate Their Aging Future," in Kohlbacher, F. and Herstatt, C. (eds.) The Silver Market Phenomenon: Business Opportunities in an Era of Demographic Change, New York: Springer, p. 56.
13 *Ibid.*, p. 63.
14 *Ibid.*

15 *Ibid.*, p. 64.
16 Charles D. Schewe, "Strategically Positioning Your Way into the Aging Marketplace," *Business Horizons* (May–June, 1991).
17 *Ibid.*
18 Dick Stroud, *The 50-Plus Market: Why the Future Is Age-Neutral When It Comes to Marketing and Branding Strategies*, Kogan Page, 2007.
19 David B. Wolfe with Robert E. Snyder, *Ageless Marketing: Strategies for Reaching the Hearts and Minds of the New Customer Majority*, Dearborn Trade Publishing, 2003, pp. 107–109.
20 Mia Oberlink, *Opportunities for Creating Livable Communities*, AARP Public Policy Institute, 2008.
21 Jean Zagrodnik, "Universal Design 101: Seven Elements of Ageless Design," *Journal on Active Aging*, 5:2 (March–April, 2006), pp. 84–85.
22 North Carolina State University, Center for Universal Design, Universal Design in Housing, 2006.
23 10 Things about Baby Boomers, p. 20.
24 David Hacket Fischer, *Growing Old in America*, Oxford University Press, 1978.
25 Amy Wallace, "True Thighs," *More* (September, 2002), pp. 90–95.
26 David B. Wolfe, *Ageless Marketing*, p. 19.
27 *Ibid.*, p. 321.
28 See Harry R. Moody, "Conscious Aging: A Strategy for Positive Development in Later Life" in Judah Ronch and Joseph Goldfield (eds.) *Mental Wellness in Aging: Strength-based Approaches*, Health Professions Services Press, 2002. See also James Hillman, *The Force of Character and the Lasting Life*, Ballantine, 2000.
29 Toni Calasanti, "A Feminist Confronts Ageism," *Journal of Aging Studies*, 22:2 (April, 2008). Virginia Polytechnic Institute and State University: Personal communication.
30 Molly Andrews, "The Seductiveness of Agelessness." *Ageing and Society*, 19 (1999), pp. 301–318.
31 Julia Twig, "The Body, Gender, and Age: Feminist Insights into Social Gerontology," *Journal of Aging Studies*, 18:1 (2004), p. 63.
32 Margaret Cruikshank, "Aging and Identity Politics," *Journal of Aging Studies* 22:2 (April, 2008).
33 Fundamental here is the work of Laura Carstensen, "Growing Old or Living Long: Take Your Pick; Research to Understand the Psychological and Emotional Processes of Aging is Essential to Creating a Society," Issues in *Science and Technology* (January 1, 2007). See also the ground-breaking work of Gene Cohen, *The Creative Age: Awakening Human Potential in the Second Half of Life*, Harper Paperback, 2001; and also Gene Cohen, *The Mature Mind*, Basic Books, 2005.
34 On behavioral economics, see *Choices, Values, and Frames*, edited by Daniel Kahneman and Amos Tversky, Cambridge University Press, 2000, and, more recently, *Nudge: Improving Decisions About Health, Wealth, and Happiness*, by Richard H. Thaler and Cass R. Sunstein, Yale University Press, 2008.
35 Kevin Clancy and Robert Shulman, "The Marketing Revolution: A Radical Manifesto for Dominating the Marketplace," *Harper Business*, 1991, p. 85 (cited by David Wolfe, *Ageless Marketing*, p. 32).

11

DESIGNING PRODUCTS FOR OLDER CONSUMERS

A Human Factors Perspective

Neil Charness, Jong-Sung Yoon, and Hellen Pham

Our goals in this chapter are to provide a brief introduction to human factors and to the Center for Research and Education on Aging and Technology Enhancement (CREATE) approach for ensuring adequate person-system fit, as well as to provide an overview of normative changes in perception, cognition, and psychomotor functioning with age that should influence product design considerations. We will look at some example products and outline how modeling can provide a useful alternative to traditional usability testing when trying to decide on the relative merits of alternative designs.

The discipline of human factors is concerned with "the role of humans in complex systems, the design of equipment and facilities for human use, and the development of environments for comfort and safety" (Salvendy, 1997). Human factors practitioners typically attempt to optimize product design from the perspective of three criteria: productivity/efficiency, safety, and comfort/enjoyment. The first two criteria are often the primary focus, particularly when the products are deployed in work settings. However, the last criterion, comfort/enjoyment (are the products easy and enjoyable to use), is possibly more important when we consider older consumers using products at home. Designers also must juggle other criteria that manufacturers hold dear, such as product quality, cost, and ease of manufacturing. As the old engineering joke goes: "You can have your product be of good quality, inexpensive, quick to get to market: good, cheap, quick. Pick any two."

There are a huge number of products available to the consuming public in developed nations. For retail giant Amazon alone, there were nearly 120 million products for sale in April 2019 (https://www.scrapehero.com/number-of -products-on-amazon-april-2019/). For convenience, we will categorize products into those used primarily in work settings, home settings, and public places.

Older consumers, the so-called "silver market," are perceived as a growing and important market for products and services. A 2016 report by Oxford Economics and the American Association of Retired Persons (AARP) suggested that the 111 million-strong cohort of those aged 50+ in the United States generated $7.6 trillion in economic activity (https://www.oxfordeconomics.com/recent-releases/the-longevity-economy).

Although we are all aging, it is convenient to segment that amorphous "age 65+" group into three sub-groups: the young-old group, typically age 65–74; the middle-old group, typically age 75–84; and the old-old group, those 85+. These groups often have different needs (and wants) in products. However, for the most part, we will contrast data from younger and older adults when it comes to looking at normative, age-related changes in functional status.

Although there are well-defined normative changes in function with age, it is not clear that self-perceptions of older adults map on very well to their own physical aging. That is, older adults do not necessarily see themselves as old (Kornadt, Hess, Voss, and Rothermund, 2016), though objective measures may indicate otherwise. The senior author, when helping an older gentleman walk down a street in Squirrel Hill in Pittsburgh a few decades ago, vividly remembers hearing the gentleman's sister complain: "Milton, you are walking like an old man!" Milton was around 90 years old at the time. Neither he nor his sister probably defined themselves as older adults. Thus, older consumers may not be attracted to products advertised as being for "older adults." Rather, products aimed at improving functional abilities may be attractive, particularly ones that improve comfort and enjoyment.

Human Factors Framework for Product Use

The Center for Research and Education on Aging and Technology Enhancement www.create-center.org, although focused primarily on technology products, provides a useful framework for conceptualizing the human-technology relationship structure. An example appears in Figure 11.1.

Users, particularly older consumers, bring a set of capabilities to performing a task with a product or system. These include cognitive, psychomotor, and perceptual capabilities. These capabilities are a product of a person's genetic endowment and their developmental and socio-cultural history (cf. Baltes, Rösler, and Reuter-Lorenz, 2006). Examples of factors that influence such capabilities include a person's age, education level, and specific experiences with the product class. The product or system that users interact with makes a set of demands on these capabilities (e.g., for technology products, via their software, hardware, and instructional support components). To the extent that the demands are met by user capabilities, the product or system is usable and enhances performance. When the demands exceed capabilities, then the system becomes difficult to use and may not help the user achieve his or her goals. This can impact not just usage, but product acceptance, attitudes toward the product, and personal feelings of competence

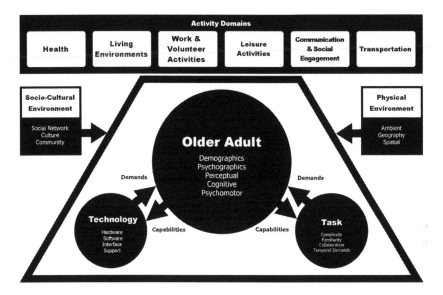

FIGURE 11.1 CREATE framework for understanding person-system interactions. Reproduced with permission from CRC Press (*Designing for Older Adults: Principles and Creative Human Factors Approaches* (3rd edition)).

(self-efficacy). CREATE research has shown that cognitive capabilities, attitudes, and self-efficacy are important predictors of technology use in a large, diverse American sample (Czaja, Charness, Fisk, Hertzog, Nair, Rogers, and Sharit, 2006).

Efficiency/productivity and safety are the usual outcomes that this demand-capability fit framework addresses. But we need to pay attention to comfort/enjoyment dimensions as well. If the controls for a product are too difficult to manipulate (think of miniaturization in electronics products such as mobile phones) or to perceive (think too small font sizes for instruction booklets or product packaging), older consumers may never purchase the product. We now focus on outlining some of the normative changes in user capabilities with increased age. There are predictable changes with age in perception, cognition, and psychomotor performance that are very likely to have an impact on whether or not the use of a product is successful (Charness and Jastrzembski, 2009; Czaja, Boot, Charness, and Rogers, 2019).

Functional Capabilities and Aging

It is worth keeping in mind that older adults comprise a very diverse group of individuals. Young-old adults are much less impaired than middle-old adults who are beginning to show some problems with instrumental activities of daily living

(IADLs) such as shopping and cleaning, whereas old-old adults are likely to suffer from multiple disabilities that lead to problems with basic activities of daily living (ADLs) such as mobility, bathing, and toileting. It is also worth remembering that although normative changes describe the general population well, not every older adult will be presbyopic, or have hearing impairment. Older adults, as a group, are more variable than younger adults for functional capabilities (show greater inter-individual variability). They also show greater within person changes across time (greater intra-individual variability, day-to-day or month-to-month variability on a task) for some cognitive tasks compared to younger adults (Hultsch, Macdonald, and Dixon, 2002). One way of capturing the latter distinction is to consider aging as a process that degrades the reliability of the information processing system. Aging processes can be conceptualized as adding unwanted noise to the system (Welford, 1981).

Vision

Despite their diversity, older adults generally do experience changes in vision that affect their ability to see as clearly as they did when they were younger. As we age we can expect to experience one or more of the following: loss of acuity particularly for near, but also for distance vision, a reduction in the field of vision, less sensitivity to light, and a reduction in the ability to distinguish colors (particularly within the short wavelengths, such as blue, green, and violet) and judge depth and distances. Although these visual impairments may occur for many reasons, typically they are due to the normal changes in eye structures (lens, pupil, cornea, and vitreous humor).

One of the most common impairments, the inability to focus effectively on nearby objects, *presbyopia or farsightedness*, results from changes in the lens and usually occurs by the mid-40s. Over time our lenses gradually become thicker and less elastic (Pinheiro and Da Silva, 2012). This thickening is often accompanied by changes in the lens that make it yellow, which limits the amount of light that can pass through the lens, impairs the refractive ability of the lens, and distorts colors.

In addition to the lens, the pupil can also limit the amount of light that enters the eye and stimulates photoreceptors as we age. Sensitivity to light declines due to age-related changes in the smooth muscles of the iris (also known as *senile miosis*) that cause the pupil to shrink in diameter. When aging, our ability to adapt to changes in light under dark or dim conditions becomes significantly worse; older adults over the age of 60 require three to ten times more light than those 20 years old and younger do, in order to perform the same visual tasks with comparable accuracy and speed (Hegde and Rhodes, 2010).

Another common visual impairment, *floaters or myodesopsia*, are loose cells that cast shadows on the retina. Patients report that these floaters can appear as small dots with linear patterns, and/or as "spider web-like" objects that are able to "float" across the visual field; this is primarily due to changes in the consistency (transforming from gel to a liquid consistency) of the vitreous humor (Milston, Madigan, and Sebag, 2016). In addition to becoming liquidlike, the vitreous humor also becomes less transparent as we age which can cause the light to be scattered throughout the posterior chamber of the eye rather than being focused on the fovea where it is converted by photoreceptors into nerve activity. Changes in the refraction of light can result in blurred vision and an increased sensitivity to glare.

For designers who are trying to accommodate these changes, as well as other age-related changes not discussed here that degrade visual acuity, there are three basic guidelines: increase illumination, minimize glare (by using matte surfaces instead of glossy ones), and use larger font sizes for text and symbols such as icons. A good guideline for adequate size is to ensure that the visual angle of subtense for a character is at least 0.6 degrees. Your thumb held at arm's length subtends about 2 degrees of visual angle for its width.

Hearing

We typically begin to notice subtle changes in our ability to hear high-frequency tones in our 40s and those losses usually progress as we age. Hearing impairments are classified in three ways: conductive (interference with the transmission of sound through the outer and/or middle ear affecting its ability to reach the inner ear), sensorineural (disorders of the inner ear affecting the transmission of sounds through auditory pathways), or mixed (both conductive and sensorineural) (Saxon, Etten, and Perkins, 2014). The most common form of sensorineural hearing loss, presbycusis, is due to degenerative changes in the cochlea and/or auditory nerve fibers that lead from the cochlea to the brain (Nelson and Hinojosa, 2006). These normal age-related changes in the ear result in a higher percentage loss in hearing across high frequencies (pitches) for older adults (Agrawal, Platz, and Niparko, 2008).

Additionally, after the age of 60 hearing loss is approximately 1dB per year (Lee, Matthews, Dubno, and Mills, 2005). This not only presents a problem for daily living and conversation; it could present problems in product use. A variety of disorders can arise, such as the perception of muddled speech (phonemes such as "s" and "th" are hard to differentiate and perceive) and tinnitus (ringing in the ears) causing interference with the perception of sound (Saxon, Etten, and Perkins, 2014).

Auditory signals (e.g., beeps) are a popular form of feedback in many products. These products range from cellular phones and digital cameras to microwave ovens. However, such feedback might be lost on older adults depending on the intensity (decibel level) and/or pitch (frequency) of such a signal. Choosing pitches in the range of 500–1000 Hz with an intensity of at least 60 dB should help keep signals audible for most older consumers.

A further difficulty for older adults is background noise. Discerning audible signals within background noise is increasingly difficult for the older user compared to younger users, with intended signals needing to be of greater intensity. However, simply boosting the volume of all sounds (e.g., with a standard hearing aid) may not improve the signal-to-noise ratio and may even result in greater masking of the signal by noise sources.

Although hearing loss is associated with age, recent findings suggest that prevalence of hearing loss in US adults is declining (e.g., Hoffman, Dobie, Losonczy, Themann, and Flamme, 2017). Possible explanations for the trend include reduction in exposure to occupational noise, less smoking, and better management of cardiovascular risk factors (Hoffman, Dobie, Losonczy, Themann, and Flamme, 2017). Despite this positive trend, the need for hearing aids and related health care will continue to increase as the older population keeps growing.

Motor Performance

Among the normative changes for the older user is a loss in fine motor control. This can be viewed as being a result of having a "noisier" motor control system. Thus, we can expect an older adult to have increased difficulty in tasks that would require selecting small targets, for example on a computer screen, based on Fitts' law (e.g., Welford, 1977). Fitts' law states that movement time (MT) is determined by the amplitude (A) or distance of the movement and the width (W) of the target, which jointly comprise the index of difficulty (ID) for the movement. This relationship is represented (Fitts, 1954; Jagacinski, and Flach, 2003) as:

$$MT = a + b\,ID$$

where

$$ID = \log_2\left(2A/W\right)$$

The Fitts' law equation implies that motor performance will improve with larger targets or smaller distances between targets, thereby lessening the index of difficulty. A meta-analysis by Jastrzembski and Charness (2007) indicated that b was about 175 milliseconds (ms)/bit for older adults compared to 100 ms/bit for younger ones. Because of the push for miniaturization, particularly in electronic products, buttons and icons may become too small (width, W, is diminished) posing a special problem for older users.

Further, essential tremor affecting arms and hands increases exponentially with age, with about 4 percent of those aged 60+ years and 20 percent of 95-year-olds exhibiting difficulties with manual activities (Louis, 2019). Essential tremor can make activities such as replacing small batteries in hearing aids very difficult. In summary, a good rule of thumb is that any given movement task can be expected to take about twice as long for older compared to younger adults.

Anthropometrics and Physical Fitness

In addition to the above changes, changes in body dimensions and functional capabilities may occur with increased age (e.g., Kroemer, 2005; Steenbekkers and van Beijsterveldt, 1998). For instance, obesity has become common in many developed countries leading to redesign to accommodate changes in weight and size, even in older adult cohorts. Sarcopenia is a term used to refer to the age-related loss of muscle that can lead to disability and functional impairment (e.g., Doherty, 2003; Visser et al., 2002). This may not only result in decreased capabilities for instrumental activities of daily living but can also affect activities of daily living, and compromise performance with products requiring physical exertion. It has been documented that even with preventative measures such as exercise, maintaining or even adding muscle mass will still result in overall loss of strength (Goodpaster, Park, Harris, Kritchevsky, Nevitt, 2006), though exercise can clearly improve both physical and mental fitness (Kramer et al., 1999).

Sarcopenia is also sometimes accompanied by osteoporosis which can diminish height due to the combination of bone loss and shrinking of the disks in the spine, though this affects women more than men. Many of these changes will show onset in middle age or later and can result in reduced ability to work or complete loss of certain abilities (Ilmarinen and Louhevaara, 1994). With this in mind—any device requiring physical exertion should aim to minimize physical effort (with the notable exception of exercise equipment).

Nationally representative US data for anthropometrics can be referenced from the National Health and Nutrition Examination Survey (NHANES) study: https://www.cdc.gov/nchs/data/series/sr_11/sr11_252.pdf. Data are also available for other nations, including Sweden (Gavriilidou, Pihlsgård, and Elmståhl, 2015), Australia (Kothiyal and Tettey, 2001), and Brazil (Almeida et al., 2013), though not always from representative samples.

Cognitive

Similar to the perceptual and psychomotor systems previously discussed, the cognitive system also changes as we grow older (Salthouse, 2012). However, unlike the other systems, these normal age-related changes in cognitive functioning can be both positive as well as negative. On the positive side, older adults benefit from their ability to draw on larger stores of previously acquired skills, knowledge, and experiences than younger adults. This accumulation of knowledge, or "crystallized intelligence" increases from the 20s and remains relatively stable throughout most of adulthood and may decline in the mid-60s (Horn, 1982). Conversely, "fluid abilities," abstract problem-solving capability, tend to decline from the 20s onward. Other more specific cognitive functions, such as working memory capacity (Maylor, 2005) and visual attention (Rogers, 2000) also show gradual decline from early adulthood and can be the source of challenges for older adults when interacting with technology products.

The term "working memory" describes a system of mental resources that must work together in order to hold and manipulate information (Baddeley, 1998). Working memory plays an important part in many cognitive tasks such as learning and understanding. Empirical evidence suggests that normal age-related cognitive changes reduce working memory capacity and that this reduction leads to an inability to inhibit irrelevant information and difficulty integrating newly acquired information (otherwise known as "executive control") with already existing knowledge (Hasher and Zacks, 1988; Engle, 2002). However, memory tasks that do not require effortful self-initiated processing (e.g., implicit memory, perceptual memory) show very mild or no age-related decline (Luo and Craik, 2008). With growing interest in identifying mechanisms that might offset age-related decline in memory, recent studies have started to focus on the effects of memory training on older adults and associated neural mechanisms underlying them.

Selective attention is defined as the ability to process one stream of information while disregarding other, concurrent streams whereas divided attention (sometimes referred to as task-switching in recent literature) requires the ability to process, maintain, and schedule two or more tasks simultaneously (Verhaeghen and Cerella, 2002). Research investigating age-related differences in divided attention has indicated performance decline when older adults are exposed to situations asking older adults to simultaneously coordinate multiple tasks. However, the emergence of performance declines in older adults depends heavily on the complexity of the task and that given sufficient practice the severity of these declines will diminish (Rogers, 2000). Age-related differences in divided attention tasks also depend heavily on working memory capacity and functioning (Salthouse, Rogan, and Prill, 1984).

The most robust change with age is slowing in the general rate of information processing (Salthouse, 1996). Some processes slow down more than others as Jastrzembski and Charness (2007) point out in their analyses of cognitive, perceptual, and motor slowing. For processes like the average fixation time of the eye during reading, slowing is minor (about 15 percent). For other perceptual, cognitive, and motor processes, older adults take from 70 to 100 percent longer. Thus, one cannot expect older product users to respond rapidly to warnings in the middle of complex procedures. One should avoid short "time-out" intervals on devices or in phone menu systems.

Generally, given the decreased reliability of the human performance system with age, products should be designed to minimize the number of cognitive, perceptual, and psychomotor operations that are needed during usage or to accomplish a goal. That should not only minimize the time to carry out an activity with the product, but more importantly, minimize the probability of error across that chain of steps.

Application of Knowledge about Aging

Given the changes outlined above, there are relatively straightforward recommendations that can be given to designers to avoid overtaxing older adult capabilities. For detailed guidelines see Czaja, Boot, Charness, and Rogers (2019). We illustrate some of these guidelines by examining products and discussing their various pros and cons.

Examples of Products in the Office: Computer Systems

A ubiquitous tool in the office is the computer (desktop or laptop) and its peripheral devices such as the mouse, monitor, keyboard, printer, scanner, webcam, and other attachments. These devices can pose challenges for the older user. If, for example, a monitor was of a smaller size (e.g., 20 inches diagonal) and the typical settings of the computer's operating system presented everything with small icons and fonts, the user could have difficulty reading from the monitor as they enter their presbyopic years. Corrections to this situation would be to increase the size of icons and fonts through software or to use a larger monitor (or to wear computer-distance reading glasses). Generally, font sizes of 12 or larger are recommended for print for older adults.

Another important component for computer use is the pointing device, usually a mouse, or trackpad. To operate a mouse, a user must make hand or arm movements to position the cursor on the screen. For an older user who may have limited movements due to arthritis, a trackball could be a superior device to help minimize physical exertion when controlling a cursor, particularly for extended time periods with repetitive tasks (Chaparro, Bohan, Fernandez, Kattel, and Choi, 1999). For those with less control over movement, perhaps due to stroke or tremor, and who merely need to select items on a screen rather than enter data, a direct positioning device, such as a touch screen would be the most efficient (Zhou and Shen, 2016). Speech-based commands coupled to speech recognition software is another option for interaction.

The keyboard could also present problems. With newer laptop/notebook computers becoming smaller than their predecessors some have keyboards with less than standard inter-key spacing, making it difficult to touch type for those with larger hands, and particularly when arthritis affects dexterity. A smaller target (recall Fitts' law) could result in overshooting causing errors and/or discomfort in typing. Thus, old and young alike should consider adding a standard keyboard to a notebook computer setup (e.g., by plugging one into a USB port or connecting with Bluetooth). Tablets pose additional problems, such as having relatively small screens that might result in added scrolling to read lines of text and may have difficult-to-read characters when set at standard resolutions. Office users of notebook computers should consider adding a docking station that would enable them to use a standard keyboard, mouse (or trackball), and larger monitor. Older adults might consider acquiring computer reading glasses that provide sharp intermediate-distance focusing (as opposed to typical bifocals designed for near or far distance) to improve vision. But product designers should not assume that everyone will have access to those aids.

Examples of Products in the Home and for Personal Use

In our daily lives we may rely on technologies big and small to help us throughout our day. Technology products these days can range from standard watches to smart devices (e.g., smart phones, smart televisions, and voice-based interface devices using digital assistants; see chapter 17 by Webster, Francis, and Antonucci on the potential benefits of smart technology to older adults). Voice-based interfaces are increasingly being adopted in US homes and most operating systems offer access to digital assistants (e.g., Microsoft's Cortana, Apple's Siri, Amazon's Alexa, Google's Assistant.) Some of these devices are relatively simple in function (i.e., the standard watch) while others can be very complex (i.e., remote controls for a Smart TV with many functions).

Our first example will be the mobile phone, comprising two classes: rapidly disappearing feature phones owned by over 80 percent of older Americans and smartphones, owned by about half in 2019 (Czaja et al., 2019). Older users will typically avoid features that are not critical to the operation of the device. Chattratichart and Brodie (2003) found that mobile phone functions were perceived to be too difficult to use (i.e., displays are too hard to read, multi-functional buttons are difficult to learn to use). Jastrzembski and Charness (2007) examined younger and older adult performance with two differently designed mobile phones. The phone with the keypad having closely positioned keys, though slightly smaller, produced quicker dialing times. Conversely, the phone that was slower in dialing was faster in a text messaging task by virtue of having fewer steps due to the more efficient menu structure. Menu structure can be an important issue when concerned with timing and usability. It was found that if a device contained a menu tree instead of changing menu screens it would reduce errors (Ziefle and Bay, 2006). However, recent studies suggest that older adults can feel disorientation and stress when the menu structure is deeper and/or complex (Petrovčič et al., 2018). Some of the early findings on mobile phone design for older adults should also be reconsidered given that smartphones have introduced new hardware and software solutions for older adults (Li and Luximon, 2019; Petrovčič et al., 2018).

Another example of increasing complexity is the menu and interface structure in Smart TV systems. Smart TV systems are replacing traditional TVs and come with a number of Internet-based streaming services along with keeping traditional over-the-air, cable, and satellite service connectivity options. A Smart TV system requires users to navigate among the different streaming services which increases the complexity of interfaces and menu structures. Accessing content in a Smart TV system frequently involves a long sequence of steps using more complex menu structures via a remote control (or multiple remote controls).

The complexity of Smart TV systems can pose challenges to older adults. It is necessary to ensure that menu text and button labels in the remote controls are large enough and have high contrast. The interface challenges can be addressed by simpler menu structures and minimizing the number of steps to access specific content (Czaja, Boot, Charness, and Rogers, 2019).

Examples of Products in Public Places

In our public lives, we interact with technology whose goal is to improve and facilitate services. Some of these devices are automated teller machines, self-service kiosks, and even the credit and debit card pay stations at registers in nearly every store. These machines can often be confusing and even daunting to those with little to no experience with them, as may be the case with older adults. In the case of public touch screen kiosks—such as airport self-check in, supermarket self-checkout, and public transportation ticket dispensers—in order to accommodate a broad range of users, these public touch screens tend to have large screen displays at a low height or with a tilted screen. The interface usually displays large target options with a combination of image and text, along with short concise instructions (Caprani, O'Connor, and Gurrin, 2012).

Another important publicly available system is the credit/debit card self-swipe or insert machines at cash registers in stores. These devices are designed to improve the efficiency of sales transactions, particularly by eliminating the slow exchange of paper money and change, and the writing and verification of paper checks. It is worth keeping in mind that low-income individuals may not have bank accounts and credit cards (~15 percent of US consumers in 2015[1]) so cash transactions may be their only option. While these devices are convenient, improperly designed devices can increase difficulty and frustration for users. Information about how to position the card to swipe or insert it should be clearly displayed. Buttons should be of adequate size, have adequate spacing, and be clearly marked (though appropriately shielded to protect against theft of a PIN). These are some of the same principles used in mobile phone designs and are transferable to any keypad design.

Ways to Design

Good design usually involves a feedback cycle where a prototype is generated in accord with accepted design guidelines, tested with the targeted user population, flaws are identified, the product is redesigned, the revised product is resubmitted to testing, etc. The cycle continues until the company is satisfied that it is marketable. The two main techniques available to designers to test product designs include usability testing and modeling. Modeling can often be used to help guide initial design choices. Usability testing, though often somewhat expensive, should be used to catch flaws that might not have been predicted through modeling or in the case where modeling is infeasible.

Usability Testing

More and more products are formally evaluated for usability before entering the marketplace, particularly health care products seeking Food and Drug Administration (FDA) approval. Usability of a product is typically assessed on five dimensions—learnability, efficiency, memorability, errors, satisfaction—forming the acronym **LEMES**. (One can cue that acronym from the phrase: "**L**et **E**very **M**ature **E**lder **S**ucceed".) Learnability refers to ease of learning to use the product. For older adults, who acquire new information more slowly than younger adults (e.g., take twice as long to learn software such as word processing: Charness, Kelley, Bosman, and Mottram, 2001), learnability of a product can be a significant factor in adoption. Testers need to consider typical uses of the product, and then assess how long it takes for a user to reach a target proficiency level for these tasks. Proficiency would include both the time to complete the task and how long it may take to perform the task without committing any errors. The latter dimension becomes most important for medical devices.

Efficiency, the second dimension, is often assessed in comparison with competitor products. It includes similar testing criteria to learnability, but also often assesses whether speed of performance can be achieved while minimizing frustration or fatigue. Memorability, the third dimension, refers to how easily the product can be used after initial learning but following a delay. Many products are only used occasionally, so products with good memorability characteristics can be used efficiently after periods of disuse. Good design will often build in "affordances," features that guide the user into the right actions. For instance, many hotel door cards include an arrow symbol that shows which of the four different vertical insertion orientations work for opening the door. (The size of the opening slot on the door helps eliminate trying the four horizontal possibilities. Superior but more costly designs can allow someone to place a card in any orientation close to a sensor panel that unlocks the door.)

Error, the fourth dimension, refers to the goal of minimizing errors in product use, with particular attention to catastrophic errors that could harm the user. Testing focuses on establishing when, where, and why errors occur. Various classification schemes have evolved to describe types of errors (e.g., Sharit, 2006), with common types being slips (unintended actions such as pressing the wrong button inadvertently), mistakes (intentionally selecting an incorrect action believed to be the correct one), and mode errors (selecting an incorrect action due to misperceiving the current state of the environment).

The final dimension, Satisfaction, refers to user perceptions about how much they enjoy using the product. Questionnaires and rating scales are typically employed to evaluate satisfaction, though some care is needed to probe for different aspects of a product, rather than to elicit a global rating.

Usability testing draws on many different techniques (Czaja, Boot, Charness, and Rogers, 2019). They include expert reviews, heuristic analysis, cognitive walkthroughs, coding video-recording of representative users who are interacting with prototypes to perform typical tasks, eliciting think aloud protocols (Ericsson, 2006) during product use, and summative post-use questionnaires and interviews. Usability often begins with focus groups (Czaja et al., 2019) being asked to comment on potential product design features. Based on user perceptions, a prototype might be produced and submitted to more intensive testing (LEMES) and then feedback from testing is used to modify the product to improve its performance. This process may iterate a number of times until the decision is made to manufacture and market the product.

Modeling

Because usability testing often involves long time frames, it may be possible to shortcut product design using simulations and models. Modeling involves abstracting human performance characteristics by deriving parameters for typical cognitive, perceptual, and motor operations, and detailing how people assemble sequences of operators to perform tasks with a product. Alternative designs will make different demands on information processing capabilities and the model or simulation should be able to predict which version results in better performance.

Card, Moran, and Newell (1983) in their book *The Psychology of Human-Computer Interaction*, described an idealized model of a person, the Model Human Processor, and outlined a first approximation modeling technique, GOMS (goals, operators, methods, selection rules). The model human processor perspective together with GOMS offer researchers and designers a means of predicting the impact of different design decisions on user performance, usually for predicting completion times for tasks with the product.

Model Human Processor

The Model Human Processor is a multi-faceted approach to making predictions about users. If we were to consider a user as a complex system, then this model breaks them down further into subsystems consisting of the perceptual, motor, and cognitive components. The overall system and subsystems are comprised of sets of memories, processors, and principles (known as "principles of operation") working together. The perceptual system as implied by its name, perceives the world through touch, visual, and auditory pathways by encoding the signals into a format that the cognitive system can understand. After the cognitive system receives the recoded signals, its job is to determine a course of action based on previous knowledge. The course of action decided upon is then carried out by the motor system. Within each of these systems, system-specific memory buffers and processors are utilized.

The usefulness of this approach is in the detailed path taken. Estimates for the duration of each process are culled from experiments and literature in psychology. For example, to read a sentence you typically fixate on one word at a time and move on. The duration of one fixation after an eye movement for older users is estimated to be about 267 ms (Jastrzembski and Charness, 2007) while a younger user's fixation duration is estimated to be about 230 ms (Card, Moran, and Newell, 1983). While the slowing of only 37 ms may seem insignificant, when repeated 100 times when reading a text passage, older adults are already 3.7 seconds behind a younger user. Such age-related changes in parameters are important to consider when designing for tasks relying on text processing.

GOMS Model

The GOMS model, which stands for Goals, Operators, Methods, and Selection rules, is a scalable model for predicting the time for user interaction with a system. A GOMS model explicitly represents goals (main goal such as turning on the TV) and sub-goals (such as finding the remote), operators (unit task operations such as pressing the power button on either the TV or remote), methods (sequences of operators to accomplish a goal), and selection rules for choosing methods (e.g., if remote is not found, go to the TV). A more detailed example is presented below. A limitation for GOMS modeling is that it best characterizes routine cognitive tasks. Unless modified, it cannot easily account for user knowledge or for errors and error recovery processes. Despite such limitations, the GOMS model is a very useful tool not only for testing existing systems, but also for creating and testing imagined systems.

GOMS example. Remote controls for Smart TV systems are growing in complexity. Modern functions of a Smart TV remote can range from the standard changing of the channel and volume to complex features such as accessing different streaming services and providing program guide listings.

For our example of GOMS modeling and Fitts' law, we are going to use the Program Guide button. Shown in Figure 11.2, a mockup of a remote for a Smart TV, is the "Home" location (i.e., "Enter" button), the area in which the user is likely to rest their thumbs, the current Guide button (Guide 1), and lastly a proposed location for the Guide button (Guide 2).

By applying Fitts' law to assess the location of the Guide buttons in relation to "Home" we would see a significant difference predicted for the index of difficulty. We can calculate this if "Home" from Guide 1 and Guide 2 is an inch and four inches apart, respectively, as follows:

Guide 1:

$$\text{Log}_2\left(2A_1/W_1\right)=2.415 \quad A_1 =1'' \quad W_1 =0.375''$$

Guide 2:

$$\text{Log}_2\left(2A_2/W_1\right) = 4.415 \quad A_2 = 4'' \quad W = 0.375''$$

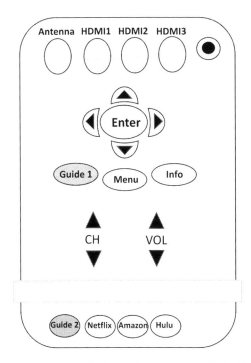

FIGURE 11.2   Mockup of remote control for Smart TV with two potential Guide button positions.

These equations show that for Guide 1 the ID is only 2.425 while Guide 2 is 4.425 if it were the same size button as Guide 1. However, in Figure 11.2, we notice that the button is much smaller, thus the equation goes as follows:

Guide 2:

$$\text{Log}_2\left(2A_2 / W_2\right) = 5 \quad A_2 = 4'' \quad W_2 = 0.25''$$

From this we can see the decreased size of the proposed guide button is not preferred due to the increase in the ID to five. We can determine that due to the increase in the ID, moving the button is not preferable.

Even though we have information for ID ratings of the proposed change, we have not evaluated time for task completion. The GOMS model lays out the steps needed to be taken in order to locate and press the Guide (either 1 or 2) button (see Figure 11.3). What we should calculate is the time for each step, based on parameters given in Jastrzembski and Charness (2007).

GOMS Example		Process*	Younger (ms)	Older(ms)
▪ Goal: Access Guide Function				
● Goal: Locate Guide Button				
○ Fixate on remote		F	230	267
○ Decision of area of interest		C	70	118
▪ Fixation on button		F	230	267
▪ Verification		C	70	118
○ *Fitts' law on time to move to button*	*Guide 1:*		312	569
	Guide 2:		570	1021
○				
○ Goal: Press button		M	70	146
Total: Given no errors in selection	**Guide 1:**		**982**	**1485**
	Guide 2:		**1240**	**1937**

*Process is the process used during each task, C = Cognitive process, F = eye fixation, and M = motor process

FIGURE 11.3   A GOMS example on accessing the program guide through the remote control with mean time parameters in milliseconds for younger and older users. Operator times taken from Jastrzembski and Charness (2007). ★Process is the process used during each task, C = cognitive process, F = eye fixation, and M = motor process.

The following calculations will be based on the usage of the remote by an older experienced user. By simply fixating on the remote in hand, the older user is expected to spend 267 ms. A cognitive process (118 ms) might then decide the area of interest from a memorized cognitive map of the remote. Next, we choose to fixate on the guide button within the area of interest (267 ms). The next step is the motor function of moving toward and then pressing the guide button. To calculate movement time, we use the Model Human Processor's version of Fitts' law as follows:

Movement Time = $b \times$ Index of Difficulty + Motor Process Cycle Time

where b = slope of line with 100 for younger adults and 175 for older adults

Motor Process Cycle = 70 ms for younger adults, and 146 for older adults

As we complete the task, assuming no errors, an older user will take nearly 1.5 seconds to use Guide 1, and approximately 1.9 seconds to use Guide 2.

It may seem that when applied to a remote, the time difference of 452 milliseconds does not seem significant. However, if this was applied to a work environment with a repetitive task, the time savings of knowing adequate placement would be worthwhile and result in significantly increased efficiency and might also increase worker comfort.

Thus, GOMS modeling can provide an estimate of the time cost for positioning a button in an array of buttons, sparing the designer from the necessity of doing costly usability testing.

Summary

Aging reduces human capabilities in predictable ways, though there will always be considerable individual differences within older samples. Because of these normative changes in perceptual, cognitive, and psychomotor abilities as a function of increased chronological age, products should be carefully designed to fit older consumers' waning capabilities. The human factors field provides useful methods, such as usability testing and modeling, as well as sound guidelines (Czaja et al., 2019) for improving product design. Better designed products hold considerable promise for improving both the quality of life of older consumers as well as the bottom line for companies. A bonus is that good design for older adults can usually be expected to improve product functioning for other consumer groups.

Note

1 https://www.pewtrusts.org/-/media/assets/2016/06/fsp_what_do_consumers_with out_bank_accounts_think_about_mobile_payments.pdf.

References

Agrawal, Y., Platz, E. A., & Niparko, J. (2008). Prevalence of hearing loss and differences by demographic characteristics Among US adults. Reprinted. *Archives of Internal Medicine*, *168*(14), 1522–1530.

Almeida, M. F., Marucci, M. F. N., Gobbo, L. A., et al. (2013). Anthropometric changes in the Brazilian cohort of older adults: SABE survey (health, well-being, and aging). *Journal of Obesity*, 1–9. Article ID 695496. doi:10.1155/2013/69549.

Baddeley, A. (1998). *Human Memory: Theory and Practice (Revised Edition)*. Boston, MA: Allyn and Bacon.

Baltes, P. B., Rösler, F., & Reuter-Lorenz, P. (Eds.) (2006). *Lifespan Development and the Brain: The Perspective of Biocultural Co-Constructivism*. New York: Cambridge University Press.

Caprani, N., O'Connor, N., & Gurrin, C. (2012). Touch screens for the older user. In: Fernando A. Auat Cheein (Ed.). *Assistive Technologies*. InTech. DOI: 10.5772/38302, https://cdn.intechopen.com/pdfs/31905/InTech-Touch_screens_for_the_older_us er.pdf.

Card, S. K., Moran, T. P., & Newell, A. (1983). *The Psychology of the Human-Computer Interaction*. Hillsdale, NJ: Lawrence Erlbaum Associates.

Chattratichart, J., & Brodie, J. (2003). The age factor in the design equation of cell phones. *Proceedings of the 12th Annual Usability Professionals' Association Conference*, June 23–27, Arizona.

Chaparro, A., Bohan, M., Fernandez, J., Kattel, B., & Choi, S. (1999). Is the trackball a better input device for the older computer user? *Journal of Occupational Rehabilitation*, *9*(1), 33–43.

Charness, N., & Jastrzembski, T. S. (2009). Gerontechnology. In: P. Saariluoma & H. Isomäki (Eds.). *Future Interaction Design II* (pp. 1–29). London: Springer-Verlag.

Charness, N., Kelley, C. L., Bosman, E. A., & Mottram, M. (2001). Word processing training and retraining: Effects of adult age, experience, and interface. *Psychology and Aging*, *16*(1), 110–127.

Czaja, S. J., Boot, W. R., Charness, N., & Rogers, W. A. (2019). *Designing for Older Adults: Principles and Creative Human Factors Approaches* (3rd edition). Boca Raton, FL: CRC Press.

Czaja, S. J., Charness, N., Fisk, A. D., Hertzog, C., Nair, S. N., Rogers, W. A., & Sharit, J. (2006). Factors predicting the use of technology: Findings from the Center for Research and Education on Aging and Technology Enhancement (CREATE). *Psychology and Aging*, *21*(2), 333–352.

Doherty, T. J. (2003). Invited Review: Aging and sarcopenia. *Journal of Applied Physiology*, *95*(4), 1717–1727.

Engle, R. W. (2002). Working memory capacity as executive attention. *Current Directions in Psychological Science*, *11*(1), 19–23.

Ericsson, K. A. (2006). Protocol analysis and expert thought: Concurrent verbalizations of thinking during experts' performance on representative tasks. In: K. A. Ericsson. In: N. Charness, P. J. Feltovich & R. R. Hoffman (Eds.), *The Cambridge Handbook of Expertise and Expert Performance* (pp. 223–242). New York: Cambridge University Press.

Fitts, P. M. (1954). The information capacity of the human motor system in controlling the amplitude of movement. *Journal of Experimental Psychology*, *47*(6), 381–391.

Gavriilidou, N. N., Pihlsgård, M., & Elmståhl, S. (2015). Anthropometric reference data for elderly Swedes and its disease-related pattern. *European Journal of Clinical Nutrition*, *69*(9), 1066–1075.

Goodpaster, B. H., Park, S. W., Harris, T. B., Kritchevsky, S. B., Nevitt, M., Schwartz, A. V., Simonsick, E. M., Tylavsky, F. A., Visser, M., & Newman, A. B. (2006). The Loss of skeletal muscle strength, mass, and quality in older adults: The health, aging and body composition study. *Journal of Gerontology: Medical Sciences*, *61A*(10), 1059–1064.

Hasher, L., & Zacks, R. T. (1988). Working memory, comprehension, and aging: A review and a new view. *The Psychology of Learning and Motivation*, Vol. *22* (pp. 193–225). New York: Academic Press.

Hegde, A. L., & Rhodes, R. (2010). Assessment of lighting in independent living facilities and residents' perceptions. *Journal of Applied Gerontology*, *29*(3), 381–390.

Hoffman, H. J., Dobie, R. A., Losonczy, K. G., Themann, C. L., & Flamme, G. A. (2017). Declining prevalence of hearing loss in US adults aged 20 to 69 years. *JAMA Otolaryngology–Head and Neck Surgery*, *143*(3), 274–285.

Horn, J. L. (1982). The theory of fluid and crystallized intelligence in relation to concepts of cognitive psychology and aging in adulthood. In: F. I. M. Craik & S. Trelub (Eds.). *Aging and Cognitive Processes* (pp.237–278). New York: Plenum Press.

Hultsch, D. F., MacDonald, S. W. S., & Dixon, R. A. (2002). Variability in reaction time performance of younger and older adults. *Journal of Gerontology: Psychological Sciences*, *57B*, P101–P115.

Ilmarinen, J., & Louhevaara, V. (1994). Preserving the capacity to work. *Aging International, 21*(2), 34–36.

Jagacinski, R. J., & Flach, J. M. (2003). *Control Theory for Humans.* Mahwah, NJ: Erlbaum.

Jastrzembski, T., & Charness, N. (2007). The model human processor and the older adult: Parameter estimation and validation Within a mobile phone task. *Journal of Experimental Psychology: Applied, 13*(4), 224–248.

Kornadt, A. E., Hess, T. M., Voss, P., & Rothermund, K. (2016). Subjective age across the life span: A differentiated, longitudinal approach. *Journals of Gerontology: Psychological Sciences, 73*(5), 767–777. doi:10.1093/geronb/gbw072.

Kothiyal, K., & Tettey, S. (2001). Anthropometry for design for the elderly. *International Journal of Occupational Safety and Ergonomics, 7*(1), 15–34.

Kramer, A. F., Hahn, S., Cohen, N., Banich, M., McAuley, E., Harrison, C., Chason, J., Vakil, E., Bardell, L., Boileau, R. A., & Colcombe, A. (1999). Aging, fitness, and neurocognitive function. *Nature, 400*(6743), 418–419.

Kroemer, K. H. E. (2005). *"Extra-Ordinary" Ergonomics: How to Accommodate Small and Big Persons, the Disabled and Elderly, Expectant Mothers, and Children.* Boca Raton, FL: CRC Press.

Lee, F. S., Matthews, L. J., Dubno, J. R., & Mills, J. H. (2005). Longitudinal study of pure-tone thresholds in older persons. *Ear and Hearing, 26*(1), 1–11.

Li, Q., & Luximon, Y. (2019). Older adults' use of mobile device: Usability challenges while navigating various interfaces. *Behaviour and Information Technology,* 1–25. DOI: 10.1080/0144929X.2019.1622786

Louis, E. D. (2019). The roles of age and aging in essential tremor: An epidemiological perspective. *Neuroepidemiology, 52*(1–2), 111–118. doi:10.1159/000492831.

Luo, L., & Craik, F. I. (2008). Aging and memory: A cognitive approach. *The Canadian Journal of Psychiatry, 53*(6), 346–353. doi:10.1177/070674370805300603.

Maylor, E. A. (2005). Age-related changes in memory. In: M. L. Johnson (Ed.). *The Cambridge Handbook of Age and Aging* (pp. 200–208). New York: Cambridge University Press.

Milston, R., Madigan, M. C., & Sebag, J. (2016). Vitreous floaters: Etiology, diagnostics, and management. *Survey of Ophthalmology, 61*(2), 211–227.

Nelson, E. G., & Hinojosa, R. (2006). Presbycusis: A human temporal bone study of individuals with downward sloping audiometric patterns of hearing loss and review of the literature. *Laryngoscope, 116*(9), 1–12.

Petrovčič, A., Taipale, S., Rogelj, A., & Dolničar, V. (2018). Design of mobile phones for older adults: An empirical analysis of design guidelines and checklists for feature phones and smartphones. *International Journal of Human-Computer Interaction, 34*(3), 251–264. doi:10.1080/10447318.2017.1345142.

Pinheiro, C., & Da Silva, F. M. (2012). Colour, vision and ergonomics. *Work, 41*(1), 5590–5593.

Rogers, W. A. (2000). Aging and attention. In: D. C. Park & N. Schwarz (Eds.). *Cognitive Aging: A Primer* (pp. 57–73). New York: Taylor & Francis Group, LLC.

Salthouse, T. A. (2012). Consequences of age-related cognitive declines. *Annual Review of Psychology, 63*, 201–226.

Salthouse, T. A. (1996). The processing-speed theory of adult age differences in cognition. *Psychological Review, 103*(3), 403–428.

Salthouse, T. A., Rogan, J. D., & Prill, K. A. (1984). Division of attention: Age differences on a visually presented memory task. *Memory and Cognition, 12*(6), 613–620.

Salvendy (Ed.) (1997). *Handbook of Human Factors and Ergonomics.* New York: John Wiley & Sons.

Saxon, S. V., Etten, M. J., & Perkins, E. A. (2014). *Physical Change and Aging: A Guide for the Helping Professions* (6th edition). New York: Springer Publishing Company.

Sharit, J. (2006). Human error. In: G. Salvendy (Ed.). *Handbook of Human Factors and Ergonomics* (3rd edition, pp. 708–760). Hoboken, NJ: Wiley.

Steenbekkers, L. P. A., & van Beijsterveldt, C. E. M. (Eds.) (1998). *Design-Relevant Characteristics of Ageing Users*. Delft, The Netherlands: Delft University Press.

Verhaeghen, P., & Cerella, J. (2002). Aging, executive control, and attention: A review of meta-analyses. *Neuroscience and Biobehavioral Reviews, 26*(7), 849–857.

Visser, M., Kritchevsky, S. B., Goodpaster, B. H., Newman, A. B., Nevitt, M., Stamm, E., & Harris, T. B. (2002). Leg muscle mass and composition in relation to lower extremity performance in men and women aged 70 to 79: The health, aging and body composition study. *Journal of the American Geriatrics Society, 50*(5), 897–904.

Welford, A. T. (1977). Motor performance. In: J. E. Birren & K. W. Schaie (Eds.). *Handbook of the Psychology of Aging* (pp. 450–496). New York: Van Nostrand Reinhold.

Welford, A. T. (1981). Signal, noise, performance, and age. *Human Factors, 23*(1), 97–109.

Zhou, X., & Shen, W. (2016). Research on interactive device ergonomics designed for elderly users in the human-computer interaction. *International Journal of Smart Home, 10*(2), 49–62.

Ziefle, M., & Bay, S. (2006). How to overcome disorientation in mobile phone menus: A comparison of two different types of navigation aids. *Human-Computer Interaction, 32*(4), 393–433.

PART IV

New Directions in Aging Research

12

SUBJECTIVE AGE AND OLDER CONSUMERS

Alessandro M. Peluso, Cesare Amatulli,
Carolyn Yoon, and Gianluigi Guido

Introduction

With the aging of modern society, academic scholars and practitioners are increasingly interested in understanding how older consumers think and behave, in order to meet better this growing segment's needs, expectations, and desires with respect to products and services (see Guido, 2014; Gunter, 1999, for reviews). The study of older consumers' behavior presumes a deep understanding of age-related processes and concepts. Aging is a fundamental aspect of human development, and *chronological age*—that is, the number of years one has lived (Barak and Gould, 1985)—has often been considered the most critical variable involved in the aging process. Yet a host of studies, conducted over the past few decades in various fields including gerontology (e.g., Kornadt et al., 2018; Kotter-Grühn, Kornadt, and Stephan, 2016), development psychology (e.g., Diehl et al., 2014; Montepare and Lachman, 1989), and consumer behavior (e.g., Kuppelwieser, 2016; Wilkes, 1992), have argued that aging is a multidimensional process, of which chronological aging represents *only one* aspect. Most of the studies have built on the notion that aging is a complex phenomenon that implicates not only biological changes (*biological aging*), but also the evolution of the social roles that individuals hold (*social aging*) and how they perceive themselves over time (*psychological aging*) (Settersten and Mayer, 1997). Therefore, an analysis limited to chronological age, its role in target marketing, and its potential effects on consumption behavior, is insufficient for a comprehensive account of how older consumers respond to marketing-related stimuli.

Prior studies have advanced the notion of *subjective age*. This concept captures individuals' perception of their own ages (e.g., Gendron, Inker, and Welleford, 2018) and has been found to predict older consumers' behaviors better than chronological age (Chaouali and Souiden, 2019; Guido, Amatulli, and Peluso, 2014). The next section focuses on the conceptualization and measurement of *subjective age*. The chapter proceeds with a discussion of a common tendency by older individuals to perceive themselves as being younger than their chronological age. We then discuss the malleability of *subjective age* and, by extension, the aforementioned tendency, by reviewing empirical findings documenting the differences across cultural contexts, age groups, individuals, and situations. The chapter concludes with a discussion of the implications of subjective age and the related tendency to feel younger of older consumers.

Subjective Age: Definition and Measurement

The concept of *subjective age* has attracted much research attention because of its relevance to some explanations of older consumers' attitudes and behaviors (e.g., Kornadt et al., 2018; Stephan et al., 2013). However, the literature on *subjective age* that has accumulated over the past few decades has proposed varied definitions and measurement instruments for this construct. This section seeks to define *subjective age* and to clarify its relation to other age-related concepts. It also discusses how it is measured and assessed in empirical studies.

Defining Subjective Age

Prior literature has provided different definitions of *subjective age*. In general, it captures the notion of individuals' perception of their own age (Gendron, Inker, and Welleford, 2018). Specifically, *subjective age* refers to the age individuals perceive themselves to be (Barrett, 2003; Shrira et al., 2019; Stephan et al., 2013), and this perception may be discrepant from their chronological age (e.g., a 70-year-old woman may perceive herself to be 60 years old). *Subjective age* reflects a psychological rather than a physical state and an integration of one's own self-concept (Brannon and Miller, 2019). Therefore, individuals of a given chronological age might have different subjective ages, as a function of the personal perception they have of themselves as well as based on contextual factors. The discrepancy between subjective and actual age reflects the extent to which individuals feel younger (or older) than their chronological age.

Some prior work conceptualized *subjective age* in a more complex manner, by defining it as a multidimensional construct. Building on a seminal study by Kastenbaum et al. (1972), Barak and colleagues (Barak, 1987; Barak and Gould, 1985; Barak and Stern, 1986; Barak, Stern, and Gould, 1988) conceptualized *subjective age* as a construct that comprised several dimensions, which tapped into different age-related perceptions. These include *identity age*, that is, the age group (i.e., young, middle-aged, old, or very old) individuals identify with; *stereotype age*, the extent to which individuals identify with old-age stereotypes (e.g., inactive, sick); and *cognitive age*, which consists of subdimensions of feel-age (i.e., how old individuals feel), look-age (i.e., how old they think they look), do-age (i.e., how old they perceive themselves to be based on their typical activities), and interest-age (i.e., how old they perceive themselves to be based on their interests). *Cognitive age* seems to be the most significant way in which *subjective age* is expressed, and *feel-age* the most relevant subdimension thereof, owing to its ability to capture individuals' perception of their own age (Kastenbaum et al., 1972; Zacher and Rudolph, 2019). Accordingly, most recent studies (e.g., Amatulli et al., 2018; Armenta et al., 2018; Guido, 2014; Stephan, Demulier, and Terracciano, 2012) have operationalized *subjective age* simply as *feel-age*.

Barak and colleagues (Barak, 1987; Barak and Gould, 1985; Barak, Stern, and Gould, 1988) have also proposed the concept of *ideal* (or *desired*) *age*, which refers to how old individuals would like to be, and introduced the notion that discrepancies between different age-related concepts can be relevant to better understanding how people perceive themselves with respect to aging. Specifically, they introduced the concepts of *youth age* and *disparity age*. *Youth age* denotes the discrepancy between *feel-age* and chronological age, thus indicating the extent to which individuals perceive themselves as younger (or older) than their actual age. *Disparity age* refers to the discrepancy between *ideal age* and chronological age, thus serving as a proxy for individuals' satisfaction with their actual ages (Hubley and Hultsch, 1994) (see Table 12.1 for a summary of the main age-related constructs). Finally, Guido, Amatulli, and Peluso (2014) proposed another construct, termed *fabricated age*, which refers to the age that individuals deliberately misrepresent as their actual chronological age, irrespective of their feel-age. This construct requires further investigation, as the potential variations in its prevalence between and within individuals and the effects on consumption are yet unknown.

Measuring Subjective Age

The literature on *subjective age* has proposed a variety of measurement approaches that differ in scale format and the number of items assessed. Regarding format, *subjective age* has been measured using semantic differential scales (e.g., "I generally feel …," 1 = extremely young, 7 = extremely old), Likert scales (e.g., "I generally feel old," 1 = strongly disagree, 7 = strongly agree), interval scales (e.g., "I feel as though I am in my ___," 1 = teen, 2 = 20s, 3 = 30s, …, 8 = 80s; Barak and Schiffman, 1981), and ratio scales (e.g., "I feel as though I am ___ years old").[1] Ratio scaling is the most frequently adopted format as it provides numerical answers, allowing a direct comparison to chronological age (Kotter-Grühn, Kornadt, and Stephan, 2016; Van Auken and Barry, 1995; Van Auken, Barry, and Bagozzi, 2006).

As for the number of items, there are both mono-item and multi-item scales. As mentioned before, most studies operationalized *subjective age* simply as *feel-age*, and assessed it using mono-item scales. Such scales consist of a single question that asks respondents to indicate the age they feel either at a given moment or in

TABLE 12.1 Main Age-Related Constructs

Construct *(Definition)*	Dimensions *(Definition)*	*Main Sources*
Chronological age (the number of years that an individual has lived)	n.a.	Barak & Gould (1985)

Subjective age (one's personal perception of their own age)	• *Identity age* (the age group an individual identifies with)
	• *Stereotype age* (the extent to which an individual identifies with old-age stereotypes)
	  • *Cognitive age* (composed of:
	  • *Feel-age* [how old an individual feels]
	  • *Look-age* [how old an individual looks]
	  • *Do-age* [the age an individual perceives themself to be based on their activities]
	  • *Interest-age* [the age an individual perceives themself to be based on their interests])
		Barak (1987)
		Barak & Gould (1985)
		Barak & Stern (1986)
		Barak, Stern, & Gould (1988)
		Kastenbaum et al. (1972)

Ideal age (how old one would like to be)	n.a.	Barak (1987) Barak & Gould (1985) Barak, Stern, & Gould (1988)
Youth age (the discrepancy between one's feel-age and chronological age)	n.a.	Barak (1987) Barak & Gould (1985) Guido, Amatulli, & Peluso (2014)
Disparity age (the discrepancy between one's ideal age and chronological age)	n.a.	Barak (1987) Hubley & Hultsch (1994)
Fabricated age (the age that one deliberately misrepresents as one's true age)	n.a.	Guido, Amatulli, & Peluso (2014)

n.a. = not applicable.

general, depending on whether *feel-age* is assessed as a temporary mental state or as an individual predisposition, respectively. Examples of questions assessing *feel-age* as a momentary mental state are: "How old do you feel right now?" (Amatulli et al., 2018), "What age do you feel now?" (Marquet et al., 2018), or "What age do you feel at this moment?" (Eibach, Mock, and Courtney, 2010). Examples of questions assessing *feel-age* as an individual predisposition are: "What age do you feel most of the time?" (Barrett, 2003; Westerhof, Barrett, and Steverink, 2003; Mock and Eibach, 2011), or "Indicate, in years, the age that most closely corresponds to the age you generally feel" (Zacher and Rudolph, 2019).

The use of multi-item scales is more common in studies that have operationalized *subjective age* as *cognitive age*. Kastenbaum et al. (1972) were among the first to propose a multi-item scale that comprised four items aimed at assessing subdimensions: feel-age (i.e., "I feel as though I were about age …"), look-age (i.e., "I look as though I were about age …"), do-age (i.e., "I do most things as though I were about age …"), and interest-age (i.e., "My interest are mostly those of a person about age …"). Barak and Schiffman (1981) slightly modified Kastenbaum et al.'s (1972) scale by asking respondents to answer those four items by indicating the decades they considered most representative of their cognitive age. Although this scale has been proved to be internally reliable and unidimensional (Chang, 2008; Montepare and Lachman, 1989; Sudbury and Simcock, 2009; Wilkes, 1992), it has not been free of criticisms. A key criticism is that the four items could reflect conceptually different aspects of a person's perception of their own age and, as such, should be kept distinct from one another (Kotter-Grühn, Kornadt, and Stephan, 2016). Another criticism is that those four items may not provide a stable representation of the underlying construct (Guido, Amatulli, and Peluso, 2014). Indeed, some studies removed one or more items (e.g., Guiot, 2001), while others added new ones (e.g., Edgar and Bunker, 2013; Zacher and Rudolph, 2019). These changes led to the development of multiple versions of the original multi-item scale.

Based on the above considerations, there are both theoretical and practical reasons for preferring mono-item scales over multi-item ones. Theoretically, *feel-age* is the most relevant dimension of *subjective age* and represents an excellent proxy for individuals' perception of their own age (Zacher and Rudolph, 2019). This implies that mono-item scales are robust enough to unambiguously capture respondents' feel-ages. Furthermore, mono-item scales can capture respondents' feel-ages in global terms, without leading them to focus exclusively on either physical or mental states (Amatulli et al., 2018). On the practical side, mono-item scales are much simpler to interpret and easier to administer than multi-item scales.

Youth Age: Operationalization and Measurement Issues

Regardless of what measurement scale is adopted, *subjective age*—even when it is operationalized as *feel-age*—makes almost no sense if it is interpreted in absolute terms. Knowing that a person feels an age of 50 conveys little information *per se*: This feel-age indeed holds different meaning if that person is 40 as opposed to 60 years old. This implies that individuals' perceptions of their ages should be considered in relation to their chronological ages. Indeed, what matters most when investigating how people feel about their ages is the discrepancy between their own *feel-age* and chronological age, that is, their *youth age*.[2]

As noted above, *youth age* indicates how younger (or older) an individual feels, relative to their actual age, and can be measured in different ways. The simplest measurement approach consists of using a comparative measure that directly asks respondents to indicate how much younger (or older) they feel compared to their chronological age on a rating scale (e.g., 1 = much younger than my actual age, 7 = much older than my actual age; see Eibach, Mock, and Courtney, 2010; Heckhausen and Krueger, 1993).

Another way of assessing *youth age* that we have found to be useful consists of asking respondents for their chronological age, followed by their feel-age, and computing discrepancy scores as the key measure of interest. Numerous studies (e.g., Armenta et al., 2018; Geraci et al., 2018; Hubley and Hultsch, 1994; Mock and Eibach, 2011) computed *youth age* as the arithmetical difference between feel-age and chronological age. Therefore, a youth-age index can be computed by subtracting feel-age from chronological age (i.e., youth-age index = chronological age − feel-age; Amatulli et al., 2018; Guido, Amatulli, and Peluso, 2014; Stephan, Demulier, and Terracciano, 2012; Weiss and Lang, 2012). Positive values on this index denote a tendency to feel younger than actual age, negative values denote a tendency to feel older, while a value of zero indicates a perfect alignment between feel-age and chronological age. For example, a 70-year-old person who feels 60 will report a youth-age index of 10, which means that they feel 10 years younger than their actual age. In contrast, the same-aged person who feels 80 years old will report a youth-age index of −10, which means that they feel 10 years older than their actual age.

Some gerontological studies (Kornadt et al., 2018; Rubin and Berntsen, 2006; Shrira et al., 2019; Stephan et al., 2016) have relativized the aforementioned arithmetical difference by computing proportional discrepancy scores. According to this approach, the youth-age index is obtained by subtracting feel-age from chronological age and dividing the resulting difference score by chronological age (i.e., youth-age index = [chronological age − feel-age]/chronological age). Positive values denote a tendency to feel younger, while negative values denote a tendency to feel older. However, in this case, the obtained values do not indicate the number of years by which individuals feel younger (or older) than their actual age, but how younger (or older) they feel in proportion to their chronological age. For example, a 70-year-old person who feels 60 will report a youth-age index of 0.14, which means that they feel 14 percent younger than their chronological age. Conversely, a same-age person who feels 80 years old will report a youth-age index of −0.14, which means that they feel 14 percent older than their chronological age.

Importantly, *feel-age* and *youth age*, which represent proxies for people's subjective age and tendency to feel younger, respectively, are malleable rather than stable constructs. Indeed, prior findings have documented malleability by examining the conditions under which it varies in magnitude. We next review the findings of malleability as a function of (1) the cultural context in which these constructs are assessed; (2) the age group to which respondents belong; (3) the individual characteristics of respondents themselves; and (4) the contingent situations in which subjective age is assessed.

Cultural Differences

One of the main findings in research on self-perception of age is that people—especially older ones—tend to feel younger than their chronological age, and are thereby shown to have positive youth-age indices. This tendency has emerged in a wide variety of studies conducted in different countries, which have employed different measures of feel-age and youth age. Even as it has been established across the globe as a universal tendency, the magnitude of this tendency varies across countries with different cultural values.

Prior literature suggests that people's tendency to feel younger than their chronological age is driven by their desire to maintain a positive view of themselves over time (Alicke and Sedikides, 2009; Brown, Collins, and Schmidt, 1988). However, at older ages, people tend to become increasingly worried about being negatively stereotyped as old. Indeed, in certain cultural contexts, age-related stereotypes are particularly negative, as aging is typically associated with undesirable attributes, such as physical and mental decline, loss of autonomy, and increased loneliness (Barnhart and Peñaloza, 2013; Nelson, 2011). Consequently, as people grow older, they are increasingly motivated to distance themselves from old-age to avoid being stereotyped accordingly. In such contexts, feeling younger than chronological age could be seen as an attempt by older people to distance themselves protectively from old-age. They seek to feel closer to the young, in response to their worry about being associated with negative aging stereotypes and to their desire to maintain a positive view of themselves (Chasteen and Cary, 2015; Weiss and Freund, 2012; Weiss and Lang, 2012).

Cultural contexts in which this phenomenon is particularly apparent are those in which it is important for people to maintain a positive image of themselves (as competent, powerful, and possessing autonomy) in the eyes of others. Interestingly, these values are typical of countries with an individualistic culture (e.g., United States), while they are less observable in countries with a collectivistic culture (e.g., Japan) (Hofstede, Hofstede, and Minkov, 2010). Because individualistic cultural contexts are youth-oriented and hold widespread negative stereotypes of old people, those who are older are particularly concerned about being associated with those stereotypes. Therefore, people from such contexts are more inclined to feel younger than their peers from collectivistic cultural contexts, where aging carries less stigma. This conclusion has received empirical support from different studies. For instance, Westerhof and colleagues (Westerhof and Barrett, 2005; Westerhof, Barrett, and Steverink, 2003) assessed youth age across two samples of respondents from the United States (a culture with very high levels of individualism) and Germany (a culture with lower levels of individualism). Their results revealed a significantly greater tendency to feel younger among U.S. adults compared to German adults.

Barak (2009) reviewed 18 different empirical studies that assessed chronological ages, feel-ages, and ideal ages in 18 different countries: Nine countries were characterized by an individualistic culture (e.g., United States, United Kingdom), while the other nine were characterized by a collectivistic culture (e.g., China, South Korea). To illustrate how people's perceptions of their ages may differ across cultural contexts, we conducted an analysis of the data concerning the aforementioned age-related variables, reported in Barak's (2009) work. Our results suggest that, on average, youth ages differed between individualistic and collectivistic cultures. Respondents' tendency to feel younger was greater in individualistic cultures than in collectivistic ones (see Figure 12.1, Panel A).

Consistent with the logic described above, our results indicate that disparity age—i.e., the discrepancy between ideal age and chronological age, as a proxy for respondents' satisfaction with their actual ages—differed between individualistic and collectivistic cultures. Respondents from individualistic cultures reported a greater disparity age, thus a lower satisfaction with their actual ages, than respondents from collectivistic cultures (see Figure 12.1, Panel B). Finally, our analysis reveals that in individualistic cultures, but not in collectivistic ones, disparity age was significantly and positively associated with chronological age. Figure 12.2 illustrates the positive relationship between chronological age and disparity age, showing that this relationship is stronger in individualistic cultures (i.e., the regression line is steeper) than in collectivistic cultures. Our results are consistent with the idea that, in individualistic cultures (but not in collectivistic ones), older people are less satisfied with their chronological ages, likely because of the negative stereotypes associated with aging. Thus, they tend to feel younger than their actual age in order to dissociate themselves from the old-age category and avoid being stigmatized or devalued as human beings.

Age Group Differences

Subjective age varies not only across cultures but also between age groups in a given cultural context. Empirical results providing support for this assertion come from two main research streams. One stream of studies has investigated age perception on single age groups (e.g., either young or older people), while the other examined different age groups, thus providing more robust evidence regarding how the phenomenon may evolve across the life span. To illustrate, studies in the first literature stream (Guiot, 2001; Hughes, Geraci, and Forrest, 2013; Kaufman

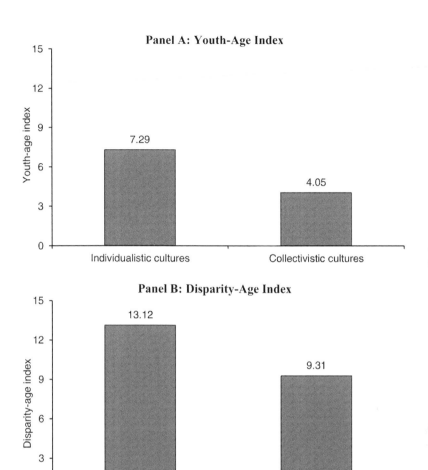

FIGURE 12.1   Cultural differences in youth age and disparity age.

and Elder, 2002; Van Auken, Barry, and Anderson, 1993) examined older people in isolation and showed that such individuals tend to feel about 8 to 16 years younger than their chronological age. Galambos, Albrecht, and Jansson (2009) analyzed a sample of adolescents and found them to feel slightly older than their actual age. The second stream compared young and older groups to better understand how subjective age (mostly operationalized as feel-age) varies across those age groups. Studies with young, middle-aged, and older age groups (Heckhausen and Krueger, 1993; Montepare and Lachman, 1989) found that adolescents tend to feel slightly older than their chronological age, middle-aged individuals tend to

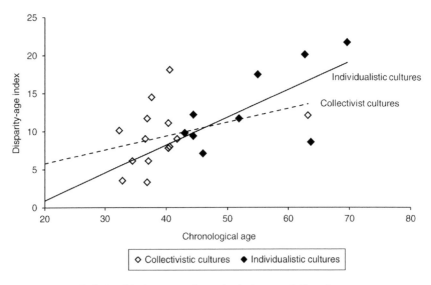

FIGURE 12.2 Relationship between chronological age and disparity age.

feel their ages as being aligned with their actual ages, and older individuals tend to feel younger than their own chronological age. The age at which individuals start feeling younger is about 25 years (Galambos, Turner, and Tilton-Weaver, 2005) and, after reaching 40, they show a consistent tendency to feel about 20 percent younger than their chronological age (Rubin and Berntsen, 2006).

A notable characteristic of these studies is their cross-sectional approach, as they assessed subjective age (i.e., feel-age) and its discrepancy from chronological age across different age groups. Therefore, although informative, these studies do not provide unequivocal evidence about how or even whether individuals' feel-ages, relative to their chronological ages, evolve over time. Some recent studies have adopted longitudinal designs. Among these, Stephan, Sutin, and Terracciano (2015b) collected data over a 10-year period from a large sample of respondents aged between 20 and 75. They found that the magnitude of people's tendency to feel younger increases as they grow older.

But why do older individuals tend to feel younger than their chronological age? Most studies converge on findings that this tendency can be explained by a self-protection account (Amatulli et al., 2018; Chasteen and Cary, 2015; Weiss and Lang, 2012; Weiss and Freund, 2012). As discussed above, older people's tendency to feel younger could be construed as a self-protective strategy through which they try to defend themselves from negative aging stereotypes that are particularly widespread in individualistic societies. Thus, feeling younger could be seen as an attempt by older people to distance themselves from their own age group and associate themselves with youth.

Individual Differences

Subjective age may also vary across individuals within a certain age group, as a function of specific individual differences in personal characteristics. Such characteristics include both socio-demographic and psychological variables.

Socio-Demographic Variables

The main socio-demographic variables examined in the literature include chronological age, gender, marital status, education, income, and health status. Regarding chronological age, past studies found a positive relationship with subjective age (i.e., feel-age) (Chéron and Kohlbacher, 2018; Kaufman and Elder, 2002; Wilkes, 1992) as well as with individuals' tendency to feel younger (Kleinspehn-Ammerlahn, Kotter-Grühn, and Smith, 2008; Stephan, Sutin, and Terracciano, 2015a; Westerhof, Barrett, and Steverink, 2003). In delving into this relationship using a sample of individuals aged 25 to 74, Barrett (2003) found also a quadratic relationship between chronological age and respondents' tendency to feel younger, suggesting that, as people grow older, they are more inclined to feel younger, but this tendency increases at a progressively slower pace. A reasonable explanation for this finding is that, at older ages, health problems may manifest, and negative changes in health serve to reduce people's tendency to feel younger (Sherman, 1994). Additional work (Logan, Ward, and Spitze, 1992; Mathur and Moschis, 2005) has shown that life transitions, accompanied by changes in lifestyle and social roles, can also reduce the tendency to feel younger (e.g., marriage, birth of children, retirement, children moving out of the household, or the birth of grandchildren).

As for other socio-demographic variables, empirical research has documented associations with gender and marital status (Guido et al., 2018). Compared to men, women are more likely to report younger feel-ages (Chéron and Kohlbacher, 2018) and, especially at older ages, are more inclined to feel younger than their chronological age (Montepare and Lachman, 1989; Stephan, Sutin, and Terracciano, 2015a; Westerhof, Barrett, and Steverink, 2003). Moreover, married individuals feel younger than their non-married counterparts (Logan, Ward, and Spitze, 1992). In terms of education and income, empirical studies (Barrett, 2003; Gwinner and Stephen, 2001; Stephan, Sutin, and Terracciano, 2015a) have shown that older individuals with high levels of education and income are particularly inclined to feel younger.

Regarding health, prior studies have suggested a positive association between good health status and one's tendency to feel younger than chronological age (Logan, Ward, and Spitze, 1992; Mathur and Moschis, 2005; Westerhof, Barrett, and Steverink, 2003). This evidence is robust across studies that used self-report measures of health (Barrett, 2003; Gwinner and Stephen, 2001) as well as objective health indicators such as grip strength, depressive symptoms, and waist circumference (Stephan, Sutin, and Terracciano, 2015a).

Psychological Variables

Feeling younger appears to be associated with a number of personality dimensions and specific individual traits. In particular, some studies (Hubley and Hultsch, 1994; Stephan, Demulier, and Terracciano, 2012; Stephan, Sutin, and Terracciano, 2015b) collected data about the Big-Five personality traits (Digman, 1990; McCrae and John, 1992), which include: agreeableness (i.e., the extent to which individuals are friendly and take care of others), conscientiousness (i.e., the extent to which they are well-organized and goal-oriented), extroversion (i.e., the extent to which they are outgoing and inclined to social interaction), neuroticism (i.e., the extent to which they are nervous and inclined to overreact to emotional stimuli), and openness (i.e., the extent to which individuals are curious and intellectually open to new ideas and ways of doing things). Interestingly, the studies documented that a greater tendency by older individuals to feel younger is associated with higher levels of extroversion, agreeableness, conscientiousness, and openness, and lower levels of neuroticism.

Regarding other, more specific individual predispositions, scholars have mainly focused on subjective well-being, sense of control, self-esteem, optimism, and loneliness. Specifically, there is a positive association between feeling younger and subjective well-being, that is, the extent to which individuals are happy based on their degree of satisfaction with life and the frequency with which they experience positive rather than negative affect (Busseri and Sadava, 2011; Diener, 1994). Prior evidence suggests that older people with a greater tendency to feel younger are more satisfied with their lives (Westerhof and Barrett, 2005) and experience higher levels of positive affect and lower levels of negative affect (Mock and Eibach, 2011). Furthermore, past studies have documented significant associations with sense of control, self-esteem, optimism, and loneliness. Indeed, older people who feel younger than their chronological age are more inclined to believe that they are able to control events in their lives (Hubley and Hultsch, 1994), hold more positive evaluations of themselves (Brannon and Miller, 2019), experience higher levels of optimism (Teuscher, 2009), and lower levels of loneliness (Gwinner and Stephens, 2001; Kleinspehn-Ammerlahn, Kotter-Grühn, and Smith, 2008).

Situational Differences

Subjective age—in particular, feel-age—also varies with situational contingencies, which may alter individuals' perceptions of their ages, making them temporarily feel younger or older as a function of the situation. Indeed, feel-age, as a malleable construct, is context-dependent; thus, it can fluctuate in relation to temporary situations, tasks, and external information cues. Older individuals, compared to people belonging to other age groups, appear to be more susceptible to such situational contingencies (Yoon et al., 2005). Therefore, temporary variations in feel-age should be more observable among older age groups.

Past research has documented situational influences on older people's tendency to feel younger than their chronological age. Real situations, such as temporary pain or health problems, can diminish this tendency (Kotter-Grühn, Neupert, and Stephan, 2015). Interestingly, Guido, Amatulli, and Peluso (2014) showed that even imagined situations could be enough to alter older individuals' tendency to feel younger. They showed that older people feel younger than their chronological age and could feel more so when they imagine themselves in situations associated with hedonic goals (e.g., at a resort), compared to situations associated with utilitarian goals (e.g., in a senior center). More recent work further demonstrated the malleability of feel-age by providing evidence in line with the self-protection account described above. For instance, a study by Kornadt et al. (2018) examined both middle-aged and older individuals, and found the latter to be more inclined to feel younger than the former, especially when feel-age was assessed with reference to domains in which aging stereotypes are particularly negative (e.g., work), compared to domains in which such stereotypes are neutral (e.g., family). Amatulli et al. (2018) showed that the mere presence of young (compared to old or same-age) social cues—in the form of real others or pictorial primes—can make older people feel younger. Moreover, they found the effect of young social cues on feel-age to be significant when such cues are described in a desirable (versus undesirable) manner and when older respondents' self-esteem is lower (versus higher). Based on this finding, feeling younger in situations when (desirable) young others are present could be seen as a strategy through which older people low in self-esteem—thus, more susceptible to others' scrutiny—seek to protect themselves from being associated with negative aging stereotypes.

The nature of the task can also play a role in temporary changes in feel-age. For instance, Eiback, Mock, and Courtney (2010) showed that making older people experience a situationally induced visual disfluency—manipulating text to appear small and blurry to read—can diminish their tendency to feel younger, likely because they misattribute their visual disfluency to their age. Analogously, engaging older individuals in cognitive or memory tests—or simply creating the expectation of participating in such tests—can have similar effects on their feel-ages (Geraci et al., 2018; Hughes et al., 2013). Conversely, engaging older individuals in a physical strength test, and telling them that their performance was better than average, can increase their tendency to feel younger (Stephan et al., 2013).

Regarding the effects of information cues, prior studies have focused primarily on age-related information that might make aging stereotypes more or less salient in the eyes of older individuals. For instance, a series of studies by Weiss and colleagues (Weiss and Freund, 2012; Weiss and Lang, 2012) showed that exposing older people to pieces of information associated with negative aging stereotypes (e.g., loss of autonomy), compared to neutral or positive stereotypes (e.g., wisdom), can instantly increase their tendency to feel younger, insofar as the evoked negative stereotypes can reinforce their desire to distance themselves from old age groups. These findings provide further support to the self-protection account illustrated above. The self-protection mechanism that underlies older people's tendency to feel younger may also drive downstream consequences on their consumption attitudes and behaviors. In the next section, we present a discussion of such consequences.

Effects of Subjective Age on Older Consumers' Behavior

Extant research on older consumers (Guido, 2014; Mathur and Moschis, 2005; Yoon, 1997; Yoon, Cole, and Lee, 2009; Yoon et al., 2005) suggests that they differ from young consumers along several cognitive, attitudinal, and behavioral dimensions. In terms of cognition, older consumers typically exhibit diminished attention, comprehension, and memory abilities. As a result of cognitive decline, their attitudes tend to be more susceptible to external influences, such as persuasive marketing communications—especially via traditional media like TV, radio, or print advertising—and social pressures—especially from family members and experts. At the same time, older consumers, compared to their younger counterparts, are less motivated to collect and process new information, and rely more on their past experiences and knowledge. This leads them to consider fewer alternatives in their purchasing decision processes (Lambert-Pandraud, Laurent, and Lapersonne, 2005), have lower expectations toward products and brands, and be less dissatisfied with their purchases (Yoon, Feinberg, and Schwarz, 2010). Behaviorally, older consumers, compared to their young counterparts, are less inclined to engage in complaining behaviors, not only because they tend to be less dissatisfied with products, but also because they think that their complaints will remain unheard (Balazs, 2004) or blame themselves for the negative performance of their products (Armenta et al., 2018). Regarding product choice, an important difference between the two consumer segments is that older consumers, compared to their younger counterparts, are far more loyal to products with which they are familiar. Older consumers have been found to prefer long-established and traditional products over modern or contemporary alternatives (Lambert-Pandraud, Laurent, and Lapersonne, 2005; Mogilner, Aaker, and Kamvar, 2012).

But how does feeling younger affect older consumers' cognition, attitudes, and behavior? Essentially, older consumers who feel younger than their chronological age tend to think and behave more similarly to their young counterparts. Indeed, feeling younger is associated with better cognitive performances (Stephan et al., 2016). Thus, older consumers who feel younger are more willing to seek information about new products, keep up with new fashion trends, and try new brands (Lia and Xia, 2012; Stephens, 1991; Wilkes, 1992). Like their younger counterparts, older consumers might be more interested in pleasurable activities (Estill et al., 2018), as well as products that are hedonic (Guido, Amatulli, and Peluso, 2014), signal status (Amatulli, Guido, and Nataraajan, 2015), and are technologically novel (Chaouali and Souiden, 2019; Chéron and Kohlbacher, 2018).

Given such critical influence of subjective age on older consumers, it is in the best interest of practitioners to understand how to communicate messages and create shopping situations that can induce older consumers to feel younger, especially if companies want to expand their young and middle-aged customer base to include older consumers. An example of this is provided in an experimental study by Amatulli et al. (2018), which showed that older consumers who are situationally induced to feel younger are more likely to choose contemporary products (typically targeted at young consumers) over traditional products (targeted at older consumers). Below we provide a description of Amatulli et al.'s (2018) findings and share an empirical generalization of the results.

Marketing Contemporary Products to Older Consumers

Amatulli et al. (2018) operationalized subjective age as feel-age and employed a social cue manipulation to induce younger feel-ages in their older participants. In one of their experiments, this manipulation consisted of exposing them to a fictitious advertisement that incorporated a pictorial prime featuring either a pair of young people (young social cue condition) or a pair of older people (old social cue condition). The featured pairs exhibited similar postures and neutral facial expressions across the two social cue conditions. The participants then indicated their feel-age and completed a choice task. The choice task consisted of asking participants to select between two pens of comparable quality and price but different designs: contemporary versus traditional. Results showed that the participants in the young social cue condition reported significantly younger feel-ages than those in the old social cue condition and, in turn, were more inclined to choose the contemporary option. They replicated this finding in a field-experiment using another product category (i.e., pastries).

To provide a further empirical generalization of this finding, we conducted another experiment to test older consumers' greater likelihood of choosing contemporary over traditional products when they are induced to feel younger. The study employed a 2 (age group: young vs. older) × 2 (social cue: young vs. old) between-group design. We recruited four hundred participants (mean age = 44; 257 females and 143 males) for an online study from a national paid pool in the United States: The young age group consisted of participants aged 35 and under (mean age = 26.11, SD = 3.25; n = 240), and the older age group consisted of those aged 65 and over (M = 71.06, SD = 5.64; n = 160). The participants were randomly assigned to either a young or old social cue condition. We manipulated the social cue using pictorial primes as in Amatulli et al. (2018).

After being exposed to the social cue, participants completed a choice task in an ostensibly unrelated part of the study session. Participants were presented with four different choice sets and were asked to choose an option from each of the choice sets. Each of these choice sets comprised two options: namely, a pair of watches, a pair of winter scarves, a pair of perfumes, and a pair of sports shoes.

Each choice set contained a contemporary and a traditional version of the same unbranded product.[3] The dependent variable was the tendency to choose the contemporary option over the traditional one across all four choice sets, measured as the percentage of times participants chose the contemporary option. Thus, the dependent variable ranged from 0 percent if participants did not choose the contemporary option for any of the choice sets, to 100 percent, if they chose the contemporary option for all four choice sets.

We analyzed the data summarized in Figure 12.3 using a likelihood ratio test. This analysis showed that the proportion of contemporary products chosen was significantly different for the two age groups: Young participants were more likely to choose contemporary products ($M = 55.42$) than older participants ($M = 34.22$), $\chi^2(1) = -70.14$, $p < 0.001$. More importantly, this effect was qualified by a significant interaction between age group and social cue, $\chi^2(1) = 11.79$, $p < 0.001$. The tendency by older consumers to choose contemporary options was higher when they were exposed to a young social cue ($M = 41.55$) than an old social cue ($M = 27.91$), $\chi^2(1) = 13.17$, $p < 0.001$. In contrast, young consumers' choice of contemporary options did not vary as a function of whether they were exposed to a young social cue ($M = 54.61$) or an old social cue ($M = 56.15$), $\chi^2(1) = 0.23$ $p = 0.63$.

The present study lends additional support to Amatulli et al.'s (2018) findings that exposure to young (versus old) social cues can prompt older consumers to feel younger and choose products that typically appeal more to younger consumer segments.

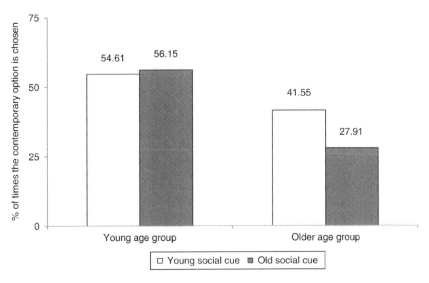

FIGURE 12.3 Proportion of contemporary choices as a function of age group and social cue.

Conclusions

Older consumers represent a disproportionately growing market segment, which is attracting considerable attention from scholars and practitioners alike. Scholars are interested in understanding how older consumers think and behave and how they perceive themselves in relation to their younger counterparts. Practitioners are interested in ways that they can appeal to this older segment by providing products and services that better meet their needs and desires.

In this chapter, we discussed the concept of subjective age, commonly operationalized as feel-age, and described the tendency to feel younger than their chronological age as a significant phenomenon to consider in characterization of older consumers. We reviewed prior research findings, which indicate that the construct is malleable insofar as it varies in magnitude across cultural contexts, age groups, individuals, and situations. Furthermore, we explained how this tendency could affect older consumers' cognition, attitudes, and behaviors. Regarding the implications on consumption, we also reviewed findings supporting the notion that older consumers with younger feel-ages tend to behave more like their younger counterparts, by exhibiting similar patterns of behaviors in consumption situations. We provided additional empirical results from a study we conducted, providing support for these prior findings.

On the theoretical side, the literature on subjective age and other age-related constructs (i.e., feel-age, youth age, etc.) is substantial, but quite fragmented. In the studies we reviewed in this chapter, we uncovered quite a bit of heterogeneity in the use of terminology, empirical design, and measurement approach. In terms of terminology, we noted that different scholars sometimes used different terms for the same construct, thus generating potential confusion in the scientific community. For example, some studies (Estill et al., 2018; Mock and Eibach, 2011; Stephan, Sutin, and Terracciano, 2015a) used the term "subjective age," rather than "youth age," to indicate the discrepancy between feel-age and chronological age. Regarding empirical work, most studies—especially those investigating individual differences—are correlational and, as such, do not allow cause-effect inferences. Therefore, longitudinal studies might be useful in future research to confer greater external validity to findings. As for the measurement approach, scholars have proposed different measurement scales of subjective age, which vary in scaling format and number of items. Future work would benefit from converging on the standard use of mono-item scales that ask respondents to indicate, in years, the age they feel in a certain moment or a given context, as they are simpler and theoretically more robust.

In terms of application, practitioners could benefit from this chapter by expanding their knowledge about this phenomenon. Knowing that older consumers may feel younger than their chronological age may be useful to design effective positioning and communication strategies aimed at appealing to this globally growing market segment. For example, positioning strategies could revolve around consumption or shopping situations that may induce older consumers to feel younger; then, companies could more efficiently use value propositions to appeal to consumers from different age groups. Similarly, if older consumers feel younger, and thereby think and behave accordingly, it may be more advantageous to communicate the same marketing strategy to speak to both young and older consumers. For example, empirical findings suggest that a young endorser might be a useful means to make older consumers feel younger and prompt them to buy more contemporary products (Amatulli et al., 2018).

In summary, older consumers' psychological aging is as relevant to understand as their biological aging. Subjective age has greater explanatory power than chronological age for a variety of older people's attitudes and behaviors, as it—and by extension individuals' tendency to feel younger—can affect their purchase and consumption behaviors. Notwithstanding the insights gained thus far, we believe that the potential of subjective age as a critical marketing variable remains underexplored. We, therefore, hope this chapter will spark interest and accelerate future research activities that will enhance knowledge about ways to address and better serve the needs of older consumers.

Notes

1 Some studies (Hughes et al., 2013; Marquet et al., 2018) adopted a ratio scale variant, whereby respondents indicated their perceived age on a continuous line of 120 millimeters, with 0-year old on the extreme left end and 120-year-old on the extreme right end of the line.
2 The discrepancy between feel-age and chronological age is also known in literature as *subjective age bias* (Armenta et al., 2018; Weiss and Lang, 2012), *relative subjective age* (Kunze, Raes, and Bruch, 2015), and *age identity* (Barrett, 2003; Westerhof and Barrett, 2005; Westerhof et al., 2014).
3 We pretested each pair of products to check that the two options were of comparable quality and price but differed significantly in design by appearing as either contemporary or traditional.

References

Alicke, M. D., & Sedikides, C. (2009). Self-enhancement and self-protection: What they are and what they do. *European Review of Social Psychology, 20*(1), 1–48.

Amatulli, C., Guido, G., & Nataraajan, R. (2015). Luxury purchasing among older consumers: Exploring inferences about cognitive age, status, and style motivations. *Journal of Business Research, 68*(9), 1945–1952.

Amatulli, C., Peluso, A. M., Guido, G., & Yoon, C. (2018). When feeling younger depends on others: The Effects of social cues on older consumers. *Journal of Consumer Research, 45*(4), 691–709.

Armenta, B. M., Scheibe, S., Stroebe, K., Postmes, T., & Van Yperen, N. W. (2018). Dynamic, not stable: Daily variations in subjective age bias and age group identification predict daily well-being in older workers. *Psychology and Aging, 33*(4), 559–571.

Balazs, A. N. (2004). Marketing to older adults. In: J. F. Nussmbaum & J. Coupland (Eds.), *Handbook of Communication and Aging Research* (pp. 329–351). New Jersey, NJ: Lawrence Erlbaum Associates.

Barak, B. (1987). Cognitive age: A new multidimensional approach to measuring age identity. *International Journal of Aging and Human Development, 25*(2), 109–128.

Barak, B. (2009). Age identity: A cross-cultural global approach. *International Journal of Behavioral Development, 33*(1), 2–11.

Barak, B., & Gould, S. (1985). Alternative age measures: A research agenda. In: E. C. Hirschman & M. B. Holbrook (Eds.), *Advance in Consumer Research*, Vol. *12* (pp. 53–58). Provo, UT: Association for Consumer Research.

Barak, B., & Schiffman, L. G. (1981). Cognitive age: A nonchronological age variable. In: K. B. Monroe (Ed.), *Advances in Consumer Research*, Vol. *8* (pp. 602–606). Ann Arbor, MI: Association for Consumer Research.

Barak, B., & Stern, B. (1986). Subjective age correlates: A research note. *The Gerontologist, 26*(5), 517–578.

Barak, B., Stern, B. B., & Gould, S. J. (1988). Ideal age concepts: An exploration. In: M. J. Houston (Ed.), *Advances in Consumer Research*, Vol. *15* (pp. 146–152). Provo, UT: Association for Consumer Research.

Barnhart, M., & Peñaloza, L. (2013). Who are you calling old? Negotiating old age identity in the elderly consumption ensemble. *Journal of Consumer Research, 39*(6), 1133–1153.

Barrett, A. E. (2003). Socioeconomic status and age identity: The role of dimensions of health in the subjective construction of age. *Journals of Gerontology: Series B, 58*(2), S101–S109.

Brannon, D., & Miller, C. J. (2019). What's my age again? The influence of subjective age on consumer health-related attitudes. *Health Marketing Quarterly, 36*(3), 254–270.

Brown, J. D., Collins, R. L., & Schmidt, G. W. (1988). Self-esteem and direct versus indirect forms of self-enhancement. *Journal of Personality and Social Psychology, 55*(3), 445–453.

Busseri, M. A., & Sadava, S. W. (2011). A review of the tripartite structure of subjective well-being: Implications for conceptualization, operationalization, analysis, and synthesis. *Personality and Social Psychology Review, 15*(3), 290–314.

Chang, C. (2008). Chronological age versus cognitive age for younger consumers: Implications for advertising persuasion. *Journal of Advertising, 37*(3), 19–32.

Chaouali, W., & Souiden, N. (2019). The role of cognitive age in explaining mobile banking resistance among elderly people. *Journal of Retailing and Consumer Services, 50*(September), 342–350.

Chasteen, A. L., & Cary, L. A. (2015). Age stereotypes and age stigma: Connections to research on subjective aging. In: M. Diehl & H.-W. Wahl (Eds.), *Annual Review of Gerontology and Geriatrics*, Vol. *35* (pp. 99–119) New York, NY: Springer.

Chéron, E., & Kohlbacher, F. (2018). Older consumers' adoption of innovation in Japan: The mediating role of cognitive age. *Journal of International Consumer Marketing, 30*(4), 244–259.

Diehl, M., Wahl, H.-W., Barrett, A. E., Brothers, A. F., Miche, M., Montepare, J. M., Westerhof, G. J., & Wurm, S. (2014). Awareness of aging: Theoretical considerations on an emerging concept. *Developmental Review: DR, 34*(2), 93–113.

Diener, E. (1994). Assessing subjective well-being: Progress and opportunities. *Social Indicators Research, 31*(2), 103–157.

Digman, J. M. (1990). Personality structure: Emergence of the five-factor model. *Annual Review of Psychology, 41*(1), 417–440.

Edgar, L., & Bunker, D. (2013). It's all in the mind: Changing the way we think about age. *International Journal of Market Research, 55*(2), 201–226.

Eibach, R. P., Mock, S. E., & Courtney, E. A. (2010). Having a "senior moment": Induced aging phenomenology, subjective age, and susceptibility to ageist stereotypes. *Journal of Experimental Social Psychology, 46*(4), 643–649.

Estill, A., Mock, S. E., Schryer, E., & Eibach, R. P. (2018). The effects of subjective age and aging attitudes on mid- to late-life sexuality. *Journal of Sex Research, 55*(2), 146–151.

Galambos, N. L., Albrecht, A. K., & Jansson, S. M. (2009). Dating, sex, and substance use predict increases in adolescents' subjective age across two years. *International Journal of Behavioral Development, 33*(1), 32–41.

Galambos, N. L., Turner, P. K., & Tilton-Weaver, L. C. (2005). Chronological and subjective age in emerging adulthood: The crossover effect. *Journal of Adolescent Research, 20*(5), 538–556.

Gendron, T. L., Inker, J., & Welleford, A. (2018). "How old do you feel?" the difficulties and ethics of operationalizing subjective age. *The Gerontologist, 58*(4), 618–624.

Geraci, L., De Forrest, R., Hughes, M., Saenz, G., & Tirso, R. (2018). The effect of cognitive testing and feedback on older adults' subjective age. *Aging, Neuropsychology, and Cognition, 25*(3), 333–350.

Guido, G. (2014). *Il comportamento di consumo degli anziani [The consumer behavior of the elderly]*. Bologna, IT: Il Mulino.

Guido, G., Amatulli, C., & Peluso, A. M. (2014). Context effects on older consumers' cognitive age: The role of hedonic versus utilitarian goals. *Psychology and Marketing, 31*(2), 103–114.

Guido, G., Pichierri, M., Pino, G., & Conoci, R. (2018). The segmentation of elderly consumers: A literature review. *Journal of Customer Behaviour, 17*(4), 257–278.

Guiot, D. (2001). Antecedents of subjective age biases among senior women. *Psychology and Marketing, 18*(10), 1049–1071.

Gunter, B. (1999). *Understanding the Older Consumer*. New York, NY: Routledge.

Gwinner, K. P., & Stephens, N. (2001). Testing the implied mediational role of cognitive age. *Psychology and Marketing, 18*(10), 1031–1048.

Heckhausen, J., & Krueger, J. (1993). Developmental expectations for the self and most other people: Age grading in three functions of social comparison. *Developmental Psychology, 29*(3), 539–548.

Hofstede, G., Hofstede, G. J., & Minkov, M. (2010). *Cultures and Organizations: Software of the Mind*. New York, NY: McGraw-Hill.

Hubley, A. M., & Hultsch, D. F. (1994). The relationship of personality trait variables to subjective age identity in older adults. *Research on Aging, 16*(4), 415–439.

Hughes, M. L., Geraci, L., & De Forrest, R. L. (2013). Aging 5 years in 5 minutes: The effect of taking a memory test on older adults' subjective age. *Psychological Science, 24*(12), 2481–2488.

Kastenbaum, R., Derbin, V., Sabatini, P., & Artt, S. (1972). "The ages of me": Toward personal and interpersonal definitions of functional aging. *Aging and Human Development, 3*(2), 197–211.

Kaufman, G., & Elder, G. H. (2002). Revisiting age identity: A research note. *Journal of Aging Studies, 16*(2), 169–176.

Kleinspehn-Ammerlahn, A., Kotter-Grühn, D., & Smith, J. (2008). Self-perceptions of aging: Do subjective age and satisfaction with aging change during old age? *Journals of Gerontology: Series B, 63*(6), P377–P385.

Kornadt, A. E., Hess, T. M., Voss, P., & Rothermund, K. (2018). Subjective age across the life span: A differentiated, longitudinal approach. *Journals of Gerontology: Series B, 73*(5), 767–777.

Kotter-Grühn, D., Kornadt, A. E., & Stephan, Y. (2016). Looking beyond chronological age: Current knowledge and future directions in the study of subjective age. *Gerontology, 62*(1), 86–93.

Kotter-Grühn, D., Neupert, S. D., & Stephan, Y. (2015). Feeling old today? Daily health, stressors, and affect explain day-to-day variability in subjective age. *Psychology and Health, 30*(12), 1470–1485.

Kunze, F., Raes, A. M., & Bruch, H. (2015). It matters how old you feel: Antecedents and performance consequences of average relative subjective age in organizations. *The Journal of Applied Psychology, 100*(5), 1511–1526.

Kuppelwieser, V. G. (2016). Towards the use of chronological age in research—A cautionary comment. *Journal of Retailing and Consumer Services, 33*(November), 17–22.

Lambert-Pandraud, R., Laurent, G., & Lapersonne, E. (2005). Repeat purchasing of new automobiles by older consumers: Empirical evidence and interpretations. *Journal of Marketing, 69*(2), 97–113.

Lin, Y.-T., & Xia, K.-N. (2012). Cognitive age and fashion consumption. *International Journal of Consumer Studies, 36*(1), 97–105.

Logan, J. R., Ward, R., & Spitze, G. (1992). As old as you feel: Age identity in middle and later life. *Social Forces, 71*(2), 451–467.

Marquet, M., Boutaayamou, M., Schwartz, C., Locquet, M., Bruyère, O., Croisier, J.-L., & Adam, S. (2018). Does negative information about aging influence older adults' physical performance and subjective age? *Archives of Gerontology and Geriatrics, 78*(September–October), 181–189.

Mathur, A., & Moschis, G. P. (2005). Antecedents of cognitive age: A replication and extension. *Psychology and Marketing, 22*(12), 969–994.

McCrae, R. R., & John, O. P. (1992). An introduction to five factor model and its applications. *Journal of Personality, 60*(2), 175–215.

Mock, S. E., & Eibach, R. P. (2011). Aging attitudes moderate the effect of subjective age on psychological well-being: Evidence from a 10-year longitudinal study. *Psychology and Aging, 26*(4), 979–986.

Mogilner, C., Aaker, J., & Kamvar, S. D. (2012). How happiness affects choice. *Journal of Consumer Research, 39*(2), 429–443.

Montepare, J. M., & Lachman, M. E. (1989). "You're only as old as you feel": Self-perceptions of age, fears of aging, and life satisfaction from adolescence to old age. *Psychology and Aging, 4*(1), 73–78.

Nelson, T. D. (2011). Ageism: The strange case of prejudice against the older you. In: R. L. Wiener & S. L. Willborn (Eds.), *Disability and Aging Discrimination* (pp. 37–47). New York, NY: Springer.

Rubin, D. C., & Berntsen, D. (2006). People over forty feel 20% younger than their age: Subjective age across the lifespan. *Psychonomic Bulletin and Review, 13*(5), 776–780.

Settersten, R. A., & Mayer, K. U. (1997). The measurement of age, age structuring, and the life course. *Annual Review of Sociology, 23*(1), 233–261.

Sherman, S. R. (1994). Changes in age identity: Self perceptions in middle and late life. *Journal of Aging Studies, 8*(4), 397–412.

Shrira, A., Segel-Karpas, D., Bodner, E., & Palgi, Y. (2019). Subjective age and emotion covariation: Findings from two daily experience studies. *Journals of Gerontology: Series B.* forthcoming. doi:10.1093/geronb/gby125.

Stephan, Y., Chalabaev, A., Kotter-Grühn, D., & Jaconelli, A. (2013). "Feeling younger, being stronger": An experimental study of subjective age and physical functioning among older adults. *Journals of Gerontology: Series B, 68*(1), 1–7.

Stephan, Y., Demulier, V., & Terracciano, A. (2012). Personality, self-rated health, and subjective age in a life-span sample: The moderating role of chronological age. *Psychology and Aging, 27*(4), 875–880.

Stephan, Y., Sutin, A. R., Caudroit, J., & Terracciano, A. (2016). Subjective age and changes in memory in older adults. *Journals of Gerontology: Series B, 71*(4), 675–683.

Stephan, Y., Sutin, A. R., & Terracciano, A. (2015a). How old do you feel? The role of age discrimination and biological aging in subjective age. *PLoS One, 10*(3), 1–12.

Stephan, Y., Sutin, A. R., & Terracciano, A. (2015b). Subjective age and personality development: A 10-year study. *Journal of Personality, 83*(2), 142–154.

Stephens, N. (1991). Cognitive age: A useful concept for advertising? *Journal of Advertising, 20*(4), 37–48.

Sudbury, L., & Simcock, P. (2009). Understanding older consumers through cognitive age and the list of values: A U.K.-based perspective. *Psychology and Marketing, 26*(1), 22–38.

Teuscher, U. (2009). Subjective age bias: A motivational and information processing approach. *International Journal of Behavioral Development, 33*(1), 22–31.

Van Auken, S., & Barry, T. E. (1995). An assessment of the trait validity of cognitive age measures. *Journal of Consumer Psychology, 4*(2), 107–132.

Van Auken, S., Barry, T. E., & Anderson, R. L. (1993). Observations: Toward the internal validation of cognitive age measures in advertising research. *Journal of Advertising Research, 33*(3), 82–85.

Van Auken, S., Barry, T. E., & Bagozzi, R. P. (2006). A cross-country construct validation of cognitive age. *Journal of the Academy of Marketing Science, 34*(3), 439–455.

Weiss, D., & Freund, A. M. (2012). Still young at heart: Negative age-related information motivates distancing from same-aged people. *Psychology and Aging, 27*(1), 173–180.

Weiss, D., & Lang, F. R. (2012). "They" are old but "I" feel younger: Age-group dissociation as a self-protective strategy in old age. *Psychology and Aging, 27*(1), 153–163.

Westerhof, G. J., & Barrett, A. E. (2005). Age identity and subjective well-being: A comparison of the United States and Germany. *Journals of Gerontology: Series B, 60*(3), S129–S136.

Westerhof, G. J., Barrett, A. E., & Steverink, N. (2003). Forever young? A comparison of age identities in the United States and Germany. *Research on Aging, 25*(4), 366–383.

Westerhof, G. J., Miche, M., Brothers, A. F., Barrett, A. E., Diehl, M., Montepare, J. M., Wahl, H.-W., & Wurm, S. (2014). The influence of subjective aging on health and longevity: A meta-analysis of longitudinal data. *Psychology and Aging, 29*(4), 793–802.

Wilkes, R. E. (1992). A structural modeling approach to the measurement and meaning of cognitive age. *Journal of Consumer Research, 19*(2), 292–301.

Yoon, C. (1997). Age differences in consumers' processing strategies: An investigation of moderating influences. *Journal of Consumer Research, 24*(3), 329–342.

Yoon, C., Cole, C. A., & Lee, M. P. (2009). Consumer decision making and aging: Current knowledge and future directions. *Journal of Consumer Psychology, 19*(1), 2–16.

Yoon, C., Feinberg, F., & Schwarz, N. (2010). Why do older consumers tell us they are more satisfied? In: A. Drolet, N. Schwarz, & C. Yoon (Eds.), *The Aging Consumer: Perspectives from Psychology and Economics* (pp. 209–228). New York, NY: Routledge.

Yoon, C., Laurent, G., Fung, H. H., Gonzalez, R., Gutchess, A. H., Hedden, T., Lambert-Pandraud, R., Mather, M., Park, D. C., Peters, E., & Skurnik, I. (2005). Cognition, persuasion and decision making in older consumers. *Marketing Letters, 16*(3–4), 429–441.

Zacher, H., & Rudolph, C. W. (2019). Just a mirage: On the incremental predictive validity of subjective age. *Work, Aging and Retirement, 5*(2), 141–162.

13

AGING ACROSS THE WORLD

The Interplay of Demographic, Economic, Historical, and Cultural Factors

Abby P. W. Yip, Julia Nolte, and Corinna E. Löckenhoff

Introduction

The world is undergoing rapid demographic transformation. Declining fertility rates and increasing longevity have resulted in unprecedented rates of population aging, with the number and proportion of older persons growing in virtually every country (Hayutin, 2007). Worldwide, the number of people aged 60 and over is projected to double by 2050, and four out of five of these older adults will be living in low- and middle-income countries (WHO, 2015). Importantly, this general trend is qualified by notable international differences in demographic dynamics, economic resources, geographic mobility, historical context, contemporary policies, and cultural values that shape the experiences of individual older adults and determine how well a given country adjusts to the aging of its population. We begin this chapter with a broad overview of potential mechanisms behind cross-national differences in aging experiences and outcomes. Next, we illustrate the interplay among such factors with respect to three key types of outcomes: perceptions and attitudes toward aging and older adults, age-related shifts in socioemotional functioning, and patterns of cognitive aging. Drawing on these insights, we conclude by considering implications for the consumer realm, identifying limitations of existing research, and formulating directions for future inquiries.

Mechanisms behind Cross-Cultural Differences

When considering international variations in population aging, it is important to differentiate between the *current percentage of older adults* in a given population and the *rates of population aging*. At present, developed countries have the oldest population profiles. Japan is making the top of the list with 26.7 percent of its population over age 65 (Japan Census Bureau, 2019) and several European countries (e.g., Italy, Portugal, Germany) are following close behind. In contrast, the most rapid *increases* in older populations are occurring in developing regions, particularly across Asia and Africa, a trend that is projected to continue over the coming decades (Hayutin, 2007).

These markers of population aging have distinct economic implications. While high percentages of older adults pose a strain on existing pension and healthcare systems, rapid population aging necessitates proactive policy changes to adapt the societal system to changing demographic realities. The failure to adapt societal opportunity structures in an age-friendly manner is known as *structural lag* (Riley, Kahn, Foner, and Mack, 1994) and levels of preparation vary widely across countries. Specifically, *The Global Aging Preparedness Index* (Jackson, Howe, and Peter, 2013) differentiates between two separate sub-indices: a "fiscal sustainability index" which measures a country's ability to afford their projected old-age dependency burdens, and an "income adequacy index" which assesses whether a country's current retirement policies are likely to be effective in maintaining or improving older adults' living standard (Jackson et al., 2013). There appears to be a trade-off between the two types of aging preparedness, with developed countries typically doing well on income adequacy and worse on fiscal sustainability and developing countries showing the opposite pattern. Only a few countries, including Australia, Chile, Canada, and Sweden are performing equally well on both dimensions, with modest reliance on pay-as-you-go state pension systems to ensure fiscal sustainability as well as large funded pension systems to maintain income adequacy (Jackson et al., 2013). High rates of older adults' labor force participation in particular, appear to be a critical factor in maintaining both living standard and societal status among older adults (Jackson et al., 2013; Vauclair et al., 2015).

Importantly, patterns of population aging may also vary across different regions within a country and this can affect opportunities for older adults and their access to relevant services. At the moment, rapidly developing countries across Asia and Africa are seeing high rates of urbanization (UN, 2019) driven by a migration of young workers from rural to urban areas. This can break up multi-generational family structures, impede familial support and caregiving, and lead to a concentration of older adults in rural areas (UN, 2002).

Of course, the aging experience is also situated within historical contexts. Countries which have seen dramatic political shifts (such as the ex-communist countries across Eastern Europe) may not only struggle to adapt healthcare and pension systems to the new contingencies but also pose challenges for the cohorts of citizens who built their lives within one political system but now enter old age under a new set of rules (Horowitz, 2010, Roaf, Atoyan, Joshi, Krogulski, and IMF Staff Team, 2014; Peterson and Ralston, 2019). More broadly, some theorists have argued that the process of modernization itself may affect the societal status of older adults (Cowgill, 1986; Street, 2012), although this association appears to take a curvilinear shape: The early stages of modernization which are characterized by rapid economic development, urbanization, and formal education can disrupt traditional multi-generational family systems and devalue the contributions of older adults. Later stages of modernization, in turn, entail the establishment of healthcare and pensions systems along with other societal support structures that tend to benefit older populations (Palmore and Manton, 1974; Street, 2012).

Finally, it is important to consider cross-cultural variations in norms, beliefs, and value systems. According to Hofstede (1980), culture constitutes an amalgamation of behavioral norms and cognitions shared by individuals within a group that are differentiated from those shared within other populations. These shared, historically derived, and socially transmitted ideas are reflective of the artifacts and practices widely distributed among a group (Tsai and Sims, 2016). On the broadest level, extant research has categorized cultures along an individualism-collectivism spectrum. People from individualistic cultures with independent self-construals tend to think of themselves as an entity separate from others and the normative imperative is to discover and express one's unique attributes. Therefore, they embrace individualistic values such as hedonism, achievement, and power and favor analytical cognitive styles and categorical thinking. In contrast, those from collectivistic cultures with interdependent self-construals tend of think of themselves as part of a larger social unit. They emphasize collectivistic values such as universalism, conformity, and tradition and engage in cognitive styles that favor tolerance for ambiguity and holistic thinking (Markus and Kitayama, 1991). With respect to aging, it has been proposed that societies with collectivistic values are more likely to endorse a positive attitude toward ancestors and older adults along with filial piety, a commitment to support one's aging parents, and thus provide more supportive environments for older adults (Nelson, 2009; Sung, 2001).

In summary, there are considerable international differences in demographic trends, economic contingencies, historical contexts, and value systems that may influence aging experiences and outcomes across the world. In the following section we first consider the role of such factors with respect to perceptions of aging and older adults and then turn to actual differences in aging trajectories and characteristics with particular emphasis on the socioemotional and cognitive domains.

Attitudes toward Aging and Older Adults

Aging-related attitudes and perceptions can be roughly divided into (1) expectations about aging and (2) views or stereotypes about older adults and their role in society, although individual studies often intertwine these concepts (North and Fiske, 2015). With respect to cross-cultural differences, initial investigations pitted the role of cultural values against the influence of demographic and economic forces. Specifically, value-based frameworks argued that collectivistic values in Eastern societies promote elder worship, filial piety, and more positive aging attitudes as compared to Western individualistic societies (Nelson, 2009; Sung, 2001). Sociodemographic perspectives, in contrast, suggested that countries embrace more negative views on aging when resources are limited and there is conflict about the allocation of resources to different age groups (Silverstein, Parrott, Angelelli, and Cook, 2000; Williams, 1997). However, a number of recent empirical studies that utilized large sample sizes to compare a wide range of cultures paint a more complex picture.

For one, cultural differences in aging perceptions appear to vary across domains of functioning. In a study comparing 26 different cultures, Löckenhoff and colleagues (2009) found that cross-cultural variations in aging perceptions were smaller for perceptions of age-related physical and cognitive changes than for perceptions of socioemotional changes. This is plausible, considering that biologically determined aspects of physiological and neural aging are most likely to be shared across cultures. In contrast, more cross-cultural variation would be expected for factors that are susceptible to life experience or that represent social constructs. The study also examined the role of culture-level indicators of demographic variables and value systems (Löckenhoff et al., 2009) and failed to find clear support for more favorable perceptions of aging within Eastern/collectivistic contexts: Although Easterners reported more positive societal views of aging, they were less likely to endorse age-related increases in wisdom. Moreover, the effects of cultural values were overshadowed by variations in population structure such that a greater proportion of older adults was associated with more negative societal views of aging.

A recent meta-analysis involving 37 studies and more than 21,000 participants from 23 cultures (North and Fiske, 2015) shed further light on the relative influence of cultural values versus sociodemographic factors on aging attitudes. Contrary to prevailing theories, Easterners endorsed more negative aging attitudes, and this was especially pronounced among East Asian as opposed to South Asian Countries. Further, there was a marked split among Western countries such that non-Anglophone European countries reported less favorable aging attitudes than Western Anglophone regions (including the U.K, North America, as well as Australia and New Zealand). An examination of sociodemographic factors implicated recent increases in population aging (rather than markers of industrialization or total proportion of older adults in the population) as a key predictor of negative aging attitudes. Perhaps most surprisingly, culture-level collectivism was associated with more *negative* views of aging, suggesting that collectivistic traditions of elder worship and filial piety are no match for the upheaval generated by rapidly changing demographic realities.

Perceived intergenerational competition is a particular concern in managing population aging. Leveraging data on 55 cultures from the *World Values Survey*, Peterson and Ralston (2017) examined cross-cultural variations in the perception that adults are societal burden and receive disproportionate support from the government. Perceptions of older adults as a burden showed a fairly low degree of cross-cultural variation with a tendency for poorer countries to report higher levels of burden. Variations were more pronounced for the perception that older adults receive disproportionate government resources. Consistent with findings by North and Fiske (2015) who found more negative aging attitudes in East Asia, Eastern countries were more likely than Western countries to report that older adults received an unfair share. In addition, there were variations based on religious orientation such that Christian countries were less likely to report that older adults were receiving disproportionate resources than Muslim and Buddhist countries. With respect to sociodemographic factors, countries with longer life expectancies, a higher proportion of older adults, and well-established pension systems were less likely to report unfair advantages for older adults. This suggests that, intergenerational competition may become less salient once a country has completed its demographic transition, people are living longer (and presumably healthier) lives, and age-friendly opportunity structures have been established.

In combination, these findings suggest that cultural variations in aging attitudes are not set in stone and certainly cannot be reduced to simple East/West dichotomies. Instead, aging views are responding dynamically to ongoing population shifts and how well a country adapts to such shifts may depend on economic resources, broadly shared cultural values, prevalent religious beliefs, and policy initiatives that avoid structural lags and establish appropriate support for an older population. Of course, cross-cultural differences in aging attitudes may also reflect actual variations in the health and functioning of aging populations, and this relationship is likely bidirectional in nature: Countries with healthier and higher functioning populations are more likely to endorse positive aging attitudes which, in turn, may promote the provision of societal support for older adults. However, the literature also shows some notable discrepancies between aging attitudes and actual aging experiences. In the following sections, we specifically consider cross-cultural variations in socioemotional and cognitive functioning across the life span.

Socioemotional Functioning

Well-Being

A broad body of prior research indicates that despite age-related losses in functional health, emotional well-being and life satisfaction are well maintained with age, an effect also known as the "the paradox of well-being" or the "paradox of aging" (Carstensen, Isaacowitz, and Charles, 1999; Carstensen, Pasupathi, Mayr, and Nesselroade, 2000; Karasawa et al., 2011; Mroczek and Kolarz, 1998). This remarkable phenomenon has been documented around the world. For instance, the Study on global AGEing and adult health (SAGE) which compares six countries (China, Ghana, India, Mexico, Russia, and South Africa) with respect to various health indicators, found sizable cross-country differences in physical morbidity and disability. In contrast, older adults' life-satisfaction was fairly high across different countries, suggesting a decoupling of life satisfaction and physical health (He, Muenchrath, and Kowal, 2012). Similarly, a large-scale analysis of data from the *World Values Survey* (Peterson and Ralston, 2019) compared age discrepancies in self-reported health and life satisfaction across 57 countries and found that, in general, older adults reported similar life satisfaction but worse physical health than their younger counterparts.

However, beyond offering general support for the "paradox of well-being," Peterson and Ralston (2019) also found that age discrepancies in self-rated health and life satisfaction were sensitive to country-level variations in material wealth, cultural context, and historical events. In particular, older adults reported relatively higher levels of well-being when they lived in wealthier countries. Also, older adults living in Buddhist and Muslim countries reported better well-being than those from Western countries. Thus, although *attitudes* toward aging and older adults do not show an advantage for Eastern over Western contexts, the *actual aging experience* may be more positive in the East. Peterson and Ralston's (2019) findings also highlighted the importance of recent historical changes in that experiencing the transition of one's home country to independence over the course of one's adulthood was associated with lower self-rated well-being and health status among older adults, possibly due to people being derailed from their expected adult pathway with respect to family relationships, career, and retirement (Peterson and Ralston, 2019; Steptoe, Deaton, and Stone, 2015).

Age differences in emotion regulatory strategies may differ by culture as well. For instance, it has been argued that age is linked with a tendency to prioritize positive over negative material in attention and memory in order to optimize positive emotional experiences in the present moment (Mather and Carstensen, 2003). A recent meta-analysis documented the presence of this age-related "positivity effect" across 100 studies from predominantly Western countries (Reed, Chan, and Mikels, 2014). However, several studies conducted with German and Hong Kong Chinese samples found cultural variations in the consistency or nature of the positivity effect (e.g., Fung, Gong, Ngo, and Isaacowitz, 2018; Fung et al., 2008; Fung and Tang, 2005; Grühn, Scheibe, and Baltes, 2007; Grühn, Smith, and Baltes, 2005). Similarly, Grossman and colleagues (Grossman, Karasawa, Kan, and Kitayama, 2014) compared adult life-span samples of Americans and Japanese who were asked to recall their emotional experiences in various social situations. Older Americans reported lower negative affect in unpleasant settings compared with their younger counterparts, but negative emotions did not differ by age among the Japanese. Instead, older Japanese reported higher levels of positive emotions in response to unpleasant experiences. Conceivably, the "linear" way of maximizing well-being (i.e., increasing positive affect and reducing negative affect) may be more common among American older adults who are steeped in independent cultural values, whereas the "dialectical" way (i.e., emphasizing the positive in negative situations) may be more prevalent among Japanese older adults (Grossmann et al., 2014) reflecting a cultural emphasis on interdependence and contextuality.

Moreover, researchers have argued that well-being encompasses not only hedonic aspects (i.e., maximizing positive emotions and avoiding negative emotions) but also eudaimonic components that capture meaning and self-realization (Ryan and Deci, 2001). In contrast to studies examining hedonic aspects of well-being (Kahneman, Diener, and Schwarz, 1999), research on eudaimonic well-being suggests sharp downward trends from midlife to old age in Western samples (Clarke, Marshall, Ryff, and Rosenthal, 2000). In one of the few cross-cultural studies of such trends, Karasawa and colleagues (2011) found that whereas hedonic aspects of well-being showed significant improvements with age in both the United States and Japan, eudaimonic aspects yielded mixed findings. Among Japanese respondents, personal growth ratings were higher in old age than in middle age whereas the opposite pattern was found in the United States (Karasawa et al., 2011). With respect to life purpose, in turn, older adults in both Japan and the United States rated themselves as having lower rates of this than their middle-aged counterparts. Further research is needed to extend findings on age differences in emotion regulatory strategies and eudaimonic well-being to a wider range of countries and identify the underlying mechanisms at the heart of such effects.

Social Relationships

Interpersonal relationships and social engagement play a key role in well-being across cultural contexts (e.g., Peterson and Ralston, 2019), but again, specific age patterns show notable variations across cultures. With respect to social network size and composition, decades of research in Western settings have shown that social networks become smaller and more focused with age such that the number of peripheral social partners declines whereas the number of close partners and family relationships remains comparatively stable (Antonucci, Akiyama, and Takahashi, 2004). As far as such broad changes in network size and composition are concerned, comparative studies find few differences among cultures (Antonucci et al., 2001, 2004). In fact, a meta-analysis spanning 277 studies and more than 175,000 individuals found that even though respondents from collectivistic cultures reported smaller average network sizes, age-related shifts in network size and composition were similar across cultures (Wrzus, Hänel, Wagner, and Neyer, 2013).

At the same time, there appear to be cross-cultural variations in the effect of life events on social network characteristics. For instance, whereas widowhood and illness were found to be associated with less robust social networks among older adults in Germany and Japan, no such effects were found within a U.S. sample (Antonucci et al., 2001). Further, losses of social network partners have different implications across cultures. For instance, widowhood had a stronger effect on depression rates in Russia as compared to the other SAGE countries (He et al., 2012).

Patterns of old age caregiving styles and living arrangements are sensitive to cultural values and norms as well. In terms of caregiving styles, the research record documents that Western samples including American and Canadian adults tend to indicate a stronger preference for formal care (i.e., paid or volunteer care provided in the context of a formal service system such as assisted living, intermediate care, or nursing facilities; Pinquart, Sörensen, and Song, 2018). In contrast, in East Asian countries influenced by Confucianism and beliefs in filial obligations, elder care provided by people other than family is perceived as improper from the traditional perspective (Pinquart et al., 2018) and thus, the norm is to use informal care which is often provided, unpaid, by a family member. As East Asians tend to view parental caregiving as a personal obligation, it is unsurprising that extended-family and multi-generational households are more prevalent among East Asian cultures such as in South Korea, China, Japan, and Taiwan (Yasuda, Iwai, Chin-Chun, and Guihua, 2011) than among Western cultures such as the United States where nuclear families are the norm. As evidence generally suggest that intergenerational co-residence and family caregiving are sources of social support which improve psychological well-being among older adults (Cong and Silverstein, 2008), these cultural norms may play a role in the aforementioned cross-cultural differences in older adults' quality of life.

In summary, broad age trends in socioemotional functioning such as decreases in social network size and the "paradox of well-being" show remarkable similarity across a wide range of cultures, but cultures may differ in the specific underlying mechanisms as well as cultural norms and practices pertaining to these broader trends. A similar pattern emerges from cross-cultural comparisons of cognitive aging.

Cognition

Societal Support Structures for Healthy Cognitive Aging

As noted previously, cognitive aging is more strongly rooted in biological mechanisms than social or emotional aging, and there is cross-cultural agreement that cognitive abilities tend to deteriorate with age (Löckenhoff et al., 2009). However, this does not imply that patterns of aging are necessarily uniform across cultures. For one, there are cross-cultural disparities in access to societal support structures. Both early educational attainment and access to healthcare are known to influence cognitive performance in later life. Specifically, childhood education helps to build up cognitive reserve, which can serve as a buffer against age-related cognitive loss or dementia (Meng and D'Arcy, 2012; Zahodne, Stern, and Manly, 2015). Further, having access to healthcare resources, such as preventive measures, can help to lower the risk of cardiovascular disease (Colleran, Richards, and Shafer, 2007; Lewey and Choudhry, 2014), which is a risk factor for cognitive decline (Deckers et al., 2017). Although cross-cultural research is still lacking, studies comparing White Americans and African Americans find that education and health, particularly cardiovascular health, can indeed help to explain racial differences in cognitive aging (Carvalho et al., 2015; Wilson, Rajan, Barnes, Weuve, and Evans, 2016). Moreover, a lack of societal support structures may counteract typical age patterns of decision preferences. For example, in a study comparing 77 countries from the *World Values Survey*, the propensity to take risks was negatively associated with age, but this effect was weakened in countries with lower societal resources and higher inequality (Mata, Josef, and Hertwig, 2016). Hence, variability in societal support structures is instrumental in understanding cross-cultural differences in age-related cognitive changes.

Cognitive Styles

Another broad body of research examines cross-cultural differences in cognitive styles which may interact with age-related changes in cognition. According to the Model of Culture and Aging (Park, Nisbett, and Hedden, 1999), interactions between culture and aging depend on the type of cognitive ability assessed. For tasks that rely on aspects of cognitive resources known to deteriorate with age including fluid cognition or "cognitive mechanics," cultural differences are likely to decrease with age because older adults have less flexibility in processing due to reduced cognitive resources (e.g., Hedden, Park, Nisbett, Ji, Jing, and Jiao, 2002). In contrast, for tasks that rely on experience-based knowledge or "cognitive pragmatics," cultural differences should remain stable or even increase with age because older adults have had a greater exposure to culturally embedded knowledge than their younger counterparts. Finally, culturally sensitive tasks that require relatively few cognitive resources may show cultural differences in older but not younger adults (e.g., Na, Huang, and Park, 2017). According to Na and colleagues (2017), this is because younger adults have sufficient cognitive resources to overcome cultural bias but older adults do not.

Studies examining the Model of Culture and Aging have primarily focused on comparisons between Easterners such as Chinese or Singaporeans and Westerners such as U.S. Americans or Canadians. Specifically, cultural values focused on interdependence are thought to lead Easterners to process information in a holistic fashion that emphasizes contextual information such as the relationships between different objects or between objects and backgrounds (Nisbett and Miyamoto, 2005; Nisbett, Peng, Choi, and Norenzayan, 2001). In turn, the cultural focus on independence among Westerners is thought to lead to a focus on the objects themselves along with an emphasis on categorical processing (Nisbett, 2004).

Empirical evidence generally supports the Model of Culture and Aging. For instance, in studies comparing U.S. and Chinese participants, cross-cultural differences in a culturally sensitive task tapping into cognitive mechanics (i.e., backward digit span) were less pronounced in older as compared to younger adults (Hedden et al., 2002). In contrast, cross-cultural differences in a culturally sensitive task tapping into cognitive pragmatics (i.e., categorical organization during free recall) were more pronounced in older as compared to younger adults (Gutchess et al., 2006). Further, in a study comparing Singaporean and U.S. samples, cultural differences in an easy categorization task only emerged for older but not for younger adults, and this was explained by older Singaporeans' reduced cognitive resources which made it harder for them to override a tendency toward intuitive judgment which is typically found within their culture (Na et al., 2017).

Cultural differences in cognitive processing also leave their traces at the neural level. In a study examining neural responses during object perception, older Singaporeans showed disproportionate decrements in object-processing regions relative to their Western counterparts (Goh et al., 2007). With respect to brain structure, Chee, Zheng, Goh, Park, and Sutton (2011) compared the object-processing regions of older Singaporeans and United States-dwelling Westerners. Consistent with a tendency among Westerners to favor analytical over holistic processing, younger, predominantly White Americans had higher cortical thickness in medial-temporal association areas than Chinese Singaporeans. Among older adults, however, these cultural differences were only found among respondents with high cognitive functioning.

Recent studies have extended research on culture by aging interactions beyond neutral laboratory stimuli to tasks involving socially relevant material including categorical memory for facial stimuli (Yang, Chen, Ng, and Fu, 2013) and memory for socially meaningful associations between items and their context (Yang, Li, et al., 2013). In particular, findings suggest that compared to older European Canadians, older Chinese adults maintain better memory for objects encoded in imaginary social contexts because they invest higher effort during encoding (Yang, Li, Wilkinson, Spaniol, and Hasher, 2018). This suggests that cultural differences in aging trajectories reflect not only an accumulation of culturally relevant knowledge but also the allocation of targeted efforts toward processing material in culturally consistent ways.

Wisdom

Cultural differences may also play a role in life-span trajectories of wisdom. Although wisdom has been defined in different ways (Sternberg and Jordan, 2005), there is a general consensus that it integrates cognitive and socioemotional factors to foster *pragmatic reasoning* which encompasses the acknowledgment of other people's points of views, the awareness of limitations in one's personal knowledge, the valuation of compromise, and the appreciation of unavoidable uncertainties in life (Baltes and Smith, 2008). One element of wise reasoning that has been explored across different age and cultural groups is dialecticism (Spencer-Rodgers, Williams, and Peng, 2010; Grossmann, 2017), the tendency to expect changes and instability and tolerate contradictions, such as reconciling divergent viewpoints and acknowledging that both sides of an argument contain a degree of truth (Nisbett et al., 2001; Spencer-Rodgers et al., 2010).

In general, older adults tend to exercise more dialectical thinking and reasoning, possibly due to more life experiences, especially in navigating challenging life dilemmas (e.g., Grossmann and Kross, 2014; Grossmann et al., 2010). Age-related increases in dialectical thinking have been found when reflecting on social issues (Basseches, 1984), conflicts and life dilemmas (Blanchard-Fields, 1986), and intergroup and interpersonal conflicts (Grossmann, Na, Varnum, Kitayama, and Nisbett, 2013). Although some studies failed to replicate age effects in dialectical thinking (e.g., Spencer-Rodgers, Peng, Wang, and Hou, 2004; Chen, Wang, Huang, and Spencer-Rodgers, 2012), this was likely the result of restriction of age range.

In addition to age effects, studies examining cultural differences consistently find that East Asians are more likely to display dialectical thinking (Spencer-Rodgers et al., 2010), presumably due to their cultural emphasis on interdependence and associated cognitive styles favoring holistic and contextual processing. To date, research on the interaction effects of age and culture on wise reasoning is limited, but an initial study by Grossmann and colleagues (2012) found age-related increments in wisdom in a U.S. sample, but not in a Japanese sample. This effect was driven by Japanese young and middle-aged adults showing significantly greater use of wise-reasoning strategies than their U.S. counterparts. In other words, the cultural focus on dialectical reasoning in Japan may have driven younger and middle-aged Japanese adults to execute and refine the use of wise-reasoning strategies earlier in the developmental trajectory. Thus, the reduced tendency to expect age-related increases in wisdom found among Eastern countries (Löckenhoff et al., 2009) may not reflect negative aging attitudes, but a realistic assessment of age trajectories in dialectical thinking.

Stereotype Threat

Beyond cross-cultural differences in societal support structures, cognitive styles, and wise reasoning, it has been debated whether cultural differences in aging stereotypes and expectations may influence patterns of cognitive aging. Meta-analytical evidence from 32 studies with almost 4,000 participants indicates that, in general, older adults' memory performance is susceptible to negative age-based stereotypes (Lamont et al., 2015). Further, consistent with research showing more negative aging perceptions in non-Anglophone Europe as compared to the United States (North and Fiske, 2015), effect sizes for age-based stereotype threat were more pronounced in Europe than in North America (Lamont et al., 2015). With respect to East-West comparisons, one initial study suggested that more positive aging views in China as compared to the United States result in better memory performance among Chinese elders (Levy and Langer, 1994), but an attempt to replicate this finding by comparing memory performance between older Chinese and Anglophone Canadians (Yoon, Hasher, Feinberg, Rahhal, and Winocur, 2000) was not successful. Instead, it was found that older Chinese Canadians only showed superior performance when the stimuli resembled written Chinese idiographs, suggesting that culture-specific cognitive skills rather than culturally shared aging views were driving the effects (Yoon et al., 2000). Importantly, although Confucian values of filial piety do not appear to protect Easterners from age-related memory decline on a societal level, eliciting such values in an experimental setting can temporarily offset the negative effects of stereotype threat among Chinese Americans (Tan and Barber, 2018). To date, much of the research on stereotype threat has focused on Western settings and further research is needed to explore such dynamics among a wider range of cultures.

In summary, although there is a general trend toward age-related cognitive decrements, especially in fluid cognition, there are noteworthy international differences in aging trajectories. which can be traced to a variety of factors ranging from societal supports structures for early education and adequate healthcare to cultural variations in cognitive styles and processing preferences. Importantly, where age by culture interactions are observed, they do not conform to a single pattern but depend on a variety of factors including the nature of the task, the length of exposure to one's cultural context, and remaining cognitive capacities among older respondents.

Conclusions and Future Directions

Taken together, the literature reviewed in this chapter reveals considerable cross-cultural concordance in key aspects of the aging experience. Expectations about aging, for example, are rather negative, but—across the world—they tend to be more positive with respect to socioemotional changes than with respect to physical and cognitive changes (e.g., Löckenhoff et al., 2009). Consistent with these expectations, most cultures show the "paradox of aging," characterized by stable or improved emotional well-being and life satisfaction in the face of physical and cognitive decrements (e.g., Peterson and Ralston, 2019). Also, older adults across the world have smaller, more dense social networks than their younger counterparts and they are more likely to prioritize family relationships (e.g., Wrzuz et al, 2013). Similarly, with respect to cognitive functioning, there are broad cross-cultural trends such that fluid processing of novel material shows age-related decrements whereas crystallized abilities that draw on experience-based knowledge remain comparatively stable (e.g., Park and Gutchess, 2006).

Superimposed on such universal trends, however, there is growing evidence of age by culture interactions and this literature paints a rather complex picture. Although certain facets of aging perceptions and specific aspects of socioemotional and cognitive aging vary across different nations and cultural contexts, the observed effects cannot be reduced to convenient single-factor explanations based on sociodemographic resources, levels of industrialization, cultural values, or societal aging stereotypes. Instead such factors appear to interact with each other: Rapid population aging is easier to adapt to if there are adequate economic resources, shifting political paradigms may shape policy responses to rural aging, and changes in multi-generational family structures may play out differently in collectivistic versus individualistic societies. Moreover, individual older adults within a given society may vary in the degree to which they conform to broader cultural patterns depending on their financial resources, functional and cognitive health, and prior exposure to culture-specific ways of living and reasoning. In addition, aging experiences may differ across regions within the same country (e.g., rural vs. urban, economically thriving vs. depressed) and—especially for countries that are currently seeing high rates of population aging—the status and well-being of older adults may shift rapidly as structural lags in creating age-friendly opportunity structures are being addressed.

Perhaps the most important conclusion to draw from this review is the imminent need for further research. The early theoretical emphasis on dichotomous East/West comparisons has drawn attention away from the considerable variability among the individual countries within broader geographic regions such as Europe and Asia. Such concerns are beginning to be addressed as large-scale cross-cultural and longitudinal datasets become available (e.g., *World Values Survey*, SAGE) and dedicated books explore aging experiences and trajectories within a given region (e.g., Cheng, Chi, Fung, Li, and Woo, 2015). However, some continents—particularly Africa and South America—remain underrepresented in the aging literature, and even less is known about age trajectories in traditional hunter-gatherer and forager farmer societies (e.g., Sorokowski et al., 2017).

As the empty spots in our "world map" of aging are being addressed, it will be important to extend assessments of cultural values beyond the broad dichotomy between individualistic and collectivistic orientations and explore additional factors. Marcus and Fritzsche (2016) for instance, have argued that levels of individualism versus collectivism interact with cultural "tightness" versus "looseness" (i.e., the strength of social norms and tolerance for deviating from such norms) and that this may influence age-based discrimination such that cultures that are both tight and collectivistic show the greatest discrimination. Conversely, when individualism is paired with a "marketized mentality" that emphasizes material success and monetary profitability above all other values, it may lead to a devaluation of groups that are deemed "unprofitable" such as the unemployed and the homeless (Hövermann, Groß, Zick, and Messner, 2015)—a tendency that may conceivably extend to older adults, especially, if they are no longer part of the workforce.

Future research is also needed to explore the implications of cross-cultural variations in aging trajectories for the consumer realm. First, cross-cultural differences have implications for the types of goods and services that may be attractive for older adults and their families. For instance, some degree of physical and cognitive decrements in later life is universal and likely to require help and support from others. However, older adults residing in individualistic Western countries are more likely to move to dedicated senior residences or utilize professional services to support continued independence in their own homes. In contrast, such options may be less popular in Eastern and Latin American cultures which emphasize family caregiving and the co-habitation of younger and older generations. Instead, older residents of such countries may be more open to services that support family caregiving and leverage community-based care (Pinquart et al., 2018; Chen and Han, 2016).

Second, there may be cross-cultural differences in optimal ways to advertise to older adults. However, given the complex patterns of interactions between age and culture, advertising strategies cannot be reduced to simple formulas. For instance, there seems to be a wide-spread trend toward a greater emphasis on positively valenced information in older adulthood, but this trend does not generalize toward all cultural settings (e.g., Fung et al., 2018; Grossmann et al., 2014; Grühn et al., 2007). More generally, as pointed out by Park and colleagues (e.g., Park et al., 1999) cultural differences in cognitive styles may increase, decrease, or remain stable depending on the type of task involved. For instance, research on people's preferred affective states shows cultural differences among younger adults, with Westerners favoring high arousal positive affect (such as excitement) and Easterners favoring low-arousal positive affect (such as calmness) and this is reflected in popular culture and leisure choices (Tsai and Sims, 2016). However, such differences may wash out with age as older Westerners become more likely to pursue low-arousal positive affect than their younger peers (Scheibe, English, Tsai, and Carstensen, 2013). Thus, although broad age and cultural trends in processing preferences can certainly inform the development of advertising campaigns that target older adults from different cultures, careful pre-testing with the intended target audience is necessary to ensure a proper match.

Perhaps the most important consideration in developing advertising campaigns for senior audiences is to reach out in ways that address the wide-spread under-representation of older adults in advertising (e.g., Prieler, Kohlbacher, Hagiwara, and Arima, 2014; Zhang et al., 2006) while counteracting negative aging views that have been shown to elicit stereotype threat across different cultures (Lamont, Swift, and Abrams, 2015; Tan and Barber, 2018). Like other advertising efforts, however, such strategies need to be culturally sensitive. For instance, activating Confucian values of filial piety may alleviate age-based stereotype threat in older Chinese Americans (Tan and Barber, 2018) but this strategy is not likely to be effective in non-Asian cultures. Moreover, presenting positive images of aging may backfire if they are perceived as unattainable. Consistent with this notion, a study conducted in Hong Kong (Fung et al., 2015) found that confronting older adults with unrealistically positive depictions of older adults resulted in less positive perceptions of personal aging and worse memory performance than exposure to positive but realistic views.

In summary, developmental and cultural findings from non-consumer contexts suggest that older consumers from different cultures are likely to have different preferences and to not take equally well to all types of advertising approaches. Because tailored advertising strategies are needed to target different groups of older consumers, research at the intersection of development, culture, and consumer preferences represents an exciting and very promising avenue for scholarship on aging.

References

Antonucci, T. C., Akiyama, H., & Takahashi, K. (2004). Attachment and close relationships across the life span. *Attachment and Human Development, 6*(4), 353–370.

Antonucci, T. C., Lansford, J. E., Schaberg, L., Smith, J., Akiyama, H., Takahashi, K., & Dartigues, J.-F. (2001). Widowhood and illness: A comparison of social network characteristics in France, Germany, Japan, and United States. *Psychology and Aging, 16*(4), 655–665.

Baltes, P. B., & Smith, J. (2008). The fascination of wisdom: Its nature, ontogeny, and function. *Perspectives on Psychological Science, 3*(1), 56–64.

Basseches, M. (1984). *Dialectical Thinking*. Norwood, NJ: Ablex.

Blanchard-Fields, F. (1986). Reasoning on social dilemmas varying in emotional saliency: An adult developmental perspective. *Psychology and Aging, 1*(4), 325–333.

Carstensen, L. L., Isaacowitz, D. M., & Charles, S. T. (1999). Taking time seriously: A theory of socioemotional selectivity. *The American Psychologist, 54*(3), 165–181.

Carstensen, L. L., Pasupathi, M., Mayr, U., & Nesselroade, J. R. (2000). Emotional experience in everyday life across the adult life span. *Journal of Personality and Social Psychology, 79*(4), 644–655.

Carvalho, J. O., Tommet, D., Crane, P. K., Thomas, M. L., Claxton, A., Habeck, C., & Romero, H. (2015). Deconstructing racial differences: The effects of quality of education and cerebrovascular risk factors. *The Journals of Gerontology: Series B, 70*(4), 545–556.

Chee, M. W. L., Zheng, H., Goh, J. O. S., Park, D., & Sutton, B. P. (2011). Brain structure in young and old East Asians and Westerners: Comparisons of structural volume and cortical thickness. *Journal of Cognitive Neuroscience, 23*(5), 1065–1079.

Chen, L., & Han, W.-J. (2016). Shanghai: Front-runner of community-based eldercare in China. *Journal of Aging and Social Policy, 28*(4), 292–307.

Chen, J., Wang, L., Huang, M., & Spencer-Rodgers, J. (2012). Naive dialecticism and Chinese employees' commitment to change. *Journal of Managerial Psychology, 27*(1), 48–70.

Cheng, S.-T., Chi, I., Fung, H. H., Li, L. W., & Woo, L. F. (2015). *Successful Aging—Asian Perspectives*. Dordrecht, Netherlands: Springer.

Clarke, P. J., Marshall, V. W., Ryff, C. D., & Rosenthal, C. J. (2000). Well-being in Canadian seniors: Findings from the Canadian study of health and aging. *Canadian Journal on Aging/La Revue Canadienne du Vieillissement, 19*(2), 139–159.

Colleran, K. M., Richards, A., & Shafer, K. (2007). Disparities in cardiovascular disease risk and treatment: Demographic comparison. *Journal of Investigative Medicine: The Official Publication of the American Federation for Clinical Research, 55*(8), 415–422.

Cong, Z., & Silverstein, M. (2008). Intergenerational support and depression among elders in rural China: Do daughters-in-law matter? *Journal of Marriage and Family, 70*(3), 599–612.

Cowgill, D. O. (1986). *Aging Around the World*. Belmont, CA: Wadsworth Pub. Co.

Deckers, K., Schievink, S. H. K., Rodriquez, M. M. F., van Oostenbrugge, R. J., van Boxtel, M. P. J., Verhey, F. R. J., & Köhler, S. (2017). Coronary heart disease and risk for cognitive impairment or dementia: Systematic review and meta-analysis. *PLoS One*, *12*(9), e0184244.

Fung, H. H., Gong, X., Ngo, N., & Isaacowitz, D. M. (2018). Cultural differences in the age-related positivity effect: Distinguishing between preference and effectiveness. *Emotion*,*19*(8),1414-1424.

Fung, H. H., Isaacowitz, D. M., Lu, A. Y., Wadlinger, H. A., Goren, D., & Wilson, H. R. (2008). Age-related positivity enhancement is not universal: Older Chinese look away from positive stimuli. *Psychology and Aging*, *23*(2), 4404–4446.

Fung, H. H., Li, T., Zhang, X., Sit, I. M. I., Cheng, S.-T., & Isaacowitz, D. M. (2015). Positive portrayals of old age do not always have positive consequences. *Journals of Gerontology. Series B—Psychological Sciences and Social Sciences*, *70*(6), 913–924.

Fung, H. H., & Tang, L. Y. T. (2005). Age differences in memory for emotional messages: Do older people always remember the positive? *Ageing International*, *30*(3), 245–262.

Goh, J. O. S., Chee, M. W., Tan, J. C., Venkatraman, V., Hebrank, A., Leshikar, E. D., Jenkins, L., Sutton, B. P., Gutchess, A. H., & Park, D. C. (2007). Age and culture modulate object processing and object-scene binding in the ventral visual area. *Cognitive, Affective and Behavioral Neuroscience*, *7*(1), 44–52.

Grossmann, I. (2017). Dialecticism across the lifespan. In: J. Spencer-Rogers & K. Peng (Eds.), *The Psychological and Cultural Foundations of East Asian Cognition: Contradiction, Change, and Holism* (pp. 135–180). Oxford, England: Oxford University Press.

Grossmann, I., Karasawa, M., Izumi, S., Na, J., Varnum, M. E., Kitayama, S., & Nisbett, R. E. (2012). Aging and wisdom: Culture matters. *Psychological Science*, *23*(10), 1059–1066.

Grossmann, I., Karasawa, M., Kan, C., & Kitayama, S. (2014). A cultural perspective on emotional experiences across the life span. *Emotion*, *14*(4), 679–692.

Grossmann, I., & Kross, E. (2014). Exploring Solomon's paradox: Self-distancing eliminates the self-other asymmetry in wise reasoning about close relationships in younger and older adults. *Psychological Science*, *25*(8), 1571–1580.

Grossmann, I., Na, J., Varnum, M. E., Kitayama, S., & Nisbett, R. E. (2013). A route to well-being: Intelligence versus wise reasoning. *Journal of Experimental Psychology: General*, *142*(3), 944–953.

Grossmann, I., Na, J., Varnum, M. E., Park, D. C., Kitayama, S., & Nisbett, R. E. (2010). Reasoning about social conflicts improves into old age. *Proceedings of the National Academy of Sciences of the United States of America*, *107*(16), 7246–7250.

Grühn, D., Scheibe, S., & Baltes, P. B. (2007). Reduced negativity effect in older adults' memory for emotional pictures: The heterogeneity-homogeneity list paradigm. *Psychology and Aging*, *22*(3), 644–649.

Grühn, D., Smith, J., & Baltes, P. B. (2005). No aging bias favoring memory for positive material: Evidence from a heterogeneity-homogeneity list paradigm using emotionally toned words. *Psychology and Aging*, *20*(4), 579–588.

Gutchess, A. H., Yoon, C., Luo, T., Feinberg, F., Hedden, T., Jing, Q., Nisbett, R. E., & Park, D. C. (2006). Categorical organization in free recall across culture and age. *Gerontology*, *52*(5), 314–323.

Hayutin, A. M. (2007). Graying of the global population. *Public Policy and Aging Report*, *17*(4), 12–17.

He, W., Muenchrath, M. N., & Kowal, P. (2012). *Shades of Gray: A Cross-Country Study of Health and Well-Being of the Older Populations in SAGE Countries, 2007–2010*. Washington, DC: US Government Printing Office.

Hedden, T., Park, D. C., Nisbett, R., Ji, L.-J., Jing, Q., & Jiao, S. (2002). Cultural variation in verbal versus spatial neuropsychological function across the life span. *Neuropsychology*, *16*(1), 65–73.

Hövermann, A., Groß, E. M., Zick, A., & Messner, S. F. (2015). Understanding the devaluation of vulnerable groups: A novel application of institutional anomie theory. *Social Science Research*, *52*, 408–421.

Hofstede, G. (1980). Culture and organizations. *International Studies of Management and Organization*, *10*(4), 15–41.

Horowitz, J. M. (2010). *The Post-Communist Generation in the Former Eastern Bloc*. Washington, DC: Pew Research Center Publications.

Jackson, R., Howe, N., & Peter, T. (2013). *The Global Aging Preparedness Index*. Lanham, MD: Rowman & Littlefield.

Japan Census Bureau (2019). *Statistical Handbook of Japan 2019*. Retrieved from https://www.stat.go.jp/english/data/handbook/c0117.html.

Kahneman, D., Diener, E., & Schwarz, N. (Eds.) (1999). *Well-Being: Foundations of Hedonic Psychology*. New York, NY: Russell Sage Foundation.

Karasawa, M., Curhan, K. B., Markus, H. R., Kitayama, S. S., Love, G. D., Radler, B. T., & Ryff, C. D. (2011). Cultural perspectives on aging and well-being: A comparison of Japan and the United States. *The International Journal of Aging and Human Development*, *73*(1), 73–98.

Lamont, R. A., Swift, H. J., & Abrams, D. (2015). A review and meta-analysis of age-based stereotype threat: Negative stereotypes, not facts, do the damage. *Psychology and Aging*, *30*(1), 180–193.

Levy, B., &, Langer, E. (1994). Aging free from negative stereotypes: Successful memory in China and among the American deaf. *Journal of Personality and Social Psychology*, *6*(66), 989–997.

Lewey, J., & Choudhry, N. K. (2014). The current state of ethnic and racial disparities in cardiovascular care: Lessons from the past and opportunities for the future. *Curr Cardiol Rep*, *16*(10), 530.

Löckenhoff, C. E., De Fruyt, F., Terracciano, A., McCrae, R. R., De Bolle, M., Costa, P. T., Yik, M. (2009). Perceptions of aging across 26 cultures and their culture-level associates. *Psychology and Aging*, *24*(4), 941–954.

Marcus, J., & Fritzsche, B. A. (2016). The cultural anchors of age discrimination in the workplace: A multilevel framework. *Work, Aging and Retirement*, *2*(2), 217–222.

Markus, H. R., & Kitayama, S. (1991). Culture and the self: Implications for cognition, emotion, and motivation. *Psychological Review*, *98*(2), 224–253.

Mata, R., Josef, A. K., & Hertwig, R. (2016). Propensity for risk taking across the life span and around the globe. *Psychological Science*, *27*(2), 231–243.

Mather, M., & Carstensen, L. L. (2003). Aging and attentional biases for emotional faces. *Psychology Science*, *14*(5), 409–415.

Meng, X., & D'Arcy, C. (2012). Education and dementia in the context of the cognitive reserve hypothesis: A systematic review with meta-analyses and qualitative analyses. *PLoS One*, *7*(6), e38268.

Mroczek, D. K., & Kolarz, C. M. (1998). The effect of age on positive and negative affect: A developmental perspective on happiness. *Journal of Personality and Social Psychology*, *75*(5), 1333–1349.

Na, J., Huang, C.-M., & Park, D. C. (2017). When age and culture interact in an easy and yet cognitively demanding task: Older adults, but not younger adults, showed the expected cultural differences. *Frontiers in Psychology*, *8*, 457.

Nelson, T. D. (2009). Ageism. In: T. D. Nelson (Ed.), *Handbook of Prejudice, Stereotyping, and Discrimination* (pp. 431–440). New York, NY: Psychology Press.

Nisbett, R. E. (2004). *The Geography of Thought: How Easterners and Westerners Think Differently and Why*. New York, NY: The Free Press.

Nisbett, R. E., & Miyamoto, Y. (2005). The influence of culture: Holistic versus analytic perception. *Trends in Cognitive Sciences, 9*(10), 467–473.

Nisbett, R. E., Peng, K., Choi, I., & Norenzayan, A. (2001). Culture and systems of thought: Holistic versus analytic cognition. *Psychological Review, 108*(2), 291–310.

North, M. S., & Fiske, S. T. (2015). Modern attitudes toward older adults in the aging world: A cross-cultural meta-analysis. *Psychological Bulletin, 141*(5), 993–1021.

Palmore, E. B., & Manton, K. (1974). Modernization and status of the aged: International correlations. *Journal of Gerontology, 29*(2), 205–210.

Park, D., & Gutchess, A. (2006). The cognitive neuroscience of aging and culture. *Current Directions in Psychological Science, 15*(3), 105–108.

Park, D. C., Nisbett, R., & Hedden, T. (1999). Aging, culture, and cognition. *Journals of Gerontology: Series B—Psychological Sciences and Social Sciences, 54*(2), 75–84.

Peterson, L., & Ralston, M. (2017). Valued elders or societal burden: Cross-national attitudes toward older adults. *International Sociology, 32*(6), 731–754.

Peterson, L., & Ralston, M. (2019). Aging well in an aging world: The impact of material conditions, culture, and societal disruptions. *Social Science and Medicine, 220*, 245–253.

Pinquart, M., Sörensen, S., & Song, Y. (2018). Older person's care-related preferences. In: T. Boll, D. Ferring & J. Valsiner (Eds.), *Cultures of Care in Aging* (pp. 123–148). Charlotte, NC: Information Age Publishing Inc.

Prieler, M., Kohlbacher, F., Hagiwara, S., & Arima, A. (2014). The representation of older people in television advertisements and social change: The case of Japan. *Ageing and Society, 35*(4), 865–887.

Reed, A. E., Chan, L., & Mikels, J. A. (2014). Meta-analysis of the age-related positivity effect: Age differences in preferences for positive over negative information. *Psychology and Aging, 29*(1), 1–15.

Riley, M. W. E., Kahn, R. L. E., Foner, A. E., & Mack, K. A. (Eds.) (1994). *Age and Structural Lag: Society's Failure to Provide Meaningful Opportunities in Work, Family, And Leisure.* Hoboken, NJ: John Wiley & Sons, Inc.

Roaf, J., Atoyan, R., Joshi, B., & Krogulski, K., & IMF Staff Team (2014). *25 Years of Transition Post-Communist Europe and the IMF: Regional Economic Issues Special Report.* Washington, DC: International Monetary Fund.

Ryan, R. M., & Deci, E. L. (2001). On happiness and human potentials: A review of research on hedonic and eudaimonic well-being. *Annual Review of Psychology, 52*(1), 141–166.

Scheibe, S., English, T., Tsai, J. L., & Carstensen, L. L. (2013). Striving to feel good: Ideal affect, actual affect, and their correspondence across adulthood. *Psychology and Aging, 28*(1), 160–171.

Silverstein, M., Parrott, T. M., Angelelli, J. J., & Cook, F. L. (2000). Solidarity and tension between age groups in the United States: Challenge for an aging America in the 21st century. *International Journal of Social Welfare, 9*(4), 270–284.

Sorokowski, P., Sorokowska, A., Frąckowiak, T., & Löckenhoff, C. E. (2017). Aging perceptions in Tsimane Amazonian forager-farmers compared with two industrialized societies: The role of gender and acculturation. *Journals of Gerontology: Psychological Sciences, 72*(4), 561–570.

Spencer-Rodgers, J., Peng, K., Wang, L., & Hou, Y. (2004). Dialectical self-esteem and East-West differences in psychological well-being. *Personality and Social Psychology Bulletin, 30*(11), 1416–1432.

Spencer-Rodgers, J., Williams, M. J., & Peng, K. (2010). Cultural differences in expectations of change and tolerance for contradiction: A decade of empirical research. *Personality and Social Psychology Review, 14*(3), 296–312.

Steptoe, A., Deaton, A., & Stone, A. A. (2015). Subjective wellbeing, health, and ageing. *The Lancet, 385*(9968), 640–648.

Sternberg, R., & Jordan, J. (Eds.) (2005). *A Handbook of Wisdom: Psychological Perspectives.* Cambridge, UK: Cambridge University Press.

Street, D. A. (2012). Sociological approaches to understanding age and aging. In: J. A. Blackburn & C. N. Dulmus (Eds.), *Handbook of Gerontology* (pp. 143–170). Hoboken, NJ: John Wiley & Sons, Inc.

Sung, K. (2001). Elder respect: Exploration of ideals and forms in East Asia. *Journal of Aging Studies, 15*(1), 13–26.

Tan, S. C., & Barber, S. J. (2018). Confucian values as a buffer against age-based stereotype threat for Chinese older adults. *Journals of Gerontology: Series B—Psychological Sciences and Social Sciences.*

Tsai, J. L., & Sims, T. (2016). Emotional aging in different cultures: Implications of affect valuation theory. In: A. Ong & C. E. Löckenhoff (Eds.), *Emotion, Aging, and Health* (pp. 119–143). Washington, DC: APA Books.

United Nations (2002). *Political Declaration and Madrid International Plan of Action on Ageing.* Madrid, Spain: United Nations.

United Nations, Department of Economic and Social Affairs, Population Division (2019). *World Urbanization Prospects: The 2018 Revision* (ST/ESA/SER.A/420). New York: United Nations.

Vauclair, C. M., Marques, S., Lima, M. L., Bratt, C., Swift, H. J., & Abrams, D. (2015). Subjective social status of older people across countries: The role of modernization and employment. *Journals of Gerontology. Series B: Psychological Sciences and Social Sciences, 70*(4), 650–660.

Williams, A. (1997). Intergenerational equity: An exploration of the 'fair innings' argument. *Health Economics, 6*(2), 117–132.

Wilson, R. S., Rajan, K. B., Barnes, L. L., Weuve, J., & Evans, D. A. (2016). Factors related to racial differences in late-life level of cognitive function. *Neuropsychology, 30*(5), 517–524.

World Health Organization (2015). *World Report on Ageing and Health.* Geneva, Switzerland: World Health Organization.

Wrzus, C., Hönel, M., Wagner, J., & Neyer, F. J. (2013). Social network changes and life events across the life span: A meta-analysis. *Psychological Bulletin, 139*(1), 53–80.

Yang, L., Chen, W., Ng, A. H., & Fu, X. (2013). Aging, culture, and memory for categorically processed information. *Journals of Gerontology. Series B: Psychological Sciences and Social Sciences, 68*(6), 872–881.

Yang, L., Li, J., Spaniol, J., Hasher, L., Wilkinson, A. J., Yu, J., & Niu, Y. (2013). Aging, culture, and memory for socially meaningful item-context associations: An East-West cross-cultural comparison study. *PLoS One, 8*(4), e60703.

Yang, L., Li, J., Wilkinson, A. J., Spaniol, J., & Hasher, L. (2018). East-West cultural differences in encoding objects in imagined social contexts. *PLoS One, 13*(11), e0207515.

Yasuda, T., Iwai, N., Chin-Chun, Y., & Guihua, X. (2011). Intergenerational coresidence in China, Japan, South Korea and Taiwan: Comparative analyses based on the East Asian social survey 2006. *Journal of Comparative Family Studies, 42*(5), 703–722.

Yoon, C., Hasher, L., Feinberg, F., Rahhal, T. A., & Winocur, G. (2000). Cross-cultural differences in memory: The role of culture-based stereotypes about aging. *Psychology and Aging, 15*(4), 694–704.

Zahodne, L. B., Stern, Y., & Manly, J. J. (2015). Differing effects of education on cognitive decline in diverse elders with low versus high educational attainment. *Neuropsychology, 29*(4), 649–657.

Zhang, Y. B., Harwood, J., Williams, A., Ylänne-McEwen, V., Wadleigh, P. M., & Thimm, C. (2006). The portrayal of older adults in advertising: A cross-national review. *Journal of Language and Social Psychology, 25*(3), 264–282.

14

THE INFLUENCE OF CREATIVITY ON OBJECTIVE AND SUBJECTIVE WELL-BEING IN OLDER ADULTHOOD

Stephanie M. Carpenter, Rebecca Chae, Yeonjin Sung, and Carolyn Yoon

The average life expectancy of adults in the United States is rising (World Bank, 2019), with the number of Americans aged 65 and older projected to reach 98 million by the year 2060 (American Psychological Association, 2017). A critical question to be addressed in aging research is how to promote the well-being of older adults, particularly given that they face an increasing number of health challenges.

Among cognitively and physically healthy older adults, there exist a number of positive consequences associated with aging (Mather and Knight, 2005). Compared to younger adults, healthy older adults experience higher levels of positive affect (Carstensen, Pasupathi, Mayr, and Nesselroade, 2000; Carstensen et al., 2011; Charles, Reynolds, and Gatz, 2001; Mroczek and Kolarz, 1998), improved emotion regulation (Mather and Knight, 2005), and boosts in cognitive flexibility and creativity (Carpenter, Chae, and Yoon, 2020; Hasher and Zacks, 1988; Hasher, Zacks, and May, 1999).

Older adults primarily experience these benefits when they do not suffer from the negative consequences of cognitive and physical aging (Charles and Carstensen, 2009; Mather and Knight, 2005). However, many older adults suffer from physical ailments, experience social isolation and loneliness (Coyle and Dugan, 2012), and undergo cognitive decline (Salthouse, 2012), all of which can have detrimental effects on their well-being. Approximately one in four older adults suffers from severe cognitive decline and mental health conditions, including depression, anxiety disorders, and dementia (Dunphy et al., 2019). Poor financial circumstances, limitations in mobility, and difficulties with everyday activities also lower older adults' quality of life (Netuveli, Wiggins, Hildon, Montgomery, and Blane, 2006). Given the age-related declines in cognitive and physical health, it is all the more important that research focuses on ways to improve well-being into older adulthood.

Well-Being across the Adult Lifespan

The construct of well-being can be defined in several ways. We focus here on two subcomponents of well-being found to be positively influenced by creativity. The first subcomponent focuses on objective outcomes related to mental health (depression, anxiety; Gortner, Rude, and Pennebaker, 2006; Flood and Phillips, 2007), physical health (Schueller and Seligman, 2010), and cognitive functioning (Mather and Knight, 2006). Objective well-being includes the effects that creative processes have on normal cognitive aging, as well as how creative processes benefit those who are experiencing severe cognitive decline and impairment (i.e., dementia, Alzheimer's disease). The second is a subjective subcomponent of well-being that includes psychosocial outcomes (Greaves and Farbus, 2006; Reynolds, 2010), emotions (Schueller and Seligman, 2010), and life satisfaction (Ryff and Keyes, 1995).

Objective and subjective subcomponents of well-being are interrelated (Schueller and Seligman, 2010). For example, older adults' objective health and cognitive decline directly impacts their subjective life satisfaction and affective states. Similarly, subjective factors (e.g., life satisfaction, positive affect) can have an impact on one's objective physical and mental health. For the purpose of the current discussion, we consider how creativity influences both objective and subjective well-being in older adults.

One potentially promising direction for improving the well-being of older adults is through their active involvement in creative processes. We define creative processes as any activity or interaction with a form of art (e.g., paintings, crafts, music, dance, expressive writing), as well as producing or bringing into being an object or outcome that requires creativity (e.g., recipes, product design, creative technology). Creativity is typically conceptualized as a process involving two modes of thinking: a combination of the experience-based "convergent" thinking, and the more disinhibited "divergent" thinking that allows an individual to integrate irrelevant and distracting information into a creative process (Kasof, 1995). Successful integration of both types of thinking produces creative outcomes that are both unique and practical enough to be executed.

The potential benefits of creativity are well-established in the aging literature and have even been discussed in terms of public policies meant to benefit aging. For example, in May of 2005, professionals in the field of creative aging made recommendations to the White House Conference on Aging that older adults be encouraged to engage in creative processes that promote successful aging (Hanna, 2006). Here we propose and outline a framework for understanding the relationship between well-being and creative processes (see Figure 14.1).

Building on this framework, we begin our discussion with a selective review of how creative processes promote and interact with objective factors to increase well-being in older adults.

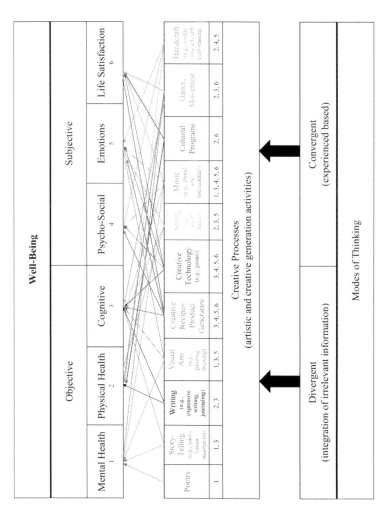

FIGURE 14.1 Framework depicting the relationship between well-being and creative processes. Creative modes of thinking (divergent, convergent) both factor into creative processes. Numbers listed below each creative process denote the well-being outcomes that are positively influenced by the respective creative process.

Creative Processes and Objective Well-Being

Mental Health

Extant research indicates that creative processes can have a number of positive benefits on mental health, and especially for older adults who suffer from depression. Interventions involving creative arts, including painting, dance movement, drama, and music modalities are utilized internationally to target depression and depressive symptoms in older adults (Dunphy et al., 2019). Creativity has also been linked to mental health recovery in older adults, where art-based practices promote both psychological and social recovery, particularly in the areas of self-discovery, self-expression, relationships, and social identity (Van Lith, Schofield, and Fenner, 2013).

These positive benefits are observed even when people are faced with end-of-life considerations and anxieties. Early research on creativity and aging suggests that older adults with more creative personalities or who engage in more creative activities cope better with aging and illness, and exhibit less denial of death (Landau and Maoz, 1978; Smith and Andersson, 1989). Creative achievement may also be an avenue for symbolic immortality (Rank, 1945; Becker, 1973), whereby creative action is viewed as a route for individualization, unique self-expression, and the opportunity to leave behind an imperishable legacy (Yalom, 1980), particularly among individuals who value creativity (Perach and Wisman, 2016).

However, the effects of creativity are mixed when one's mortality is salient. Some extant research has shown that creativity can buffer the negative effects of mortality salience. In one study, when mortality salience was activated, conforming to others' opinions led to increased defensiveness about worldview, but engaging in a creative task decreased this tendency (Routledge, Arndt, and Sheldon, 2004). However, other existing research has shown that when mortality is salient, people who complete a creative task express more guilt and feel less connected to others, as compared to those who do not complete a creative task (Arndt, Greenberg, Solomon, Pyszczynski, and Schimel, 1999). These findings suggest that creative processes may not be universally beneficial and that more work is needed to understand the ways in which mortality salience interacts with creative processes to impact well-being.

Several opportunities exist for developing mental health interventions and creative courses for older individuals. Indeed, creativity interventions positively affect mental and physiological health indicators (Flood and Phillips, 2007). Even the act of creating an artistic product has been suggested to be more important than the actual product outcome (Flood and Phillips, 2007). Many creative interventions include mainstream art endeavors, such as painting. There are, however, a number of other useful interventions that are not traditionally thought of as creative but can, in fact, be classified as creative processes. These include participation in choral groups, rhythm and dance exercises, poetry, group storytelling, and journaling, to name a few (see Flood and Phillips, 2007, for a complete review).

Courses designed to provide "art as therapy" improve self-esteem and self-confidence, as well as provide a safe space for reflection on mental health concerns. Participants in these programs describe them as cathartic and as a springboard for engaging in a wide range of further creative projects (Heenan, 2006). Indeed, programs that involve creativity as a means for promoting positive mental health outcomes in a supportive, non-clinical environment encourage and facilitate empowerment and recovery (Heenan, 2006).

While many of these effects have been demonstrated in older adults, similar effects are found even in younger adult populations. For example, vulnerable college students with both a history of, and/or current, depressive symptoms who engaged in expressive writing showed significantly lower depression symptoms when assessed after six months (Gortner, Rude, and Pennebaker, 2006). Creative programs and initiatives thus hold the potential to contribute to addressing mental health and social care needs (Spandler, Secker, Kent, Hacking, and Shenton, 2007) across the entire adult lifespan.

General Physical Health/Disease Prevention

Creativity has positive benefits on objective well-being beyond mental health. As people age, they tend to focus more on general physical health concerns and disease prevention. Creativity, including participatory art and dance programs, promotes better health, prevents disease, and reduces the risk factors associated with the need for long-term care in older adulthood (Cohen, 2006; Cohen et al., 2006; McHugh, 2016).

Moreover, involvement in creative processes through participatory art programs can reduce doctor visits, medication use, falls, and loneliness, and improve morale (Cohen, 2006). Among women with a long-term physical illness, textile arts provide "cultural capital," as some women returned to the textile art skills they learned and developed when a long-term health crisis occurred. These findings indicate that involvement in creative processes during a negative event, such as illness, may have life-enhancing effects, and suggest that rehabilitation specialists should focus more on the arts as a resource for older adults living with physical illness (Reynolds, 2004).

Cognitive Outcomes

Beyond mental and physical health, another important issue to consider is the decline in cognition associated with aging (Salthouse, 2012). A major consideration in research on cognitive aging is how best to support older adults facing cognitive decline. Much of this decline is considered to be along the normal spectrum of cognitive aging, characterized by greater distractibility (Hasher and Zacks, 1988; Hasher et al., 1999), reductions in executive functioning (Salthouse, 2012), and changes in decision-making. The literature also suggests that creative processes can help buffer the potentially negative consequences of cognitive aging (Carpenter et al., 2020; Hasher et al., 1999). This is especially important given that creative activity requires higher-order cognition that can promote brain health and psychological well-being into older adulthood (Patterson and Perlstein, 2011).

Normal Cognitive Functioning in Older Adulthood

Studies of dance, expressive writing, music (singing and instrumental), theater arts, and visual arts have all documented participant improvements in a number of important cognitive abilities, including memory, creativity, problem-solving, everyday competence, reaction time, balance/gait, and quality of life (Noice, Noice, and Kramer, 2014). One model grounded in theories of cognitive and social psychology suggests that expressive writing reduces intrusive and avoidant thinking about a stressful experience, thus freeing working memory resources (Klein and Boals, 2001).

There is even evidence of age-related neural changes in response to engaging in creative tasks. For example, neural networks have been found to be more functionally coupled during creative thinking for older than for younger adults (Adnan, Beaty, Silvia, Spreng, and Turner, 2019). Even when older and younger adults performed similarly on a creativity task, increased network efficiency was associated with creative ability only for older adults. This suggests the existence of a default-executive coupling associated with creative ability in older adulthood (Adnan et al., 2019).

A growing body of literature has also shown that age-related declines in the ability to inhibit distracting information can benefit older adults' creative processes more than younger adults (Hasher and Zacks, 1988; Hasher et al., 1999). Even when both younger and older adults perform the same set of creative tasks, older adults, who have difficulty inhibiting distracting information, display greater cognitive flexibility and creativity than younger adults (Carpenter et al., 2020; Hasher et al., 1999). Research on divergent thinking suggests that older and younger adults are similarly capable of integrating distracting information into a creative product, even if older adults ultimately produce a smaller number of creative products (Palmiero, Di Giacomo, and Passafiume, 2014). These findings suggest that engaging in creative processes enhances cognitive functioning across the adult lifespan, but may benefit older adults more than younger adults.

Severe Cognitive Decline in Older Adulthood

Up to this point, we have reviewed the benefits of creative processes for older adults with relatively high levels of cognitive functioning. However, recent research suggests that creative processes can also be beneficial for those facing more severe and debilitating cognitive decline. For instance, patients with dementia are still able to produce and appreciate visual art, and art therapy interventions may be especially promising for promoting well-being in dementia patients (Chancellor, Duncan, and Chatterjee, 2014). Several studies have suggested that art therapy engages attention, elicits positive feelings, and improves neuropsychiatric symptoms, social behavior, and self-esteem (Chancellor et al., 2014; see Bellass et al., 2019 for a review).

However, much of the research on the positive benefits of creativity for dementia patients has overlooked more context-specific and mundane everyday activities that are crucial to overall well-being. Dementia patients, their caregivers, and family members may benefit from employing creativity in their daily activities. Examples include generating neologisms when memory loss affects word retrieval, using humor to cope with difficult situations, inventing new forms of self-expression, and making practical adaptations to other daily struggles (Bellass et al., 2019).

We have thus far discussed the ways that creative processes can play a critical role in promoting various forms of objective well-being in older adults. Another important subcomponent of well-being is more subjective in nature and includes outcomes that are psychosocial, emotional, and based on perceptions of life satisfaction. Such subjective forms of well-being are also linked in a number of important ways to creativity and aging. Next, we provide a selective review of the ways in which creative processes promote and interact with subjective factors to increase well-being in older adults.

Creative Processes and Subjective Well-being

Psychosocial

As people age, their social networks become smaller and more close-knit (cf. Charles and Carstensen, 2009), and creative interpersonal activities involving close others may promote subjective well-being. Creative processes offer a number of psychosocial benefits. For instance, the creation of art and handicrafts as social leisure activities enriches older adults' mental life, promotes the enjoyment of art, presents new challenges for older adults to overcome, allows for play and experimentation, and provides new goals and ambitions (Reynolds, 2010). Furthermore, creative activities completed with others lead to the development of a positive group identity, confidence, and self-efficacy, which can reverse the downward trends in well-being and health that are expected to accompany aging (Greaves and Farbus, 2006). Interpersonal connections that older adults create outside of their home and immediate family can also help protect them against stereotyping and exclusions they encounter (Reynolds, 2010). Especially among older women, research has shown that those who participate in art and craft activities report more purpose in their lives and feeling more appreciated by others (Liddle, Parkinson, and Sibbritt, 2013).

The benefits of creative interpersonal activities are generalizable across different domains of art and even age groups. Beyond art- and craft-making, engaging with music (e.g., listening, singing, or making music) provides a way for older adults to participate in enjoyable and personally meaningful activities and can be a source of personal empowerment, social cohesion, and social contact (Sixsmith and Gibson, 2007). Even research with younger adults suggests a substantial amount of emotional, psychological (e.g., self-efficacy), and social well-being associated with participation in creative processes, such as art-making (Tamannaeifar and Motaghedifard, 2014). Taken together, the evidence suggests an important influence of the arts on psychosocial outcomes across the adult lifespan.

Emotions

Emotions and self-regulation are a critical component to successful aging, and positive emotional processes are often preserved or even enhanced in older adults (cf. Charles and Carstensen, 2009). Substantial literature has suggested that creative processes are especially likely to elicit positive emotions in older adulthood. Indeed, art-making (De Petrillo and Winner, 2005) and acting (Burroughs and Mick, 2004) lead to increases in positive mood and pleasurable feelings. Drawing has been shown to repair mood to a greater extent than writing (Drake, Coleman, and Winner, 2011). Music and singing also enhance morale, increase positive mood, and reduce depression and anxiety across the adult lifespan (Daykin et al., 2018).

Life Satisfaction

One critical factor in subjective well-being is the extent to which people experience life satisfaction. Creative processes have been shown to increase life satisfaction as people age (Goff, 1993; McHugh, 2016). Dance and movement training boosts life satisfaction (Osgood, Meyers, and Orchowsky, 1990), and improves physical fitness, especially in older women (Cruz-Ferreira, Marmeleira, Formigo, Gomes, and Fernandes, 2015). Music (Hays and Minichiello, 2005) and participation in cultural programs that involve creativity (Cohen, 2006) help older adults maintain a higher quality of life. Creating art contributes to successful aging by enhancing a sense of competence, purpose, personal growth, problem-solving skills, and motivation, all of which improve life satisfaction (Fisher and Specht, 1999). These findings suggest that taking part in various artistic activities increases life satisfaction among older adults.

Thus, as with objective well-being, creative processes play a critical role in promoting several forms of subjective well-being in older adults. However, older adults may also be able to find creative outlets in daily life beyond artistic endeavors. For instance, research in consumer behavior has recently begun investigating ways in which consumers can benefit from interacting creatively with products during their consumption experiences (cf. Sellier and Dahl, 2011). It is plausible that engaging older adults in creative activities during their interactions with everyday products could also benefit their well-being. Our focus now turns to the ways in which older adults can benefit as creative consumers.

Implications for Improving Older Adults' Well-Being: Consumer Creativity

Consumer creativity is defined as a consumer's ability to generate innovative ideas in a consumption context (Burroughs and Mick, 2004; Moreau and Dahl, 2005). For example, consumers can cleverly mix different food ingredients to make a special dish (Finke, Ward, and Smith, 1992; Jay and Perkins, 1997; Treffinger, Isaksen, and Dorval, 1996) or get involved in the design and development of new products, such as handbags or toys (Burroughs, Dahl, Moreau, Chattopadhyay, and Gorn, 2011; Burroughs and Mick, 2004; Moreau and Dahl, 2005; Sellier and Dahl, 2011). Interacting creatively with products also promotes consumer competence and positive affect when assembling (Mochon, Norton, and Ariely, 2012; Norton, Mochon, and Ariely, 2012) or designing (Dahl and Moreau, 2007) products.

Other extant research suggests that creativity is integral to consumer problem-solving. Both situational factors (i.e., time constraints, situational involvement) and person factors (i.e., locus of control, metaphoric thinking ability) can improve creative problem-solving, which in turn increases positive affect (Burroughs and Mick, 2004). Restricting the choice of creative inputs (e.g., decreasing the number of ingredients for a cook) has also been found to enhance creativity for consumers who have experience in a creative domain. These restrictions boosted enjoyment in the creative process and led to products that received higher ratings by expert judges (Sellier and Dahl, 2011).

One domain in which consumers have a substantial opportunity to be creative is through interactive technologies. Older adults are the fastest growing consumer segment of Internet users (Hart, Chaparro, and Halcomb, 2008). For example, in 2003 only 25 percent of Americans over the age of 65 were "online," as compared with 56 percent of 30 to 49 year-olds and 36 percent of 50 to 64 year-olds (Pew Internet and American Life Project, 2005). As of 2017, 67 percent of Americans over the age of 65 report going "online," and smartphone ownership in older adulthood ranges from 59 percent ownership among 65 to 69 year olds, 49 percent among 70 to 74 year olds, 31 percent among 75 to 79 year olds, and 17 percent among those aged 80 or older (Pew Internet and American Life Project, 2017). This suggests that the opportunities to involve older adults in creative technologies have been increasing. However, most research on consumer interaction with technology has focused on younger adults, and largely ignored the many opportunities for engaging older adults with creative technology.

There are a number of ways in which older adults could benefit from the use of creative forms of technology to improve social interactions, health, and safety (Fozard, Bouma, Franco, and Bronswijk, 2009; Fozard, Rietsema, Bouma, and Graafmans, 2000). Older adults use various types of online communication including email, instant messaging, and online forums (Xie, 2008) in order to connect with family and friends (Thayer and Ray, 2006), cope with grief (Opalinski, 2001), and deal with limited mobility (Alexy, 2000). Older adults also use computers and the Internet to seek information (Blake, 1998; Opalinski, 2001), particularly in the areas of health, education, and productivity (Rosenthal, 2008; White and Weatherall, 2000). Creative technologies, including mobile applications, may improve older adult experiences of fun and life satisfaction (Fozard et al., 2000, 2009). For example, older adults tend to use the Internet to engage in hobbies like genealogy (White and Weatherall, 2000).

As an open, interactive advertising platform, the Internet provides ample opportunities for consumers to participate in firms' online marketing communications (Bruner and Kumar, 2000; Liu and Shrum, 2009; Macias, 2003; Singh and Dalal, 1999; Van Doren, Fechner, and Green-Adelsberger, 2000). An increasing number of companies are indeed encouraging consumers to apply their creativity and contribute to firms' online marketing activities.

If consumers have autonomy and feel competent while engaging in creative activities, they are more likely to enjoy the experience (Dahl and Moreau, 2007). However, older adults do not always feel a sense of autonomy and competence when using technology (Wagner, Hassanein, and Head, 2010). Thus, special considerations are needed when developing technologies for older adults to ensure that the technology suits their needs and preferences (Wagner, Hassanein, and Head, 2010). This includes using easy-to-read fonts, making functions and applications user-friendly and easy to interact with (e.g., layouts that require less precise mouse movements, interfaces that use low frequency sounds; cf. Hawthorn, 2000), and ensuring that the technology resonates with what they find interesting. Designing technologies that meet the needs and preferences of older adults will likely increase their use of technology as a medium for engaging in creative activities.

Possible Downsides to Engaging Older Adults in Creative Processes

This chapter has largely focused on the positive associations with and consequences of creativity on different facets of well-being. However, evidence suggests that in some circumstances, creativity can both elicit and arise from negative emotions. As mentioned earlier, engaging in creative activities when mortality is salient can lead to negative emotions like guilt (Arndt et al., 1999). Evidence suggests that intense negative emotions can generate powerful, self-reflective thought and perseverance, leading to increased creativity (De Dreu, Baas, and Nijstad, 2008; Kaufman and Baer, 2002; Verhaeghen, Joorman, and Khan, 2005). Biological vulnerability to depression, social rejection, and negative emotions have also all been shown to lead to greater artistic creativity (Akinola and Mendes, 2008).

Similarly, people in creative professions tend to have decrements in both their objective and subjective well-being. Historical figures in a variety of creative domains, ranging from Emily Dickinson to Robert Schumann to Vincent Van Gogh, suffered from depression and other mood disorders (Goodwin, Jamison, and Goodwin, 1990; Ramey and Weisberg, 2004; Weisberg, 1994). Clinical, empirical, and biographical studies of creative individuals have shown that those in the creative arts suffer from significantly higher rates of mood disorders compared to matched controls (Andreasen, 1987; Ludwig, 1995). Mood disorders have been reported to be eight to ten times more prevalent in writers and artists than in the general population (Jamison, 1993). On a practical level, excess creativity may be detrimental if creators invest in unproven ideas at the expense of improving or expanding upon already proven ideas (Gabora and Tseng, 2017).

These findings, together, suggest that creative processes may not be universally beneficial or necessarily linked to well-being. More research is needed to understand to what extent these findings generalize to creativity and well-being in older adulthood. Future research should elucidate the psychological and contextual conditions in which creativity can provide the greatest benefits to older adults' well-being and those in which it would be best for older adults to avoid creative endeavors.

Future Research on Creativity and Aging

This chapter has reviewed a number of ways in which creative processes positively benefit both objective and subjective well-being across the adult lifespan and into older age. However, there is a critical need for future research on creativity and aging to better understand when and how creative processes promote greater well-being, as well as when and how creativity can lead to reductions in well-being. Several broad questions and directions for future research are proposed here:

1. What is the ideal type of creative process for promoting well-being? Future research should investigate the contexts in which different forms of creativity (e.g., artistic activities, product generation) are more beneficial than others. In some contexts, optimal creative performance may require elaboration and analytic processing with close attention to detail (Mackie and Worth, 1991; Schwarz, Higgins, and Sorrentino, 1990). In other contexts, creative states and performances may require reliance on rapid, less effortful heuristic strategies that do not require systematic and analytic processing (Fiedler, 2000; Isen, Daubman, and Nowicki, 1987). Future research could directly examine the processing styles underlying creativity to determine when the different types of creative processes are most effective for enhancing older adults' well-being.

2. How do emotional states interact with creativity to impact well-being? Although the scope of this discussion has focused on ways in which creativity elicits positive emotions, there is also evidence to suggest that creativity can elicit negative emotions in some situations (e.g., when mortality is made salient; Arndt et al., 1999), and that negative emotions (Akinola and Mendes,

2008) can enhance creativity. Ambient mood states that are unrelated to the creative task can also strongly influence how people approach creative problems. In one meta-analysis, Baas, De Dreu, and Nijstad (2008) proposed a dual pathway model of creativity. In this model, activating negative moods enhanced creative fluency and originality through increased perseverance, whereas activating positive moods enhanced creative fluency and originality through greater cognitive flexibility. Future research should aim to determine how different emotional states influence creativity and associated well-being across the lifespan.

3. What is the optimal level of creativity for promoting different types of well-being? Despite extensive research showing the positive impact of creativity on several facets of older adults' well-being, empirical studies of creative individuals suggest that high levels of creativity can be associated with poor mental health (e.g., Akinola and Mendes, 2008; Andreasen, 1987; Ludwig, 1995) and wasted effort (Gabora and Tseng, 2017). Future research should seek to elucidate what level of creativity is most likely to enhance well-being in older adults.

4. How should creative activities be framed to enhance well-being? Research has shown that not all approaches to creativity are equivalent. For instance, if the creative problems are too well-defined or structured (e.g., there is a very specific goal), the creativity of the product suffers (Moreau and Engeset, 2016). However, providing restrictions for creativity in domains of expertise (e.g., cooking) can also boost creativity (Sellier and Dahl, 2011). Future research should seek to understand different approaches to creative activities that may enhance well-being in older adults.

5. Is well-being an antecedent or an outcome of creativity? We have largely focused on examining the role of creativity in improving well-being. However, it is likely that the relationship between creativity and well-being is more complex. For example, people who are physically or mentally healthier or feel more life satisfaction may also be more willing to engage in creative activities for enjoyment. Future research should seek to understand to what extent well-being is an antecedent (versus outcome) of creativity. Research should also determine how best to engage people in creative activities when they are already lower on objective and/or subjective well-being.

6. In what ways can creative technology be used to promote well-being in older adults? As discussed earlier, older adults can benefit from the use of creative forms of technology for improving social interactions, health, and safety (Fozard et al., 2000, 2009). There are a number of creative ways that consumers can interact with technology. Recent reports have suggested that older adults are becoming savvier with the use of technology, notwithstanding their greater difficulty engaging with technology compared to younger adults (see Wagner et al., 2010 for a review). Some older adults refrain from or are incapable of engaging with technology because they do not perceive

a benefit (Mann, Belchior, Tomita, and Kemp, 2005; Melenhorst, Rogers, and Bouwhuis, 2006), and/or lack motivation (Carpenter and Buday, 2007; Morris, Goodman, and Brading, 2007; Peacock and Künemund, 2007; Selwyn, Gorard, Furlong, and Madden, 2003), knowledge (Ng, 2007; Opalinski, 2001), access (Peacock and Künemund, 2007) or physical support (Carpenter and Buday, 2007; Saunders, 2004). Future research should explore how new forms of creativity (e.g., "creative technology") affect the well-being of older adults and how older adults can better adapt to these new forms of creative technology.

Conclusion

This chapter reviews the existing literature on the positive influences of creativity on objective and subjective forms of well-being in older adulthood, considers the implications of creativity on consumer behavior across the adult lifespan, discusses possible negative consequences of creativity, and highlights a number of future research directions.

Our framework outlining the influence of creativity on subjective and objective well-being is organized around extant research related to creativity and aging. We wish to acknowledge that other metrics of well-being, or different forms of objective and subjective well-being, exist and would be essential to test in future investigations.

Future research on creativity and aging should seek to test the ideas proposed herein and any additional questions that will advance our understanding of how and when creative processes influence both objective and subjective well-being in older adults. These investigations will provide valuable information about the contexts in which creativity not only improves objective and subjective well-being, but when it can be detrimental to older adults' well-being.

References

Adnan, A., Beaty, R., Silvia, P., Spreng, R. N., & Turner, G. R. (2019). Creative aging: Functional brain networks associated with divergent thinking in older and younger adults. *Neurobiology of Aging, 75*, 150–158. doi:10.1016/j.neurobiolaging.2018.11.004.

Akinola, M., & Mendes, W. B. (2008). The dark side of creativity: Biological vulnerability and negative emotions lead to greater artistic creativity. *Personality and Social Psychology Bulletin, 34*(12), 1677–1686. doi:10.1177/0146167208323933.

Alexy, E. M. (2000). Computers and caregiving: Reaching out and redesigning interventions for homebound older adults and caregivers. *Holistic Nursing Practice, 14*(4), 60–66. Retrieved from https://journals.lww.com/hnpjournal/Fulltext/2000/07000/Comp uters_and_Caregiving__Reaching_Out_and.9.aspx.

American Psychological Association (2017). *Older Adults' Health and Age-Related Changes: Reality Versus Myth* [PDF File]. Retrieved from https://www.apa.org/pi/aging/resour ces/guides/myth-reality.pdf.

Andreasen, N. C. (1987). Creativity and mental illness: Prevalence rates in writers and their first-degree relatives. *The American Journal of Psychiatry*, *144*(10), 1288–1292. doi:10.1176/ajp.144.10.1288.

Arndt, J., Greenberg, J., Solomon, S., Pyszczynski, T., & Schimel, J. (1999). Creativity and terror management: Evidence that creative activity increases guilt and social projection following mortality salience. *Journal of Personality and Social Psychology*, *77*(1), 19–32. doi:10.1037/0022-3514.77.1.19.

Baas, M., De Dreu, C. K. W., & Nijstad, B. A. (2008). A meta-analysis of 25 years of mood-creativity research: Hedonic tone, activation, or regulatory focus? *Psychological Bulletin*, *134*(6), 779–806. doi:10.1037/a0012815.

Becker, E. (1973). *The Denial of Death*. New York, NY: Free Press.

Bellass, S., Balmer, A., May, V., Keady, J., Buse, C., Capstick, A., Burke, L., Bartlett, R., & Hodgson, J. (2019). Broadening the debate on creativity and dementia: A critical approach. *Dementia*, *18*(7–8), 2799–2820. doi:10.1177/1471301218760906.

Blake, M. (1998). Libraries, the internet and older people. *New Review of Information Networking*, *4*(1), 23–38. doi:10.1080/13614579809516915.

Bruner, G. C., & Kumar, A. (2000). Web commercials and advertising hierarchy-of-effects. *Journal of Advertising Research*, *40*(1–2), 35–42. doi:10.2501/jar-40-1-2-35-42.

Burroughs, J. E., Dahl, D. W., Moreau, C. P., Chattopadhyay, A., & Gorn, G. J. (2011). Facilitating and rewarding creativity during new product development. *Journal of Marketing*, *75*(4), 53–67. doi:10.1509/jmkg.75.4.53.

Burroughs, J. E., & Mick, G. D. (2004). Exploring antecedents and consequences of consumer creativity in a problem-solving context. *Journal of Consumer Research*, *31*(2), 402–411. doi:10.1086/422118.

Carpenter, B. D., & Buday, S. (2007). Computer use among older adults in a naturally occurring retirement community. *Computers in Human Behavior*, *23*(6), 3012–3024. doi:10.1016/j.chb.2006.08.015.

Carpenter, S., Chae, R., & Yoon, C. (2020). Creativity and aging: Positive consequences of distraction. *Psychology and Aging*. Forthcoming.

Carstensen, L. L., Pasupathi, M., Mayr, U., & Nesselroade, J. R. (2000). Emotional experience in everyday life across the adult life span. *Journal of Personality and Social Psychology*, *79*(4), 644–655. doi:10.1037/0022-3514.79.4.644.

Carstensen, L. L., Turan, B., Scheibe, S., Ram, N., Ersner-Hershfield, H., Samanez-Larkin, G. R., Brooks, K. P., & Nesselroade, J. R. (2011). Emotional experience improves with age: Evidence based on over 10 years of experience sampling. *Psychology and Aging*, *26*(1), 21–33. doi:10.1037/a0021285.

Chancellor, B., Duncan, A., & Chatterjee, A. (2014). Art therapy for Alzheimer's disease and other dementias. *Journal of Alzheimer's Disease*, *39*(1), 1–11. doi:10.3233/JAD-131295.

Charles, S. T., & Carstensen, L. L. (2009). Socioemotional selectivity theory. In: H. T. Reis & S. Sprecher (Eds.), *Encyclopedia of Human Relationships* (pp. 1578–1581). Thousand Oaks, CA: Sage.

Charles, S. T., Reynolds, C. A., & Gatz, M. (2001). Age-related differences and change in positive and negative affect over 23 years. *Journal of Personality and Social Psychology*, *80*(1), 136–151. doi:10.1037/0022-3514.80.1.136.

Cohen, G. (2006). Research on creativity and aging: The positive impact of the arts on health and illness. *Generations*, *30*(1), 7–15. Retrieved from http://proquest.umi.com, Document ID: 1070989031.

Cohen, G. D., Perlstein, S., Chapline, J., Kelly, J., Firth, K. M., & Simmens, S. (2006). The impact of professionally conducted cultural programs on the physical health, mental health, and social functioning of older adults. *The Gerontologist, 46*(6), 726–734. doi:10.1093/geront/46.6.726.

Coyle, C. E., & Dugan, E. (2012). Social isolation, loneliness and health among older adults. *Journal of Aging and Health, 24*(8), 1346–1363. doi:10.1177/0898264312460275.

Cruz-Ferreira, A., Marmeleira, J., Formigo, A., Gomes, D., & Fernandes, J. (2015). Creative dance improves physical fitness and life satisfaction in older women. *Research on Aging, 37*(8), 837–855. doi:10.1177/0164027514568103.

Dahl, D. W., & Moreau, C. P. (2007). Thinking inside the box: Why consumers enjoy constrained creative experiences. *Journal of Marketing Research, 44*(3), 357–369. doi:10.1509/jmkr.44.3.357.

Daykin, N., Mansfield, L., Meads, C., Julier, G., Tomlinson, A., Payne, A., Grigsby Duffy, L., Lane, J., D'Innocenzo, G., Burnett, A., Kay, T., Dolan, P., Testoni, S., & Victor, C. (2018). What works for wellbeing? A systematic review of wellbeing outcomes for music and singing in adults. *Perspectives in Public Health, 138*(1), 39–46. doi:10.1177/1757913917740391.

De Dreu, C. K. W., Baas, M., & Nijstad, B. A. (2008). Hedonic tone and activation level in the mood-creativity link: Toward a dual pathway to creativity model. *Journal of Personality and Social Psychology, 94*(5), 739–756. doi:10.1037/0022-3514.94.5.739.

De Petrillo, L., & Winner, E. (2005). Does art improve mood? A test of a key assumption underlying art therapy. *Art Therapy, 22*(4), 205–212. doi:10.1080/07421656.2005.101 29521.

Drake, J. E., Coleman, K., & Winner, E. (2011). Short-term mood repair through art: Effects of medium and strategy. *Art Therapy, 28*(1), 26–30. doi:10.1080/07421656.2 011.557032.

Dunphy, K., Baker, F. A., Dumaresq, E., Carroll-Haskins, K., Eickholt, J., Ercole, M., Kaimal, G., Meyer, K., Sajnani, N., Shamir, O. Y., & Wosch, T. (2019). Creative arts interventions to address depression in older adults: A systematic review of outcomes, processes, and mechanisms. *Frontiers in Psychology, 9*(2655). doi:10.3389/fpsyg.2018.02655.

Fiedler, K. (2000). Toward an integrative account of affect and cognition phenomena using the BIAS computer algorithm. In: J. Forgas (Ed.), *Feeling and Thinking: The Role of Affect in Social Cognition* (pp. 223–252). New York, NY: Cambridge University Press.

Finke, R. A., Ward, T. B., & Smith, S. M. (1992). *Creative Cognition: Theory, Research, and Applications*. Cambridge, MA: The MIT Press.

Fisher, B. J., & Specht, D. K. (1999). Successful aging and creativity in later life. *Journal of Aging Studies, 13*(4), 457–472. doi:10.1016/S0890-4065(99)00021-3.

Flood, M., & Phillips, K. D. (2007). Creativity in older adults: A plethora of possibilities. *Issues in Mental Health Nursing, 28*(4), 389–411. doi:10.1080/01612840701252956.

Fozard, J. L., Bouma, H., Franco, A., & Bronswijk, V. J. E. M. H. (2009). Homo ludens: Adult creativity and quality of life. *Gerontechnology, 8*(4), 187–196. doi:25-f1b1c0e3-340a -4094-aaac-05008da9c583.

Fozard, J. L., Rietsema, J., Bouma, H., & Graafmans, J. A. M. (2000). Gerontechnology: Creating enabling environments for the challenges and opportunities of aging. *Educational Gerontology, 26*(4), 331–344. doi:10.1080/036012700407820.

Gabora, L., & Tseng, S. (2017). The social benefits of balancing creativity and imitation: Evidence from an agent-based model. *Psychology of Aesthetics, Creativity, and the Arts, 11*(4), 403–419. doi:10.1037/aca0000132.

Goff, K. (1993). Creativity and life satisfaction of older adults. *Educational Gerontology, 19*(3), 241–250. doi:10.1080/0360127930190304.

Goodwin, F. K., & Jamison, K. R. (1990). Suicide. In F. K. Goodwin & K. R. Jamison (Eds), *Manic Depressive Illness* (pp. 227–244). New York, NY: Oxford University Press.

Gortner, E.-M., Rude, S. S., & Pennebaker, J. W. (2006). Benefits of expressive writing in lowering rumination and depressive symptoms. *Behavior Therapy, 37*(3), 292–303. doi:10.1016/j.beth.2006.01.004.

Greaves, C. J., & Farbus, L. (2006). Effects of creative and social activity on the health and well-being of socially isolated older people: Outcomes from a multi-method observational study. *The Journal of the Royal Society for the Promotion of Health, 126*(3), 134–142. doi:10.1177/1466424006064303.

Hanna, G. (2006). Focus on creativity and aging in the United States. *Generations, 30*(1), 47–49. Retrieved from https://www.ingentaconnect.com/content/asag/gen/2006/00 000030/00000001/art00011.

Hart, T. A., Chaparro, B. S., & Halcomb, C. G. (2008). Evaluating websites for older adults: Adherence to 'senior-friendly' guidelines and end-user performance. *Behaviour and Information Technology, 27*(3), 191–199. doi:10.1080/01449290600802031.

Hasher, L., & Zacks, R. T. (1988). Working memory, comprehension, and aging: A review and a new view. In: G. H. Bower (Ed.), *Psychology of Learning and Motivation* (Vol. 22, pp. 193–225). San Diego, CA: Academic Press.

Hasher, L., Zacks, R. T., & May, C. P. (1999). Inhibitory control, circadian arousal, and age. In D. Gopher & A. Koriat (Eds.), *Attention and Performance XVII: Cognitive Regulation of Performance: Interaction of Theory and Application.* (pp. 653–675). Cambridge, MA: The MIT Press.

Hawthorn, D. (2000). Possible implications of aging for interface designers. *Interacting with Computers, 12*(5), 507–528. doi:10.1016/S0953-5438(99)00021-1.

Hays, T., & Minichiello, V. (2005). The contribution of music to quality of life in older people: An Australian qualitative study. *Ageing and Society, 25*(2), 261–278. doi:10.1017/S0144686X04002946.

Heenan, D. (2006). Art as therapy: An effective way of promoting positive mental health? *Disability and Society, 21*(2), 179–191. doi:10.1080/09687590500498143.

Isen, A. M., Daubman, K. A., & Nowicki, G. P. (1987). Positive affect facilitates creative problem solving. *Journal of Personality and Social Psychology, 52*(6), 1122–1131. doi:10.1037/0022-3514.52.6.1122.

Jamison, K. R. (1993). *Touched with Fire.* New York, NY: Free Press.

Jay, E. S., & Perkins, D. N. (1997). Problem finding: The search for mechanism. In: M. A. Runco (Ed.), *The Creativity Research Handbook* (Vol. 1, pp. 257–293). Cresskill, NJ: Hampton.

Kasof, J. (1995). Explaining creativity: The attributional perspective. *Creativity Research Journal, 8*(4), 311–366. doi:10.1207/s15326934crj0804_1.

Kaufman, J. C., & Baer, J. (2002). I bask in dreams of suicide: Mental illness, poetry, and women. *Review of General Psychology, 6*(3), 271–286. doi:10.1037/1089-2680.6.3.271.

Klein, K., & Boals, A. (2001). Expressive writing can increase working memory capacity. *Journal of Experimental Psychology: General, 130*(3), 520–533. doi:10.1037/0096-3445.130.3.520.

Landau, E., & Maoz, B. (1978). Creativity and self-actualization in the aging personality. *American Journal of Psychotherapy, 32*(1), 117–127. doi:10.1176/appi.psychotherapy.1978.32.1.117.

Liddle, J. L. M., Parkinson, L., & Sibbritt, D. W. (2013). Purpose and pleasure in late life: Conceptualising older women's participation in art and craft activities. *Journal of Aging Studies, 27*(4), 330–338. doi:10.1016/j.jaging.2013.08.002.

Liu, Y., & Shrum, L. J. (2009). A dual-process model of interactivity effects. *Journal of Advertising, 38*(2), 53–68. doi:10.2753/JOA0091-3367380204.

Ludwig, A. M. (1995). *The Price of Greatness: Resolving the Creativity and Madness Controversy.* New York, NY: Guilford Press.

Macias, W. (2003). A beginning look at the effects of interactivity, product involvement and web experience on comprehension: Brand web sites as interactive advertising. *Journal of Current Issues and Research in Advertising, 25*(2), 31–44. doi:10.1080/10641734.2003 .10505147.

Mackie, D., & Worth, L. (1991). Emotion and social judgments. In: J. Forgas (Ed.), *Emotion and Social Judgments* (pp. 201–219). Elmsford, NY: Pergamon.

Mann, W. C., Belchior, P., Tomita, M. R., & Kemp, B. J. (2005). Computer use by middle-aged and older adults with disabilities. *Technology and Disability, 17*(1), 1–9. doi:10.3233/ TAD-2005-17101.

Mather, M., & Knight, M. (2005). Goal-directed memory: The role of cognitive control in older adults' emotional memory. *Psychology and Aging, 20*(4), 554–570. doi:10.1037/0882-7974.20.4.554.

Mather, M., & Knight, M. R. (2006). Angry faces get noticed quickly: Threat detection is not impaired among older adults. *The Journals of Gerontology: Series B, 61*(1), 54–57. doi:10.1093/geronb/61.1.P54.

McHugh, M. C. (2016). Experiencing flow: Creativity and meaningful task engagement for senior women. *Women and Therapy, 39*(3–4), 280–295. doi:10.1080/02703149.201 6.1116862.

Melenhorst, A.-S., Rogers, W. A., & Bouwhuis, D. G. (2006). Older adults' motivated choice for technological innovation: Evidence for benefit-driven selectivity. *Psychology and Aging, 21*(1), 190–195. doi:10.1037/0882-7974.21.1.190.

Mochon, D., Norton, M. I., & Ariely, D. (2012). Bolstering and restoring feelings of competence via the IKEA effect. *International Journal of Research in Marketing, 29*(4), 363–369. doi:10.1016/j.ijresmar.2012.05.001.

Moreau, C. P., & Dahl, D. W. (2005). Designing the solution: The impact of constraints on consumers' creativity. *Journal of Consumer Research, 32*(1), 13–22. doi:10.1086/429597.

Moreau, C. P., & Engeset, M. G. (2016). The downstream consequences of problem-solving mindsets: How playing with lego influences creativity. *Journal of Marketing Research, 53*(1), 18–30. doi:10.1509/jmr.13.0499.

Morris, A., Goodman, J., & Brading, H. (2007). Internet use and non-use: Views of older users. *Universal Access in the Information Society, 6*(1), 43–57. doi:10.1007/s10209-006-0057-5.

Mroczek, D. K., & Kolarz, C. M. (1998). The effect of age on positive and negative affect: A developmental perspective on happiness. *Journal of Personality and Social Psychology, 75*(5), 1333–1349. doi:10.1037/0022-3514.75.5.1333.

Netuveli, G., Wiggins, R. D., Hildon, Z., Montgomery, S. M., & Blane, D. (2006). Quality of life at older ages: Evidence from the English longitudinal study of aging (wave 1). *Journal of Epidemiology and Community Health, 60*(4), 357–363. doi:10.1136/jech.2005.040071.

Ng, C.-H. (2007). Motivation among older adults in learning computing technologies: A grounded model. *Educational Gerontology, 34*(1), 1–14. doi:10.1080/03601270701763845.

Noice, T., Noice, H., & Kramer, A. F. (2014). Participatory arts for older adults: A review of benefits and challenges. *The Gerontologist, 54*(5), 741–753. doi:10.1093/geront/gnt138.

Norton, M. I., Mochon, D., & Ariely, D. (2012). The IKEA effect: When labor leads to love. *Journal of Consumer Psychology, 22*(3), 453–460. doi:10.1016/j.jcps.2011.08.002.

Opalinski, L. (2001). Older adults and the digital divide: Assessing results of a web-based survey. *Journal of Technology in Human Services, 18*(3–4), 203–221. doi:10.1300/ J017v18n03_13.

Osgood, N. J., Meyers, B. S., & Orchowsky, S. (1990). The impact of creative dance and movement training on the life satisfaction of older adults: An exploratory study. *Journal of Applied Gerontology, 9*(3), 255–265. doi:10.1177/073346489000900302.

Palmiero, M., Di Giacomo, D., & Passafiume, D. (2014). Divergent thinking and age-related changes. *Creativity Research Journal, 26*(4), 456–460. doi:10.1080/10400419.2014.961 786.

Patterson, M., & Perlstein, S. (2011). Good for the heart, good for the soul: The creative arts and brain health in later life. *Generations, 35*(2), 27–36. Retrieved from https://www.ing entaconnect.com/content/asag/gen/2011/00000035/00000002/art00005.

Peacock, S. E., & Künemund, H. (2007). Senior citizens and internet technology. *European Journal of Ageing, 4*(4), 191–200. doi:10.1007/s10433-007-0067-z.

Perach, R., & Wisman, A. (2016). Can creativity beat death? A review and evidence on the existential anxiety buffering functions of creative achievement. *The Journal of Creative Behavior, 53*(2), 193–210. doi:10.1002/jocb.171.

Pew Internet and American Life Project (2005). *The Mainstreaming of Online Life.* Retrieved from http://www.pewintenet.org/pdfs/internet_status_2005.pdf.

Pew Internet and American Life Project (2017). *Tech Adoption Climbs Among Older Adults.* Retrieved from http://www.pewinternet.org/2017/05/17/tech-adoption-climbs-a mong-older-adults/.

Ramey, C. H., & Weisberg, R. W. (2004). The "poetical activity" of Emily Dickinson: A further test of the hypothesis that affective disorders foster creativity. *Creativity Research Journal, 16*(2–3), 173–185. doi:10.1080/10400419.2004.9651451.

Rank, O. (1945). *Will Therapy; and, Truth and Reality.* Oxford, England: Knopf.

Reynolds, F. (2004). Conversations about creativity and chronic illness ii: Textile artists coping with long-term health problems reflect on the creative process. *Creativity Research Journal, 16*(1), 79–89. doi:10.1207/s15326934crj1601_8.

Reynolds, F. (2010). 'Colour and communion': Exploring the influences of visual art-making as a leisure activity on older women's subjective well-being. *Journal of Aging Studies, 24*(2), 135–143. doi:10.1016/j.jaging.2008.10.004.

Rosenthal, R. L. (2008). Older computer-literate women: Their motivations, obstacles, and paths to success. *Educational Gerontology, 34*(7), 610–626. doi:10.1080/03601270801949427.

Routledge, C., Arndt, J., & Sheldon, K. M. (2004). Task engagement after mortality salience: The effects of creativity, conformity and connectedness on worldview defence. *European Journal of Social Psychology, 34*(4), 477–487. doi:10.1002/ejsp.209.

Ryff, C.D., & Keyes, C.L.M. (1995). The structure of psychological well-being revisited. *Journal of Personality and Social Psychology, 69*(4), 719–727. doi:10.1037/0022-3514.69.4.719.

Salthouse, T. (2012). Consequences of age-related cognitive declines. *Annual Review of Psychology, 63,* 201–226. doi:10.1146/annurev-psych-120710-100328.

Saunders, E. J. (2004). Maximizing computer use among the elderly in rural senior centers. *Educational Gerontology, 30*(7), 573–585. doi:10.1080/03601270490466967.

Schueller, S. M., & Seligman, M. E. P. (2010). Pursuit of pleasure, engagement, and meaning: Relationships to subjective and objective measures of well-being. *The Journal of Positive Psychology, 5*(4), 253–263. doi:10.1080/17439761003794130.

Schwarz, N. (1990). Feelings as information: Informational and motivational functions of affective states. In: E. T. Higgins & E. M. Sorrentino (Eds.), *Handbook of Motivation and Cognition* (Vol. 2, pp. 527–561). New York, NY: Guilford.

Sellier, A.-L., & Dahl, D. W. (2011). Focus! Creative success is enjoyed through restricted choice. *Journal of Marketing Research, 48*(6), 996–1007. doi:10.1509/jmr.10.0407.

Selwyn, N., Gorard, S., Furlong, J., & Madden, L. (2003). Older adults' use of information and communications technology in everyday life. *Ageing and Society*, *23*(5), 561–582. doi:10.1017/S0144686X03001302.

Singh, S. N., & Dalal, N. P. (1999). Web home pages as advertisements. *Communications of the ACM*, *42*(8), 91–98. doi:10.1145/310930.310978.

Sixsmith, A., & Gibson, G. (2007). Music and the wellbeing of people with dementia. *Ageing and Society*, *27*(1), 127–145. doi:10.1017/S0144686X06005228.

Smith, G. J., & Andersson, G. (1989). Creativity as a key factor in adaptation to old age. *Psychological Research Bulletin*, *29*(7), 24.

Spandler, H., Secker, J., Kent, L., Hacking, S., & Shenton, J. (2007). Catching life: The contribution of arts initiatives to recovery approaches in mental health. *Journal of Psychiatric and Mental Health Nursing*, *14*(8), 791–799. doi:10.1111/j.1365-2850.2007.01174.

Tamannaeifar, M. R., & Motaghedifard, M. (2014). Subjective well-being and its sub-scales among students: The study of role of creativity and self-efficacy. *Thinking Skills and Creativity*, *12*, 37–42. doi:10.1016/j.tsc.2013.12.003.

Thayer, S. E., & Ray, S. (2006). Online communication preferences across age, gender, and duration of Internet use. *Cyberpsychology and Behavior*, *9*(4), 432–440. doi:10.1089/cpb.2006.9.432.

The World Bank, World Development Indicators (2019). *People*. Retrieved from http:// datatopics.worldbank.org/world-development-indicators/themes/people.html#which -indicators-are-new.

Treffinger, D. J., Isaksen, S. G., & Dorval, B. K. (1996). Creative problem solving: An overview. In: M. A. Runco (Ed.), *Problem Finding, Problem Solving, and Creativity* (pp. 223–235). Norwood, NJ: Ablex.

Van Doren, D. C., Fechner, D. L., & Green-Adelsberger, K. (2000). Promotional strategies on the World Wide Web. *Journal of Marketing Communications*, *6*(1), 21–35. doi:10.1080/135272600345534.

Van Lith, T., Schofield, M. J., & Fenner, P. (2013). Identifying the evidence-base for art-based practices and their potential benefit for mental health recovery: A critical review. *Disability and Rehabilitation*, *35*(16), 1309–1323. doi:10.3109/09638288.2012.732188.

Verhaeghen, P., Joorman, J., & Khan, R. (2005). Why we sing the blues: The relation between self-reflective rumination, mood, and creativity. *Emotion*, *5*(2), 226–232. doi:10.1037/1528-3542.5.2.226.

Wagner, N., Hassanein, K., & Head, M. (2010). Computer use by older adults: A multi-disciplinary review. *Computers in Human Behavior*, *26*(5), 870–882. doi:10.1016/j.chb.2010.03.029.

Weisberg, R. W. (1994). Genius and madness?: A Quasi-experimental test of the hypothesis that manic-depression increases creativity. *Psychological Science*, *5*(6), 361–367. doi:10.1111/j.1467-9280.1994.tb00286.x.

White, J., & Weatherall, A. (2000). A grounded theory analysis of older adults and information technology. *Educational Gerontology*, *26*(4), 371–386. doi:10.1080/036012700407857.

Xie, B. (2008). Multimodal computer-mediated communication and social support among older Chinese internet users. *Journal of Computer-Mediated Communication*, *13*(3), 728–750. doi:10.1111/j.1083-6101.2008.00417.

Yalom, I. D. (1980). *Existential Psychotherapy I*. New York, NY: Basic Books New York.

15

ARE YOUNG ADULTS MORE NARCISSISTIC THAN OLDER ADULTS?

*Cassandra D. Davis, Alexandra Polyakova,
Anand V. Bodapati and Aimee Drolet*

Introduction

Older generations often characterize younger generations as self-centered, caring only about themselves with little regard for others or society as a whole. The Depression-era generation labeled its Baby Boomer offspring the "Me Generation," which is essentially the same label that the Baby Boomer generation now uses to characterize its own Millennial offspring ("Generation Me"). The recurring theme is that young adults are more narcissistic (i.e., egoistic vs. altruistic) in comparison to their older adult counterparts. However, research findings regarding the relationship between age and having narcissistic values and goals are mixed. Some past studies have shown that young (vs. older) adults are more likely to: (1) hold values that align with sub-clinical narcissism, a "self-admiration that is characterized by tendencies toward grandiose ideas, fantasied talents, exhibitionism, and defensiveness in response to criticism; interpersonal relationships … characterized by feelings of entitlement, exploitativeness, and a lack of empathy" (Raskin and Terry, 1988, p. 896); and (2) pursue narcissistic goals, such as being in a position of leadership or authority and having high self-esteem (e.g., Twenge, Campbell, and Freeman, 2012). Yet, other studies find no relationship between age and the possession of narcissistic values and goals (Trzesniewski, Donnellan, and Robins, 2008; Donnellan, Trzesniewski, and Robins, 2009; Wetzel et al., 2017) or a positive relationship (e.g., Arnett, Trzesniewski, and Donnellan, 2013).

Interestingly, irrespective of studies' mixed findings regarding the nature of the relationship between age and narcissism, research reveals that *both* older adults and young adults view young adults as more narcissistic compared to older adults (c.f., Trzesniewski and Donnellan, 2014). Understanding potential differences due to age in the possession of more egoistic tendencies (e.g., materialism) versus altruistic tendencies (e.g., civic engagement) is important from both a marketing and public policy perspective. For example, in order to target consumers more efficiently, marketers frequently rely on psychographic segmentations plans which are derived from data on consumers' personal traits, values, and goals, in addition to socioeconomic and demographic data (age, race/ethnicity, income, etc.). By specifically targeting consumers' personal values, advertisers can increase consumers' motivation to process an advertisement and felt involvement with the advertised product, thereby increasing ad effectiveness.

Overview of Chapter

This chapter reviews the mix of empirical findings with respect to the nature of the relationship between age and expressions of sub-clinical narcissism. Our review suggests that young (vs. older) adults may exhibit more narcissistic characteristics compared to older adults, but these differences and their underlying causes may be more complex than is generally acknowledged. First, we discuss numerous past studies that investigated differences in the incidence of narcissistic values (e.g., high self-esteem) among young adults and then older adults, paying special attention to whether age per se or cohort effects. Second, we consider whether the higher incidence of narcissistic behavior among young adults is driven by egoism (self-interest) whereas the lower incidence among older adults is driven by altruism (selflessness), focusing specifically on the complexities of altruism (and the inherent vagueness of behavior). We then follow-up by examining two domains of behavior: materialism and civic engagement. This chapter concludes with a discussion of potential future research opportunities.

Age and Narcissism

Elevated Narcissism among Young Adults

Numerous studies document differences in values based on age. Most studies show that young adults and younger age cohorts hold more narcissistic values. For example, previous studies have found that older adults are less likely to exhibit psychological entitlement, a narcissistic personality trait characterized by selfish, aggressive, and unethical behavior across domains (Campbell et al., 2004; Boyd and Helms, 2005; Butori, 2010). In general, psychological entitlement is viewed as having a negative impact on social behavior. Both social investment theory (Roberts and Wood, 2006) and the maturity principle (Caspi, Roberts, and Shiner, 2005) suggest that psychological entitlement decreases with age as younger individuals engage with social institutions and reach societal milestones such as entering the workforce, getting married, and caring for children and elderly parents. This suggestion is supported by research that finds a negative association between psychological entitlement and age-related roles (e.g., parent) (Roberts, Edmonds, and Grijalva, 2010).

In addition, young adults place more value on achieving narcissistic goals, such as acquiring fame and fortune (Twenge et al., 2012). They place more emphasis on social status. However, regardless of their desire for higher social status, young adults have a lower need for social approval (Twenge et al., 2008). Young adults also value leisure more than older adults do. Correspondingly, young adults exhibit a poorer work ethic, perhaps because older adults view work as more central to their lives (e.g., Twenge and Kasser, 2013). Young adults hold fewer altruistic work values, such as having a job that helps others and or a job with societal worth.

The importance placed on narcissistic values can be harmful to individuals and society given that behaviors based on these values may lead to risky health behaviors (Williams, Hedberg, Cox, and Deci, 2000), bad spending habits (Roberts and Pirog, 2004), poor learning outcomes due to lower persistence (Vansteenkiste et al., 2008), and lower well-being (Kasser and Ryan, 1996). Moreover, the possession of narcissistic values leads to incivility and a pronounced tendency to objectify, derogate, and exploit others (Kasser et al., 2004).

However, there are three things to note regarding studies that find more pronounced narcissistic tendencies among young (vs. older) adults. First, young adults also hold values that that are viewed as less egocentric. For example, young adults are more likely to support gender equality (Huddy, Neely, and Lafay, 2000). They are also less likely to endorse prejudicial views (Firebaugh and Davis, 1988). However, this age difference may be the result of self-regulatory failure among older adults rather than lower levels of prejudice among young adults (Gonsalkorale, Sherman, and Klauer, 2009).

Second, although most studies find that young adults are more narcissistic, several do not (e.g., Arnett, Trzesniewski, and Donnellan, 2013; Trzesniewski, Donnellan, and Robins, 2008; Wetzel et al., 2017). The mix in findings appears at least partly due to differences in testing methods, specifically whether they tested for the effect of (chronological) age versus generational cohort. Age effects are the result of influences related to the biological aging process, whereas cohort effects are the result of influences of membership in a generational cohort and socialization differences across generations. Indeed, some findings can be attributed an age effect whereby narcissistic values decline over the lifespan, from adolescence to maturity. Other studies based on qualitative interviews suggest that differences in narcissistic tendencies are due to a cohort effect whereby younger generations exhibit stronger narcissistic tendencies compared to older generations. However, this conclusion is clearly an oversimplification. Members of the older Baby Boomer generation (Me Generation) appear more egoistic than members of the middle-aged X-Generation, yet members of the younger Millennial generation (Generation Me) view narcissistic values and goals more favorably compared to Gen-Xers.

Third, previous studies have relied on a variety of data analytic methods. In particular, some studies rely on cross-sectional data analysis, for example a comparison of different cohorts at a specific point in time. Other studies use time-lag data analysis that allows one to compare different groups at a specific age. Studies also use longitudinal data to compare individuals over time. For example, Chopik and Grill (2019) followed individuals from adolescence to old age. Their longitudinal analysis challenges the notion that individuals become less narcissistic as they age. Specifically, their analysis shows that narcissism remains relatively stable across the lifespan.

Increased Altruism among Older Adults

Generally speaking, older (vs. young) adults appear to behave more altruistically, i.e., in a less self-focused and more other-focused way.

Older Adults' Social Behavior

In particular, older adults place greater value on the quality rather than the quantity of their social relationships versus the quantity. Indeed, there are significant age effects on the composition and size of their social networks. Older adults tend to have smaller social networks but report experiencing more positive emotions when interacting with their social partners (Charles and Piazza, 2007) and rate their social networks as more satisfying (Lansford, Sherman, and Antonucci, 1998). Older (vs. young) adults are more concerned about maintaining close personal connections and exert more effort on maintaining social relationships (Lang, Wagner, Wrzus, and Neyer, 2013). They are also more selective with respect to whether a relationship should be closer or more distant (Carstensen and Charles, 1998). These findings may be explained by the composition of the social networks of older adults versus young adults. Young adults' social networks consist of more novel acquaintances and weaker ties that reflect a lower interest in and desire for strong close relationships.

Socioemotional selectivity theory provides a causal account for these social network changes that occur over the adult lifespan (Carstensen, Isaacowitz, and Charles, 1999). When time is perceived as limited, emotional goals assume primacy and close social relationships become more important and receive more attention. Older adults, who are nearer the end of their lives, tend to view time as more limited, whereas younger adults tend to view time as more expansive. As a result, older (vs. younger) adults generally have smaller social networks composed primarily of family and friends (vs. novel acquaintances) who tend to be more positive and reliable relationship partners. Increasing age leads individuals to put more effort into maintaining and supporting their relationship partners, which accords with the widely held perception that older adults are more altruistic.

In part, older adults appear more altruistic insofar as they express greater care for the community and greater interest in community matters in comparison to young adults. For example, older adults donate more of their time to the community They volunteer and vote at higher rates. Older adults also help younger adults successfully transition to adulthood. From a community standpoint, this help is extremely valuable (Erikson, 1985). In addition, older adults are more likely to engage in more informal kinds of volunteering with respect to their social networks (Martinez, Crooks, Kim, and Tanner, 2011). For example, research on digital gaming demonstrates that older individuals are more desirous of socializing and their socializing is relatively more focused on helping other players versus competing with them (Gajadhar, Nap, de Kort, and IJsselsteijn, 2010).

Older Adults as Caregivers

Another key reason why older adults are generally viewed as more altruistic is that older adults are more likely than young adults are to occupy the role of caregiver. Accordingly, the perception that older adults are less selfish and more compassionate than young adults (Plutzer and Berkman, 2005) may be a result of seeing older adults as caregivers for children and elderly parents more often (Grundy and Henretta, 2006). Further, perception that older adults are warmer and friendlier may also be due to older adults' more frequent appearance in the caregiving role.

Although older (vs. younger) individuals are generally viewed as warmer and friendlier, they also may be viewed as less competent (Cuddy and Fiske, 2002). This, of course, does a disservice to older adults, especially considering the many societal contributions they make. The perception of older adults as warm and friendly but less competent may be driven by older individuals' declining participation in competitive social roles, as well as by the impression that older individuals have fewer agentic goals and a relatively low status in society.

Workplace Behavior

In the workplace, older employees are viewed as more reliable, hard-working, and loyal. They are less tardy, less likely to engage in workplace aggression, and have fewer instances of on-the-job substance use (Steinberg et al., 1994).

However, older employees are less interested in transactional contracts (economic exchanges) and relational contracts (economic exchanges that are tied to relationships) (Bal and Kooij, 2011). This disinterest may result in a shift in work-life balance and close social relationship goals. This supposition fits with socioemotional selectivity theory (Carstensen and Charles, 1998). As people age, they focus more on close personal relationships that provide positive emotional benefits; presumably fewer of these relationships are workplace relationships.

In addition, research on older employees' organizational citizenship behaviors, which are prosocial behaviors that promote organizational effectiveness and efficiency support mixed findings (Jones and Schaubroeck, 2004; Li, Liang, and Crant, 2010). For example, Streufert, Pogash, Piasecki, and Post (1990) show that teams with more older employees and fewer young and middle-age employees are slower to respond, less likely to search for information, make fewer decisions, and act less strategically.

Many of the complaints about older team members may be due to inter-generational differences. For example, older (vs. younger) employees may be less familiar with newer ideas, methods, and technologies, causing them to feel less confident and more hesitant to make decisions. Older individuals may also have difficulty relating to, understanding, and appreciating younger individuals' views, ideas, and opinions, thereby making group cohesion and group decision-making more difficult. Thus, in the workplace context, older adults can appear less altruistic and more narcissistic.

This mix of results with respect to the workplace may not be due to a generational cohort effect rather than an age effect given that older adults examined in the aforementioned studies on workplace behavior are members of the Baby Boomer generation. Baby Boomers have been characterized as more materialistic and status-seeking than (younger) Gen-Xers. Some past research implicates the trait of individualism as a cause of young adults' narcissistic values and goals (e.g., Konrath, O'Brien, and Hsing, 2011), and Baby Boomers have been characterized as valuing individualism highly (Williams, Page, Petrosky, and Hernandez, 2010). However, Gen-Xers also value individualism (e.g., self-expression and anti-conformity) even though they appear less narcissistic compared to Baby Boomers.

Egoism or Altruism?

As mentioned in the introduction, both young and older adults view young adults as more egoistic compared to older adults who are more altruistic. And, most empirical studies (e.g., Frankenberger, 2000) show that younger adults, especially adolescents, are more egotistical (self-focused and self-interested) in comparison to older adults. For example, research by Sze, Gyurak, and Levenso (2012) reveals that empathic concern is higher among older (vs. younger) individuals. Further, older individuals are more likely to donate to charitable causes (Carpenter, Connolly, and Myers, 2008; Pornpattananangkul, Chowdhury, Feng, and Yu, 2019), although this could be due to the fact that older (vs. younger) individuals tend to be wealthier. These studies along with other studies find that altruistic behavior increases with age (Rushton et al., 1986; Matsumoto, Yamagishi, Li, and Kiyonari, 2016).

However, although older adults behave more altruistically, their reasons for doing so may be the result of egoistic goal pursuit. Research by Hubbard, Harbaugh, Srivastava, Degras, and Mayr (2016) demonstrates that neural activities in the value and reward sections of the brain are stimulated when people witness money being transferred to charities. Further, individuals experience a robust increase in these neural activities as they increase in age. Hubbard et al. (2016) suggest that this phenomenon is one reason why older (vs. young) adults are more altruistic: They derive more physical pleasure from altruistic behavior. Socioemotional selectivity theory offers another (egoistic) reason why older people behave more altruistically. Specifically, as people age, they seek more emotionally fulfilling activities. Older people who engage in these activities are viewed more favorably by others (Freund and Blanchard-Fields, 2014) which benefits them emotionally (Musick et al., 1999). The altruistic behavior of older adults has other emotional benefits, including increased feelings of autonomy, vitality, well-being, and self-esteem (Sheldon and Kasser, 1995). Accordingly, altruistic conduct has a positive effect on older individuals' ego-integrity (Van Hiel and Vansteenkiste, 2009).

Thus, one is left to wonder whether the increase in altruistic behavior among older adults actually reflects an increased desire to help others or increased egoism. In other words, should people (of any age) be considered selfish for performing good deeds just because those acts may also provide emotional or physical benefits to themselves? Are these acts in fact a reflection of altruism versus egoism? These questions have caused some researchers to redefine altruism. In particular, Batson (1991) defines altruism as a motivational state that causes people to promote the welfare of others. This redefinition focuses on the good acts that people perform without consideration of the root causes of these acts.

This redefinition is an implicit acknowledgement of three realities. The first is that the textbook definition of altruism as behavior that is motivated by a selfless desire to help others solely for others' sake is difficult to confirm because it is very difficult to identify and disentangle human motives. The second reality is that good acts do not have to fit the textbook definition of altruism in order to be acknowledged and appreciated. The third reality is that good acts can be performed by bad people. For example, drug lords who terrorize communities will also make donations to these communities and its religious institutions (Sheridan, 1997). And, although widely scorned, tobacco manufacturers also engage in socially responsible public initiatives. A significant portion of their revenue pays for state governments' anti-tobacco initiatives.

Regardless of how altruism is defined, it is clear that older adults benefit greatly from behaving altruistically. For example, volunteering is associated with higher life satisfaction (Van Willigen, 2000) and lower depression levels (Musick and Wilson, 2003). It also has positive physical benefits (Moen, Dempster-McClain, and Williams, 1992). Volunteering increases physical functionality (Moen et al., 1992) and decreases the risk of disability (Mendes de Leon, Glass, and Berkman, 2003). Researchers have also linked volunteering to reduced mortality rates (Musick et al., 1999).

The fact that older adults benefit personally from volunteering does not lessen the benefits that communities gain from older adults' increased volunteerism. These communities also benefit from older adults' increased generosity.

Compared to middle-age and young adults, older adults contribute substantially more to charitable causes (cf. Center on Philanthropy, 2007). However, it should be noted that young adults' volunteering likewise benefits their communities. Indeed, the majority of older adult volunteers first began volunteering when they were young adults (Toppe et al., 2002).

Interestingly, older adults aged 70 and older exhibit higher levels of egoism (Havighurst, Neugarten, and Tobin, 1968). Their stronger egoism may be attributable to an increase in self-preoccupation and a decrease in the willingness to devote energy to their relationships with others, both of which may be a cause or effect of decreased social interaction (Havighurst et al., 1968; Pressey and Pressey, 1969). Also, some studies find a quadratic effect of age on altruism. Specifically, their results reveal a positive relationship between age and charitable giving. The strength of this relationship decreases after older adults reach a specific age (e.g., Landry, Lange, List, Price, and Rupp, 2006).

The Effect of Context

In the above two sections of this chapter, we reviewed studies on the general relationship between age and narcissism (which appears on average to be an increasing one) and whether older adults' increased tendency to behave less selfishly is indeed the result of altruism or instead due to egoism. Our earlier review found an effect of context on whether the relationship between age and narcissism is indeed positive and why. Specifically, older adults appear to behave less altruistically in the workplace than in a personal context. In this section, we examine the effect age has on the incidence of narcissism and its positive and negative consequences in two other contexts: (1) civic engagement, and (2) materialism.

Age and Civic Engagement

There are interesting differences with respect to the effect of age on the frequency with which older (vs. young) adults appear to engage in certain civic-oriented behaviors; civic engagement behaviors are generally viewed as altruistic versus egoistic in nature.

Community Involvement

Most previous studies reveal that older adults have a relatively stronger service orientation with respect to community (Omoto, Synder, and Martino, 2000). They are more likely to participate in community activities. They are also more likely to volunteer in order to help their community achieve its prosocial goals, as discussed above. Again, participation in community activities and community volunteering can be beneficial to older individuals' well-being (Musick, Herzog, and House,

1999; Van Willigen, 2000). Communities benefit greatly from the wisdom and spare time and effort older individuals have to offer.

It is worth noting that sometimes young adults are as likely or more likely than older adults are to participate in community activities and volunteerism. Primary and secondary institutions often encourage students to engage in civic behaviors, especially volunteering. For example, some high schools require students to volunteer for a specific number of hours in order for them to graduate. And, many colleges and universities take community volunteerism into account when deciding which students they should admit.

Voting Behavior

Contrary to the notion that older (vs. younger) individuals are more altruistic (vs. narcissistic), studies show that older individuals are more inclined to vote for policies that benefit themselves rather than others, in particular younger others. Specifically, older voters are more inclined to vote for increases in public healthcare and pensions, which disproportionately benefit them at a cost to younger voters who are generally less likely to have pensions and have less need for expansive healthcare services, at least in the short-run. Older individuals are also less likely to vote against increases in education spending, which disproportionately benefits younger and middle-age individuals (Cattaneo and Wolter, 2009).

However, an analysis of the influence of age on the tendency to vote for or against increases in education funding should take several factors into account. First, there is heterogeneity among older voters, i.e., they are not a homogeneous voting bloc. Older voters with higher levels of interpersonal trust are more likely to support funding education through increased taxation (Busemeyer and Lober, 2019). Longstanding (vs. newer) residents are more supportive of education funding (Berkman and Plutzer, 2004). Second, older individuals are more likely to support education funding when the demographic makeup of community residents is less homogenous (Roch and Rushton, 2008).

Third, older voters may be more financially constrained than younger and middle-age voters are, which then influences their voting preferences. For example, older voters are more likely to have a fixed income. Indeed, Torres-Gil (1992) reveals that older individuals are more fearful of economic insecurity. These fears are prompted by increased life expectancy as well as smaller and fewer pension and retirement programs. Also, older voters are more likely to own their own homes, which is a source of wealth. However, due to a fixed income or decreased income after retirement, they may be more likely to vote against any increases in property taxes. It is common for state and local educational institutions to rely on property tax revenues for funding. Having stated that, there is also evidence that older individuals favor increased education funding but disagree that property taxes are the best source for funding schools (MacManus, 1995).

Longitudinal (vs. cross-sectional) research suggests that age differences in voting behavior with respect to education funding is due to cohort effects rather than age effects. Plutzer and Berkman (2005) reveal that every birth cohort save the most senior (i.e., early Baby Boomers in their 70s and 80s) are more likely to support increased spending on education. Accordingly, in the long term, cohort replacement may lead to an increase in support for education spending, even by their oldest voters (Plutzer and Berkman, 2005).

In summary, young voters appear to be more supportive of increases in education funding in comparison to older voters. Past research reveals that difference in voting behavior is driven by both age and cohort effects.

Materialism

Richins and Dawson (1992) define materialism as "the importance a person places on possessions and their acquisition as a necessary or desirable form of conduct to reach desired end states, including happiness" (p. 307). In general, materialism is viewed as a narcissistic trait. Theories, such as Erikson's (1950) theory of eight psychosocial stages across life, propose that younger individuals care more about acquiring material possessions, especially those associated with high social status. Materialism has many negative consequences, including compulsive buying (Dittmar, 2005), overdrawn credit (Richins, 2011), loneliness, depression, and anxiety (Pieters, 2013; Kasser and Ryan, 1993), and lower subjective well-being (Dittmar, Bond, Hurst, and Kasser, 2014).

The above notwithstanding, there is considerable heterogeneity in the importance individuals place on having high-status possessions. After all, individuals of all ages need material possessions and enjoy those of superior quality. Higher quality goods tend to be more expensive, and expensive possessions are associated with having higher social status. Indeed, some studies show that older individuals are more materialistic compared to younger middle-aged adults. For example, Jaspers and Pieters' (2016) large longitudinal study finds systematic variation across the lifespan. In particular, the level of materialism is highest at a young age, decreases with middle adulthood, and then increases again in later life.

However, materialism is not a unidimensional construct. Accordingly, materialism may manifest itself differently in different age groups, and age differences in materialism may reflect different aspects of materialism. The material values scale (MVS, Richins, and Dawson, 1992), has three factors: "acquisition centrality," "possession-defined success," and "acquisition as the pursuit of happiness." Richins and Dawson describe "acquisition centrality" as the degree to which people's possessions are central to their lives, "possession-defined success" as the degree to which people treat their possessions as determinants of success in life, and "acquisition as the pursuit of happiness" as the degree to which people's belongings are necessary for happiness and life satisfaction. Jaspers and Pieters (2016) find different effects of aging on the importance placed on each of the three factors. Specifically, the importance of "acquisition centrality" declines steadily over the adult life span. Alternatively, "acquisition as the pursuit of happiness" remains relatively stable across the lifespan; individuals of all ages rate this factor as the least important. Alternatively, younger individuals rate "possession–defined success" as the most important factor. Last, the importance of "possession–defined success" is higher among young adults but decreases during middle-age but then slowly increases after middle-age.

Several studies suggest that materialism benefits older individuals in multiple ways. Acquiring and having possessions are one way for people to feel less dependent on others, more in control of their lives, and more successful (Heckhausen et al., 1989; Richins, 2011). Materialism is also a way for older individuals to reduce stress levels (Chang and Arkin, 2002; Roberts, Manolis, and Tanner, 2003). Recent research on the relationship between age and use of various coping strategies reveals that older (vs. young) adults are less likely to cope with stressful life events by reaching out to friends for (explicit) emotional support because they are disinclined to disturb close others (Jiang, Drolet, and Kim, 2018). Shopping can be a therapeutic activity, a pleasurable distraction that can enhance self-esteem.

Of course, it is important to take into account the significant role that income plays in the acquisition of possession, irrespective of age. Poorer individuals are simply less able to afford high-status goods which tend to be more expensive. Indeed, studies suggest that age differences in materialistic behavior are due to changes in income more so than other factors (Abdel-Ghany and Sharpe, 1997; Lee, 2001). For example, Denton, Mountain, and Spencer (2006) find that differences in older individuals' pre-retirement versus post-retirement spending are driven by changes in income rather than changes in taste. Post-retirement, income has a large effect on expenditures related to healthcare, travel, and housing, as well as spending on apparel and technological innovations (Zeithaml and Gilly, 1987; Lee et al., 1997).

General Discussion

This chapter provides a solid foundation for understanding difference in the prevalence of narcissism among younger versus older individuals. On the whole, our review suggests that (sub-clinical) narcissism is more prevalent among young individuals and younger generations. In contrast, older adults appear more altruistic. For example, they prioritize close social relationships and donate more time and money to their communities.

Implications

It is important for marketers to understand the prevalence of narcissism across different groups and contexts because narcissism underlies many consumer values and behaviors, such as materialism. Marketers who seek to target older consumers benefit from knowing whether narcissism increases with age, what drives age differences, and how narcissism influences older (vs. younger) consumers' reaction to marketers' actions. Indeed, in a 2016 study, SYZYGY, which is a media agency headquartered in Germany, commissioned a study of the effect of age cohort on narcissistic tendencies. They relied on sample of over 5000 adults from three generational cohorts. They found that Millennials scored higher on Emmons' (1984) Narcissistic Personality Inventory (NPI-16). Their study also revealed a significant relationship between narcissism and consumers' use of so-called "EgoTech," i.e., new technology that is designed to flatter the ego and appeal to the cult of the self.

Future Research

This review suggests several avenues for future research. For example, studies might focus more efforts on disentangling age effects from cohort effects. In contrast to age effects, cohort effects persist over the entire lifespan. The distinction is important for the design of customer relationship management (CRM) programs. These programs tend to focus on the long run.

In addition, future research might focus on issues related to consumer protection from financial fraud. As our review suggests, older consumers' altruistic behaviors may be driven by their desire to appear socially attractive. However, this desire can result in negative consequences. For example, studies find that older individuals are more vulnerable to affinity fraud, an investment scam that disproportionately targets older individuals (Deason, Rajgopal, and Waymire, 2015). In this scam, fraudsters rely on kinship or on likeness with a positive reference group. It is possible older individuals are more susceptible to this type of fraud due to their greater desire for close social relationships.

Another avenue for future research relates to the workplace. Older individuals make up an increasingly important segment of workers as the population of older adults continues to grow and retirements are increasingly delayed. Future research might focus on finding employers and employment opportunities that best match older individuals' skill set and work objectives. Older adults may be better suited for individual-level roles rather than group-level roles. It may also be the case that older adults are better suited for work that requires emotional skills and find this work to be more rewarding.

References

Abdel-Ghany, M., & Sharpe, D. L. (1997). Consumption patterns among the young-old and old-old. *Journal of Individual Affairs*, *31*(1), 90–112. doi: 10.1111/j.1745-6606.1997. tb00828.x.

Adler, R. P., & Goggin, J. (2005). What do we mean by "civic engagement"? *Journal of Transformative Education*, *3*(3), 236–253. doi: 10.1177/1541344605276792.

Arnett, J. J., Trzesniewski, K. H., & Donnellan, M. B. (2013). The dangers of generational myth-making: Rejoinder to twenge. *Emerging Adulthood, 1*(1), 17–20. doi: 10.1177/2167696812466848.

Bal, P. M., & Kooij, D. (2011). The relations between work centrality, psychological contracts, and job attitudes: The influence of age. *European Journal of Work and Organizational Psychology, 20*(4), 497–523. doi: 10.1080/13594321003669079.

Batson, C. D. (1991). *The Altruism Question: Toward a Social-Psychological Answer.* Hillsdale, NJ: Lawrence Erlbaum.

Berkman, M. B., & Plutzer, E. (2004). Gray peril or loyal support? The effects of the elderly on educational expenditures. *Social Science Quarterly, 85*(5), 1178–1192. doi: 10.1111/j.0038-4941.2004.00270.x.

Boyd III, H. C., & Helms, J. E. (2005). Individual entitlement theory and measurement. *Psychology and Marketing, 22*(3), 271–286. doi: 10.1002/mar.20058.

Busemeyer, M. R., & Lober, D. (2019). Between solidarity and self-interest: The elderly and support for public education revisited. *Journal of Social Policy,* 1–20. doi: 10.1017/S0047279419000382.

Butori, R. (2010). Proposition for an improved version of the individual entitlement inventory. *Psychology and Marketing, 27*(3), 285–297. doi: 10.1002/mar.20327.

Campbell, W. K., Bonacci, A. M., Shelton, J., Exline, J. J., & Bushman, B. J. (2004). Psychological entitlement: Interpersonal consequences and validation of a self-report measure. *Journal of Personality Assessment, 83*(1), 29–45. doi: 10.1207/ s15327752jpa8301_04.

Carpenter, J., Connolly, C.`, & Myers, C. K. (2008). Altruistic behavior in a representative dictator experiment. *Experimental Economics, 11*(3), 282–298. doi: 10.1007/ s10683-007-9193-x.

Carstensen, L. L., & Charles, S. (1998). Emotion in the second half of life. *Current Directions in Psychological Science, 7*(5), 144–149.

Carstensen, L. L., Isaacowitz, D. M., & Charles, S. T. (1999). Taking time seriously: A theory of socioemotional selectivity. *American Psychologist, 54*(3), 165–181. doi: 10.1037/0003-066X.54.3.165.

Caspi, A., Roberts, B. W., & Shiner, R. L. (2005). Personality development: Stability and change. *Annual Review of Psychology, 56*(1), 453–484. doi: 10.1146/annurev.psych.55 .090902.141913.

Cattaneo, M. A., & Wolter, S. C. (2009). Are the elderly a threat to educational expenditures? *European Journal of Political Economy, 25*(2), 225–236. doi: 10.1016/j. ejpoleco.2008.10.002.

Center on Philanthropy (2007). *American Express Charitable Gift Survey.* Indianapolis, IN: Indiana University. Retrieved from www.philanthropy.iupui.edu [Accessed 8 February 2020].

Chang, L., & Arkin, R. M. (2002). Materialism as an attempt to cope with uncertainty. *Psychology and Marketing, 19*(5), 389–406. doi: 10.1002/mar.10016.

Charles, S. T., & Piazza, J. R. (2007). Memories of social interactions: Age differences in emotional intensity. *Psychology and Aging, 22*(2), 300–309. doi: 10.1037/0882-7974.22.2.300.

Chopik, W. J., & Grimm, K. J. (2019). Longitudinal changes and historic differences in narcissism from adolescence to older adulthood. *Psychology and Aging, 34*(8), 1109–1123. doi: 10.1037/pag0000379.

Cuddy, A. J., & Fiske, S. T. (2002). Doddering, but dear: Process, content, and function in stereotyping of older persons. In: T. D. Nelson (Ed.), *Ageism* (pp. 3–26). Cambridge, MA: MIT Press.

Deason, S., Rajgopal, S., & Waymire, G. B. (2015). Who gets swindled in Ponzi schemes? Available at SSRN 2586490.

Denton, F. T., Mountain, D. C., & Spencer, B. G. (2006). Age, retirement, and expenditure patterns: An econometric study of older households. *Atlantic Economic Journal, 34*(4), 421–434. doi: 10.1007/s11293-006-9028-8.

Dittmar, H. (2005). Compulsive buying–a growing concern? An examination of gender, age, and endorsement of materialistic values as predictors. *British Journal of Psychology, 96*(4), 467–491. doi: 10.1348/000712605X53533.

Dittmar, H., Bond, R., Hurst, M., & Kasser, T. (2014). The relationship between materialism and personal well-being: A meta-analysis. *Journal of Personality and Social Psychology, 107*(5), 879–924. doi: 10.1037/a0037409.

Donnellan, M. B., Trzesniewski, K. H., & Robins, R. W. (2009). An emerging epidemic of narcissism or much ado about nothing? *Journal of Research in Personality, 43*(3), 498–501. doi: 10.1016/j.jrp.2008.12.010.

Emmons, R. A. (1984). Factor analysis and construct validity of the narcissistic personality inventory. *Journal of Personality Assessment, 48*(3), 291–300.

Erikson, E. H. (1950). *Childhood and Society.* New York, NY: Norton.

Erikson, E. H. (1985). *The Life Cycle Completed.* New York, NY: Norton.

Firebaugh, G., & Davis, K. E. (1988). Trends in antiblack prejudice, 1972–1984: Region and cohort effects. *American Journal of Sociology, 94*(2), 251–272. doi: 10.1086/228991.

Frankenberger, K. D. (2000). Adolescent egocentrism: A comparison among adolescents and adults. *Journal of Adolescence, 23*(3), 343–354.

Freund, A. M., & Blanchard-Fields, F. (2014). Age-related differences in altruism across adulthood: Making personal financial gain versus contributing to the public good. *Developmental Psychology, 50*(4), 1125–1136. doi: 10.1037/a0034491.

Gajadhar, B. J., Nap, H. H., de Kort, Y. A., & IJsselsteijn, W. A. (2010, September). Out of sight, out of mind: Co-player effects on seniors' player experience. In: *Proceedings of the 3rd International Conference on Fun and Games* (pp. 74–83). Academic Medicine, Leuven, Belgium.

Gonsalkorale, K., Sherman, J. W., & Klauer, K. C. (2009). Aging and prejudice: Diminished regulation of automatic race bias among older adults. *Journal of Experimental Social Psychology, 45*(2), 410–414. doi: 10.1016/j.jesp.2008.11.004.

Grundy, E., & Henretta, J. C. (2006). Between elderly parents and adult children: A new look at the intergenerational care provided by the 'sandwich generation.' *Ageing and Society, 26*(5), 707–722. doi: 10.1017/S0144686X06004934.

Havighurst, R. J., Neugarten, B. L., & Tobin, S. S. (1968). Middle age and aging. In: Robert J. Havighurst, Bernice L. Neugarten, & Sheldon S. Tobin (Eds.), *Middle Age and Ageing.* Chicago, IL: University of Chicago Press.

Heckhausen, J., Dixon, R. A., & Baltes, P. B. (1989). Gains and losses in development throughout adulthood as perceived by different adult age groups. *Developmental Psychology, 25*(1), 109–121. doi: 10.1037/0012-1649.25.1.109.

Hubbard, J., Harbaugh, W. T., Srivastava, S., Degras, D., & Mayr, U. (2016). A general benevolence dimension that links neural, psychological, economic, and life-span data on altruistic tendencies. *Journal of Experimental Psychology: General, 145*(10), 1351–1358. doi: 10.1037/xge0000209.supp.

Huddy, L., Neely, F. K., & Lafay, M. R. (2000). Poll trends: Support for the women's movement. *Public Opinion Quarterly, 64*(3), 309–350.

Jaspers, E. D., & Pieters, R. G. (2016). Materialism across the life span: An age-period-cohort analysis. *Journal of Personality and Social Psychology, 111*(3), 451–473. doi: 10.1037/pspp0000092.

Jiang, L., Drolet, A., & Kim, H. S. (2018). Age and social support seeking: Understanding the role of perceived social costs to others. *Personality and Social Psychology Bulletin, 44*(7), 1104–1116.

Jones, J. R., & Schaubroeck, J. (2004). Mediators of the relationship between race and organizational citizenship behavior. *Journal of Managerial Issues, 16*(4), 505–527.

Kasser, T., & Ryan, R. M. (1993). A dark side of the American dream: Correlates of financial success as a central life aspiration. *Journal of Personality and Social Psychology, 65*(2), 410–422. doi: 10.1037/0022-3514.65.2.410.

Kasser, T., & Ryan, R. M. (1996). Further examining the American dream: Differential correlates of intrinsic and extrinsic goals. *Personality and Social Psychology Bulletin, 22*(3), 280–287. doi: 10.1177/0146167296223006.

Kasser, T., Ryan, R. M., Couchman, C. E., & Sheldon, K. M. (2004). Materialistic values: Their causes and consequences. In: T. Kasser & A. D. Kanner (Eds.), *Psychology and Individual Culture: The Struggle for a Good Life in a Materialistic World* (pp. 11–28). Washington, DC: American Psychological Association.

Konrath, S. H., O'Brien, E. H., & Hsing, C. (2011). Changes in dispositional empathy in American college students over time: A meta-analysis. *Personality and Social Psychology Review, 15*(2), 180–198. doi: 10.1177/1088868310377395.

Landry, C. E., Lange, A., List, J. A., Price, M. K., & Rupp, N. G. (2006). Toward an understanding of the economics of charity: Evidence from a field experiment. *The Quarterly Journal of Economics, 121*(2), 747–782.

Lang, F. R., Wagner, J., Wrzus, C., & Neyer, F. J. (2013). Personal effort in social relationships across adulthood. *Psychology and Aging, 28*(2), 529–539. doi: 10.1037/a0032221.

Lansford, J. E., Sherman, A. M., & Antonucci, T. C. (1998). Satisfaction with social networks: An examination of socioemotional selectivity theory across cohorts. *Psychology and Aging, 13*(4), 544–552. doi: 10.1037/0882-7974.13.4.544.

Lee, Y. G. (2001). Consumption patterns of elderly households: Are they different between younger and older elderly in Korea? how do they differ between Korea and the US. *Individual Interest Annual, 47*, 1–11.

Lee, J. K., Sherman, D. H., Mok, C. J., & Wang, H. (1997). Apparel expenditure patterns of elderly individuals: A life-cycle consumption model. *Family and Individual Sciences Research Journal, 26*(2), 109–140. doi: 10.1177/1077727X970262002.

Li, N., Liang, J., & Crant, J. M. (2010). The role of proactive personality in job satisfaction and organizational citizenship behavior: A relational perspective. *Journal of Applied Psychology, 95*(2), 395–402. doi: 10.1037/a0018079.

MacManus, S. A. (1995). Taxing and spending politics: A generational perspective. *The Journal of Politics, 57*(3), 607–629. doi: 10.2307/2960185.

Martinez, I. L., Crooks, D., Kim, K. S., & Tanner, E. (2011). Invisible civic engagement among older adults: Valuing the contributions of informal volunteering. *Journal of Cross-Cultural Gerontology, 26*(1), 23–37. doi: 10.1007/s10823-011-9137-y.

Matsumoto, Y., Yamagishi, T., Li, Y., & Kiyonari, T. (2016). Prosocial behavior increases with age across five economic games. *PLOS ONE, 11*(7).

Mendes de Leon, C. F., Glass, T. A., & Berkman, L. F. (2003). Social engagement and disability in a community population of older adults: The New Haven EPESE. *American Journal of Epidemiology, 157*(7), 633–642. doi: 10.1093/aje/kwg028.

Moen, P., Dempster-McClain, D., & Williams Jr., R. M. (1992). Successful aging: A life-course perspective on women's multiple roles and health. *American Journal of Sociology, 97*(6), 1612–1638. doi: 10.1086/229941.

Musick, M. A., Herzog, A. R., & House, J. S. (1999). Volunteering and mortality among older adults: Findings from a national sample. *Journal of Gerontology: Social Sciences*, *54B*(3), 769–784. doi: 10.1093/geronb/54B.3.S173.

Musick, M. A., & Wilson, J. (2003). Volunteering and depression: The role of psychological and social resources in different age groups. *Social Science and Medicine*, *56*(2), 259–269. doi: 10.1016/S0277-9536(02)00025-4.

Omoto, A. M., Snyder, M., & Martino, S. C. (2000). Volunteerism and the life course: Investigating age-related agendas for action. *Basic and Applied Social Psychology*, *22*(3), 181–197. doi: 10.1207/S15324834BASP2203_6.

Pieters, R. (2013). Bidirectional dynamics of materialism and loneliness: Not just a vicious cycle. *Journal of Individual Research*, *40*(4), 615–631. doi: 10.1086/671564.

Plutzer, E., & Berkman, M. (2005). The graying of America and support for funding the nation's schools. *Public Opinion Quarterly*, *69*(1), 66–86. doi: 10.1093/poq/nfi010.

Pornpattananangkul, N., Chowdhury, A., Feng, L., & Yu, R. (2019). Social discounting in the elderly: Senior citizens are Good Samaritans to strangers. *The Journals of Gerontology: Series B*, *74*(1), 52–58. doi: 10.1093/geronb/gbx040.

Pressey, S. L., & Pressey, A. D. (1969). "Insider" longitudinal evaluations of institutional living [Summary]. In: *Proceedings of the 77th Annual Convention of the American Psychological Association*, Washington, DC (Vol. 4, pp. 451–458).

Raskin, R., & Terry, H. (1988). A principal-components analysis of the narcissistic personality inventory and further evidence of its construct validity. *Journal of Personality and Social Psychology*, *54*(5), 890–902. doi: 10.1037/0022-3514.54.5.890.

Richins, M. L. (2011). Materialism, transformation expectations, and spending: Implications for credit use. *Journal of Public Policy and Marketing*, *30*(2), 141–156.

Richins, M. L., & Dawson, S. (1992). A consumer values orientation for materialism and its measurement: Scale development and validation. *Journal of Consumer Research*, *19*(3), 303–316. doi: 10.1086/209304.

Roberts, B. W., Edmonds, G., & Grijalva, E. (2010). It is developmental me, not generation me: Developmental changes are more important than generational changes in narcissism— Commentary on Trzesniewski & Donnellan. *Perspectives on Psychological Science: A Journal of the Association for Psychological Science*, *5*(1), 97–102. doi: 10.1177/1745691609357019.

Roberts, J. A., & Pirog III, S. F. (2004). Personal goals and their role in individual behavior: The case of compulsive buying. *Journal of Marketing Theory and Practice*, *12*(3), 61–73. doi: 10.1080/10696679.2004.11658525.

Roberts, B. W., & Wood, D. (2006). Personality development in the context of the neo-socioanalytic model of personality. In: D. Mroczek & T. Little (Eds.), *Handbook of Personality Development* (pp. 11–39). Mahwah, NJ: Lawrence Erlbaum.

Roberts, J. A., Manolis, C., & Tanner Jr, J. F. (2003). Family structure, materialism, and compulsive buying: A reinquiry and extension. *Journal of the Academy of Marketing Science*, *31*(3), 300–311. doi: 10.1177/0092070303031003007.

Roch, C. H., & Rushton, M. (2008). Racial context and voting over taxes: Evidence from a referendum in Alabama. *Public Finance Review*, *36*(5), 614–634. doi: 10.1177/1091142107313826.

Rushton, J. P., Fuller, D., Neale, M., Nias, D., & Eysenck, H. J. (1986). Altruism and aggression: The heritability of individual differences. *Journal of Personality and Social Psychology*, *34*, 146–158. doi: 10.1037/0022-3514.50.6.1192.

Sheldon, Kennon M., & Kasser, Tim. (1995). Coherence and congruence: Two aspects of personality integration. *Journal of Personality and Social Psychology*, *68*(3), 531.

Sheridan, M. B. (1997). Drug lords buy way into church's heart. *Los Angeles Times*, 21. Retrieved from https://www.latimes.com/archives/la-xpm-1997-oct-21-mn-44987 -story.html.

Steinberg, M., Najman, J., Donald, K., McChesney-Clark, G., & Mahon, C. (1994). *Attitudes and Practices of Employers and Employees Towards Older Workers in a Climate of Anti-Discrimination*. Brisbane: Department of Social and Preventative Medicine, University of Queensland.

Streufert, S., Pogash, R., Piasecki, M., & Post, G. M. (1990). Age and management team performance. *Psychology and Aging*, 5(4), 551–559. doi: 10.1037/0882-7974.5.4.551.

Sze, J. A., Gyurak, A., Goodkind, M. S., & Levenson, R. W. (2012). Greater emotional empathy and prosocial behavior in late life. *Emotion*, 12(5), 1129–1140. doi: 10.1037/a0025011.

Toppe, C., Golombek, S., Kirsch, A., Michel, J., & Weber, M. (2002). *Engaging Youth in Lifelong Service: Findings and Recommendations for Encouraging a Tradition of Voluntary Action among America's Youth*. Washington, DC: Independent Sector.

Torres-Gil, Fernando M. (1992). *The New Aging: Politics and Change in America*. New York, NY: Auburn House.

Trzesniewski, K. H., & Donnellan, M. B. (2014). "Young people these days...": Evidence for negative perceptions of emerging adults. *Emerging Adulthood*, 2(3), 211–226. doi: 10.1177/2167696814522620.

Trzesniewski, K. H., Donnellan, M. B., & Robins, R. W. (2008). Do today's young people really think they are so extraordinary? An examination of secular trends in narcissism and self-enhancement. *Psychological Science*, 19(2), 181–188. doi: 10.1111/j.1467-9280.2008.02065.x.

Twenge, J. M., Campbell, W. K., & Freeman, E. C. (2012). Generational differences in young adults' life goals, concern for others, and civic orientation: 1966–2009. *Journal of Personality and Social Psychology*, 102(5), 1045–1062. doi: 10.1037/a0027408.

Twenge, J. M., & Kasser, T. (2013). Generational changes in materialism and work centrality, 1976–2007: Associations with temporal changes in societal insecurity and materialistic role modeling. *Personality and Social Psychology Bulletin*, 39(7), 883–897. doi: 10.1177/0146167213484586.

Twenge, Jean M., Konrath, Sara, Foster, Joshua D., Keith Campbell, W., & Bushman, Brad J. (2008). Further evidence of an increase in narcissism among college students. *Journal of Personality*, 76(4), 919–928.

Van Hiel, A., & Vansteenkiste, M. (2009). Ambitions fulfilled? The effects of intrinsic and extrinsic goal attainment on older adults' ego-integrity and death attitudes. *The International Journal of Aging and Human Development*, 68(1), 27–51. doi: 10.2190/AG.68.1.b.

Van Willigen, M. (2000). Differential benefits of volunteering across the life course. *Journal of Gerontology: Social Sciences*, 55(5), S308–S318. doi: 10.1093/geronb/55.5.S308.

Vansteenkiste, M., Timmermans, T., Lens, W., Soenens, B., & Van den Broeck, A. (2008). Does extrinsic goal framing enhance extrinsic goal-oriented individuals' learning and performance? An experimental test of the match perspective versus self-determination theory. *Journal of Educational Psychology*, 100(2), 387. doi: 10.1037/0022-0663.100.2.387.

Wetzel, E., Brown, A., Hill, P. L., Chung, J. M., Robins, R. W., & Roberts, B. W. (2017). The narcissism epidemic is dead; long live the narcissism epidemic. *Psychological Science*, 28(12), 1833–1847. doi: 10.1177/0956797617724208.

Williams, G. C., Hedberg, V. A., Cox, E. M., & Deci, E. L. (2000). Extrinsic life goals and health-risk behaviors in adolescents 1. *Journal of Applied Social Psychology*, *30*(8), 1756–1771. doi: 10.1111/j.1559-1816.2000.tb02466.x.

Williams, K. C., Page, R. A., Petrosky, A. R., & Hernandez, E. H. (2010). Multi-generational marketing: Descriptions, characteristics, lifestyles, and attitudes. *Journal of Applied Business and Economics*, *11*(2), 21–36.

Zeithaml, V. A., & Gilly, M. C. (1987). Characteristics affecting the acceptance of retailing technologies: A comparison of elderly and nonelderly individuals. *Journal of Retailing*, *63*(1), 49–68.

16

SMART LIVING FOR OLDER PEOPLE AND THE AGING CONSUMER[1]

Noah J. Webster, Jess Francis and Toni C. Antonucci

Introduction

We live in extraordinary and rapidly changing times. These changes are both global and local. They offer unprecedented opportunities to adjust, create, and innovate. Although we focus in this chapter on the older adult, it should be noted that these changes involve and have consequences for people of all ages. In this chapter, we highlight changes in population demographics including important age, race, and ethnic distributions. We then consider changes in the individual life span as well as in family structure. We note that some people are living longer and in better health than ever before while simultaneously others are living with increasing chronic illnesses and functional limitations. We also note that the very nature of the family has changed in significant ways. These changes result in very different experiences, needs, and preferences of the older adult population. In addition, people are living in very different circumstances. For example, older people are much more likely to live alone or in couples than in previous generations although there are now increasing numbers of racial and ethnic groups that are much more likely to live in multi-generational families. These individual and living circumstances result in unique, changing, and developing consumption patterns.

We propose that smart living offers a new and exciting approach to adapting to our changing society both for older people and for people of all ages. For the first time, we have the opportunity and capability to use emerging technology to address the needs of our population in real and evolving time. As a result, U.S. businesses and corporations are developing new products and offering new services to address the needs of this changing and increasing population. We focus on the potential of smart living as a unique and productive approach to meeting the challenges we are facing. The potential of smart living is considerable, given that recent and ongoing developments create ever new possibilities, e.g., complex and diverse health and family contexts. We consider examples from a variety of smart living settings, including the home, workplace, and public domain. We discuss how these developments can promote healthy aging, improve the functioning of the workforce, and facilitate transportation. We note that smart living is useful for single individuals living alone, for families, as well as for communities and societies. The proposed approach provides a new perspective on design and consumption that addresses the needs of an aging society and will, for the first time, address multiple domains including prevention, intervention, adaptation, and rehabilitation. As the needs of our changing society evolve, so do its consumption patterns. Hints from the present and anticipation of the future suggest that smart living can influence how goods and services can be developed in order to meet the specific needs of an individual and/or family. Especially exciting is the use of smart living to facilitate healthy aging and potentially reduce socioeconomically driven health disparities that are currently quite profound among older adults.

We propose a new approach to design and consumption that addresses the needs of an aging society from a life span perspective, thus including the aging individual as well as people of other ages, to address multiple needs of our society. Finally, we recognize the importance of psychological factors, most notably the need for individuals of all ages to feel that their life has meaning, their behavior matters, and that they have a role and purpose in society. We note that smart living can address health, convenience, and safety needs as well as the individual's need to matter by creating products and services that meet these diverse needs and reach a wide spectrum of consumers. To do so, we need to face the demographic revolution with new and innovative ideas and proposals for the design and marketing of goods and services that meet the challenges of an aging society. We turn first to a consideration of the population demographics and other societal trends.

Changing Demographics and Other Trends

Population Aging

U.S. Population Aging

The aging of America is dramatic. Some have called it a demographic revolution (Diczfalusy, 2001). The average life expectancy was 47 years in 1900 and 79 years in 2000. In 2005, 37 million people were 65+. Between 2010 and 2030, this number will increase to 72 million. From 1995 to 2050 the population of Americans aged 85 and older will increase by over 400 percent (Antonucci, Blieszner, and Denmark, 2009). While these population changes highlight the extraordinary success of increasing longevity, several National Research Council (NRC; e.g., Pew and Van Hemel, 2004) reports describe some of the challenges that these unprecedented aging-related changes will bring to the structure of our society.

These challenges, if not anticipated and planned for, could threaten many valued aspects of our society, including our economy, social security, and health care. These changes will create new opportunities, but also will impose new burdens on people and institutions who provide a wide range of goods as well as personal and social services. These challenges also have important implications for family life and the ways in which many local communities are organized. An aging society will require that our country rethink and reinvent vital institutions. Our nation has no precedent for the societal transition that is to come. These population changes, while posing many challenges, also represent opportunities for innovation. As we have met previous "revolutions" (e.g., the Industrial Revolution), we will undoubtedly meet this one but it will require innovation and ingenuity as well as unique collaborations between industry and academic partners.

Global Population Aging

The United States is not unique in undergoing population-level shifts in the age distribution of its population. Japan began on this path earlier than any other country. By 2030 in Japan, it is expected that the number of people aged 85 and older will outnumber those under the age of 15 (Powell, 2010). According to the United Nations, by the year 2030, more than 60 countries worldwide will have 2 million or more people aged 65 and older. Specifically, the global population of those aged 85 and older is expected to increase 151 percent from 2005 to 2030. Comparatively, the population of adults aged 65 and older is projected to only increase by 104 percent. Population aging is increasing most rapidly in Asia. In particular, China is aging at an unprecedented rate (Du & Tu, 2000) due to a number of factors, including the government's one-child policy in effect from 1979 to 2015. The impact of the aging population on the size of the workforce is going to be strong, particularly in Europe. For example, the number of people aged 15 to 64 is expected to decline in Spain by 10 percent, in Germany by 11 percent, and in Italy by 15 percent (Powell, 2010). In Africa, population aging is occurring in a different economic context with African economies heavily dependent on subsistence agriculture (Powell, 2010), which relies less on technology and more on the labor of people. While older adults comprise a small percentage of the population in Africa compared to other parts of the world, declining fertility rates and high death rates due to AIDS, especially among young adults, are leading to decreases in the number of eligible workers (c.f. Estes, Biggs, Phillipson, 2003).

These population changes are causing important shifts in consumption patterns. From an industry perspective, one conclusion to be drawn from these population shifts is that there will be increased demand for goods and services to meet the specific needs, preferences, and lifestyles of older adults. For example, demand for health care services and specialized housing accommodations (Powell, 2010) as well as additional goods and services to facilitate lifestyle, work, and leisure activities are expected to increase dramatically in concert with increases in the size of the older adult population.

Other Societal Trends

While the United States and many countries around the world are undergoing population-level aging, other related trends are occurring simultaneously. Together in context with increasing numbers of older adults, these trends will also have profound influences on consumption patterns, need for specific goods and services, as well as industry approaches to addressing these needs, including product design, development, and marketing. First, the U.S. population will have greater racial and ethnic diversity. For example, from 2005 to 2050, the proportion of the population comprising Hispanics is projected to grow from 14 to 29 percent, while the proportion of Whites will shrink from 67 to 47 percent (Perez and Hirschman, 2009). This will significantly increase the market for products that consider the customs and preferences of the Hispanic community. Examples include specialized food, clothing, housing, employment, and educational needs, as well as leisure time and unique traditional family activities. Second, socioeconomic disparities are projected to increase. The share of income earned by the top 1 percent of the population increased from 9 percent of total income in 1970 to about 30 percent in 2010 (Rice and Obama, 2009). This is creating a significant market for luxury goods and services as well as for low cost and cost-saving products. Third, more people will be living with chronic conditions than ever before, a trend driven, in part, by the success of longer life spans. For example, the number of people with a chronic illness (e.g., hypertension, diabetes, asthma) increased from 125 million in 2000 to 149 million in 2015. People living with chronic diseases have special health and lifestyle product needs that create and increase the size of new markets. Fourth, disability is increasing. Among households in which the oldest member is 85 or above, the percentage of households with a member who is disabled increased from 8.8 percent in 2000 to 11.6 percent in 2010 (U.S. Census Bureau, 2015). This has created an increased need for universal design and assistive devices. Fifth, obesity rates in the United States have increased among both adults and children. The prevalence of obesity among adults increased from just under 15 percent in 1970 to 35 percent in 2010 and from 5 percent to 15 percent among children (Frieden et al., 2013). This is critical as obesity is a risk factor for many acute and chronic diseases. Further, it also creates new markets for example, in plus size clothes and furniture, as well as requires adaptations to design necessary for people with limited physical functioning.

Beyond demographic changes and population health, two other significant changes are occurring in both living arrangements and the workforce. In terms of living arrangements, the number of Americans living in multi-generational households increased dramatically from 1940 when just over 30 million people were living in this type of housing situation to nearly 50 million in 2008

(Heimlich, 2009). Some of this is due to ethnic and/or racial traditions, but it is also the result of reduced incomes and standards of living mentioned previously. This means that homes will need to accommodate the needs of a wide age range and be adaptive to meet these needs as they change.

In terms of the workforce, more Americans will work well past the age of 55. Specifically, the percentage of the workforce aged 55 and older increased from about 12 percent in 1988 to almost 25 percent in 2018 (U.S. Department of Labor, Bureau of Labor Statistics, 2019). Similarly, the percentage of the U.S. population aged 50 and older who had "not given retirement much thought" increased from about 37 percent in 2008 to over 45 percent in 2010, a dramatic jump (Health and Retirement Study, 2010). This trend is expected to further to increase as people are anticipating financial needs over a longer life span. Longer work lives also produce consumer demands for new products that accommodate changing preferences for transportation to and from work as well as the possibility of higher discretionary income for leisure and non-essential goods and services.

Implications of the Aging Population - Challenges and Opportunities

The changes detailed above in demographics, health, and related trends will have far-reaching consequences for how the individual, family, and society consume goods and services. We propose that these changes will also have a dramatic impact on different aspects of the U.S. economy, such as the age distribution of the workforce, and changing demand for specific prevention, intervention, and rehabilitative health and home services. Simultaneously, changing norms and lifestyles are also affecting the demand for goods and services. For example, sustainability concerns, emerging technologies, and decreased interest in driving or owning personal vehicles are fundamentally changing people's views about transportation. These changes will pose both challenges and opportunities. To paraphrase Charles Dickens, it will be the best of times and the worst of times. With knowledge and planning, the scale can be tipped in the direction of the former, with minimization of the latter.

Individual and the Family

Changes in life expectancy and family structure are creating ripple effects across all aspects of life. Of course, more people living into middle- and late-life will, simply put, mean more consumers. This is especially noteworthy when fewer children are being born (Ryan et al., 2012) creating new consumption patterns for goods and services to assist older people in meeting their changing needs. To underscore this point, the estimated ratio of caregivers (both formal and informal) to older adults will decline from about 9 to 1 to 3 to 1 (Avison et al., 2018). However, the needs and preferences of this older group are specific. In this section, we consider some of these specific needs by outlining additional ongoing changes at the individual and family levels and discussing how these might impact the aging consumer. We focus on two important illustrative issues: individual health and multi-generational families.

Health

While we do not review the specifics of changing health and disease experiences with aging, it is useful to consider their implications. Interestingly, changes in health among older people tend to be bifurcated. Some people are living longer and in better health, while others are experiencing disease and disability at younger ages (Olshansky et al., 2012). These different trajectories usually do not simply emerge in later life but rather are the direct extension of differences in resources, opportunities, and risk exposures over a lifetime. Both have implications for consumption but we focus here on adults in middle and later life.

Aging in Good Health

The probability of reaching later life in good health is higher among those who are more educated and better off financially. They are also likely to have steadier work histories and more leisure time in later life. Both have implications for their consumer behavior in later life. People who are well educated are more likely to be better informed about how to engage in healthy behavior (Cutler and Lleras-Muney, 2010; Cowell, 2006). They are more likely to be proactive about their health and will, therefore, engage in more preventive health practices such as exercising and maintaining a balanced diet and avoid preventable risks associated with unhealthy behavior such as smoking or drinking (Cutler and Lleras-Muney, 2010; Cowell, 2006). Older people seeking to maximize their preventive health behaviors are, for example, more likely to purchase exercise equipment, have gym memberships, and engage personal trainers. Evidence of this preoccupation is apparent with the number of older people who can be seen wearing Fitbits or tracking their steps on their phones. Older people are thus contributing to the 32-billion-dollar health and fitness industry in the United States., a trend that is likely to continue well into the future and to become more specialized to accommodate the heterogeneous needs and preferences of older people.

Healthy older people are also more likely to be engaged in medical preventive health care. This is important because screening can identify health issues requiring attention before symptoms become apparent. Examples include cancer and high blood pressure screening, both of which often are asymptomatic. Periodic health screening can also identify health problems that are associated with symptoms that might be ignored during regular health care visits. Examples include hearing loss, visual impairment, depression, falls, or substance abuse. Periodic vaccines and medication checks are also important, as they can prevent possible health problems. Each is associated with recommended uses of specific goods and services, such as hearing aids, glasses, and/or recommended surgeries for such age-related conditions as glaucoma and cataracts.

Awareness of certain risk factors suggests specific interventions. For example, falls are one of the most serious problems experienced by older people not just because of the immediate effect, but because they often result in an expanding and downward spiral (Pynoos, Steinman, Nguyen, and Bressette, 2012). However, careful consideration of both personal and situational factors can be helpful (Kra mer, Creekmur, Mitchell, Rose, Pynoos, and Rubenstein, 2014). Thus, engaging in exercise programs, stretching, yoga, and similar programs can be very helpful for improving gait and balance—two factors often associated with falls among older people. At the same time, adjustments of the physical circumstances in which older people live often require adaptation of their environment such as the instal-lation of handrails, removal of barriers and addition of ramps to offset the danger of stairs, or moving from multistory to single floor housing. As more and more people live in multifamily households and communal environments, modifica-tions and circumstances that increase safety for the older persons and facilitate their ability to engage in regular social interactions become critical. Older people and their families often adopt such changes as they can help promote an engag-ing, meaningful, and healthy lifestyle through interactions with family, friends, and neighbors as well as participation in the local community or religious groups and/ or travel with other seniors who have similar interests.

These changes in circumstances, needs, and preferences all have implications for consumption. Older people and their families are often interested, willing, and able to purchase goods and services that address their health needs, ensure their safety, and improve their lifestyle. Independence is a highly valued attribute in our society, hence any neighborhood, household, or individual adaptations or devices that enhance one's ability to maintain independence either completely or in part, will be highly valued by all. Hence, communities are increasingly providing local public transporta-tion options for older people that include vans, special fare taxis, and of course, inde-pendent ride companies such as Uber and Lyft are increasingly used by people of all ages. Local community centers, religious groups, and professional trade organizations are increasingly providing goods and services to meet the needs of their commu-nity elders. Families are increasingly adapting customs and making choices that are safe for their multi-generational household members. These often include choosing single level homes or homes with separate but attached apartments or locations that permit easy access to stores, religious institutions, or medical facilities.

Smart living has the potential to increase the older person's ability to live independently for an extended period of time. A particular benefit is that smart living is customizable to meet the specific changing needs and preferences of the individual. For the relatively healthy older person, convenience and preventive safety might be a priority. An automated system can be put in place to order and deliver groceries or medications, and safety features can be added to the home that prevents falls and/or notifies a concerned party if a fall does take place. For people with more specific needs, services can be retained to assist with bathing, dressing, and household chores, etc. Home visits by medical professionals might be arranged as well as transportation to and from appointments. The potential to meet the changing needs of older people, to reassure them and their families, and to adjust as needs change further would make smart living an important tool for promoting the health and well-being of the older population.

Corporate World

Most corporations are already well versed in responding to and providing for the needs of specific populations. There is a long history of targeting and positioning products and marketing to different segments of the population. It is well known that different communities and circumstances have different needs, for example, rural/urban communities, warm and cold weather climates, active participant versus passive observers of various sports including golf, football, tennis, basketball, and soccer; different religious groups often have specific food, transportation, and other customs that require special attention.

Consumption

As noted above, population aging will alter consumption patterns, and this will increase the need and demand for universal design of goods and services. Racial and ethnic population shifts will also be accompanied by changing needs for goods and services. Higher health care costs will mean lower-income individuals might be pressured to choose between health care services and medications and non-essential goods and services. However, having a pension, social security, and/or Medicare may now leave some people with a lifetime of low or uncertain income with more discretionary, dependable income than when they were younger. The increased number of multi-generational households, caused either by custom or necessity, will also change consumption patterns, requiring that goods and services meet the needs of multi-generational households and have universal designs to satisfy multiple age groups and lifestyles. Taking technology as an example, households now need much better electrical wiring, multiple electrical sockets, and access to desktop computers, handheld devices, smartphones, iPads, and the like. All members of the household, young and old alike, are likely to require an Internet connection. Children watch entertaining and educational shows, younger people use these devices for work or to play video games while older people might connect with family and friends through email, use the Internet to seek medical information or access telemedicine, and/or simply catch up on the news. Some of these changes will require minor adaptations while others are much more significant. Each has implications for consumption patterns and quality of life for older people and their families.

Workforce

New age structures will require rethinking how people work, when they will work, workplace accommodations, and career (re)training. Older adults in good health are likely to work longer, past the usual retirement age to the overall benefit of the individual, company, and overall productivity given the experience, efficiency, and generally reduced absences of the older worker. On the other hand, chronic illnesses and disabilities (e.g., from obesity) may go unchecked and may mean higher employer/employee costs and loss of productivity. Changing contractual obligations for pensions and health care, plus continued pressure for lower production costs, will apply further pressures around decisions about full-time employment. Shifting from manufacturing goods to a service-based economy will result in the need for (re) training in secondary or tertiary careers for individuals of all ages.

Interestingly, while many have worried that a multi-generational workforce will be dysfunctional and the cause for much age-based conflict, recent research has shown that these multi-generational workforce teams actually function quite well, benefiting from the different skills and experiences each member brings to the team. In a recent review of generational diversity at work, Woodward, Vongswasdi, and More (2015) found that intergenerational teams benefit from different experiences, which leads to greater innovation and creativity, although some have reported, if not addressed, the probability of misunderstandings and miscommunications are increased. However, if handled correctly and with proper intergenerational teamwork development, the increased diversity, experience, and skills may serve to improve the overall creativity and productivity of a team.

What Is Smart Living?

Smart living refers to the integration of various innovations and advancements to promote a lifestyle that is more connected, efficient, economical, and sustainable (Kor, Pattinson, Yanovsky, and Kharchenko, 2018). These innovations are often bolstered by smart, digital, and assistive technologies that promote bi-directional communication between user and device by generating data through the implementation of sensors, intuitive user interfaces, and remote control via Wi-Fi or other means of Internet connectivity (Kor, Pattinson, Yanovsky, and Kharchenko, 2018). Such data can be especially relevant and valuable to marketers when tailoring their services to different consumers. In order for marketers to understand the future landscape of our digital society, it is essential for researchers to recognize the consumer power and influence of the aging population, specifically the Baby Boomer generation, that is considered to be unique from previous and future generations of older adults (Eastman, Iyer, and Thomas, 2013). The rapid expansion and specific needs of the older adult population pose contemporary issues that have not presented themselves as challenges for previous older generations before the widespread use of digital and smart technologies.

According to U.S. Census data, roughly 66 percent of older adults, defined here as individuals aged 65 and older, report problems with climbing the stairs, 47 percent of older adults report trouble with independent living activities such as visiting the doctor or going grocery shopping, 40 percent of older adults report trouble hearing, and 28 percent report cognitive difficulties such as trouble remembering and making decisions (He and Larsen, 2014). The development of such impairments or disabilities can lead older adults to rely heavily on some form of caregiving from others (either formally or informally). As older adults are at particular risk for social isolation, they are at increased risk for cognitive impairment (Cacioppo and Hawkley, 2009; Dolen, and Bearison, 1982). If older adults encounter age-related functional impairment, they might also experience a shrinkage in the size of their social networks and thus, have fewer resources to aid them in living independently. In such situations customized smart living may be particularly effective.

Smart Living and Social Isolation

There is currently an increased focus among academics and community partners on the impact of social isolation on older adults. AARP launched the "Connect2Affect" initiative to promote awareness about the effects of social isolation as well as a digital interface for older adults to connect with others and provide information about how to diminish social isolation among older adults (AARP, 2017). AARP reports that roughly half of adults aged 50 and older experience some degree of loneliness and that, perhaps not surprisingly, loneliness is more common among those who are unmarried and living alone (2017). Moreover, social isolation may be more prevalent among older adults living in rural locations (Kaye, 2017), those living in high-crime areas (Portacolone, 2017), and those of lower socioeconomic status and in poor health (Czaja, 2017; Kaye, 2017; Portacolone, 2017). Although some researchers are hesitant to advise the use of digital and smart technologies to help mitigate the threat of social isolation due to the potential deleterious effects on social relationships, many researchers still acknowledge the benefits of such technology use for overall well-being and social connectedness among older adults (Czaja, 2017; Kaye, 2017). Furthermore, using technology to promote older adults' continued participation in modern society should have an overall positive effect on consumption as it will result in a greater number of consumers over a longer portion of the life course.

In order to understand how to promote participation in smart living among the aging Baby Boomers, it is first important to understand the antecedents and barriers to technology adoption among them (cf. Charness, Yoon, and Pham). Older adults' technology use and adoption are driven by factors that are as diverse and varied as the backgrounds of the older adults themselves. Technology use and adoption can be traced to older adults' particular socioeconomic status, race, usability preferences and needs, demographics, and environment (Buse, 2009;

Czaja, Fiske, Hertzog, Charness, Nair, Rogers, and Sharit, 2006). For example, 59 percent of older adults between the ages of 65 and 69 report owning a smartphone whereas only 17 percent of the eldest older adults, aged 80 and above, report smartphone ownership (Anderson and Perrin, 2017). Moreover, 81 percent of older adults with annual incomes of $75,000 or higher report owning smartphones. On the other hand, only 27 percent of older adults with annual incomes of $27,000 or less report smartphone ownership. Higher education is also positively associated with smartphone ownership for older people (Anderson and Perrin, 2017). Likewise, regarding older adults' Internet use and broadband adoption, younger older adults, defined here as individuals between the ages of 65 and 74 years old, are more likely to use the Internet and adopt broadband than individuals 75 years and older; annual income and education are both positively related to Internet use and broadband adoption among older adults (Anderson and Perrin, 2017).

Older adults' perspectives on the consistency and capabilities of digital and smart technology account for some of the lag in older adults' technology adoption. For instance, one of the most prominent concerns related to technology use, specifically smart technology use, among older adults, is the issue of privacy and surveillance. Many older adults express apprehension regarding smart technology's data monitoring capabilities and the safety of their personal information (Caine, Fisk, and Rogers, 2006; Francis, Hussain, and Cotten, 2018). Furthermore, some older adults have expressed concern about the reliability of technologies, specifically that technology will fail to work when it is needed the most (Francis, Kadylak, Makki, Rikard, and Cotten, 2018). Despite these concerns, older adults also realize the perceived value of receiving technological assistance and training from younger family members and express a desire to use technology to connect with their children and grandchildren (Francis et al., 2018).

The ability for technology use to connect older adults to their family and other social network ties has a myriad of benefits for older adults' health, both physical and emotional. Among older adults, technology use has been linked to decreased feelings of loneliness and depression and increased connection to social network support and care (Blit-Cohen and Litwin, 2004; Chopik, 2016; Cotten, Anderson, and McCullough, 2013). Using technology to connect to social network members has also been shown to promote feelings of mattering among older adults (Francis, Kadylak, Cotten, and Rikard, 2016; Francis, Rikard, Cotten, and Kadylak, 2017). To expand on the notion of mattering, it refers to the belief that we are the object of attention, importance, and dependence in the lives of significant others (Rosenberg and McCullough, 1981). The foundation of this concept can be found in Durkheim's (1933) assertion that individuals are social animals who thrive on the belief that they are relevant contributors to society. For older adults who are at higher risk for social isolation, using technology to connect with meaningful others can promote mattering by communicating that they are a significant part of those individuals' lives and they are a part of a social contract with those specific others, signaling that they are not alone. Moreover, mattering is a motivational force that encourages us to actively seek out relationships and behaviors that will further promote our feeling of mattering to others. Therefore, it can be argued that those older adults who feel as though they matter will pursue behaviors, products, and services that facilitate a healthy, productive, and independent lifestyle. Doing so will help them maintain an active role in the lives of those to whom they feel they matter. This, in turn, should lead to sustained and even increased consumption of those goods and services that aid in the older adults' implicit mission to matter. This is where smart living may create the most relevant benefit to older adults. The key for researchers and marketers alike is to effectively communicate that relevance to the older adult community in order to circumvent any perceived barriers to the adoption of digital and smart technology.

Marketing of Smart Living

We argue that approaches to marketing smart living products and services to older people should be grounded in three primary principles that have been informed by research from the social sciences. They should: (1) be applicable across life domains (e.g., health, mobility); (2) be universal in design while still customizable to the individual; (3) promote intergenerational integration. These features maximize their usefulness and therefore their marketability and are most likely to be adopted by the largest number of people.

Applicable across Life Domains

For products to be useful and usable for an aging and increasingly diverse population, technologies need to cut across multiple life domains. Therefore, we argue smart living should be marketed not as a specific technology for a particular purpose, but rather as a toolkit of strategies and product and service solutions addressing the challenges and opportunities of a changing and aging society. Next, we provide two examples of how the broader concept of smart living can be tailored to promote two different but intertwined life domains of health and mobility. While these examples are beneficial to older people, we chose these examples because they clearly address the needs of individuals of different ages, thus demonstrating how to integrate rather than isolate an intergenerational family and/ or community.

Health

Health includes issues of prevention, intervention, and rehabilitation/recovery. Customizable smart living can address every aspect of health. Under prevention, smart living might translate into suggestions for and facilitation of nutritious meals, physical activity, or preventive health care to address the needs of functionally limited adults, elite athletes, or busy families. Thus, healthy meal choices or an individual's physiological responses to physical activity might be recorded or monitored through individualized programming, home-based sensors, wearables, or assistive devices. Similarly, products could address individual preferences for the types of meals they wish to consume as well as any special dietary needs or restrictions. Assistive devices or apps could help cognitively or physically impaired people of all ages, as well as busy families, order groceries and have them delivered, prepare appropriate meals, or remember to turn the stove off. Wearable devices could warn of low glucose levels, high blood pressure, or the likelihood of an impending seizure, thus preventing potentially dangerous events. Smart living might include strategies and products to offset cognitive decline, or to assist with training for new jobs, learning new hobbies, or preparing for and recovering from a stressful day.

Mobility and Transportation

A multi-generational family might need a plan to transport family members using various forms of transportation, or a device to warn one family member of gait unsteadiness associated with falls and another of drowsy driving associated with accidents. We envision products that allow individuals to safely walk to the store or nearby bus stop, or a device that assists people with specific limitations getting in and out of vehicles. This toolkit could also help achieve practical family goals, such as reduced mileage and gas use. A multi-generational family may need to get children to school, adults to work, and elders to appointments. Transportation could be arranged in advance and include getting children to a bus stop and setting up a ride via a ride-share or autonomous vehicle. A non-rush hour service such as community vans or taxis can get any non-driver to appointments without the need for a second or third vehicle or a dedicated driver. Assistive devices, sensors, and smartphone apps can make sure the children are on time for their bus, and adults get to work on time, while those with medical or other appointments can be both reminded of and transported to the doctor's office on their own schedule. Everyone is provided with the transportation they need in a safe, practical, and efficient manner that is ultimately more sustainable than individual transportation provided by private vehicles.

Universal and Personalized Design

Often, when a product or service is designed and marketed specifically for older adults (e.g., Lifeline, Meals on Wheels) a stigma is attached to that product or service. The stigma may serve as a disincentive for older adults to purchase and use the product or service, regardless of how well-meaning or impactful the product or service may be on the quality of life outcomes. This stigma is driven by ageism in our culture, which is perpetuated by negative aging stereotypes. This includes thinking of aging as negative, with the view that older age is a time of declining health and well-being accompanied by loss of productivity, cognition, and ultimately independence. Moreover, in a recent review of assistive technologies marketed to older adults, researchers found that the attributions to aging projected onto the design of these technologies by developers tended to be paternalistic in nature and devoid of the user's perspective altogether (Bechtold and Capari, 2019). Theories and research on aging (e.g., successful aging model; Rowe and Kahn, 1998) have helped to combat these negative stereotypes of aging by demonstrating how aging and later life can be a time of growth, associated with positive health outcomes. It is worth noting that healthy and happy people are more active and engaged consumers.

To minimize these potentially negative effects, we argue that it is necessary to be careful to avoid product or service stigma. Unfortunately, products that are marketed to the older population tend to be accompanied by messages highlighting negative aspects of aging. Pervasive advertisements emphasizing the weak, fallen, or helpless elders are clear and discouraging examples. Rather, we suggest that those wishing to target the aging consumer should develop and advertise products and services that are universal, that is, useful and useable for people of all ages. At the same time, the product or service should be customizable to the needs and situational context of the person using them. This approach can benefit companies as it creates a larger target population to consume the product or service. This approach to design and marketing also benefits older adults through the reduction of stigma, which may, in turn, increase the likelihood of use and allows all to benefit from the product or service. One example is the use of a smartwatch to achieve the same objectives and functionality as a Lifeline. The smartwatch has broad appeal and uses across the life span. It can be tailored to the specific needs of older adults who may have mobility issues and be at risk of falling. However, the smartwatch does not carry with it the same age-specific negative stigma as a Lifeline.

Another example is the well-meaning and impactful service of Meals on Wheels. This non-profit service provides essential nutrition and social interaction for homebound older adults. However, older adults may be reluctant to sign up for this service until absolutely needed, given that it connotes both poverty and a lack of independence. In contrast, some companies have become quite successful marketing door-to-door delivery of food (e.g., Uber Eats, Grubhub, Door Dash) or, for those interested in preparing the meal but limited in the ability to go to a grocery store to purchase the ingredients, services like Blue Apron or Home Chef can be extremely useful. Marketing these services for people of all ages, while at the same time allowing for the slightly different provision of service for older adults (e.g., the natural occurrence of a delivery person interacting for a short time with the older adult) could expand the use of these products and allow another population to utilize these services.

We assert that the goal in marketing smart living should be to develop universal designs (i.e., intended use for people of all ages, while at the same time being customizable to the needs and context of the individual). It is important to note that we see customizable as fundamentally different from personalized. The latter suggests it was personalized at design (e.g., Lifeline for older adults that has no use for younger adults), while customizable indicates the ability to be flexible going forward, and for individuals to use it differently to meet their specific and changing needs at any particular point in time.

Intergenerational

The three approaches we advocate for effective marketing of smart living products and services in the context of an aging and changing society are not independent. This is especially true for our third proposed component of having an intergenerational focus. By this, we mean smart living products can be positioned to address consumers' needs to facilitate and promote intergenerational interactions (e.g., video calling to connect non-proximate family members). Smart living products can also work to indirectly facilitate intergenerational exchanges of knowledge and information for how to use a product or service that is relevant and useful to all generations (e.g., as noted in the example above regarding mobility and transportation).

We expect that products and services developed to cut across multiple life domains and to be universally useful across the life span can provide increased opportunities for intergenerational exchanges and interactions. Most often in such situations, we might think of grandchildren showing their grandparents how to use or make adjustments to a product (e.g., adding apps to a smartphone to connect and share pictures with them). However, the directionality of the communication transmission can work both ways allowing older adults the opportunity to reciprocate and play an integral and meaningful role in the lives of younger generations. This may include sharing stories or reading to grandchildren via video chat, sharing family photos or family history of previous generations.

The use of smart living products and services as vehicles for facilitating intergenerational exchanges and interactions can have far-reaching societal impacts. This includes a potential reduction in feelings of loneliness and social isolation among older adults as well as enhanced intergenerational solidarity through reciprocal exchanges, socialization, and mentoring of the younger generations (Bengtson and Roberts, 1991). Further, intergenerational relations may help increase older adults' sense of purpose and mattering, which also impacts health and well-being in later life (Fazio, 2007). Intergenerational exchanges with non-relatives may also promote reciprocity in support exchanges through, as noted above, opportunities for older adults to share their knowledge and experience in ways that benefit younger generations. Experience Core brought elders in a low-income neighborhood in Baltimore to nearby schools to offer one-on-one time for reading and play with very young children (Fried et al., 2013). The children benefited from individualized attention otherwise not affordable in these low-income school districts while the elders experienced the benefit of having close relationships with the children which increased their activity, mobility, and intellectual acuity. The increased activity motivated these older adults to engage in other positive activities, such as eating healthier. A side benefit was that elders were able to use bus passes they were issued from the program to get to other parts of the city, thus increasing their visiting and social engagement as well as their ability to purchase and consume goods and services from different parts of the city. Intergenerational exchanges are also good for younger generations in that they can facilitate a greater sense of connectedness to older family members during a time when geographic distances between family members may be increasing.

Beyond the societal impact, smart living products and services with a value proposition that facilitates intergenerational exchanges and interactions can be good for business in that they will have a larger target audience. Research suggests that one of the major motivators cited by older adults for purchasing and learning how to use new technologies is to connect and interact with younger family members (Francis et al., 2018).

A number of initiatives, approaches, and models have been developed, which address the major demographic shifts (e.g., aging society) and implications described in this chapter. We briefly summarize two of these perspectives below, which inform our call for smart living to address the challenges and opportunities of an aging society.

Illustrative Innovative Perspectives

University-Industry Collaborations

In 2009, the University of Tokyo's Institute of Gerontology launched an initiative that sought to address the needs and challenges of Japan's rapidly aging society (Institute of Gerontology, University of Tokyo, 2013). The initiative led by Dr. Hiroko Akiyama brought together representatives from 60 companies spanning multiple industries (e.g., automotive, food, construction, finance) to jointly develop a roadmap for an aging society. One approach being used to promote university-industry collaboration in Japan is that of the "living lab." This concept developed and widely used in Europe is being utilized in Japan to address the challenges and opportunities of its rapidly aging population. The approach involves a model of co-creation through a "public-private-people partnership" (Kyodo, 2018).

Age-Friendly Cities Initiative

In 2002, The World Health Organization (WHO) released a policy framework focused on active aging (World Health Organization, 2010). This framework has since been used by the WHO to promote the need for primary health care to be more age-friendly (i.e., responsive and specific to the needs of older persons). This approach has since expanded to emphasize the environments in which older adults live, with a focus on cities. It has been argued that making cities more age-friendly is one of the most effective approaches to addressing the needs of the increasing number of older adults discussed previously in this chapter. Some key components of the age-friendly community initiative that can be facilitated through smart living include barrier-free and enabling interior and exterior spaces, accessible and appropriate health services, accessible home-safety designs and products, and services to assist with household chores and home maintenance.

Future Directions

A Model for the 21st Century

In this chapter, we have provided an overview of the significant demographic shifts our society is currently undergoing. This is highlighted by the fact that the size of the older adult population is increasing dramatically. This is not a temporary shift driven by a large aging cohort (i.e., the Baby Boomers), but is a trend that will remain and potentially increase in future generations. Additional changes are occurring simultaneously, many of which are interrelated to an aging society (e.g., need for multi-generational housing among those with fewer resources, increasing chronic illnesses) and some which are not (e.g., climate change). These trends, while posing unique and unprecedented challenges, also pose an opportunity for innovation and collaboration.

One area prime for innovation that can help address many of the needs of our changing society is the role of new technologies to promote smart living. This entails the integration of technological advances to promote and facilitate lifestyles that are connected, efficient, economical, and sustainable (Kor, Pattinson, Yanovsky, and Kharchenko, 2018). Our model for smart living in the 21st century includes proposed approaches to marketing, research, and inclusivity, which have been discussed throughout this chapter and are summarized below.

Marketing of Smart Living in the 21st Century

Informed by the aforementioned models as well as current and future societal challenges, we propose that marketers adopt a model of consumption of smart living products and services for the 21st century. This model reflects a marketing perspective that incorporates the consideration of major societal changes. Using the three principles noted above of applicability across domains, universal design that is customizable and promotes intergenerational integration, we consider a particularly relevant and contemporary example: Lyft, the ridesharing service. Lyft is useful to people of all ages. However, certain barriers exist to a more widespread consumption of the service by older adults. In response, Lyft has been working to customize their universal service to older adults. This does not include marketing its service to just older adults. Rather this includes working to make adjustments to the service that allows it to remain useful and useable across the life span, while at the same time be more useable and inclusive for all, including older adults. One specific way Lyft is doing this is by enabling older adults the ability to reserve a ride via a phone call as opposed to only through a smartphone app. This is designed to both increase profits for Lyft as well as improve mobility for many older adults, a pressing societal challenge.

Research to Facilitate Smart Living in the 21st Century

We advocate for a research approach that not only uncovers insights about the emerging challenges facing society but also leverages research partnerships and collaborations to address these challenges through well-designed products and services for smart living. This includes interdisciplinary collaborations among academic researchers. For example, to more effectively anticipate and address the needs of a changing society, research teams need to include social scientists, engineers, and clinicians. The social sciences have important roles to play on these interdisciplinary research teams. For example, sociologists working to understand population-level trends (e.g., demography) can help anticipate future population shifts. Psychologists can help understand not only older adults' needs, but also their preferences, attitudes, and other factors that may drive consumption patterns and describe how they are similar to or different from other age groups while meeting the needs and preferences of people with other specific characteristics (e.g., race, ethnic, religion). This can inform designs that are more reflexive and customizable and as well as marketing approaches with successful outcomes.

The industry also has a vital role to play in this process through engaging with both academic researchers as well as industry partners across sectors (e.g., fast-moving consumer goods industry, automotive industry, technology, social media). In order to accomplish this goal, new perspectives on collaboration are needed. This could involve consortia comprised of diverse academic and industry partners working together to solve broad societal challenges in mutually beneficial ways.

Opportunity and Need to Address Health Disparities

In order for smart living to accomplish the goal we have set forth in this paper of addressing the challenges linked with an aging and changing society, it needs to be inclusive. This means being relevant and affordable for people with varying access to resources. Doing so can help not only address future challenges associated with an aging society but simultaneously help to address longstanding disparities linked to unequal access to resources.

In sum, we live in a rapidly changing world with many challenges and opportunities. We are fortunate to live in a time of extraordinary new technologies, products, and services, with clear possibilities for ever-emerging new developments. Aging consumers will have multiple needs that are specific to their life stage but also needs that are diverse with respect to their preferences, goals, and experiences. Careful consideration of the individual's lifetime experiences and their societal circumstances can result in an unprecedented ability to reach this newly emerging group, the aging consumer, in a manner that is beneficial to the health and well-being of the individual, reciprocally supportive of intergenerational goals, while at the same time optimizing how responses to the changing demographics optimally contribute to society.

Note

1 Author note: The authors would like to thank the Life Course Development Program at the University of Michigan for their feedback on earlier drafts of this chapter.

References

AARP (2017). Connect2Affect: End social isolation among seniors. https://connect2affect
.org.

Anderson, M., & Perrin, A. (2017). *Technology Use among Seniors*. Washington, D.C.: Pew Research Center. https://www.pewresearch.org/internet/2017/05/17/technology-u se-among-seniors/.

Antonucci, T. C., Blieszner, R., & Denmark, F. (2009). Psychological perspectives on older women. In: H. Landrine & N. F. Russo (Eds.), *Handbook of Diversity in Feminist Psychology* (pp. 233–260). New York, NY: Springer Publishing Company.

Avison, C., Brock, D., Campione, J., Hassell, S., Rabinovich, B., Ritter, R., Severynse, J., Yang, D. H., & Zebrak, K. (2018). Outcome evaluation of the national family caregiver support program. https://connect2affect.org.

Bechtold, U., & Capari, L. (2019). Paternalistic rather than assistive? Concepts and social attributions of older adults represented in Active Assisted Living technology project descriptions. *Gerontechnology, 18*(4), 193–205.

Bengtson, V. L., & Roberts, R. E. (1991). Intergenerational solidarity in aging families: An example of formal theory construction. *Journal of Marriage and the Family*, 856–870.

Blit-Cohen, E., & Litwin, H. (2004). Elder participation in cyberspace: A qualitative analysis of Israeli retirees. *Journal of Aging Studies, 18*(4), 385–398.

Buse, C. E. (2009). When you retire, does everything become leisure? Information and communication technology use and the work/leisure boundary in retirement. *New Media and Society, 11*(7), 1143–1161.

Cacioppo, J. T., & Hawkley, L. C. (2009). Perceived social isolation and cognition. *Trends in Cognitive Sciences, 13*(10), 447–454.

Caine, K. E., Fisk, A. D., & Rogers, W. A. (2006). Benefits and privacy concerns of a home equipped with a visual sensing system: A perspective from older adults. *Proceedings of the Human Factors and Ergonomics Society Annual Meeting, 50*(2), 180–184. SAGE Publications.

Chopik, W. J. (2016). The benefits of social technology use among older adults are mediated by reduced loneliness. *Cyberpsychology, Behavior, and Social Networking, 19*(9), 551–556.

Cotten, S. R., Anderson, W. A., & McCullough, B. M. (2013). Impact of Internet use on loneliness and contact with others among older adults: Cross-sectional analysis. *Journal of Medical Internet Research, 15*(2), 215–227.

Cowell, A. J. (2006). The relationship between education and health behavior: Some empirical evidence. *Health Economics, 15*(2), 125–146.

Cutler, D. M., & Lleras-Muney, A. (2010). Understanding differences in health behaviors by education. *Journal of Health Economics, 29*(1), 1–28.

Czaja, S. (2017). The role of technology in supporting social engagement among older adults. *Public Policy and Aging Report, 27*(4), 145–148.

Czaja, S. J., Charness, N., Fisk, A. D., Hertzog, C., Nair, S. N., Rogers, W. A., & Sharit, J. (2006). Factors predicting the use of technology: Findings from the Center for Research and Education on Aging and Technology Enhancement (CREATE). *Psychology and Aging, 21*(2), 333.

Diczfalusy, E. (2001). The demographic revolution and our common future. *Maturitas, 38*(1), 5–14.

Dolen, L. S., & Bearison, D. J. (1982). Social interaction and social cognition in aging. A contextual analysis. *Human Development, 25*(6), 430–442.

Du, P., & Tu, P. (2000). Population aging and old age security. In: X. Peng (Ed.), *The Changing Population of China* (pp. 77–90). Hoboken, N.J.: Blackwell.

Durkheim, E. (1933). *The Division of Labor in Society*. New York City, N.Y.: Macmillan.

Eastman, J., Iyer, R., & Thomas, S. P. (2013). The impact of status consumption on shopping styles: An exploratory look at the millennial generation. *Marketing Management Journal, 23*(1), 57–73.

Estes, C., Biggs, S., & Phillipson, C. (2003). *Social Theory, Social Policy and Aging*. Milton Keynes: Open University Press.

Fazio, E. M. (2007). *Role Occupancy, Physical Health and the Diminishment of the Sense of Mattering in Late Life* (Doctoral dissertation).

Francis, J., Kadylak, T., Cotten, S. R., & Rikard, R. V. (2016). When it comes to depression, ICT use matters: A longitudinal analysis of the effect of ICT use and mattering on depression among older adults. In: C. Stephanidis (Ed.), *HCII 2016 Posters, Part II, CCIS 611* (pp. 1–6). New York City, N.Y.: Springer.

Francis, J., Kadylak, T., Makki, T. W., Rikard, R. V., & Cotten, S. R. (2018). Catalyst to connection: When technical difficulties lead to social support for older adults. *The American Behavioral Scientist, 62*(9), 1167–1185.

Francis, J., Rikard, R. V., Cotten, S. R., & Kadylak, T. (2017). Does ICT use matter? The effect of information & communication technology (ICT) use on perceived mattering among older adults. *Information, Communication and Society, 22*, 1281–1294.

Fried, L. P., Carlson, M. C., McGill, S., Seeman, T., Xue, Q. L., Frick, K., Tan, E., Tanner, E. K., Barron, J., Frangakis, C., & Piferi, R. (2013). Experience corps: A dual trial to promote the health of older adults and children's academic success. *Contemporary Clinical Trials, 36*(1), 1–13.

Frieden, T. R., Harold Jaffe, D. W., Moolenaar, R. L., Leahy, M. A., Martinroe, J. C., & Spriggs, S. R. (2013). CDC health disparities and inequalities report-united states, 2013, supplement morbidity and mortality weekly report supplement centers for disease control and prevention MMWR editorial and production staff MMWR editorial board.

He, W., & Larsen, L. J. (2014). *Older Americans with a Disability, 2008–2012*. Washington, DC: U.S. Census Bureau.

Health and Retirement Study (2010). (2008 Core, Final, Version 1.0) public use dataset. Produced and distributed by the University of Michigan with funding from the National Institute on Aging (grant number NIA U01AG009740). Ann Arbor, MI.

Heimlich, R. (2009). *Housing Crisis*. Washington, D.C.: Pew Research Center. https://www.pewresearch.org/fact-tank/2009/02/17/housing-crisis/.

Institute of Gerontology, University of Tokyo (2013). Toward active living by a centenarian generation. A large-scale social experiment for a Highly-Aged Society. https://www.u-tokyo.ac.jp/focus/en/features/f_00048.html.

Kaye, L. (2017). Older adults, rural living, and the escalating risk of social isolation. *Public Policy and Aging Report, 27*(4), 139–144.

Kor, A. L., Pattinson, C., Yanovsky, M., & Kharchenko, V. (2018). IoT-enabled smart living. In: M. Dastbaz, H. Arabnia & B. Akhgar (Eds.), *Technology for Smart Futures* (pp. 3–28). Cham: Springer.

Kramer, B. J., Creekmur, B., Mitchell, M. N., Rose, D. J., Pynoos, J., & Rubenstein, L. Z. (2014). Community fall prevention programs: Comparing three InSTEP models by level of intensity. *Journal of Aging and Physical Activity, 22*(3), 372–379.

Kyodo (2018). Living labs bring old and young together to tap community expertise. https://www.japantimes.co.jp/news/2018/06/25/national/living-labs-bring-old-young-gtogether-tap-community-expertise/#.Xe6lt-hKhaR.

Olshansky, S. J., Antonucci, T. C., Berkman, L., Binstock, R. H., Boersch-Supan, A., Cacioppo, J. T., Carnes, B. A., Carstensen, L. L., Fried, L. P., Goldman, D. P., & Jackson, J. (2012). Differences in life expectancy due to race and educational differences are widening, and many may not catch up. *Health Affairs, 31*(8), 1803–1813.

Perez, A. D., & Hirschman, C. (2009). The changing racial and ethnic composition of the US population: Emerging American identities. *Population and Development Review, 35*(1), 1–51.

Pew, R. W., & Van Hemel, S. B. (Eds.), National Research Council. (2004). *Technology for Adaptive Aging. National Research Council of the National Academies.* Washington, DC: The National Academies Press.

Portacolone, E. (2017). Structural factors of elders' isolation in a high-crime neighborhood: An in-depth perspective. *The Public Policy and Aging Report, 27*(4), 152–155.

Powell, J. L. (2010). The power of global aging. *Ageing International, 35*(1), 1–14.

Pynoos, J., Steinman, B. A., Do Nguyen, A. Q., & Bressette, M. (2012). Assessing and adapting the home environment to reduce falls and meet the changing capacity of older adults. *Journal of Housing for the Elderly, 26*(1-3), 137–155.

Rice, D. (2009). *What to Look for in HUD's 2010 Budget for Low-Income Housing.* Washington, D.C.: Center on Budget and Policy Priorities. https://www.cbpp.org/sites/default/files/atoms/files/5-4-09hous.pdf.

Rosenberg, M., & McCullough, B. C. (1981). Mattering: Inferred significance and mental health among adolescents. *Research in Community and Mental Health, 2,* 163–182.

Rowe, J. W., & Kahn, R. L. (1998). *Successful Aging.* New York, NY: Pantheon.

Ryan, L. H., Smith, J., Antonucci, T. C., & Jackson, J. S. (2012). Cohort differences in the availability of informal caregivers: Are the Boomers at risk? *The Gerontologist, 52*(2), 177–188.

U.S. Census Bureau (2015). *Desire to Move and Residential Mobility: 2010–2011* (Report No. P70-140). http://www.census.gov/library/publications/2015/demo/p70-140.html.

U.S. Department of Labor, Bureau of Labor Statistics (2019). *Employment Projections 2018–2028.* https://www.bls.gov/news.release/pdf/ecopro.pdf.

Woodward, I., Vongswasdi, P., & More, E. (2015). Generational diversity at work: A systematic review of the research.

World Health Organization (2010). *Global Age-Friendly Cities Project.* https://www.who.int/ageing/projects/age-friendly_cities.pdf?ua=1.

INDEX

Note: page references in bold indicate tables; italics indicate figures.